masculinity

Previously published in the AFI Film Readers Series
edited by Charles Wolfe and Edward Branigan

The Persistence of History
Vivian Sobchack

Classical Hollywood Comedy
Henry Jenkins and Kristine Brunovska Karnick

Disney Discourse
Eric Smoodin

Black American Cinema
Manthia Diawara

Film Theory Goes to the Movies
Jim Collins, Ava Preacher Collins, and Hilary Radner

Theorizing Documentary
Michael Renov

Sound Theory/Sound Practice
Rick Altman

Psychoanalysis and Cinema
E. Ann Kaplan

Fabrications
Jane M. Gaines and Charlotte Herzog

The Revolution Wasn't Televised
Lynn Spigel and Michael Curtin

Black Women Film and Video Artists
Jacqueline Bobo

Home, Exile, Homeland
Hamid Naficy

Violence and American Cinema
J. David Slocum

masculinity

bodies,

movies,

culture

edited by

peter lehman

.

routledge
new york and london

Published in 2001 by
Routledge
29 West 35th Street
New York, NY 10001

Published in Great Britain by
Routledge
11 New Fetter Lane
London EC4P 4EE

Routledge is an imprint of the Taylor & Francis Group

Printed in the United States of America on acid-free paper.
Typography: Jack Donner

Library of Congress Cataloging-in-Publication Data

Masculinity: bodies, movies, culture / edited by Peter Lehman.
    p. cm. — (AFI film readers)
Includes bibliographical references and index.
ISBN 0-415-92323-9 — ISBN 0-415-92324-7 (pbk.)
1. Men in motion pictures. 2. Machismo in motion pictures. 3.
Homosexuality in motion pictures. 4. Masculinity—United States—
History—20th century.
I. Lehman, Peter. II. Series.

PN1995.9.M46 M34 2000
791.43'652041 —dc21
                                                        00-030827

In Memory of Paul A. Thom

contents

Acknowledgments   ix

Introduction   1
    Peter Lehman

1.   "Someone Is Going to Pay":   7
    Resurgent White Masculinity in *Ransom*
    Krin Gabbard

2.   Crying Over the Melodramatic Penis: 25
    Melodrama and Male Nudity in Films of the 90s
    Peter Lehman

3.   The Saviors and the Saved: 43
    Masculine Redemption in Contemporary Films
    Amy Aronson and Michael Kimmel

4.   Identity, Queerness, and Homosocial Bonding: 51
    The Case of *Swingers*
    Justin Wyatt

5.   Rape Fantasies: 67
    Hollywood and Homophobia
    Joe Wlodarz

6.   Choosing to Be "Not a Man":   81
    Masculine Anxiety in Nouri Bouzid's
    Rih Essed/Man of Ashes
    Robert Lang and Maher Ben Moussa

7.   T(he)-Men's Room: 95
    Masculinity and Space in Anthony Mann's *T-Men*
    Susan White

8.   The Talented Poststructuralist: 115
    Heteromasculinity, Gay Artifice, and Class Passing
    Chris Straayer

9.   "Emotional Constipation"   133
    and the Power of Dammed Masculinity:
    ***Deliverance* and the Paradoxes of Male Liberation**
    Sally Robinson

10. "As a Mother Cuddles a Child":   149
    Sexuality and Masculinity
    in World War II Combat Films
    Robert Eberwein

11. The Nation and the Nude: 167
    Colonial Masculinity and the Spectacle
    of the Male Body in Recent Canadian Cinema(s)
    Lee Parpart

12. Lynching Photography and the "Black Beast Rapist" 193
    in the Southern White Masculine Imagination
    Amy Louise Wood

13. Screening the Italian-American Male   213
    Aaron Baker and Juliann Vitullo

14. "Studs Have Feelings Too":   227
    Warren Beatty and the Question
    of Star Discourse and Gender
    Lucia Bozzola

15. James Bond's Penis   243
    Toby Miller

16. Oliver Stone's *Nixon* and the Unmanning   257
    of the Self-Made Man
    Dennis Bingham

17. Suck, Spit, Chew, Swallow: 279
    A Performative Exploration of Men's Bodies
    Tim Miller

Contributors   301

Index   305

acknowledgments

First, thanks go to Edward Branigan and Chuck Wolfe for inviting me to propose an anthology for their series. I have great respect for Edward, Chuck, and the series. When they approached me years ago and I proposed a volume on masculinity, the idea was received with what I interpreted as polite disbelief. Sometime later I proposed a volume on an unrelated topic only to be asked to do the one on masculinity. I thank them for their confidence in me as an editor and their willingness to go with the topic. I hope the results justify their confidence. All of my work on masculinity and the male body owes a special acknowledgment to Susan Hunt. Countless hours of telephone conversation with her (unfortunately counted by the long-distance telephone carrier) have enabled me to clarify my thinking and to benefit from hers. Finally, everything I publish is indebted to Melanie Magisos for her valuable revision suggestions, and my introduction and essay in this volume are no exception.

introduction

Peter Lehman

About 1980 a colleague remarked to me that she thought feminist film theory and criticism provided men and women within our culture an opportunity to have a conversation about sexual topics that they would not otherwise have. In other words, we were talking to each other about topics of importance in our lives that we could not speak to each other about directly, so we talked about them indirectly through film. While we seemed to be talking about sexuality in films, we were in reality talking about our lives. My immediate response was to write off her perspective as a generation issue; even though she was only a few years older than me, I felt that I was part of a generation where men and women had no problem talking to each other openly about sexual issues. If feminist criticism fulfilled that function for her, fine, but it seemed inapplicable to me. In the following years, however, I thought back many times to that comment, realizing its perceptiveness and my naivete. Not only had I underestimated how much we talked about sexual issues to each other as men and women through film theory and criticism, but I simultaneously overestimated the degree of openness with which men and women of my generation spoke to each other about issues of sexuality.

If the above was true of men and women speaking to each other about female sexuality and the female body within a heterosexual context (which was the focus of academic attention at the time), it was even truer of talking about the male body and male sexuality. This was the case whether it was men or women talking, and if the mode of address or the intended audience was gay or straight. Even my generation couldn't fool itself on that topic. Important essays on the male body appeared, however, in the '80s (Richard Dyer and Steve Neal) and were followed by a number of books on the subject (Studlar, Silverman, Cohan and Hark, Lehman, Bingham, Jeffords).

The context, then, for another book about masculinity and the male body at the end of the decade is quite different than it was at the beginning. When I told a male colleague about my work, then in progress, on the manuscript for *Running Scared,* he lost no time in replying, "Who needs it?" I was, therefore, pleasantly surprised that, when the book was published, he praised it and recommended it to his students. By the end of the decade, I think the question "Who needs it?" is less likely to come up, and there is a growing consensus that many of us, men and women, straight and gay or lesbian, need it and want it. And while the essays in this volume extend previous work and push in new directions, some central aspects of work in this area haven't changed all that much. As several of these essays make clear, both in the movies and within our culture, representing, showing, and even talking about many areas of masculinity, sexuality, and the male body are still nearly taboo. Indeed, as I prepared to write this introduction, I received an e-mail message from Tim Miller, a performance artist and contributor to this volume, in which he writes of a recent experience performing in Tennessee with hateful, homophobic protestors outside the theater.

Tim Miller's inclusion in this anthology is of extreme importance to me precisely within the context of the manner in which men and women, straight or gay/lesbian, talk to each other about masculinity and the male body through film theory and criticism. Miller is not a film scholar nor even primarily an academic but, rather, a gay performance artist whose performances frequently include nudity. In addition to performing a one-man show on stage, he conducts community-based group workshops on sexuality. His account of working with primarily gay men in the workshop/performance context reveals precisely how many of the theoretical and critical issues taken up elsewhere in this volume are part of men's lived experiences. Furthermore, Miller has brought much attention to legal issues of public funding for the arts through his political activism for the "NEA Four," artists who were denied grant funding due to the controversial sexual content of their work. In his work, Miller blurs lines between creative performance and self-help workshops, and between "art" and social activism; I hope his inclusion in this volume blurs lines between film theory and cultural theory, between theory and practice, and between straight and gay modes of address and audiences.

I have not grouped the essays in this volume into formal categories for several reasons. If one has a category on "race" or one on "homosexuality," the implication may be that the essays are easily contained in those groupings. But that is far from the case. Indeed, such categorizing tends to create artificial barriers. I prefer to emphasize the interconnectedness of these essays. Most of them address more than one issue. Nevertheless, certain directions emerge from them, and I have ordered them accordingly. The collection begins with recent trends and then moves to the representation of gay characters and issues. The next essays blur the line between the homosexual and the homosocial. These are followed by essays on race, ethnicity, and nationality, and finally to essays dealing with individual men and male characters in relationship to power. The volume concludes with Tim Miller's touching account of his work with men and issues of masculinity and sexuality.

Krin Gabbard focuses his attention on race in recent films in his analysis of the manner in which *Ransom*, starring Mel Gibson, represents black masculinity in relation to white masculinity. Gabbard argues that *Ransom* fits into the "angry white male" genre. Even though the kidnappers are white, an African-American FBI agent attempts to control the negotiations and Gibson's heroics are directed at that character. Gabbard shows that the film displaces its racism in a manner that enables identification with Gibson against the hypermasculine black character. My essay identifies a new pattern of showing the penis in films of the '90s, which I term the "melodramatic penis." Starting with *The Crying Game*, a number of films show the penis within the context of extreme melodrama. Although these films avoid the conventional polarity of either trying to make the penis an impressive phallic spectacle or an object of pathetic or comic collapse, they still imply that showing the penis has to be of great importance.

Other essays focus on recent films that represent gay characters. Amy Aronson and Michael Kimmel argue that in the '90s it has become the function of gay, asexual men to save heterosexual romance. In such films as *My Best Friend's Wedding*, a gay man replaces what had earlier been the function of a female character or even a child—to bring the heterosexual couple together. Justin Wyatt directs his attention to the "new queer cinema." He describes patterns of friendship among men in the gay community and argues that seemingly straight films such as *Swingers* co-opt that model. At a time when the conventional heterosexual family is under siege, the gay model of friendship resonates deeply within the culture. One of the early films of male homosocial bonding that Wyatt identifies is Barry Levinson's *Diner*. This is especially interesting in light of Joe Wlodarz's analysis of Levinson's later film, *Sleepers*. Whereas Wyatt is sympathetic to *Diner*, Wlodarz identifies a homophobic subtext within *Sleepers*. The proliferation of gay characters in recent Hollywood films in general is, Wlodarz argues, easily assimilated. Serious homophobia, however, is particularly related to anal sex between men. Recent Hollywood films including *Sleepers* represent such sex as rape, dangerously collapsing the meanings of homosexual sex with rape.

Robert Lang and Maher Ben Moussa also take up the subject of homosexuality but within a quite different cultural context. They argue that Nouri Bouzid's *Man of Ashes* (1986) is a particularly daring Tunisian film on the subject of male sexuality. Homosexual rape is, however, also central to that film in which two childhood boyfriends are raped. Lang and Ben Moussa, however, argue that the rape is merely a device to show what happens when someone rejects societally approved sexual roles, as one of the boys does when he chooses to be a homosexual or "not a man."

Several other essays reveal how often work on masculinity and the male body in general blurs clear, comfortable distinctions between straight and gay. Susan White identifies a strong homosocial subtext in Anthony Mann's *T-Men*, a film that she notes perfects the pleasures and threats of looking at the male body. The film's strong homosocial and homoerotic overtones result from a narrative trajectory that places many scenes in public bathhouses and restrooms. The homoerotic body in *T-Men* is tied to horrific forms of brutal punishment. Chris Straayer analyzes the character of Ripley in the film *Purple Noon* and the Patricia Highsmith novel *The Talented Mr. Ripley* upon which the film is based. Straayer examines the two texts in relation to masculinity, homosexuality, and class, arguing that the novel endorses a notion of freedom that contrasts with the film's emphasis on determination. Sally Robinson analyzes cultural discourses about masculinity that see it as naturally possessing sexual energies which, if blocked, will cause physical and psychological damage. Concentrating on *Deliverance,* the film that Wlodarz identifies as the first of the homosexual rape films, Robinson argues that these films have contradictory ideological implications about masculinity. On the one hand, they legitimize various forms of masculine behavior as natural in light of the dangers of a blocked masculinity lacking release. On the other hand, they reveal a post–women's liberation notion of a willingness to abdicate and renegotiate male power, even to the point of considering the pleasures of the loss of power.

Robert Eberwein turns his attention away from recent cinema and analyzes the representation of masculinity in a series of World War II films that show men engaged in such nontraditional male gender roles as nursing each other and dancing together. Eberwein argues against previous readings of such films as always signifying homosexuality by placing them within a number of historical discourses such as training films and advertisements. By examining the relationship of the misé-en-scène to the narrative, he shows how these films negotiate complex, historical gender issues.

Yet another group of essays emphasize race, ethnicity, and nationality. Lee Parpart makes an important case for paying careful attention to nation and region when considering such issues as the representation of the nude male body. She notes that images of the penis are relatively common in Canadian cinema and that their presence doesn't provoke the anxieties and the strategies so commonplace for containing those anxieties in U.S. cinema. Parpart relates this to Canada's position in relation to the world's powerful nations, arguing that Canadians are not heavily invested in notions of empowered nationhood and dominant masculinity, concepts which bear upon when, how and what types of nude male bodies can be represented. Amy Wood provides an analysis of one of the most deeply disturbing sets of images of the male body ever created—lynching photographs taken by white Southerners of their black victims. Comparing them to hunting photographs, she analyses the functions these photographs fulfilled for the men who took them. Wood's essay does not deal with cinema but along with Tim Miller's essay clearly shows the need to consider related areas such as photography and performance. For all their obvious differences, the lynching photographs and the racial subtext in *Ransom* bear a sad similarity, both testifying to white male attempts to control their perceived threat of black male sexuality.

Aaron Baker and Juliann Vitullo analyze the representation of Italian Americans in such successful films of the '70s and early '80s as *The Godfather* and *Rocky*, which they then compare and contrast with such '90s films as *A Bronx Tale* and *Household Saints*. Baker and Vitullo argue that the earlier films focused on physical and violent urban, ethnic, working-class men in contrast to overcivilized, weak, white men, while the latter films question that dichotomy and adopt more complex ideas about identity.

The final group of essays focuses upon individual men and power, but does so in a variety of contexts: an actor, a fictional character, and a well-known nonfictional character. Lucia Bozzola analyzes Warren Beatty's star persona by considering the relationship between his private life and movie roles during two distinct periods, the mid-'70s when he made *Shampoo* and the mid- to late '90s when he made *Love Affair* and *Bulworth*. During the '70s, Beatty was notorious for being a legendary lover and *Shampoo* draws upon that and presents his body in a manner that assumes its desirability for women. By the mid-'90s his marriage to Annette Bening, and his image of a man who has settled down, is seen in *Love Affair* where sex is replaced by love. By the late '90s, Beatty's place in the public eye had shifted entirely from the area of sexuality to politics, another area of traditional male power.

Toby Miller directs his attention to a fictional character of great power—James Bond. Or perhaps, it would be more accurate to say, to his penis, a part of that fictional character's body and potential source of power. Miller notes that in the novels, Bond runs away from sex, his penis representing a threat of the loss of control. In the films, on the other hand, Bond is highly sexual. Miller places this shift within an historical, political, and economic context. Dennis Bingham's subject is also a figure of great power—a president of the United States. Bingham shows how in *Nixon,* Oliver Stone represents the man as one driven by a host of insecurities about his masculinity and a desperate need to overcompensate for them. Stone's Nixon can be understood in relationship to the historical, cultural discourse of the self-made man, one who is given nothing and has contempt for those born with a silver spoon in their mouths. This leads Nixon to embrace "compulsive manhood," a never-ending quest to prove his masculinity.

It is perhaps fitting to end this introduction with Bingham's drawing on Michael Kimmel's notion of "compulsive manhood" because it indicates how sadly troubled many common conceptions of masculinity are. Most of the essays in this collection deal with cultural texts that can only be understood within such troubling contexts of masculinity, or represent masculinity and male sexuality within cultures that embrace such troubling notions. Thus, at the end of one millennium and the beginning of another, masculinity remains a disturbingly complex and shifting category that the essays in this book help us to better understand.

works cited

Bingham, Dennis. 1994. *Acting Male: Masculinities in the Films of James Stewart, Jack Nicholson, and Clint Eastwood.* New Brunswick: Rutgers University Press.

Cohan, Steven and Ina Rae Hark. 1993. *Screening the Male: Exploring Masculinities in Hollywood Cinema.* New York: Routledge.

Dyer, Richard. [1982] 1992. "Don't Look Now: The Male Pin-Up." In *The Sexual Subject: A Screen Reader in Sexuality.* New York: Routledge: 265–76.

Jeffords, Susan. 1994. *Hard Bodies: Hollywood Masculinity in the Reagan Era.* New Brunswick: Rutgers University Press.

Neale, Steve. [1983] 1992. "Masculinity as Spectacle" In *The Sexual Subject: A Screen Reader in Sexuality.* New York: Routledge: 277–87.

Lehman, Peter. 1993. *Running Scared: Masculinity and the Representation of the Male Body.* Philadelphia: Temple University Press.

Silverman, Kaja. 1992. *Male Subjectivity at the Margins.* New York: Routledge.

"someone

is going

to pay"

resurgent

white masculinity

in *ransom*

k r i n   g a b b a r d

An early scene in *Ransom* (directed by Ron Howard in 1996) presents an image that powerfully symbolizes the masculine anxieties of both the hero and the film.[1] We see Tom Mullen (Mel Gibson), the wealthy owner of an airline company, his wife, Kate (Rene Russo), and their son, Sean (Brawley Nolte) at a science fair in New York's Central Park. The boy has built an airborne device in which a video camera is attached to two helium-filled orange balloons. Using a remote unit, Sean, who looks about nine years old, controls the flight of the balloons as well as the direction of the video camera. Suddenly, kidnappers seize the boy while both parents are momentarily distracted. We then see the balloons drifting slowly out of the park. The possibility that his son has been kidnapped begins to dawn on Tom just as the balloons collide with the cornice of an apartment building. One of the balloons bursts, sending the video camera plummeting to the sidewalk. The falling camera functions as a synecdoche for the son, who has been seized while deploying that camera over the rooftops of

New York City. With its two large circular balloons, the contraption is also a metaphor for Tom's prominent but threatened masculinity: his "balls."

Those who threaten Tom and his status as a member of a white ruling class include not only the group of working-class kidnappers but also an African-American FBI agent who seeks to control Tom's negotiations with them. The racial thematics of the film function entirely apart from the narrative, but they create similarities between *Ransom* and the growing number of films in the "angry white male" genre. The familiar white male heroics of Mel Gibson are deployed primarily against the persona of Delroy Lindo, who plays Special Agent Lonnie Hawkins. Lindo's character speaks with a slight accent associated with working-class black people, but otherwise he comports himself very much as an assimilated member of the American middle class. The white kidnappers, however, are much more likely to engage in signifying practices associated with African Americans. Nevertheless, it is Lindo's black FBI agent who embodies white anxieties about black masculinity and its imagined threat to the dominance of white men, particularly for a character played by Mel Gibson, whose lack of physical stature may be partially responsible for his desire to project a hypermasculine image in most of his films.[2] In the case of *Ransom*, Gibson's character encounters a man whose size (and color) threaten his quest for masculine dominance.

Sean's attempts at urban surveillance foreshadow a series of gazes directed at Tom Mullen as he endures the pain and humiliation caused by the kidnapping and attempts to regain control of his life. As the large body of psychoanalytic film theory suggests, looking in movies usually involves empowerment while being looked at often means the opposite. From his penthouse apartment near Central Park, Mullen can look out over the city from a privileged location consistent with his financial and social position.[3] Once his son has been kidnapped, however, that lofty position becomes systematically less available. Tom learns that his movements are being carefully monitored not only by the kidnappers but also by the FBI, the media, and random onlookers, almost all of them from the working class. Although the plot of *Ransom* is driven by Tom's attempts to retrieve his son, the film is in many ways much more involved with Tom's needs to retrieve his manhood, in particular that version of manhood that has little to do with the daily demands of fatherhood. The film repeatedly dramatizes Tom's paranoia as he confronts emasculating forces linked to family, class, and—most disturbingly in a film that presents the familiar face of "liberal" Hollywood multiculturalism—race.

my father the hero

The prominent image of large but fragile balls floating inexorably toward destruction can also be read as a symbol for Tom's vulnerability as a father. Although the film repeatedly pays lip service to the importance of families, *Ransom* reveals the tension between life in the nuclear family and the aspirations of the American hero, especially the familiar type that Robert B. Ray calls "the outlaw hero," the ubiquitous figure in American narratives who runs away from home and rejects values associated with domesticity and conventional social organization. American heroes of this breed make their own laws, answering to an internal but infallible sense of right and wrong. The hero often risks his life to save the people he cares about, but he usually moves on as the narrative ends, still resisting the compromises and entanglements that come with family and stability.[4] Clark Gable, Humphrey Bogart, and John Wayne made careers playing this character. More recently, Mel Gibson has joined Clint Eastwood, Tom Cruise, Bruce Willis, and various others who continue the tradition. It is difficult to imagine any of these actors playing a domesticated man in a stable relationship with a wife and child. Eastwood, the oldest of the current crop of outlaw heroes, has never once played such a character in all thirty-eight of his starring roles since 1967. Eastwood may spend large portions of a film pursuing a woman, and he may ride off with a woman at a film's conclusion, but if an Eastwood character is ever married in a film's "back story," he is inevitably estranged, divorced, or widowed. Because Eastwood's masculine presentation is incompatible with the daily frustrations and accommodations of conventional family life, a stable loving relationship becomes for his characters an unrepresentable element in an impossible past. Although Gibson plays a family man in *Ransom*, he spends most of the film asserting his manhood in violation of the family conventions that are missing from the films of Eastwood and the other male stars of the action cinema. The fundamental and incoherent project of *Ransom* is to represent Tom Mullen as, simultaneously, a family man and a "real" man of the action cinema.

Frank Krutnik understands paradoxes of masculine representation through Freud's account of the male child's oedipal crises. For Freud, the child must renounce the mother and accept the authority of the father in order to escape the threat of castration and ultimately to achieve masculine autonomy. To maintain his autonomy, the man must avoid a return to the body of the mother—or her surrogates— who hold out that promise of plenitude, the "oceanic" feeling. Freud says that even "normal" male desire returns the man to his "infantile fixation on tender feelings on the mother" (Freud 168–69). These feelings, however, must always coexist with the fear of castration as punishment for violating the father's law. For Krutnik *The Maltese Falcon* (1941) is the purest representation of "redeemed" masculinity, especially at the climax when Sam (Humphrey Bogart) overcomes his desire for the murderous Brigid (Mary Astor) and hands her over to the agents of patriarchal law on the police force. Krutnik is more interested, however, in the more masochistic scenario of certain *films noirs* of the mid- to late 1940s that reflect the inevitable dissatisfaction with traditional representations of masculinity in postwar America. In films such as *Out of the Past* (1947) and *The Killers* (1946), even stars who would later become macho icons like Robert Mitchum and Burt Lancaster betray their father figures and submit to the will of phallic women. Although these films tend to be moral fables about what happens to men who swerve from the true path of masculinity, the films also reveal male anxieties about living up to the impossible standards of manliness presented by American culture. Films such as *Bonnie and Clyde* (1967), *Body Heat* (1982), and *Basic Instinct* (1992) have continued to offer audiences the complex experience of identifying with men who violate the laws of patriarchy on multiple levels as they submit to sexual and powerful women.

Ransom is much more typical of the mainstreams of the Hollywood cinema in which men achieve masculine autonomy by resisting union with a woman, but it is unusual in creating a character like Tom Mullen who does so from *within* an idealized family structure. While the fathering of children gives men a certain degree of phallic authority, it also erodes their autonomy and draws them back into the world of the child, the mother, and the oceanic feeling from which the adult male in dominant American narrative must escape. *Ransom* dramatizes what happens when myths of the American hero are superimposed on myths of the bourgeois family. Something's got to give.[5] In the script by Richard Price, Jonathan Gold, and Alexander Ignon, the hero defies his wife and agent Hawkins by refusing to pay a $2 million ransom. Convinced that the kidnappers will kill his son as soon as they receive the ransom money, Mullen appears on television and promises the ransom money to anyone who provides information leading to the capture of the kidnappers, dead or alive. If the kidnappers return his son, Mullen will withdraw the reward.[6]

Mullen makes this decision entirely on his own. His wife, Kate, and Agent Hawkins are flabbergasted when they see Tom on the television broadcast, and they both look for ways to pay off the kidnappers with or without Tom's cooperation. In a conversation with Kate, Tom explains his decision: if the Mullens pay, they are likely to lose their son; but if the kidnappers know that a huge bounty has been put on their heads, they will return the child "in mint condition" and live the rest of their lives without being targets for bounty hunters. As an essential element in the gender and racial politics of the film, Tom's logic is meant to be more convincing to the audience than to the film's other characters. By daring the kidnappers to kill his son, Tom can resist the voice of the Other—in this case a woman and a black man—and remain the audacious, autonomous protagonist of his own narrative rather than a passive player in the kidnappers' drama. As several critics pointed out, a crucial scene in *Ransom* recalls the final shots of *The Godfather* (1972): Tom and his advisors are photographed from his wife's point of view as she discovers that she has been excluded from Tom's deliberations. A major difference, however, is that *Ransom* does not, like *The Godfather*, characterize Tom's decision to exclude his wife from "family business" as a descent into evil. Quite the contrary. Tom's gamble pays off when Jimmy Shaker (Gary Sinise), a corrupt police detective who is the leader of the kidnappers, kills his co-conspirators and attempts to collect the reward money as if he were an honest cop who had stumbled upon the kidnappers' lair. Tom soon discovers Jimmy's deception and dispatches him in a long and bloody fight scene that climaxes the film. The credits role with the family reunited, the kidnappers destroyed, and the hero vindicated. Any suggestion that Tom has irreparably damaged his marriage by ignoring his wife and risking the life of his son is drowned out by the sound of bullets and by the cathartic drama of Tom's triumphant fight to the death with Jimmy Shaker.

a morlock ascends

The white hero in *Ransom* reestablishes his autonomous masculinity not just because he resists the feminizing effects of family and not just because he kills the mastermind behind the kidnapping of his son. As I have suggested, Tom Mullen also overcomes the attempts of a powerful black man to control his dealings with the kidnappers. Furthermore, Tom enhances his success by escaping the gaze and control of members of the American working class, both black and white.

The film begins at a party in the Mullens' penthouse in which well-heeled guests are served by caterers, one of whom wears a tattoo on her neck, usually a marker of lower-class status and ethnicity. This is Maris (Lili Taylor), later revealed to be one of the kidnappers. Also in a clearly subservient role is a Latina woman, Fatema (Iraida Polanco), the Mullens' housekeeper. Once the kidnapping plot is under way, Tom can no longer interact with members of the working class in so rigidly a hierarchical fashion. In order to deliver the money to the kidnappers, Tom must follow the elaborate orders given to him by Jimmy Shaker, who speaks into a masking device attached to the telephone that gives

11

his voice a deep, demonic resonance. The odyssey on which Jimmy sends Tom takes him first to a swimming pool in a Harlem recreation center where Tom must dive into the water fully clothed in order to retrieve a key to a locker where he will find a change of clothes. Jimmy has also sent Tom into the water to disable the listening device that Tom is likely to be wearing and to change Tom's appearance so that the FBI will have more difficulty following him. This plan also gives Jimmy the pleasure of imagining Tom as he confronts the startled black bathers in and around the pool. The film's construction of an ascendant white masculinity here explicitly contrasts the trim, well-dressed body of Mel Gibson with the dark, partially clothed bodies of Harlem residents, many of them aged and overweight.

After Tom Mullen has emerged from the recreation center, he listens on a portable telephone as Jimmy directs him to a stone quarry in New Jersey. As he drives along the same highway unnoticed by Tom, Jimmy overtly categorizes his relationship with Tom in terms of a class struggle by describing George Pal's 1960 film *The Time Machine*. As Jimmy says, *The Time Machine* foresees a world in the distant future divided into two groups, the Eloi and the Morlocks. The beautiful, blonde, toga-clad Eloi live a carefree existence above ground while the ugly, apelike Morlocks live beneath the surface. The Morlocks provide all the necessities of life for the Eloi, but the Morlocks occasionally ascend to the surface and bring back one of the Eloi for food. Jimmy explains that New York is like the world foreseen in *The Time Machine*. He is a Morlock, and Tom is one of the Eloi: "Every now and then one of you gets snatched." Although Pal's film draws upon Cold War ideology of the 1950s and early 1960s and explains the Morlock/Eloi division in terms of a nuclear holocaust, Jimmy's reading of the film is more faithful to H. G. Wells's 1895 novel on which the film is based. A committed socialist, Wells projected a capitalist economy that would banish workers to underground factories, leaving the surface of the earth a vernal paradise for industrialists and their families. Eventually, the workers revolt and overpower the Eloi on the surface, but only after their long confinement by the forces of capital causes them to evolve into troglodytes who cannot survive above ground. *Ransom*, however, like Hollywood's *The Time Machine*, gives the working-class little sympathy, consistently associating its working-class characters with predators and criminals while portraying the powerful and the elite as their victims.

After finishing his exegesis of *The Time Machine*, Jimmy says to Tom, "See you at the Whitney, see you at the Four Seasons, see you at the Met," ultimately chanting only the mantralike phrase, "See you." Jimmy's look at Tom is tinged with envy and class hatred, but it is only one of many looks that are directed at Tom from the lower classes. Tom is also watched by members of the press corps who camp outside his apartment building as well as by African Americans at the swimming pool. The film even dwells on a medley of gazes in a scene that might otherwise seem gratuitous. Immediately after Tom announces on television that he is transforming the ransom money into a bounty, he is filmed in slow motion picking up the money he has dramatically spread out on the table before him. The music in James Horner's score becomes atonal and percussive, connoting confusion and disorientation. Slow motion shots of Mel Gibson's face are then intercut with three separate shots of employees at the television station staring at him with varying degrees of disbelief. The camera then shoots Gibson from behind so that the TV spotlights are on either side of his body, emphasizing the extent to which he has become a media spectacle. Leaving the station, Tom's image is doubled as he walks past the mirrorlike exterior of the building while a crowd shouts at him. Symbolically in danger of becoming fragmented by the plenitude of refracted images of himself, Tom is trying to seize control of the narrative so that he is once again the one who looks down on the people and not the one at whose multiple images the people can freely gaze.

The tension between Tom and the working class is also central to one of *Ransom*'s more important subplots. When Sean is first seized, Tom suspects the involvement of Jackie Brown, a union official who had accused Tom of bribing him to prevent a strike at Tom's company, Endeavor Airlines. We learn that Brown was imprisoned after a sting operation involving union deals at another airline. In negotiations with prosecutors, Brown offered to testify against Mullen in exchange for a shorter sentence. Tom denied offering a bribe, and an extensive investigation by the FBI declared that Tom was innocent of the charge. When the FBI arrive at his home after Sean has been kidnapped, Tom reluctantly explains to Agent Hawkins that he did, in fact, arrange to give Brown a payoff, and he attempts to justify the denial he made when Brown's accusations became public. "See, most guys at the top, they acquire their airline. Not . . . not me. I built Endeavor from the ground up, and it's mine. No bastard's taking it away from me. No union, no government, and no two-bit gangster like Jackie Brown. . . . I paid him off. I initiated the bribe. I had a business to run. I had two thousand employees, God knows how many customers, and I didn't have time for a goddamned strike."

Tom and Lonnie Hawkins then ask Jackie Brown in prison if he is involved in the kidnapping. Jackie Brown is played by Dan Hedaya, a rough-hewn actor who is more likely to play a scrappy schemer than a graceful aristocrat. Wearing bright orange prison coveralls, a bad haircut, and a day's growth of stubble, Brown is at first confused by a visit from his antagonist but soon becomes enraged when he hears Tom accusing him once again. He crawls over a table and strikes Tom on the

13

face, loudly proclaiming his innocence. As he is dragged back to his cell, he shouts, "I got six of my own kids, and I would die for every one of them, and I haven't seen them since I got locked up in here because of YOU. Why aren't you in here?" Whatever sympathy the audience may have for Jackie Brown at this point is left unexplored. He disappears from the film after this scene. We later discover, however, that Jackie Brown is at least indirectly involved with the kidnapping. During the same conversation in which Jimmy Shaker explains *The Time Machine* to Tom, Jimmy says that he had seen Tom on television professing his innocence in the Brown affair. Once again the gaze of the Other is stigmatized when Jimmy says that he looked into Tom's eyes and could tell that he was not telling the truth: "You're a lyin' ass dog, pal." Jimmy felt certain that Tom was the kind of man who would buy his way out of trouble.

The fact that Tom paid off Jackie Brown and then lied about it helped to bring about the kidnapping crisis that Tom endures. But there are no other important repercussions, at least not in the film's diegesis. When Kate finds out that Tom had lied even to her about his innocence, she expresses disappointment in one brief scene. But like Tom's unilateral decision to withhold the ransom money from the kidnappers, his deception of his wife in the Jackie Brown affair is forgotten, and presumably forgiven when the family is united at the end of the film. It can even be argued that Tom has learned from his mistakes—he paid off Jackie Brown, but now he knows better and will not pay off the kidnappers. The only other person who knows the truth about Jackie Brown is Agent Hawkins, but in a scene that seems awkwardly tacked on to the script, he tells Tom that he may never tell anyone what he knows about the affair.

The class issues raised by the Brown affair—and much else in the film—are further effaced by suggestions that Tom and his wife both come from the working class, or at least that they have only recently joined the ranks of the super rich. We learn that Kate was once a grade school teacher, and a TV commercial for Tom's airline that runs early in the film portrays Tom dressed in a cowboy hat, as a self-made man. It even seems that they have only recently moved into a Fifth Avenue penthouse that is still undergoing renovations. Although Tom and Kate are elegantly dressed during the initial party scene, they spend most of the film wearing blue jeans, and in the case of Tom, a T-shirt with a school insignia, the kind of "legible clothing" usually associated with the working class.[7] When Tom visits Jackie Brown in prison, he wears a black leather jacket. All of this fuzzes over *Ransom*'s important class dialectic and allows audiences to see Mel Gibson as another working-class action hero fighting for his family and not as a white-collar criminal.

not a love story

The person in *Ransom* who seems most concerned about social and economic class is Jimmy Shaker. In the American cinema, as in much of American political life, members of the white haute bourgeoisie are seldom marked as possessing "class," just as they are almost never marked as having "race." A term such as "class warfare" inevitably suggests insurrections by the lower elements rather than measures taken at the top to eliminate opportunities for those on the bottom. When Tom Mullen argues that he wanted to prevent a "goddamned strike" at his company, Endeavor Airlines, there is no suggestion that he may have prevented his employees from winning better salaries and working conditions. The film takes the side of the attractive captain of industry, not that of his workers. So, Jimmy Shaker, who compares himself to one of H. G. Wells's Morlocks, is the one unattractively obsessed with class issues, not unlike black characters in many Hollywood films who can't stop talking about race in the presence of white people who seem completely oblivious to racial distinctions. In *Die Hard with a Vengeance* (1995), for example, the constant harangues of Zeus Carver (Samuel L. Jackson) finally lead to the outburst by John McClane (Bruce Willis): "Just because I'm white, you don't like me. Have I oppressed you? Have I oppressed your people somehow?"[8] Similarly, Tom Mullen is irritated by Jimmy Shaker's concern with class because he does not see himself involved in any class struggle. The American cinema has perpetuated the notion that the white ruling class is not itself a class but a legitimate element of the status quo. Like the members of that class, the American cinema often categorizes those who talk of race and class as, at best, misguided malcontents. The extent to which white American paranoia lies behind this pattern of representation is especially clear when films such as *Die Hard with a Vengeance* and *Ransom* foreground an obsessed Other full of anger about race or class.

FBI Agent Hawkins briefly alludes to class difference when he is shown speaking sweetly to his wife on the telephone, urging her to hug their daughter and expressing satisfaction with his own middle-class status: "I'm so glad we're not rich. You just got to thank God for what you have." He then breaks off the conversation when Tom Mullen enters. Throughout the film Hawkins never once mentions race. Nevertheless, the central conflict in *Ransom* does not simply match Tom Mullen/Mel Gibson with a group of white kidnappers. Symbolically, Agent Hawkins is the *real* obstacle to Mullen's attempts to regain the manhood that is in danger of floating away like fragile balloons.

Hiring Delroy Lindo to play Hawkins was an inspired bit of casting. Very few actors, black or white, carry themselves with as much phallic power. For *Ransom*, Lindo even adopts the look of many urban black males who have shaved their heads while retaining some facial hair. Because of the long association of hair with sexuality, baldness often symbolizes castration. Consequently, bald men face three choices: they can cover the tops of their heads with wigs or with elaborate combing strategies in hopes of denying their castration; they can leave the top of the head bare while grooming the hair on the sides in a conventional fashion, thus refusing to acknowledge the association of baldness with castration; and finally, they can completely disavow castration by shaving off all of their remaining hair in order to *become* the phallus. White male stars such as Yul Brynner and Telly Savalas embraced this third choice in the 1950s and 1970s, but in the 1990s a completely shaved head was associated primarily with black men, most notably star athletes such as Michael Jordan and gangsta rappers such as Tupac Shakur. As has been the case in American culture at least since the nineteenth century, white men have looked to black men as masculine role models even as they fear their hypersexuality.[9] Not surprisingly, many young white men in the 1990s followed African-American fashion by shaving their heads. Appropriately, one of the white kidnappers in *Ransom* sports a hairless pate.

In *Ransom*, the phallic head of Delroy Lindo bears a commanding and even threatening countenance. If you know Spanish, you know that Lindo is not *lindo*. But at the same time that Lindo can *look* extremely menacing, he can also be gentle and accommodating. In his public appearances, Delroy Lindo is good-natured and personable. Obviously a gifted actor rather than a "natural" performer, Lindo has given convincing performances as evil characters who seem at first to be reasonable men. In *Get Shorty* (1995) his Bo Catlett initially presents himself as a Runyonesque gangster and an aspiring screenwriter. He is soon revealed, however, to be a sociopathic killer. In a crucial scene, he holds the young daughter of his henchmen Bear (James Gandolfini) on his lap, speaking sweetly to her while clearly implying that he is capable of hurting her if Bear does not do his bidding. Because of Lindo's engaging manner, the child is completely unaware that she is in any danger. In *Clockers* (1995), Lindo plays the drug dealer Rodney, who initially seems good-hearted, even functioning as a father-surrogate for the young hero Strike (Mekhi Phifer). Once again, Lindo's character eventually reveals a murderous side, and as in *Get Shorty*, his violent death is obligatory. As Lonnie Hawkins, Lindo never reveals a dark side, but he is assertive and forceful when necessary. For the ideological project of the film, however, he must carry a great deal of racial menace in his face and body, not to mention the intertextual baggage from earlier roles in films such as *Get Shorty* and *Clockers*.

In the narrative of *Ransom*, Agent Hawkins continually attempts to rein in the heroics of Tom Mullen, assuring him that he's only there "to get your boy back." Nevertheless, the tension begins early when Hawkins slams his own hand down on top of Mullen's when the phone first rings and Tom is anxious to speak with the kidnappers before the FBI staff is fully prepared to trace the call. Later, after Hawkins and Mullen visit Jackie Brown in prison, Mullen wonders if the same FBI that failed to catch him for the Brown payoff is capable of finding his son. Hawkins chooses a curious means of reassuring Tom: "Take a good look at me. Take a *real* good look at me. I got to be real good at what I do to be in the position I'm in. See, they didn't assign me to the Endeavor investigation. But if I had been, if it's any consolation to you, I'd have nailed you." It's not exactly clear why Hawkins asks Mullen to look at him. Alongside this powerful but unacknowledged registering of his race, Hawkins could be suggesting that a black man must be extremely talented in order to rise through the ranks of an organization with a racist past such as the FBI, or he could simply be asking that Mullen observe the determination in his face. Either way, Hawkins is saying that he would win in an adversarial relationship with Mullen. In the racial and gender dynamics of the film, this is a challenge that Tom Mullen accepts. After the FBI intervenes and botches Tom's attempt to deliver the money to the kidnappers, Mullen feels sufficiently betrayed to strike Hawkins in the face as soon as he returns to his penthouse. Tom had insisted that he make the drop unassisted, but a small army of agents watched his every move. Although it is clear that Hawkins is not giving all the orders, Tom holds him personally responsible for preventing him from handing over the ransom money. In the narrative, Tom is simply taking out his anger on the person he feels is most guilty. But it is significant that the target of his anger is a black man seeking control. After Tom strikes him, Hawkins immediately immobilizes Tom by holding his arm behind his back and pinning him to the floor face down. This is the last time that Tom will find himself under the control of the black FBI agent.

When Mullen subsequently decides not to pay the kidnappers, he is not only overcoming the impotence brought on by his life as a family man. He is also overcoming the impotence he feels in the face of constant attempts by a black man to restrain him. Hawkins even works on Kate by telling her that Tom lied to her about Jackie Brown in hopes that she might dissuade him from withdrawing the ransom. Nevertheless, toward the end of the film, when Jimmy Shaker holds a gun on Tom and tells him to drive to the bank for the reward money, Tom surreptitiously finds a way to summon Hawkins. On one level, this is simply an obligatory moment in the American action cinema in which the purposes of the "outlaw hero" and the "official hero" converge. For Robert B. Ray, the reconciliatory finale is essential to the Western and various "disguised westerns." In *Shane* (1953), for example, the title character comes to the rescue of Joe Starrett; in *Casablanca* (1942) Rick saves Victor Laszlo; and in *Star Wars* (1977) Han Solo extricates Luke Skywalker from a near-death situation. As Ray points out, this narrative strategy is especially satisfying because it allows the audience to have it both ways, relieving them of the anxiety of choosing one hero over the other. The reconciliatory finale also functions ideologically by justifying the antisocial, even paranoid behavior of the more glamorous outlaw hero. According to this syntax, however, Tom Mullen should be rescuing Lonnie Hawkins and not the other way around.

Furthermore, the phallic male competition between Mullen and Hawkins continues right up until the last seconds of the film. Before Hawkins has arrived on the scene, Tom has taken charge once again and severely beaten Shaker with his fists. When Hawkins and the police finally do arrive, they hold Shaker at gunpoint and repeatedly tell Mullen to drop the gun he has acquired in the struggle. Mullen is still resisting, refusing to relinquish the pistol. As is almost always the case in this film, Mullen is vindicated: like most movie villains of recent vintage, Shaker is capable of one last murderous assault even after he appears to be near death. Just when Shaker seems on the verge of collapse, he reaches for a gun strapped to his ankle and takes a shot at Mullen. Although Agent Hawkins puts three bullets into Shaker's body, Mullen strikes first, quickly getting off a shot that hits Shaker in the heart. Tom wins again.

In many ways, Lindo's Lonnie Hawkins recalls the many black judges and police captains who regularly appear in Hollywood films. These figures are often allowed a great deal of anger and power as they deliver rebukes or bark orders at white defendants and subordinates. (The convention was even parodied in *Last Action Hero* [1993].) As Ella Shohat has written, black characters in movies are often "'guests' in the narrative" (240), placed there simply to give presence to African Americans rather than to serve the needs of the diegesis. Sharon Willis points out that the ubiquitous black judge or police chief does more than just affirm a film's multicultural pretensions; as "the embodiment of legal authority or moral surveillance" these characters "operate as indexes of paranoid fantasies that situate African Americans as the ones who know the truth about race, while avoiding any occasion for a reciprocated gaze that would cause the dominant culture to look at itself through another's eyes" (Willis 5–6). But rather than efface the implied threat these characters must carry, *Ransom* brings the paranoid fantasy to the surface by allowing Agent Hawkins to confront the hero with his transgressions. Although the narrative displaces class and racial elements into purely legal conflicts, Tom Mullen does more than just refuse the "reciprocated gaze" that action heroes such as Bruce

Willis usually avoid; Mullen actively works to triumph over the judgmental gaze of the black FBI agent. In this way, the film makes Hawkins the double of Jimmy Shaker, another figure associated with the law who gazes at Jimmy and passes judgment on him.

In fact, Jimmy Shaker and the other white kidnappers fill in many aspects of the film's paranoia about the empowerment of African Americans that are missing from actual black characters. As is often the case in *Ransom*, negative associations attached to blacks, women, and the working class slide together and overlap; like highly charged elements in the culture's dreamwork, they are displaced and condensed. One of the kidnappers has "boom" tattooed on his hand with one letter on each finger, recalling the "love" and "hate" on the hands of Radio Raheem (Bill Nunn) in Spike Lee's *Do the Right Thing* (1988) (a quotation by Lee of Robert Mitchum's hands in *Night of the Hunter* [1955]). While Agent Hawkins never uses ghetto language, the kidnappers regularly adopt speech patterns and a metalanguage associated with African Americans. The kidnapper with the shaved head says, "Hey, ya know what the brothers call this? 'Some more draaama.'" Maris refers at one point to the power of her lover, Jimmy Shaker, by saying, "My man is runnin' shit." When Shaker appears in Tom's apartment to claim the reward money, he holds a gun on Tom and at one point gestures with his arm and shoulder in the style of a black rap artist.

Of the many films in which white males face challenges from blacks, women, immigrants, and other previously disempowered groups, *Falling Down* (1993) is most often mentioned by critics. But this film problematizes the confusion of D-Fens, the white protagonist played by Michael Douglas. The audience is invited to appreciate the irony in his final remark, "*I'm* the bad guy?" Films such as *Ransom*, however, invite almost total sympathy for the white hero and do not acknowledge his paranoia toward the Other. In this sense, *Ransom* has more in common with *Forrest Gump* (1994), another film with a sympathetic white hero and carefully coded racist sentiments. Early on, the film includes a clip from *Birth of a Nation* (1914), surely the most important Angry White Male film ever made. As part of a catalogue of Forrest's ancestors, the old black-and-white footage from *Birth of a Nation* is doctored so that the face of Forrest/Tom Hanks digitally replaces that of Henry Walthall as he leads the charge of the Ku Klux Klan. Although viewers with a knowledge of film history may watch this scene with ironic bemusement, a later scene is meant to be taken much more seriously. John Groch has said that Forrest perfectly embodies the angry white male when he encounters his beloved Jenny (Robin Wright) with a group of student radicals during the Vietnam War years. Forrest watches Jenny being slapped by her white activist boyfriend at the same time that a black militant is directing a nonstop verbal harangue at Forrest. Seemingly oblivious to the African-American man, Forrest runs to the side of Jenny and repeatedly punches the boy who had hit her. The voluble black man does not commit violence, and Forrest does not direct any hostility toward him, but as Groch argues, the black militant's contiguity to the violence and his aggressive participation in the same antiwar harangue as the abusive white peacenik suggest that Forrest might as well be beating up the black man.

Ransom adopts the same practice of racist displacement as *Forrest Gump*. While *Gump* finesses its racial thematics by having the angry white hero ignore the black militant while foregrounding his race, *Ransom* can allow its angry white hero to strike the black man because the narrative has *not* foregrounded his race. In both films, however, the violent outbursts allow audiences to see white men righteously asserting themselves over hypermasculine black characters. Although Mel Gibson has played opposite Danny Glover in all four of the *Lethal Weapon* films, his relationship with Lindo in *Ransom* does not suggest the homosocial, interracial romance of the *Lethal Weapon* films, not to mention the many other American narratives that allow white men to bond in significant ways with men of color. *The Last of the Mohicans, Moby Dick, Two Years before the Mast,* and *Huckleberry Finn* are the most commonly cited American novels in this tradition. Similarly, in the Hollywood films *Casablanca* (1942) and *The Man Who Shot Liberty Valance* (1964), the outlaw heroes have faithful black companions. The familiar interracial relationship has been updated and conventionalized in the three *Die Hard* films (1988, 1990, 1995), the two *48 Hrs* (1982, 1990), *Unforgiven* (1992), *The Last Boy Scout* (1991), *Dave* (1993), *Seven* (1995), *The Glimmer Man* (1996), and even *The Long Kiss Goodnight* (1996), in which Geena Davis plays a secret agent on the run assisted by a private detective played by Samuel L. Jackson. All of these films in one way or another speak to the need among white people to imagine that they can be redeemed by winning the love and devotion of a single powerful, dark-skinned man.[10] All those centuries of hatred and oppression can be wiped away by this one pure act of love. If only it were so. But unlike Danny Glover in the *Lethal Weapon* films, Delroy Lindo in *Ransom* has little in common with Queequeg, Chingachgook, or Nigger Jim. On the one hand, Lindo superficially resembles the Glover character in the *Lethal Weapon* series, who is also a happily married family man whose failed attempts at constraining the Gibson character only add to the white man's luster. On the other hand, at no time in *Ransom* does Tom show even mild affection for the black FBI agent, while Hawkins himself is less concerned about the personal situation of Tom and much more concerned about the displeasure of his superiors at the FBI. *Ransom* vaguely resembles canonical American narratives that speak to misgivings about the feminizing effects of family and childrearing, but the film has much more to do with arousing and containing white male uneasiness about perceived threats from hypermasculine black men.

Although the racist underpinnings of the *Die Hards*, the *Lethal Weapons*, and the rest have been thoroughly unmasked by critics such as Fred Pfeil, Sharon Willis, and Robyn Weigman, *Ransom* is an especially malign contribution to this tradition. The racial and gender dynamics of *Ransom* might be considered alongside the hypermasculine posturings in many of Mel Gibson's films (Luhr 227–46). But *Ransom* should also be compared to other screenplays by Richard Price, who wrote scripts for *Sea of Love* (1989), *Kiss of Death* (1995), and *Clockers* (1995), as well as *Ransom*. Price may have brought an urban, race-conscious style to the script for *Ransom* that became paranoid in the hands of Gibson and Ron Howard. The obsessions of director Howard surely play a role in *Ransom*'s desperate reinscription of discredited forms of masculinity. His earlier films such as *Gung Ho* (1986), *Backdraft* (1991), *Far and Away* (1992), and *Apollo 13* (1995) are all driven by a concern with male bravado and reactionary, but unexamined notions of heroism. He may even have been seeking to revise the public's memory of him as the young Opie on *The Andy Griffith Show* and the nerdy Richie on *Happy Days*. After the release of *Ransom*, Bernard Weinraub wrote in the *New York Times*,

> Mr. Howard acknowledged that his acting persona, especially on "Happy Days," and his smiling, easy demeanor had helped shape the impression that he was a film maker without an edge. "I've always been involved in sort of pop entertainment," he said. "You live with a little bit of frustration that that kind of work is not taken as seriously as other kinds of work. I mean, there's great feedback, but yeah, sure, I was sort of legitimately categorized and typed as the all-American guy." (C11)

Howard also told the *New York Times* that he identified with Mel Gibson's character in the film: "He's a winning character but flawed" (Weinraub C11). But Gibson's flaws in *Ransom* are the kind that audiences can tolerate, especially when they complement qualities that speak to conscious and unconscious anxieties about social, racial, and gender hierarchies. With a fantasy about a hardworking couple fighting their way to Fifth Avenue splendor and a climactic death struggle against an implacable villain, almost anyone can identify with an attractive white man struggling to prevent his masculinity from floating away.

1. I thank Peter Lehman, William Luhr, and Susan White for their extremely helpful contributions to this chapter.

2. Although the vertical measurements of male stars are zealously guarded secrets, Mel Gibson appears to be about 5' 7" tall. In Hollywood, faces clearly matter more than bodies; the industry has thoroughly mastered the art of disguising the diminutive physical stature of leading men such as Gibson, Alan Ladd, Paul Newman, Kirk Douglas, Al Pacino, and Tom Cruise. In the case of Mel Gibson, however, height may have something to do with his strident attempts to present himself as manly. Gibson spent much of the 1990s making films that insist on male perseverance, often, as William Luhr has pointed out, to the point of extreme masochism. In *The Man without a Face* (1993) and *Braveheart* (1995), two films that Gibson has directed, the hero attempts to live up to what Luhr accurately characterizes as an idealized if not impossible notion of masculinity.

3. For a revealing account of how specific paintings were chosen to make the Mullens' apartment look opulent but viewer friendly, see Berman.

4. Among the many commentators on the myth of the American hero, see Fiedler, Slotkin, Chase, and Ray.

5. The emasculating and feminizing pressures of family life that bear down on Tom Mullen in *Ransom* have even drawn the attention of critics in the popular press. Here is an excerpt from Aaron Gill's review in *Time Out New York*:

   > Like so many Hollywood thrillers, *Ransom* is built on a reactionary psychological subtext. If Tom (Mel Gibson) is the archetypal father, rendered impotent by his feminine love for his son (just indulge me for one minute), only by denying that love and reasserting his masculine impulse can he again find his rightful place in the universe (i.e., on top). Hey, it worked for Agamemnon, right? (59)

   Agamemnon killed his daughter not his son, but the reviewer has correctly identified the film's ambivalence about family.

6. *Ransom* (1996) is based on a 1956 film called *Ransom!*, directed by Alex Segal. The screenplay was by Cyril Hume and Richard Maibaum, who get credit for "story" in the 1996 version. There is of course no black FBI agent in the original film, and the plot culminates simply with the decision by the protagonist (Glenn Ford) to change the ransom money into reward money, which soon results in the return of his son.

7. According to an only partially facetious book by Paul Fussell, clothing inscribed with written letters marks the wearer as belonging to the "prole" classes, those who seek to gain prestige by associating themselves with the name of a university or a successful product printed on their T-shirts and baseball caps.

8. I have relied on Sharon Willis's *High Contrast* for this citation as well as for much of the argument in this section of the essay.

9. Eric Lott has documented the appropriation of black forms of masculinity by whites, beginning at least in the 1840s when minstrel shows were the most popular entertainment in America. Lott also argues that black men are still masculine role models for working-class white American men: "this dynamic, persisting into adulthood, is so much a part of most

American white men's equipment for living that they remain entirely unaware of their participation in it" (53).

10. Leslie Fiedler is the critic most associated with this tradition in American literature. For cinema and television, also see Pfeil (1–36), Willis (27–59), Weigman (149–202), and Penley (86–98).

works cited

Berman, Avis. 1996. "In the Script, the Art Says, 'They're Rich.'" *New York Times*, Nov. 3, II: 43.

Chase, Richard Volney. 1980. *The American Novel and Its Traditions*. Baltimore: Johns Hopkins University Press.

Fiedler, Leslie. 1960. *Love and Death in the American Novel*. New York: Stein and Day.

Freud, Sigmund. 1974. "A Special Type of Object Choice Made by Men" (Contributions to the Psychology of Love I) [1910]. *The Standard Edition of the Complete Psychological Works of Sigmund Freud*. Trans and ed. James Strachey, 11: 165–75. London: Hogarth.

Fussell, Paul. 1983. *Class: A Guide through the American Status System*. New York: Summit.

Gill, Aaron. 1996. Review of *Ransom*. *Time Out New York*, Nov. 1–14, 59.

Groch, John. 1996. "Afterbirth of a Nation: The Angry White Male's Ride to the Rescue in Contemporary American Cinema." Society for Cinema Studies Annual Conference. University of North Texas, Dallas. March 7.

Krutnik, Frank. 1991. *In a Lonely Street: Film Noir, Genre, Masculinity*. New York: Routledge.

Lott, Eric. 1993. *Love and Theft: Blackface Minstrelsy and the American Working Class*. New York: Oxford University Press.

Luhr, William. 1999. "Mutilating Mel: Martyrdom and Masculinity in *Braveheart*." In *Mythologies of Violence in Postmodern Media*, ed. Christopher Sharrett. Detroit: Wayne State University Press, 227–46.

Penley, Constance. 1997. *NASA/Trek: Popular Science and Sex in America*. New York: Verso.

Pfeil, Fred. 1995. *White Guys: Studies in Postmodern Domination and Difference*. New York: Verso.

Ray, Robert B. 1985. *A Certain Tendency of the Hollywood Cinema: 1930–1980*. Princeton: Princeton University Press.

Shohat, Ella. 1991. "Ethnicities-in-Relation: Toward a Multicultural Reading of American Cinema." In *Unspeakable Images: Ethnicity and the American Cinema*, ed. Lester Friedman, 215–50. Urbana: University of Illinois Press.

Slotkin, Richard. 1973. *Regeneration through Violence: The Mythology of the American Frontier, 1600–1860*. Middletown, Conn.: Wesleyan University Press.

Weigman, Robyn. 1995. *American Anatomies: Theorizing Race and Gender*. Durham, N.C.: Duke University Press.

Weinraub, Bernard. 1996. "The Dark Underbelly of Ron Howard." *New York Times*, Nov. 12. C11.

Willis, Sharon. 1997. *High Contrast: Race and Gender in Contemporary Hollywood Film*. Durham, N.C.: Duke University Press.

crying

over the

melodramatic

penis

melodrama

and male nudity

in films of the 90s

peter lehman

Over the opening credit sequence of Neil Jordan's *The Crying Game* (1992), we hear Percy Sledge singing "When a Man Loves a Woman." The song we later learn is used ironically since the film deals centrally with Fergus, a man who discovers that Dil, the woman he loves, is really a man. The song points to how carefully Jordan uses music in the film. Over the film's closing credit sequence, for example, he returns to ironic use of music with Lyle Lovett's cover version of the Tammy Wynette classic, "Stand by Your Man." Clever as this selection of songs is, however, it is the title song, "The Crying Game," that points to a significant central feature of the film: melodrama and the male body.

Traditionally, melodrama has been associated with women and the female spectator. There are, however, interesting traditions of male melodrama and one of them is a somewhat minor and overlooked pop/rock music tradition, songs which frequently have the word "crying" in their titles. Johnnie Ray's "Cry" (1952) probably marks the beginning of that tradition, and many of Roy Orbison's songs, including his classic hit "Crying" (1962), are the most artistically significant recordings within that tradition. Perhaps not coincidentally, Orbison himself recorded a cover version of "Cry."[1] Jordan's choice of Dave Berry's "The Crying Game" (1964) as the title song of his film invokes this male melodramatic rock tradition, and it does so in a manner which relates to the film's shocking and now famous revelation scene.

In *Running Scared: Masculinity and the Representation of the Male Body*, I argued that images of men and the male body are caught within a polarity not unlike the mother/whore dichotomy which structures so many representations of women. At one pole, we have the powerful, awesome spectacle of phallic masculinity, and at the other its vulnerable, pitiable, and frequently comic collapse. The stars of male action films (e.g., John Wayne, Clint Eastwood, Arnold Schwarzenegger, Sylvester Stallone) and hard-core porn (John Holmes and Jamie Gillis), for example, typify the former. Short actors with rounded bodies (e.g., Edward G. Robinson, Peter Lorre), certain comic actors (e.g., Dudley Moore and Woody Allen) as well as the countless characters who are the butt of penis-size jokes typify the latter. This polarity not surprisingly also structures much of the representation of the penis in those rare instances when it is represented. The oft-noted requirement that porn stars be well endowed stems from the manner in which hard-core porn attempts to represent the male as an awesome, phallic spectacle. With the exception of such stars as John Holmes who are unusually large even when flaccid, hard-core porn generally minimizes or even totally elides flaccid penises, favoring an emphasis on large erections. The opposite side of the coin is the epidemic of penis-size jokes in U.S. films of the '80s and '90s (e.g., "Pee Wee" in *Porky's*, 1981, and the Pierce Brosnan character in *Mrs. Doubtfire*, 1993) in which characters with small penises, never seen, become the butts of such jokes. Implicitly, the message is that if the penis is going to be shown it had better be an impressive spectacle or, if it fails to live up to that standard, it had better be the unrepresented object of scornful humor.

While I still believe that such a polarity functions centrally within current Western representations of the penis, the extreme critical praise and box-office success surrounding David Henry Hwang's play *M. Butterfly* and Neil Jordan's film *The Crying Game* suggest the emergence of a third category which I call the melodramatic penis. These representations of the penis, which are neither the phallic spectacle nor its pitiable and/or comic collapse, on the one hand challenge conventional representations, and on the other hand constitute a troubled site of representation that contains disturbing contradictions. The much-publicized Bobbitt case that centered on a severed and reattached penis is part of this melodramatic penis discourse. Penises, it seems, must elicit an extremely strong response from us, and if awe and laughter do not define the full range of such responses, melodrama is standing by.

Why is the sight of the penis such a problem, and what significance does the mini-epidemic of melodramatic penises that I will analyze below have? There are three major reasons for the difficulty of representing the penis in our culture. First, because of the gap between the penis and the phallus, the latter threatens to underwhelm the former. In Richard Dyer's memorable words, "the penis isn't a patch on the phallus" (274). The privileged signifier of the phallus most easily retains its awe and mystique when the penis is hidden. The sight of the actual organ threatens to deflate and make ludicrous the symbolic phallus. Second, since so many areas of representation in our culture, including mainstream cinema, are male dominated, two other problems arise, one linked to heterosexuality and one to homosexuality. Men may fear that the representation of the penis gives women a basis for comparison and judgment and, although men have long engaged in such behavior toward women, the thought of the tables being turned on them is close to unbearable. Finally, the representation of the penis creates a great deal of anxiety for homophobic men who may become intensely disturbed at finding themselves fascinated by it or deriving pleasure from looking at it.

Within this triple layer of fearfulness, the easiest thing to do is not represent the penis but, if the penis must be shown or even spoken about, its representation must be carefully regulated. Various discourses have sprung up to fulfill precisely that function; they include a medical discourse, an artistic discourse, a pornographic discourse, and even a comic discourse. In a desperate attempt to collapse the distinction between the penis and the phallus, pornography limits the representation of the penis to the large, ever-present, long-lasting erection. This, pornography asserts, is what women want and need. Twentieth-century medical discourse, on the other hand, virtually fetishizes the normal, average penis, which it defines statistically as the 4-inch flaccid penis and the 6-inch erection, with a normal range of 5 to 7 inches. Such discourse assures nearly everyone that their penis is normal and limits its photographs, diagrams, drawings, and so on, to penises within this normal range. Penis-size jokes, on the other hand, seem to acknowledge that not all penises are in fact so much the same and that some look noticeably smaller than others. In most of that humor, however, the small penis is the butt of the joke. In a sense, penis-size jokes are the other side of the pornography coin: if the latter affirms the penis as the glorious phallus, the former ridicules those penises that, though invisible in representation, fall short of maintaining the sight of the penis as a dramatic spectacle. Small, retracted, shriveled penises are pathetic objects of ridicule, unworthy of being worshiped on the pornographic throne of the phallic penis or even the medical throne of the normal penis.

How does the melodramatic penis fit into these discourses and why has it made its appearance at this moment? Precisely because the penis has remained hidden for so long, in some ways it has become the last great taboo in our culture. The media typically maintain a tense contradictory relationship with such taboos: on the one hand, there are cultural imperatives for respecting the taboo and, on the other hand, there are the journalistic and artistic motives for breaking the taboos by creating new images which bring attention to themselves, sometimes in a shocking manner. Indeed, John Wayne Bobbitt's penis may well be the ultimate melodramatic penis: first it is severed, then it is lost, then it is found, then it is miraculously reattached, then it becomes a star in porn films, and then it is enlarged! While I am hard put to imagine what other melodramatic events can befall that penis, it is important to note the obsessive media coverage of this story. In 1993, for the first time, the word *penis* became common in much journalistic discourse, including prime-time, network newscasts (Grindstaff and McGaughey). In one sense, the Bobbitt case gave the media the opportunity they needed to assault the last taboo and utter the word *penis.* We are currently undergoing a media feeding frenzy about penises. No sooner had the Bobbitt case died down than the media began detailed coverage of new techniques in penis-enlargement surgery. Indeed, the *Wall Street Journal* gave front page coverage to the penis-enlargement business in 1996! I have been interviewed and quoted countless times about the representation of the penis by the media since publishing *Running Scared.*

This flurry of media attention to the penis clearly relates to the representation of the penis in films of the '90s. There is currently a widespread assault on this taboo and, of course, work like my own within academia is part of that context: scholars, artists, and journalists alike contribute to the total picture. It is worth noting that the films I will analyze here are extremely diverse: *Cobb* (1994) and *Boogie Nights* (1997) are mainstream Hollywood productions; *Angels and Insects* (1995) and *The Crying Game* (1992) have strong affinities with the European art cinema; *Carried Away* (1996) is an American independent, low-budget feature directed by Bruno Barretta, a Brazilian filmmaker; and *The Governess* (1999) is a British costume drama written and directed by a woman, Sandra Goldbacher.

I begin my analysis with *The Crying Game* since that film inaugurated this cycle. The opening scene of the film contains a conventional reference to penises when Jody urinates at a fair. He stands in such a manner that the view of his body is blocked by a tent, though he remarks that he has never urinated while holding a woman's hand. A similar scene occurs when he is held captive and has to urinate. The camera is positioned in such a manner that his genitals are offscreen at the bottom of the frame. Yet the unusual circumstances of the scene bring extraordinary attention to his penis. Since he is handcuffed, he asks Fergus, his guard, to unzip his pants, take out his penis, and hold it while he urinates. Fergus eventually does so, but only with great reluctance and discomfort. These scenes lull the audience into a false sense of conventional expectations—no matter how much talk of and attention to the penis, the film positions its spectators to expect that the organ will not be shown. No experience in the film, in other words, has shattered the expectation that the conventions will be followed. This even further heightens what would under any circumstances be the shockingly unexpected representation of the penis in the revelation scene. In a film where we are positioned to expect to not see the penis even when we hear about it, we are hardly prepared to see it in a scene where we do not even know it is present. Not surprisingly, that scene is one of intense melodrama.

After going to Dil's apartment, Fergus lies back on the bed as Dil goes into the bathroom preparatory to lovemaking. Dil reemerges, comes over to the bed, and Fergus rises, kisses her, and begins to take her robe off. As he slides it down he sits on the edge of the bed. With the camera placed behind him we see both him looking and the sight of male genitals simultaneously; his stunned reaction coincides with ours. This camera positioning doubly heightens what is already a highly dramatic moment. Jordan could, of course, easily have shot the scene in a conventional manner where the spectator would have learned that Dil is a man without seeing his genitals or, in a less conventional scenario, at least have learned that information before seeing the genitals. Jordan's strategy maximizes the shock value of the moment by making it a perceptual experience for the spectator. This is further heightened by keeping Fergus in the frame, since the spectator's shock is intensified through character identification with the heterosexual man who finds himself in this distressful situation.

At this point, the more conventional moments of melodrama begin. Fergus becomes violently ill. As he jumps up from the bed to rush to the bathroom, he pushes Dil over, and we see Dil fall to the bed. We hear the sounds of off-screen vomiting and then cut to a graphic medium shot of Fergus vomiting into the bathroom sink. Cut to a long shot with the bathroom at the far left rear of the frame. Dil sits on a sofa in the foreground, blood trickling from his nose. As Dil speaks we continue to see Fergus vomiting through the open bathroom door. He then slams it shut. When he emerges, apologizes, and prepares to leave, he walks past Dil, who grabs his pants and is pulled to the floor, begging, "Don't go, say something." Fergus does not respond and Dil falls from supporting his upper body with his hands on the floor to lying completely prostrate with his head on the floor. As he falls to this position, non-diegetic music reappears to heighten the moment. He says, "Jesus," as Fergus leaves, and the shot holds for a moment after the door in the rear of the frame has closed, and we are left with the sight of Dil lying distraught in the left foreground of the frame.

Several elements in this scene are reminiscent of classic melodrama, the most obvious being illness and images of bodies being knocked down and lying prostrate (e.g., *Way Down East*, 1920). The violence with which Fergus knocks Dil down the first time and bloodies his nose, the manner in which Dil gets pulled to the floor and remains partially propped up before fully collapsing, and the explicit imagery of Fergus vomiting combine to create a melodramatic spectacle. Camera positioning and the use of the soundtrack further mark the scene's melodrama stylistically. The sounds of Fergus's retching are a constant reminder of how violently sick he becomes, and the last shot of the scene, as he exits, is extremely unbalanced in a manner characteristic of classical melodrama. Thomas Elsaesser has shown how the tensions in Hollywood melodrama are frequently reflected in compositions that give extreme emphasis to foregrounded objects. In Jordan's variation, rather than an object such as a liquor bottle, Dil's body looms in the left foreground. Had Jordan placed the camera further back or, in a more likely variation, changed the angle and the distance so that, for example, Dil lies in the center of the frame as Fergus walks off to the right, the melodramatic effect would have been lessened. All stylistic decisions in the revelation scene, however, convert the drama inherent in the moment to melodrama, which appears to be the only mode appropriate to the unexpected sight of the penis.

David Henry Hwang's play *M. Butterfly* supplies a similar moment in a seemingly opposite context since there the sight of the penis, far from being a surprise, is expected by both the character in the play and the audience. The revelation that Song, one of the play's central characters, is a man rather than a woman comes near the end of the play. When the play opened it was, however, widely known that it dramatized an internationally publicized case that led to the arrests of a French diplomat and a Chinese opera singer on espionage charges. Being unaware of Chinese opera performance traditions, the male diplomat mistakenly believed that the singer with whom he fell in love was a woman. Whereas the advertising campaign for *The Crying Game* was built around the secret which it urged all who had seen the film to keep to themselves, *M. Butterfly* opened in 1988 amid publicity which referred to the then well-known story. Rather than being caught unaware, theatergoers were positioned to wonder how such a thing could happen.

The scene itself is further structured as a kind of dramatized striptease. Song appears before Gallimard, the diplomat, after the latter has learned of his true identity. Referring to Gallimard's request years earlier that Butterfly (as he calls her) strip for him, Song promises to do it now. Although Gallimard begs him not to do it, Song strips. The stage directions are simple: "Song drops his briefs. He is naked" (Hwang, 88). There are no prior stage directions indicating how Song has come to be in his briefs. He has previously been described as wearing a "well-cut suit" (80). As the scene is commonly staged, however, the play comes to a virtual halt as Song announces, "Monsieur Gallimard—the wait is over" (88) and slowly and deliberately takes off his tie, shirt, and suit before dropping his underpants. Both Gallimard and the audience watch in mounting suspense for what they know is coming. Song is positioned frontally for both Gallimard and the audience and the scene is fully lit. Song remains naked for the remainder of the scene until the stage directions indicate, "He puts on his briefs and slacks" (90) before Gallimard removes him from the stage.

Patterns of showing and/or talking about the penis in general within the theater are, not surprisingly, linked closely to that of movies. *The Shock of Recognition* by Robert Anderson, a brief one-act play written in 1966 and produced in New York in 1967 as part of the play *You Know I Can't Hear You when the Water Is Running,* almost ludicrously summarizes the "problem" presented by showing the penis in the theater at that time. Indeed, the play is about nothing else! It concerns a playwright who has the shocking idea of showing a naked man on stage. Much of the play is taken up with discussion by the playwright, the producer and others about how unacceptable this is, with particular emphasis given to the issue of showing the penis. What actor could possibly agree to do it? What do women think of penises? What do men think of penises? Although no penis is shown in this play, the play is about virtually nothing else but the seemingly revolutionary idea of doing so.

The Shock of Recognition, so titled because the playwright wanted the nude actor to be an Everyman rather than a masculine ideal, is dated in the worst and most extreme sense of the term. What is of interest today about the play is that it was written and staged in 1966 and 1967—the last possible moment in U.S. history when such a play could be written. Soon the Broadway production of *Hair* would conclude with the entire cast of men and women coming out on stage completely nude and lined up facing the audience. Other plays such as *Tom Paine* and *Oh! Calcutta* would quickly follow. The whole notion of making such a big deal out of frontal male nudity was suddenly ancient history, part of another era. This coincided with a larger cultural climate of late '60s and '70s casual male nudity that had faded by the '90s. The melodramatic revelation of the penis is the polar opposite of casual (Lehman and Hunt).

Heather MacDonald's *Dream of a Common Language* (1993), for example, also stages male nudity in a highly melodramatic way. In the play, set in 1874, Clovis, the wife of a well-known artist and herself a former artist, asks Marc, a male friend, to pose nude for her. Even though he is an artist himself, he doesn't understand at first why a woman would want a completely nude model, and he only begins to fully disrobe after Clovis holds a gun on him. According to the stage directions, "Clovis points the gun at each garment indicating which he should remove next" (88). He stops with his underwear still on and she fires a shot to get him to continue. The other major characters, all of whom are offstage, hear the shots and rush onstage. When he understands the gravity of the situation, Victor, her husband, starts to disrobe while Marc remarks, "You want to point guns at men, make us take off our clothes" (90). The stage directions then read, "VICTOR has removed all his clothing and stands naked, wide open to Clovis" (90). She then poses and paints the nude man.

This melodramatic scene of a seemingly crazed woman artist waving a gun at a man to get him to strip for her is the climax of the play, which ends shortly afterward. In this play, the appearance of the penis is motivated by the historical setting, a time during which it was unacceptable for female artists to paint male nudes. That is, it appears that all the gun waving, drum-beating melodrama surrounding the penis belongs to the late nineteenth century, but it speaks loudly and clearly to the '90s. Indeed, the parallels with *M. Butterfly* are most interesting: the latter motivates its male nudity with reference to actual recent events and leads up to it with a striptease; the former motivates its male nudity with general reference to an earlier era and leads up to it with an enforced version of a striptease. In both cases, the audience *of* the plays watches in rapt attention along with the characters *in* the plays as the slow removal of clothing leading up to the revelation of the penis takes place.

It is difficult to imagine scenes being structured in a manner that would bring more attention to a penis than these. Indeed, much of *M. Butterfly* leads up to this moment of revelation where Gallimard is faced with the indisputable evidence that both he and the audience find so incredible. As in *The Crying Game*, the revelation also produces a strong response from the heterosexual male character in the scene. According to the stage directions, after Song is naked, "Sound cue out. Slowly we and Song come to realize that what we had thought to be Gallimard's sobbing is actually laughter" (88). Once again, the scene could easily have been staged in a much more conventional manner. Song could, for example, stand with his back to the audience so that only Gallimard sees his genitals. As with *The Crying Game*, the audience who has been watching this "woman" throughout the play is now forced to acknowledge that physiologically "she" is a he. Song's penis is not the butt of Gallimard's laughter as in a penis-size joke; the laughter, rather, is directed at the situation in which he finds himself.

Clearly, neither Jordan nor Hwang position the spectator to view the penis as an awesome spectacle of phallic power nor as its pitiable or comic collapse. Nor do they fall into the equally conventional and limiting position of not showing the spectator the penis that is the center of such dramatic attention within their narratives (as in, for example, *The Full Monty*, 1997, which, as many critics pointed out, does not deliver the full monty to the spectators of the film). Something of the limitation of this latter position ironically emerges in David Cronenberg's film of *M. Butterfly* (1993) which was written and produced by Hwang. Since unlike the play, the film adopts a linear narrative which fits the classical Hollywood style, perhaps it comes as no surprise that the revelation scene is shot in such a manner that Song is seen nude only from behind or from the waist up. This conventional approach simply contributes to the awe and mystique of the penis by keeping it hidden.

When the penis is represented or shown or even referred to it is nearly always part of a discourse which attempts to carefully regulate that representation or reference: hard-core porn represents large, mostly erect penises; sexology represents statistically average, "normal" penises; penis-size jokes usually refer to small inadequate penises. What is lost amid all this careful regulation is the variety of actual penises that are not asked to bear the burden of representing anything other than what they are—penises, in other words, which are neither more nor less than penises. While the recent emergence of what I have called the melodramatic penis at least challenges norms of representation, it perpetuates the cultural assumption that the sight of the penis has to be provoked by an extraordinary event that guarantees the sight will have a major impact. These are still penises that are not just penises.[2]

When *The Crying Game* appeared in 1992, its representation of the penis was, to say the least, unique in the history of mainstream feature filmmaking; no other films had similarly shown the "shocking" revelation of a penis where the spectator didn't expect one. As I have indicated, at that time, the larger cultural significance of the representation of the penis in that film seemed to relate to a Broadway play and a news story, not other films. Things, however, have changed drastically in the last seven years. After *The Crying Game*, at least five other films with related melodramatic representations of the penis had appeared by 1999. Two of them, *Cobb* (1994) and *Angels and Insects* (1995), are closely related in that the scenes in question are not only shocking surprises but excessively melodramatic. The others, *Carried Away* (1996), *Boogie Nights* (1997), and *The Governess* (1998) are more closely related to the theatrical version of *M. Butterfly*.

Cobb is an unusual sports biopic about the famous baseball player Ty Cobb. What makes the film unusual is its dark representation of one of the greatest heroes of America's national pastime. Cobb is portrayed as an unappealing, out-of-control, mentally disturbed, racist, anti-Semitic, misogynistic egomaniac—hardly the stuff of conventional hero worship. As he recounts his life's story to a reporter, he talks about how wonderful his father was and reveals that he was murdered. We then see a brief image of a man falling. Later, Cobb returns to the subject and we see a full flashback of his father's murder, including the brief snippet we had earlier seen. Now he narrates that his father, suspecting his mother of having an affair, tells his wife that he is going out of town on a business trip. He sneaks back to the house at night and approaches the bedroom window through which we see a naked woman. Upon discovering the intruder, the woman grabs a rifle and shoots him. When we return to the frame story, the reporter blurts out with astonishment, "Your mother killed your father!" From the flashback we surmise this has been an accident since she is startled by the intruder and acts in what appears to be self-defense.

Within Hollywood convention, we always accept flashbacks as revealing the truth, something that, as Kristin Thompson has argued, makes Alfred Hitchcock's *Stage Fright* (1950) transgressive. Similarly, near the end of *Cobb*, when we finally learn the truth about Cobb's father's death, an already classically melodramatic scene is made more shockingly so by the simultaneous revelation that we, the spectators of the film, have been tricked by the earlier lying flashback and are only now learning the truth. The situation is pure classic melodrama: once again, we are told that Cobb's father suspects his wife of infidelity, announces a business trip and, on a stormy night, sneaks home to spy on her activities. This time, however, when he watches through the bedroom window, he catches his wife in the act of adultery—the melodramatic moment *par excellence*. Precisely at this moment we get the shocking view not only of what is going on inside the room but simultaneously we see the lover in frontal nudity as he picks up a rifle and shoots Cobb's father. The melodramatic moment par excellence, a spouse catching a partner in the act of adultery, is displaced by the only thing that could top it: someone being murdered on the spot.

The unexpected sight of the penis here clearly contributes to and is embedded within an intensely melodramatic moment. The audience is already in something of a state of shock from the double whammy of the lying flashback and the revelation of the adulterous act when it is treated in quick succession to the surprising spectacle of frontal male nudity followed quickly by murder.[3] The film does offer a motive for the lying flashback: Cobb, a psychological wreck of a man, cannot easily admit to the true nature of his mother's adultery and his father's death. In an attempt to preserve his own legend, he tries to conceal the truth. The lying flashback, however, creates yet another parallel with *The Crying Game*. I mentioned above that in the latter film, the audience is lulled into conventional expectations by two earlier urination scenes that no penis will be shown. The lying flashback similarly lulls the audience since it leads us to believe that Cobb's mother is alone in her bedroom. She is the only person we have seen in the previous flashback. The last thing we expect to see the next time we revisit the scene is a man, let alone a penis. In one sense, then, we are just as surprised to see a man in the scene in *Cobb* as we are in *The Crying Game*. The added shock of surprise intensifies the melodramatic effect in both films.

Between the revelation that a woman is a man in *The Crying Game* and the revelation that a man we thought was shot without malice was in fact killed by his wife's lover after catching them together, it would seem we have pretty well reached the peaks of melodramatic possibilities for the surprise appearance of the penis: what, after all, can equal transvestism and adultery/murder for supplying such juicy melodramatic contexts? Incest can. *Angels and Insects*, set during the Victorian era, involves a young man who is a long-term visitor in a family that includes a brother and sister. He falls in love with the young woman, and they are married. Suddenly, however, she withdraws her sexual favors from her husband and even sleeps in another room. One day the husband leaves the house but returns home unexpectedly. He frantically searches through the house, looking for his wife. When he enters a bedroom, he interrupts her in the midst of intercourse with her brother. The brother turns around and frontally faces the camera, his genitals fully exposed.

The scene has a quite literal parallel with the nude scene in *Cobb* since it is structured around a husband returning home unexpectedly and discovering his wife in the act of adultery. Once again, it is not just the central character who is shocked in this film but also the spectators. Indeed, once again we have been lulled into complacency since everything we have seen about this family fits an image of propriety and extreme sexual repression. We are once again doubly shocked: no sooner do we realize that the wife is having sex with her brother than we are presented with the spectacle of his penis, this time erect. Much like we were shocked to discover the presence of the male lover in the bedroom during the last flashback in *Cobb*, here we are shocked to discover the presence of the brother. It is precisely these contexts of a similar series of shocks in which we see the penis that make these moments so similar in all three films. On the surface, the penis itself never appears to be the cause of the shocks but, rather, accompanies the revelation of something shocking: transvestism, adultery, and incest.

Carried Away tells the story of a relationship between two middle-aged schoolteachers. The man lives with his aging mother, and the woman lives alone. The man has a torrid affair with one of his high school students which leads him to question the nature of his relationship with the schoolteacher. In one scene, he goes over to her house and confronts her about his dissatisfactions: they have a boring, predictable love life, and since they make love in the dark they have never even seen each other's nude bodies. Working himself into a virtual hysteria about this state of affairs, he begins to dramatically turn on all the lights in the room and to disrobe in front of her until he stands naked. He repeatedly tells her to look at him and then commands her to undress, which she does. Throughout the scene there are several well-lit, frontal and side-view long shots of the man's body as he stands waiting for her to look at him and then undress and join him. The scene ends as they embrace and fall to the floor to make love.

In some ways, this scene appears to be nearly the opposite of the scenes in *The Crying Game*, *Cobb*, and *Angels and Insects*; rather than the sudden unexpected appearance of the penis surprising us, its appearance is announced with great flourish. Indeed, *Carried Away* beats drums and literally shines spotlights on the penis. Furthermore, unlike the scenes in those other films, this scene lacks excessive melodrama. Nothing more dramatic happens than the lovers taking off their clothes, embracing, and falling to the floor—no one intrudes with a gun, for example.

Within the context of *Carried Away*, however, the nude scene is in fact fairly melodramatic; it, like the scene in *Cobb*, even takes place during a thunderstorm, a fairly classic element of melodrama. Furthermore, throughout much of the film, the Dennis Hopper character is quite staid; he thus appears quite agitated, indeed nearly hysterical, during this scene. One of the very points of *Carried Away* is that, contrary to genre conventions, affairs and sexual transgressions do not have to end in melodramatic excess. This is seen in several ways. The climax of the film occurs after everyone has learned of the affair between the man and the teenage girl. In the expectation that the girl's father will attempt to kill him, the man takes a rifle and prepares himself for the inevitable, violent confrontation. Yet, when the father, accompanied by the mother, arrive, all they want to do is talk. They do not threaten physical violence or legal action. Indeed the film ends with no severe consequences for any of the three lovers; the girl returns to her family, and the teachers are reunited as a couple. There is not even any suggestion that the underage girl has been traumatized by her sexual experiences with the much older man. The closest thing to conventional melodrama occurs when the girl sets fire to a horse barn.

Within the context of this film, then, the love scene between the teachers is in fact marked as somewhat excessive. More important, however, the strategy of virtually announcing the penis will be revealed before actually showing it has a curiously similar effect to its surprise appearance: it imbues the sight of the penis with a sense of great significance. Far from being casual, this is a nearly overwhelming moment.

The notorious "dick" shot in *Boogie Nights* (1997) can also best be understood within this '90s discourse of the melodramatic penis (Lehman, 1998). The need to talk about and show the penis is everywhere, including an entire episode of *Ally McBeal* during the 1997–98 season and *Chicago Hope* during the 1998–99 season. In this regard, Paul Thomas Anderson's dwelling on it throughout the film and showing it in the last shot can best be understood as part of the time in which his film was made, rather than the time period it represents. In 1975 or even 1985 it is highly unlikely that a Hollywood film that spoke of its central character's penis would end with a graphic shot of it.

On the surface, it might seem that the final shot of *Boogie Nights* falls not into the melodramatic category but, rather, that of the awesome spectacle of phallic power. But within the context of a Hollywood film, the shot is also quite melodramatic—a sort of hybrid of the two categories. After soliloquizing in front of a mirror while waiting to shoot a porn scene, Dirk Diggler (Mark Whalberg) unzips his pants and pulls out his penis, which we see as a frontal, close shot in the mirror. And what a penis it is—there is no question that part of the shot's effect derives from this "impressive" spectacle. I have argued elsewhere that this kind of emphasis on the large flaccid penis results from a slippage of the erect penis onto the flaccid penis (Lehman, 1993). If we are going to show the flaccid penis, in other words, it had better look as much like the supposed awesome spectacle of an erection as possible. And, indeed, the flaccid penis in *Boogie Nights* seems virtually indistinguishable from the 13-inch erection we have been hearing about. The brutally frontal, nearly confrontational manner in which the penis is directly revealed for the camera relates the shot to the excesses of melodrama I have described in the other films. Like the scenes in *Carried Away* and the theatrical version of *M. Butterfly*, this scene is structured in such a manner that the revelation of the penis is much heralded.

In a newspaper article devoted entirely to discussing the penis shot in *Boogie Nights*, journalist Barry Koltnow discusses moments in the history of film that have "shocked" audiences sexually: Clark Gable removing his shirt in *It Happened One Night* and Sharon Stone crossing her legs in *Basic Instinct*. "This time the shocking moment will come in the last few frames," Koltnow notes. It is precisely this element of shock that aligns the last shot of *Boogie Nights* with the melodramatic shocks of transvestism, adultery, murder, and incest in the films described above.

The Governess, written and directed by Sandra Goldbacher, supplies yet another variation on the above pattern. In this film, Minnie Driver plays a young Jewish woman who hides her true identity and takes a job as a governess in the home of a wealthy family. The husband, a scientist and inventor, is working on the discovery of the photographic process. The governess ingratiates herself with her employer, and they work together and have an affair. On one occasion, he passes out after too much drink, and she takes nude pictures of him. She leaves them for him in the spirit of a lover's gift. Later, however, we see him examining the pictures with a magnifying glass. He seems focused on the image of his penis, and a deeply disturbed expression appears on his face.

The penis is shown both in the photo-session scene and later in the photograph as the man studies his image. Neither is a particularly melodramatic moment. Indeed, during the session, the woman enjoys herself and suffers no response at all from the sleeping man. And although the man is troubled as he looks at the picture, nothing further happens at that moment. The pause, however, is brief. The appearance of the penis precipitates the most intense melodrama for the remainder of the film.[4] First, the employer immediately banishes the governess from his laboratory and breaks off his entire relationship with her, both as a coworker and a lover. In further retribution, he denies her contribution to their joint research and takes full credit himself within scientific circles for work they shared. In revenge for these actions, the governess melodramatically disrupts a family dinner by marching in with a print of the nude photograph and giving it to the wife.

The Governess departs slightly from the pattern in the above films in two ways. First, the penis is neither a big shock nor is it a highly heralded event. Second, when it appears it seems anything but melodramatic—there is a brief pause before the melodrama erupts. Like *Dream of a Common Language*, *The Governess* thematizes the melodramatic penis within an historical context—all the turmoil surrounding it appears attributable to the nineteenth century. And even though the film supplies a profound investigation into historical issues of gender and representation (it is a highly accomplished, important film), it also nevertheless speaks to the contemporary context I have been describing.[5]

All of these films and plays featuring melodramatic penises certainly suggest that the taboo against showing the penis is crumbling. Yet, this is not a simple occasion for joy. The melodramatic penis may in part be a reaction to the women's movement. At a time when women have made major inroads upon areas of male privilege such as the workplace, politics, and the military, asserting the importance of the penis seems to affirm the significance of the one thing women can't have (Lehman and Hunt).

The current moment involves tension between conflicting ideologies in a manner that recalls the nineteenth century and the invention of photography and then cinema. Stephen Heath has noted that, prior to the invention of photography, the problem of anxiety produced by representing the female genitals was avoided in art by painting and sculpting the female body as complete without any sign of the genitals, not even the suggestion of a slit or opening in the body. The main drive behind the invention of photography, however, was to reveal everything, including what the naked eye could not see. Suddenly, photography demanded that female genitals be open, exposed to view and ceaselessly explored. Linda Williams has shown how early hard-core film pornography was similarly driven by a need to show everything. Thus, the camera's ideology of showing everything conflicted with the cultural tradition of representing the female body as complete without being fully sexed. From such a perspective, acknowledging the female genitals gave rise to castration anxieties and the resultant representations had to develop strategies to contain those anxieties—various forms of fetishism, for example, and scenarios of narrative reassurance.

Something similar is happening in the late twentieth century, but now it is the penis and not the vagina that is the site of the anxiety producing conflict. The dominant ideological drive to retain the awe and mystique surrounding the penis is crumbling before the journalistic and artistic drive to break down the final taboo. The melodramatic penis is the result. The melodrama surrounding the representation of the penis paradoxically cries out to reaffirm the spectacular importance of the penis even as the very assault on the taboo seeks to dislodge that importance. The melodramatic penis can, on the one hand, be read in a positive manner as avoiding such simple structuring dichotomies as the large, awesome phallic spectacle versus its pathetic, comic collapse. In that sense, the melodramatic penis is far removed from either the pornographic phallic penis or the small penis that is the butt of jokes. On the other hand, the melodramatic penis continues to insist that the very act of representing the penis is somehow monumental. The penis may no longer be called upon to look impressive or sound pathetic but in a different manner it is still marked as being of extraordinary significance. The discourse of the melodramatic penis still seeks to block a penis from merely being a penis. In this regard the seemingly opposite strategies of surprise in *The Crying Game*, *Cobb*, and *Angels and Insects* and prior expectation in *M. Butterfly*, *Carried Away*, *Boogie Nights*, and *The Governess* are really the same: whether by shocking us or preparing us, all these works insist that showing the penis is of excessive dramatic importance. That is something to cry about.

notes

1. Jordan titled his film *In Dreams* (1999), after a Roy Orbison song, which he used over the closing credits.

2. Signififcantly, *The Crying Game*, *M. Butterfly* and the Bobbitt case all involve racial and crosscultural elements. From the perspective of issues of the male body to which I have limited my remarks here, I think that all of these examples would remain fundamentally unchanged if all the characters were white. Narratives and images of racial and cultural difference that center strongly on the penis, however, suggest that racial and sexual difference frequently become intertwined, as with Robert Mapplethorpe's photographs and the media coverage of the controversy surrounding them.

   Since writing this essay, Richard Lucht has brought to my attention the 1983 teen slasher film *Sleepaway Camp*. It ends in a graphically shocking scene with full frontal nudity revealing that the central female character is a teenage boy, not a girl. Given the often radical vitality of the "disreputable" slasher genre, it is not surprising to find a film in it prefigure the melodramatic penis nearly a decade before an "art" film such as *The Crying Game*.

3. Although my main interest in this scene at the moment relates to the connection between the surprising revelation of the penis and melodramatic excess within the narrative, the scene includes another peculiar element in relationship to the representation of the male genitals. If the sight of the male genitals is rare enough in any context within the Hollywood cinema, the sight of a naked man holding a rifle may be unique. The reason this image is particularly bizarre is due to a certain redundancy within Hollywood logic whereby a rifle is commonly viewed as a phallic symbol. The usual rules of representation governing masculinity and the male body preclude simultaneously revealing both the literal organ, the penis, and its symbolic dimension, the phallus, in this case represented by the rifle. As we shall see, this risks opening a ludicrous space between the penis and the phallus, a space which patriarchy desperately tries to deny. Indeed, the scene in *Cobb* minimizes the penis/phallus contrast by showing both only briefly as the lover receives the rifle from the woman and moves toward her; the very phallic shots of him pointing the shotgun at and shooting Cobb's father are mid-shots.

4. *American History X* (1998) also fits this pattern. During what appears to be a peaceful shower scene in a prison, we see several apparently casual shots of the penises of showering inmates, including that of the main character. Moments later, however, he is the victim of a shocking and graphic rape.

5. *The Governess* also includes another scene of male nudity. The son in the family is a young man who falls in love with the governess and is rejected by her. Near the end of the film, after she leaves the family, we see the distraught young man emerging naked from a swim in the ocean. The glimpse of his penis in this shot is tied to the emotional anguish highly visible on his face. His nakedness, a sign of excessive vulnerability, along with his behavior and intense emotional distress are signs of melodramatic illness.

works cited

Anderson, Robert. 1967. *You Know I Can't Hear You when the Water's Running*. New York: Dramatists Play Service Inc.

Dyer, Richard. [1982] 1992. "Don't Look Now." In *The Sexual Subject: A Screen Reader in Sexuality*, 265–76. London: Routledge.

Elsaesser, Thomas. [1972] 1985. "Tales of Sound and Fury: Observations on the Family Melodrama." In *Movies and Methods, Vol. 2*, ed. Bill Nichols, 166–89. Berkeley: University of California Press.

Grindstaff, Maura, and Martha McGaughey. 1998. "Feminism, Psychoanalysis, and (Male) Hysteria over John Bobbitt's Missing Manhood." *Men and Masculinities* 1, 2 (October): 173–92.

Heath, Stephen. [1978] 1992. "Difference." In *The Sexual Subject: A Screen Reader in Sexuality*, 47–106. London: Routledge.

Hwang, David Henry. 1994. *M. Butterfly*. New York: Penguin.

Koltnow, Barry. 1997. "BOOGIE NIGHTS Leaves a Big Question" *Orange County Register*, Oct. 20, Knight-Ridder/Tribune Information Services.

Lehman, Peter. 1993. *Running Scared: Masculinity and the Representation of the Male Body*. Philadelphia: Temple University Press.

———. 1998. "Will the Real Dirk Diggler Please Stand Up?" *Jump Cut* 42: 32–38.

Lehman, Peter, and Susan Hunt. 1999. "From Casual to Melodramatic: Changing Representations of the Penis in Films of the 70s and 90s." *Framework* 40 (April): 69–84.

McDonald, Heather. 1993. *Dream of a Common Language*. New York: Samuel French.

Thompson, Kristin. 1988. *Breaking the Glass Armor: NeoFormalist Film Analysis*. Princeton, N.J.: Princeton University Press.

Williams, Linda. 1989. *Hardcore: Power, Pleasure, and the "Frenzy of the Visible."* Berkeley: University of California Press.

the

saviors

and the

three | # saved

masculine redemption

in contemporary films

a m y a r o n s o n a n d m i c h a e l k i m m e l

During her reign as resident feminist on the op-ed page of the *New York Times*, Anna Quindlen once asked her women readers which man they'd prefer for a mate: a short, thin, reedy man, careful, committed, and chivalrous, always sexually faithful; or a dark, roguishly handsome, self-interested scoundrel who would never be faithful. Readers, of course, chose the former (though when posed to our students, several women always note that they wouldn't mind having sex with the latter before they got married).

But what if, Quindlen asked, you gave them names. Call the first one Ashley Wilkes, the second Rhett Butler. Now whom would you choose?

"Well, that's different," said one woman student. "Rhett Butler's never been loved by me. When I love him, he'll change."

In a heartbeat, Quindlen had exposed the consequences of women's romantic fantasies: a woman's love can change a bad man into a good man. When Rhett is loved by that woman, he may physically remain Rhett (indeed, he'd better), but emotionally he'll become Ashley.

This romantic fantasy—"the angel in the house," in Virginia Woolf's famous phrase—is the centerpiece of feminine fiction;[1] Charlotte Brontë's *Jane Eyre* (1847), which many see as the great mother of all women's novels, is a *locus classicus*. And it's been a Hollywood staple for decades: *Eyre* itself has been made into a film an astounding eight times. Think of *Magnificent Obsession* (1954) in which Rock Hudson renounces his wastrel ways and dedicates himself to medicine for the love of Jane Wyman. (And this was a remake of the 1935 film with Robert Taylor and Irene Dunn.) Or *San Francisco* (1936), where the bad gin-joint proprietor (Gable again) is transformed in his battle with the saintly priest (Spencer Tracy) for Jeanette MacDonald's soul (and other body parts).

Like Gable, Humphrey Bogart made a virtual career out of this transformation. In *Casablanca* (1942) his infernal abiding love for Ingrid Bergman leads him to act heroically, the renunciation of love as its ultimate confirmation. In *African Queen* (1951), it's Katherine Hepburn who elicits the move; in *To Have and Have Not* (1944), it's Lauren Bacall (who is also the vehicle for the plunge into depravity and ruin in *The Big Sleep* [1946]).

The transformative power of women's pure love has been one of America's most resilient cultural tropes. Except it doesn't work anymore. Because it wasn't really femininity that transformed those bad guys. It was innocence. And once upon a time, women embodied that innocence—on screen and in real life.

Not anymore. Feminism changed all that.[2] In the movies, feminism changed good girls, innocent and pure, into worldly women—corrupted by power (*Disclosure*, 1994), tainted by greed (the bony climber Sigourney Weaver compared to the zaftig wannabe Melanie Griffith in *Working Girl*, 1988), inured to the needs of their children (*Kramer vs. Kramer*, 1979). Some have even become murderous (*Thelma and Louise*, 1991.)

And they've got better things to do with their time than changing bad men into good ones. In *An Unmarried Woman* (1978), Jill Clayburgh opts to stay that way, while in *Waiting to Exhale* (1995), the ensemble waits for men who are already good. In *She's Gotta Have it* (1986), girls just wanna have fun too.

About the only recent movie in which good women turn bad men into good men is *The First Wives Club* (1996)—but that's after they've been dumped, and against the men's wills. About the best today's women can get from men is grudgingly ethical behavior, which, fortunately, is more than compensated by sisterly solidarity.

So what's a bad man to do? What force is innocent and virtuous enough to change him? In Hollywood these days, it's a little child who will lead him.

Only young children embody the virtuous innocence that can change bad men into good men.[3] This is easily observable in several recent Hollywood hits. In *Liar Liar* (1997), for example, it is shyster corporate attorney Jim Carrey's revelation that he's a bad father to his five-year-old son that leads him to the righteous path. His Dantean descent into the depravity of unbridled honesty, occasioned by Justin Cooper's birthday wish that his father couldn't lie for twenty-four hours, transforms a bad father into a good man, literally overnight.

And the pivotal scene in *Jerry Maguire* (1996), an Oscar-nominated smash hit, comes not through a magical romantic moment or ecstatic sexual passion between Tom Cruise and Renee Zellweger, and not even in the racial healing generated by his friendship with Cuba Gooding Jr. It's when Cruise is sitting on the sofa with Jonathan Lipnicki, Zellweger's adorably bespectacled and nerdy son, that he realizes the meaning of life and the importance of acting like a mensch.

It's doubly significant that in both cases, the guy then gets the girl. Not only must he prove himself worthy as a father figure to her children, but he can only accomplish that, only be changed, by the boys.

And what about some other recent "classics," like *Vice Versa* (1988) in which Judge Reinhold is changed from a demanding workaholic to an understanding boss, and a bumbling boyfriend into a loving mate, by walking a mile in his son's moccasins and listening to his sage advice. Or *Made in America* (1993) in which the conniving cracker used-car salesman Ted Danson becomes a smoke-free, teetotaling, virtuous father to his part-black daughter. And what about *Bye Bye Love* (1987), in which three divorced dads (Randy Quaid, Paul Reiser, and Matthew Modine) suffer more from being away from their children than from their divorcees, and after painful revelation, become better fathers, and therefore better men. Even Oscar Schindler (*Schindler's List*, 1993) is haunted by that little girl in the red dress, whose terror transfixes and then transforms him. (In case viewers missed the point, Spielberg colorizes her image in the stark black and white world of the Holocaust.) Spielberg has made a virtual cottage industry celebrating childhood innocence against the corruptions of adulthood. In his *E.T.* (1982), only the love and faith of children enables that elfin extraterrestrial to escape from the prodding and poking invasions of grownup researchers. And then there's another film, *Three Men and a Baby* (1987), in which gurgling infantile innocence tames three devoutly philandering bachelors the way no women ever could.

This trope shows no signs of fading out. One of the first big summer movies of the new millennium was *The Kid* (2000), starring diehard action hero Bruce Willis. In this film, he plays a middle-aged jerk who gets his shot at redemption when he meets a ten-year-old boy who reminds him of himself.

In a sense, *Kramer vs. Kramer* is the touchstone text of this new genre. There, Dustin Hoffman, an absentee landlord of domestic patriarchy, is converted to devoted daddydom by making breakfast and sitting by the playground, while his ex-wife, Meryl Streep, is climbing the corporate ladder. Not only can men be nurturing fathers, the film suggested, but they can be better *mothers* than modern women.

And *Kramer* evokes another timeless theme: it is the sons who will heal the pain of the fathers. Fatherhood is thrust upon the Hoffman character unwittingly, and he gradually transforms himself in the role to become a nurturing parent. Far more than in *Tootsie* (1982), it is in *Kramer vs. Kramer* that Dustin Hoffman "learns to do it without the dress." He learns not to be a woman, whom he can merely imitate, but to be a "mother." As, of course, does Robin Williams, in *Mrs. Doubtfire* (1993), although he also needs the asexuality of the frumpy British nanny in order to get in touch with his "feminine" side.

Nowhere is this theme of the son healing his father's wounds, and, in the process healing his own "father wound," clearer than in *Field of Dreams* (1989) a film that ushered in a new genre, the male weepie. (This film was a perfect cipher for the sexes, a John Gray interplanetary gender difference moment: women watched, almost stupefied, at the ending, saying, "I don't get it, they're having a catch?" while their husbands/dates/boyfriends/friends wept openly and said, "They're having a catch!") It is through baseball, America's game, that father and son are reconciled, that the pain of both father and son is finally healed.

Taken together, these fatherhood fables can be read as part of the "backlash-bind" against women. Women have abandoned their role as nurturing mother in their rush toward self-fulfillment professionally or sexually. If women would only leave the workplace and go back home, where they belong, they could do their job of taming men and raising children, who would not be placed at such risk that they have to transform men themselves. (Of course, women can keep working and being independent, but they'll never get a man that way.) Women can either be powerless, long-suffering saving graces (as of old), or powerless, manless figures on the margin—ultimately to be rescued by their children as well. Writing men in can mean writing women out.

Women can no longer be counted on to transform bad men into good men, since they have abandoned their natural roles. So who is going to help them return to innocence, to their naturally virtuous state which they abandoned when they left the home and went off to the workplace? Men obviously can't do it: they're programmed to be violent rapacious beasts until some force constrains them. And children failed at the task, or at least they can't be counted on since feminism—the glamorous world of work, sexual fulfillment, and individual identity—has seduced women away from their families, homes and most important, motherhood.

To be sure, there are exceptions, such as *Baby Boom* (1987), the yup-pie-becomes-mommy confection starring Diane Keaton. There, the necessity of child care transforms a corporate career climber into a nurturing mother substitute, whose business savvy suddenly makes her more successful than she could ever have dreamed earlier. Kids are good for business when you make kids *the* business.

But these days, children can be counted on to help teach bad men to be good men, but not bad career women to be good nurturing maternal figures. That task would have to go to someone who really knows the values of domesticity, someone who can really express feelings and has his or her priorities right. Of course, it's gay men! Gay men have stepped into the breach and are teaching straight women how to hold onto their men, their families and reset their priorities so that domestic bliss takes priority over career hustles.

In Hollywood's current rendition, gay men are not the sex-crazed near-maniacal predators of *Cruising* (1980), nor even the genuinely maniacal female-wannabes of *Silence of the Lambs* (1991). Gay men are kind, considerate, nurturing, and, most important, domestic. They like the home, they know how to decorate it, and they know that domestic bliss is the only real happiness. Gay men have become today's women.[4] And like women, they may be an object of desire, but they are not its subject—these gay men do not have gay sex. Their goal is not to change men—men are far too homophobic for that!—but to help women realize the errors of their ways and to come back to the home.

This is evident in several recent films.[5] In *Four Weddings and a Funeral* (1993), while the feckless Hugh Grant stumbles toward amorous rapprochement with Andie MacDowell, it is the caring, committed relationship between the two gay male characters that illustrates the kind of love and caring that straights can only envy.

But in that film, gay male intervention is only indirect, by way of illustration. In *My Best Friend's Wedding* (1997), it is Rupert Everett (an openly gay man playing an openly gay man) who shows the relationship-phobic Julia Roberts that she can balance work and family. Only with his guidance can Roberts, portraying a food critic, have her (wedding) cake and eat it too.

The gay man–straight woman model pairing appears to be a cinematic match made in heaven. Or at least the act won't be breaking up soon. In *The Next Best Thing* (2000), Everett teams up with Madonna, who portrays a thirtysomething single woman who convinces her best friend, Everett, to be the father of her child before time runs out on her biological clock. Alas, five years later, she falls in love with another man. (This is said to be a work of fiction, and not at all based on the life of the pop diva.).

In the hit comedy *In and Out* (1998), after her fiancé, Kevin Kline, comes out as gay, Joan Cusak is helped by another gay character, a television reporter played by Tom Selleck, to find a man who loves her for exactly who she is—without myths, lies, or diets. And in *The Object of My Affection* (1998), Jennifer Aniston learns what she really needs in a husband and father for her child—someone with whom she won't have sex!

It is interesting, and perhaps not coincidental, that the emergence of gay men as the nurturing role models who can teach heterosexual women how to keep their priorities straight, almost always takes place in anticipation of a heterosexual wedding. Every one of these films centers on a forthcoming nuptial ceremony, in which the bride's ambivalence, or some other equally contrived plot device, signals the need for gay male intervention. (Even in *The Birdcage* [1996], Robin Williams's son's impending wedding leads to the relationship crisis—in which, as we find out, it is the amorous lovebird relationship between Williams and Nathan Lane that provides the real role model to the young couple, not the upper-class chill between Gene Hackman and Diane Wiest.) What gay men represent is clear priorities—relationships always come first, before commitment to work.

Even television, long a holdout against gay characters that were remotely sympathetic, has jumped on the gay bandwagon. Several spinoffs of the very successful *Will and Grace* are in the pipeline—each one pairing a confused heterosexual career woman and her happy, healthy gay male roommate. Whereas gay men and lesbians were virtually invisible only a few years ago, today there are thirteen gay men (one lead, seven regular, and five recurring) characters on major television shows, and nine lesbians (one regular and eight recurring).[6] Of course, in order for Will (played by Eric McCormick) to be a credible lead, he must play off his far more flamboyant sidekick, Jack (played by Sean Hayes), who so exaggerates camp stereotypes of gay masculinity that Will seems, well, normal. That normalization is crucial to his ability to transform Grace—or at least provide ongoing relationship counsel. Will is quite close to the man of Grace's dreams, which explains why she can't seem to find a straight man who has all of Will's virtues.

What makes gay men such good advisors to straight women is that they know the pleasures of the home, and are uncorrupted by lust for women, which, as we all know, is the major thing that makes men behave badly.

Of course, making children and gay men the repository of Rousseauian innocence and virtue may make plots simpler, but also blurs the politics. Gone are the little monsters of Puritanism, whose wills must be broken; gone, too, the Freudian bundles of sexual energy and infantile aggression. In the depoliticized world in which everything you really needed to know you learned in kindergarten, compassionate politics has become a form of infantile regression. And the costs for gay men are simple: they can never fall in love or have sex. In order for gay men to reorient heterosexual women's botched priorities, they must, themselves, be as virtuous as children, innocent and asexual.

Such fables thus fit snugly into a right-wing family values agenda, almost suggesting that children need fathers more than they need mothers (if not fathers, at least patriarchs). There are no "feminist" marriages here, with two good parents balancing career and family, working as equals for the good of all concerned. And as the Christian Coalition counsels, we're able to "love the sinner and hate the sin," separating homosexuals from homosexuality, because we don't ever allow them to express their own sexuality.

Of course, *Ellen* (with Ellen DeGeneres in the title role) breaks that mold, and, in so doing, reinforces it. It is permissible (with much right-wing squawking, of course) for a woman to kiss another woman. But a passionate kiss is a long way off for two men in a major television show.

In these films and TV shows, both heterosexual women and heterosexual men are in desperate need of transformation. Women have been seduced by the workplace and have abandoned their natural nurturing roles; men never had those roles to begin with and have no way to get in touch with their feelings. Yes, it's true that such films show that men can love children and even do housework and child care, without sacrificing their masculinity. And they also show that women can remember that it is love and family that provide the center of one's life.

But they also show that men and women require some external agent to prompt the transformation, something outside themselves. Men and feminist women won't get better unless they are pushed, we're told; left to themselves, they can barely manage a nudge toward being better fathers and mothers, husbands and wives. Nary a whiff of compassion or nurturing wafts upward from these men or women on their own. In the world of Hollywood masculinity and postfeminist femininity, ethics seem still to reside in some mythic Other, waiting to be inhaled.

notes

1. See Virginia Woolf, "Professions for Women," in Michele Barrett, ed., *Virginia Woolf: Women and Writing* (New York: Harcourt, Brace, Jovanovich, 1979), 57–63. A definition appears on 58–59.

2. One book that in some ways anticipates this discussion is Tania Modleski's *Feminism without Women* (New York: Routledge, 1991).

3. Vivian Sobchack, discussing the role of the child within the genres of contemporary horror film and the family melodrama, argues that the child in the horror film "shows us the terror and rage of *patriarchy in*

decline . . . ," while the "popular family melodrama shows us a sweetly problematic *paternity in ascendance.*" See Sobchack, "Child/Alien/Father: Patriarchal Crisis and Generic Exchange." *Camera Obscura* 15 (1986): 7–36. See also Thomas DiPiero, "The Patriarch Is Not (Just) a Man." *Camera Obscura* 25–26 (1991): 101–24.

4. The literary critic Leslie Fiedler has elaborated a related theme, wherein gay men function as a form of female surrogate, thus releasing straight men from the confines of marriage and letting them off the hook for generations of oppressing the Other. Several other literary scholars have usefully explored this theme, particularly Richard Slotkin, *Regeneration through Violence: The Mythology of the American Frontier, 1600–1800* (Middletown: Wesleyan University Press, 1973); and Richard Volney Chase, *The American Novel and Its Traditions.* (Baltimore: Johns Hopkins University Press, 1980).

5. Sharon Willis further elaborates Fiedler's theme, and does so in terms of contemporary film genres. In her chapter, "Mutilated Masculinities and Their Prostheses: Die Hards and Lethal Weapons," she argues that "what these films put forward as the central figure of masculinity in crisis is really white heterosexual masculinity desperately seeking to reconstruct itself within a web of social differences, where its opposing terms include not only femininity but black masculinity and male homosexuality." See Willis, *High Contrast: Race and Gender in Contemporary Hollywood Film* (Durham, NC: Duke University Press, 1997), p. 31.

6. Tallies come from GLAAD. Web site, www. GLAAD.org

identity,

queerness,

and

homosocial

bonding

the case

of *swingers*

j u s t i n   w y a t t

Several years ago, a friend of mine living abroad began a correspondence with me attempting to solidify a friendship that had been dormant for several seasons. As part of the letter exchange, we compared experiences of discovering our gayness during our undergraduate careers, a process complicated considerably by having the closet door half open, half closed. His journey differed from mine in one rather significant way: during his college years, he was an active member of a fraternity, Alpha Tau Omega (ATO), at a time not so long ago when being out would mean immediate social ostracization. While the fraternity years were indeed marked by very careful bracketing of certain portions of his life, my friend unearthed several other guys in the fraternity who were also gay or at least curious. The result was a vibrant, hidden subculture referred to as the "GayTOs" by its members. To me, the reminiscence offered a life lesson, first and foremost, in the boundaries drawn between the homosocial and the homosexual. Nevertheless, the story also demonstrated how the realms of homosociality and homosexuality are potentially fluid, with the male bonding at the heart of the homosocial flirting at the possibility of homosexuality. The division between the two is bolstered by social convention and dominant social norms, but undermined time and again by attraction and desire.

Like any potentially illicit activity, male bonding is negotiated on screen with great care and under meticulous guidelines. As the line between *Boys in the Band* and *Boys in the Sand* illustrates, the presentation of cinematic male bonding inevitably depends at least partly on the expected audience, venue, and prevailing political and social climate at the time of production. Perhaps the largest partition between representations is the straight versus gay variation—that is, those films intended primarily for a straight audience versus those directed to a gay audience. In this essay, I would like to address the social, political, and narrative potential inherent in male groups depicted on screen: in straight films, gay films, and most particularly in those films which elude simple classification along these lines. Indeed, in the current era, the most politically charged films in terms of gay representation and male bonding might well be those that refuse to be labeled as such. The comedy of unemployed heterosexual actors on the fringes of Hollywood, *Swingers*, offers a particularly striking example of such an interstitial film—perhaps the queerest film never tagged as belonging to the "New Queer Cinema." *Swingers* demonstrates the cooptation of gay male friendship within a supposedly "straight" comedy, signaling that queerness can be accommodated openly within increasingly conventional media texts.

bonding: straight, gay, and other

Traditionally, films have presented male bonding within set generic frameworks. The male group and bonding between individual males within that group are central to those films with a strong male institutional bias: generically the war film, western, police/detective film, as well as variants such as the prison, fraternity, or sports film. Within this framework, the buddy picture—particularly the action or police/detective film featuring a mismatched pair—has been a staple of the male group film. Scholars such as Yvonne Tasker, Cynthia Fuchs, Susan Jeffords, and Chris Holmlund have investigated male pairings in action cinema, demonstrating that the genre of the action buddy movie facilitates the erasure of difference between the male partners and, as Tasker notes, the threat of other types of difference, especially racial (1993, 43–47). While the homoerotic plays through films such as the *Lethal Weapon* series, *The Rookie*, and *Black Rain*, the films virulently attempt to heterosexualize their homosocial protagonists through secondary romantic liaisons. Nevertheless, the homoerotic tension remains, creating a space for the violent spectacle that ironically sometimes allows key moments of physical contact between the male pair.

As Vito Russo notes, a common characteristic of the male buddy film is the open homophobia among the male characters: *Thunderbolt and Lightfoot*, *The Choirboys* and *Slap Shot* are offered as examples. This homophobia is matched on occasion by openly homosexual minor characters who can be differentiated immediately from the male buddy protagonists (Russo 1987, 84–85). The presence of the gay characters within the straight male friendship films is to disavow the potential of a gay bond between the straight friends and to bolster their heterosexual friendship. Crucially, the converse also holds true: in the gay male variation, the presence of a straight person within the gay group serves to strengthen the bond between the gay friends. This scenario is played comically in Richard Lester's film of Terrence McNally's *The Ritz*. Cleveland garbageman Gaetano Proclo, middle-aged, rotund, and heterosexual, flees his murderous Mafia brother-in-law by hiding in the Manhattan gay bathhouse the Ritz. Proclo continually misreads cues in heterosexual terms within the gay environment, creating the space for farce and illuminating the strongly coded verbal and nonverbal communicative forms that elude straight decoding within the gay environment. The misreading begins when Gaetano, completely unaware of the sexual component to the Ritz, is asked by the front desk attendant if he has ever been in a "place like this before." Gaetano cheerily replies, "Oh sure. We've got a Jack LaLanne's in Cleveland." Ritz regular Chris must eventually explain the rules of the bathhouse to Gaetano, who responds with wide-eyed amazement at the myriad activities in the steam room, the sauna, and the dormitory.

The straight-as-Other also structures the classic gay male friendship film *The Boys in the Band*. Much of the drama derives from the impending arrival of heterosexual Alan at Michael's gay birthday party. The panicked host explains the situation to his friend Donald by claiming that the straight and "square" Alan belongs to a class at odds with the exclusively gay guests: "I mean they look down on people in the theater— so whatta you think he's going to feel about this freak show I've got booked for dinner." Alan serves to highlight the gay identity of the other characters and the degree to which they are comfortable assuming such an identity. Meeting Alan, the gay friends are forced to act "straight," constraining any signs betraying their gayness. The most effeminate one, Emory, simply cannot make the transition from gay to straight acting, constantly referring to his male friends with female pronouns and as queens. Not surprisingly, Alan's internalized homophobia finds an outlet through Emory—after a wisecrack about his wife performing oral sex, Alan brutally punches Emory while calling him a "goddamn little mincing swish." The other friends refuse to intervene in the altercation. The inaction can be interpreted as a sign of the friends' fear of being gay bashed, their own discomfort with stereotypical gay behavior, or perhaps some combination of the two. Clearly, though, the bond between the gay friends is mediated by the structures guiding straight society—they expect anger, alienation, and even violence when confronted with a person outside their gay circle of friends.

The male group films—gay and straight—illustrate the crucial distinction between friendship in the gay and straight worlds. The model for male bonding within the straight world develops from gender differences in childhood. Boys in early adolescence are less eager for intimacy compared with girls. For boys, the male gang is more important than one-on-one friendship, but the gang members require little closeness and rely on other abilities (e.g., athletic) for membership. In contrast to girls, boys are less likely to seek loyalty from their male friends, and the loss of a friend is easily accommodated by the presence of another male gang member (Farr 1992). This trajectory continues throughout the physical and emotional development of the straight male. By late adolescence, the male group diminishes in importance as interactions with the opposite sex fill the void. The male group dynamic is retained, however, in a slightly altered form for heterosexual males. Kathryn Ann Farr traces this process by identifying the role played by exclusionary adult male groups "to learn and celebrate the masculinity of camaraderie, competition, aggressiveness and independence" (1992, 403). Referring to these male groups as "Good Old Boys Sociability Groups" (or, to use Farr's acronym, GOBS), Farr analyzes the ways through which these informal male groups perpetuate masculine identity and masculine privilege throughout adulthood. A key element of the Good Old Boy Group is that the members are "gender successful"—that is, the members are masculine, heterosexual, and have enjoyed considerable popularity with women. This male bonding is facilitated by the ritualized activity of joking, used by the members to negotiate latent tension and aggression felt toward other members.

Friendship for gay males carries a much greater significance, in large part because the distinction between friendship and kinship is lost for many gay people. As Kath Weston suggests, gay people's alienation from heterosexual society and, often, from family leads us to replace biological/blood family with families we choose or create (1991, 28). The role of friendship in this process is, of course, central: for gay people, friendship becomes a fluid category that helps to create social networks and community. Limiting his analysis to gay males, Peter Nardi foregrounds the transgressive quality of gay male friendship in overcoming "traditional" male socialization stereotypes (1995). Nardi's model of gay male friendship embodies three major characteristics: the familial, the sexual, and the political (1992). Friends are frequently viewed as family, especially by people estranged from their biological family. Sexual attraction plays a role in the early stages of many of these friendships. The political, legal, religious, economic, and health concerns are routinely affected by dominant society, and in addition gays function through friendship as a political group to combat this harassment. The AIDS epidemic has consolidated many of these friendships into institutional frameworks. As Nardi explains, "Friends become more salient as primary sources of social and emotional support when illness strikes" (1992, 118). "AIDS buddies" as a crucial form of support blur the boundaries between community assistance and friendship.[1] Friendship between gay males is also characterized by an emotional intimacy unlike that between heterosexual male friends. Nardi suggests that one consequence of these deviations from the norm of straight male friendship is a possible reconfiguration of social interaction affecting all males, gay and straight.

in between straight and gay:
trespassing friendship and the cinema

Given these models of straight and gay male friendship, represented in several examples from film, what about those cinematic cases that cannot be typed so readily—films falling supposedly within the domain of "straight male" friendship, yet which cannot adequately contain the threat of homosocial bonding? To be more precise, more problematic to the models of straight and gay male friendship are those films that feature the straight male group yet cannot be classified immediately by genre (war, sports, action, etc.). In these cases, the straight male group cannot be "explained" immediately by institutional factors—the police force, the Army, the basketball team, and so on—and therefore the potential for homosocial bonding is not defused by the institutional and generic frameworks. Among the films that defy such simple labeling are Barry Levinson's nostalgic tale of postcollege friends in 1959 Baltimore, *Diner* (1982), and Doug Liman's comedy of unemployed straight actors adopting a hip, retro-swing lifestyle, *Swingers* (1996). In both cases, the male group acts as a haven for a particular male pairing, one couple of male friends veers toward a more intimate relationship advanced by the "safety" of the larger heterosexual male group. Certainly neither film presents an overtly gay relationship, yet both suggest that homosociality unconstrained by social conventions can foster a homosexual relationship. The two films differ in a most significant manner in their depiction of the lines between homosociality and homosexuality. Whereas *Diner* hints at unresolved romantic feelings between the friends, *Swingers*, produced fifteen years later, incorporates a queer aesthetic in its presentation of a straight male friendship.

Diner spins around the fate of five friends in their mid-20s—Eddie (Steve Guttenberg), Boogie (Mickey Rourke), Fenwick (Kevin Bacon), Shrevie (Daniel Stern), and Billy (Timothy Daly)—during the period leading to Eddie's wedding on New Year's Eve 1959. Unlike the similar period friendship film *American Graffiti*, *Diner*'s female characters are supporting or peripheral to the major group (Ellen Barkin playing Shrevie's neglected wife has the only female role of consequence). The friends spend endless nighttime and early morning hours at Fells Point Diner, debating the relative merits of Frank Sinatra, Johnny Mathis, and Elvis Presley, sports trivia, and dating rituals. Levinson paints the male bonding in *Diner* as a failed attempt to extend adolescence through a GOBS structure. The friends, individually and collectively, cannot function beyond their group: the recently married Shrevie finds that he cannot talk to his wife, Fenwick wallows in alcoholism rather than choosing a career, and Boogie gambles and womanizes, thereby squandering his chance at a career in law.

While the friends certainly are pictured as heterosexual, the form of their relationships with women, sexual and platonic, are inevitably troubled. Time after time, these liaisons are transformed from the serious, which might threaten the male friendships, into comical games to score points with the other friends. In the first scene, during a Saturday night dance, Boogie confronts Fenwick about "selling" his date, Diane, to David Frazier for $5. Boogie facilitates a reunion between Fenwick and Diane, while Fenwick pockets the money and impresses his friends with his outrageous behavior. Although he acts as peacekeeper in this exchange, Boogie, the Lothario of the group, presents the most frequent examples of translating his heterosexual conquests into forms of male one-upmanship. The most vivid example involves his date with Carol Heathrow, an inhibited blonde. Late one night at the diner, the friends bet that she will not touch Boogie's penis on the first date—a topic that inspires continual riffs on how the act will be validated. As Shrevie deadpans, "What are you going to do—get fingerprints? I'm not going to do the dusting!" Taking bets from his disbelieving pals, Boogie invites all of them to attend a screening of *A Summer Place* where the sexual act will take place for all to witness. Through inserting his erect penis into the popcorn container, Boogie scores a technical victory, yet he simultaneously transforms the supposed passionate connection into a farcical one, treating sex and bonding with women as valuable only through the perspective of his male friends.

Eddie and Billy are probably the most forlorn of the bunch: Eddie requires his fiancée to pass a football quiz before consenting to the wedding, and Billy cannot untangle his feelings, romantic and otherwise, for a longtime female confidante. The most conflicted and potent example of homosocial bonding exists between Eddie and Billy: Eddie has not informed Billy, his best friend, about his wedding, for reasons unexplained by either character. The implication is that Billy does not want to alienate his friend or to shift the terms of their relationship. Crucially, all the action excludes Eddie's fiancée, Elyse, altogether, focusing instead on the moments of bonding between Eddie and Billy. Eddie is obsessed with two aspects at this turning point: his own virginity and, in light of the impending marriage, his potentially altered friendship with Billy. Billy continually reassures Eddie that their bond will change only if Eddie permits it.

In the most telling scene between the two, on his stag night, Eddie describes a failed attempt at an adolescent seduction, and, in the process, he drapes his arm around his best friend. After a drunken Billy starts to play piano onstage, Eddie follows, dancing cheerfully until he is stopped in his tracks by the female stripper on the runway. He freezes—momentarily shocked and dismayed by his inability to interact with the scantily clad older woman. The scene illustrates the potential transformation of the homosocial to the homosexual: a threat inherent in any moment of homosocial bonding. In this case, Billy's jump to the stage can be seen, literally and figuratively, as an attempt to evade the advances of his confused best friend. As Eddie nonetheless pursues his friend on stage, he is halted by heterosexuality-on-display: the stripper whose territory he has just invaded by jumping on the runway. This moment captures Levinson's understanding of the power of homosocial bonding and the institutional structures enacted to separate the homosocial from the homosexual. Significantly, the next scene shows the friends drinking coffee with the stripper in a diner. Until the early morning, Eddie tells corny jokes— "sixth-grade humor," according to the stripper—and any vestige of sexual tension between the three is dissipated. By returning to a diner, the privileged space of male bonding, the friends are able to negotiate the potential threat of the heterosexual to their homosocial bonding. *Diner* depicts the exclusionary quality of homosocial bonding— women are either elided or valued only in terms of their relation to the male group members. The potential threat of homosexuality hidden behind the homosocial bonding is also clearly pictured within the film. This threat is mediated, however, by the period setting and moreover by the date of the film's release, 1982.[2]

Certainly, the major studios were still guarded about presenting homosexuality on screen at that time. While the sexual revolution had broadened the representation of all sexuality on screen, gayness was still largely taboo. One significant exception to the majors' timidity was *Cruising* (1980), remarkable for featuring a star, Al Pacino, in a fairly graphic depiction of the gay S&M scene. United Artists was not rewarded for this daring, however: the film failed miserably at the box office and was ravaged by most critics. In the spring of 1982, *Diner's* release date, several studios began to flirt with gayness as a topic. These attempts were generally quite guarded though. *Making Love*, for example, presented an exceedingly timid depiction of a gay husband leaving his wife, and it can be seen as an appropriate barometer for Hollywood's comfort with overt depictions of homosexual relationships. Other films from that season engaged gayness in varying degrees, all firmly within a generic framework: *Victor/Victoria* (musical comedy), *Deathtrap* (thriller), and *Partners* (comedy). The juxtaposition of the homosocial and homosexual in *Diner* follows in this burgeoning movement of studio filmmaking aware of potential gay themes and readings of mainstream films.

While *Diner* embodies many of the traditional characteristics of the straight male friendship, such as the social group, joking, and shared rather than individual support, in its exploration of homosocial bonding, *Swingers* adopts the model of the gay male friendship, though none of its lead characters self-identify as gay. Like *Diner*, *Swingers* revolves around a group of friend in their mid-20s: in this case, actors on the fringes of contemporary Hollywood who spend their nights frequenting swing clubs and adopting the "lifestyle" of Sinatra's Rat Pack. The group consists of Trent, the lanky social organizer; Mike, the forlorn stand-up comic; Sue (named for Johnny Cash's song "A Boy Named Sue"), hot-tempered and libidinous; and Rob, a naive former New Yorker vying for a theme park acting engagement as Goofy.

While the boys spend inordinate time discussing the rules of dating and the possibility for romance, *Swingers* nevertheless qualifies as a queer text in several ways. Queerness resides primarily in the forms of communication and interaction between the friends in the group. First, the friends speak in highly coded conversation: they have adopted a vocabulary requiring a glossary at the back of the published screenplay. In the world of the *Swingers* friends, *baby* has a dual purpose, referring either to a girl or woman (e.g. "Look at all the beautiful babies") or as a term of endearment for a close personal friend, usually male. *Money* could refer to currency, but more likely is an adjective of praise for something or someone (to cheer up the dejected Mike, Trent exclaims, "You're so money and you don't even know it"). To be *business class* is not a compliment: it indicates that one's posterior is large enough to require flight arrangements other than coach seating (e.g., "He's got a great face, but he's business class").

The lexicon is matched with a full evocation of a past era, specifically the cocktail-intensive, laid-back attitude from the 1950s Rat Pack (Sinatra, Dean Martin, Sammy Davis Jr., Peter Lawford, Joey Bishop).

Admittedly, the Rat Pack also has been embraced by contemporary mainstream popular culture, as evidenced by the resurgence of interest in lounge music, the 1998 HBO movie *The Rat Pack*, and the publication of books such as Shawn Levy's *Rat Pack Confidential* (1998). The friends of *Swingers* revel in the outer surfaces of the Rat Pack: borrowing the look of canvas jackets and starched white undershirts, the narrow ties, and the cardigans; drinking only the finest liquor (scotch must be any "glen"); driving only a vintage Comet convertible. The vocabulary can be traced back to the Rat Pack as well—from the politically incorrect turn of phrase to the title of the film (Sinatra's discography includes such albums as "Come Swing with Me!," "Songs for Swingin' Lovers!," and "A Swingin' Affair!").

The connections are made explicitly within the text: near the beginning, Trent and Mike drive from Hollywood to Las Vegas, changing into their retro-suits along the way. Hoping that their effortless style and looks will ensure the adoration of the casino managers, Trent insists on gambling in an authentic '50s casino, which has clearly seen better days. He explains to Mike, "Back in the day this place was a contender. Now they appreciate the business. They'll fall all over themselves for class clientele like us. You want to be fresh on the scene, right, baby?" With a montage of the casinos set against the arriving buddies in their vintage convertible, the *Swingers* friends are transformed, in their own minds at least, into the Rat Pack (as a *Newsweek* article more accurately describes them, "the mouse pack strutting their retro stuff" [Marin 1998, 64–65]).

While the heterosexuality of the Rat Pack was one of its defining characteristics, with *Swingers*, flirtation rather than seduction is most significant. Although the friends endlessly flirt with young women, the goal does not appear to be a fling, merely the acquisition of a phone number (or "digits" in the Swingers' terms). Trent even rips up one girl's number right after receiving it—the challenge is to attain the number rather than to actually connect with the opposite sex. Flirtation is constructed as an elaborate game, but a game nevertheless, as meaningful as the video hockey games which the friends endlessly play. In this spirit, *Swingers* writer and star Jon Favreau has even developed the Swingers rules: a list of absurd guidelines for those wanting advice on how to meet women. Critically, "team play," helping your buddy to find a date, is listed near the top of the rules (Vaughn and Favreau 1996).

Ultimately, what is the result of these characteristics—the reveling in surface and style, the evocation of times past, the coded communication? *Swingers* falls into the domain of camp, one of the privileged sites for gay men. After the publication of Susan Sontag's "Notes on Camp" in 1964, many scholars have debated the definitional boundaries of

59

From Left to right, Vince Vaughn, Jon Favreau and Patrick Van Horn in Doug Liman's *Swingers*.

camp and the intersection between camp and gayness. Jack Babuscio's outline of four primary features of camp—irony, aestheticism, theatricality, and humor—offers a useful framework for understanding *Swingers'* venture into this territory (1993). The ironic contrast between the young pals and their incongruous appearances, their highly developed and exotic retro-aesthetic, and certainly the humorous and very theatrical means of self-presentation and communication evidenced within the group overlap with Babuscio's explication of camp. The functioning of *Swingers* as camp also connects in a clear fashion to gayness. Richard Dyer lists the positive aspects of camp as "identity and togetherness, fun and wit, self-protection and thorns in the flesh of straight society" (1992, 136). *Swingers* operates in this register, creating the means through which to negotiate one's experience of the world. Just as camp serves to undercut straight society in the gay world, camp also renders the world of "straights" (defined broadly as non-Swingers) powerless for the cinematic friends.

The stress of identity and togetherness functions in the Swingers group as a whole, but even more powerfully in the bond created by Trent and Mike. The camp affectations of their world sever the two from the outside—indeed, Trent and Mike seem the least able to interact with those outside the group. Although the dynamic between the two centers on Trent buoying Mike's spirits over and over, there is sufficient variation to reveal an intimacy between the friends. While Trent urges Mike to seek digits from "beautiful babies," Trent's own love life seems at a standstill—particularly after his attempted seduction of a Vegas cocktail waitress is ruined by Mike's constant interruptions at the waitress's trailer home. Curiously, when Mike does make contact with the opposite sex, by dancing with Lorraine in the swing club, Trent's response is excessively emotional: he bursts into tears. Whether the tears are for joy (his best friend has found a date) or sorrow (the bond between the men may be broken) is left unanswered by the film. Interestingly, Vince Vaughn (Trent) has commented, "I do think that *Swingers* is a love story. I don't think there's a sexual relationship between Trent and Mike ... but undoubtedly it's a love story about them" ("Going, Going, Vaughn," 115). The degree of support and personal contact between the two again aligns the pair with the model of gay male friendship. As Nardi concludes from his ethnographic research on gay male friendship, "This expression of intimacy and emotional support between men appears to be more typical of gay men than heterosexual men. . . . For gay men, expressive and instrumental support, as well as self-disclosing feelings and emotions, come from their friendship with other men, unlike what traditional male norms about friendship suggest" (1992, 111).

Critically, the integration of gay male friendship into straight society reflects one of the most compelling arguments in John D'Emilio's seminal essay "Capitalism and Gay Identity" (Lancaster and di Leonardo 1997). D'Emilio contends that capitalism has splintered the nuclear family by pushing individuals into roles outside the family unit while simultaneously enshrining the family as the center of all life. The contradictions at the heart of capitalism call for a newly configured model of society and new social roles. Gays and lesbians have pioneered the development of "affectional communities," in D'Emilio's terms, for support and development outside the structure of the nuclear family. In this manner, D'Emilio posits that gays and lesbians have the potential to lead society with new social formations.

The intense and emotional friendship between Mike and Trent, added to the camp quality and the importance on community, suggests that *Swingers* is operating from the model of gay male friendship despite the attested heterosexuality of the friends. In this manner, gay male friendship has been usurped by a straight text, leading to the possibility of a connection between the homosocial and the homosexual and to the innovative social formations envisioned by D'Emilio. Eve Kosofsky Sedgwick (1985) argues that male bonding has been traditionally characterized by an intense homophobia, with the homosocial depending on a separation from the homosexual. In contrast, *Swingers* offers a significant point of connection between the homosocial and homosexual: through its adoption of the model of gay male friendship and, with one exception, through the absence of homophobic references within the text.[3] This possibility makes me think that *Swingers* may actually be part of the New Queer Cinema: queerer still for not being calculated as such within the marketplace and for covertly introducing aspects of gay culture into the mainstream.[4]

While *Swingers* does blur the boundaries between the homosocial and the homosexual, not all contemporary films centering on male bonding demonstrate such an enlightened view.[5] *The Full Monty* (1997), for instance, arguably falls into the same terrain as *Swingers* through focusing on male bonding without a generic safety net. The tale of unemployed steelworkers forming an unlikely local striptease company definitely is structured around moments of the male friends connecting, sometimes around very personal issues, such as impotence and sexual dysfunction. Ostensibly all the characters are heterosexual, yet the two most withdrawn characters, Guy and Lomper, fall into an off-screen affair (a rather chaste kiss is the only physical affection between the two). Until the initiation of the affair, the film does suggest, like *Diner* and *Swingers*, that the homosociality is threatened by an underlying current of homosexuality. Regardless, after the two men are seen holding hands at a funeral, the suspicion of an affair or merely gay tendencies between the two is seized for an extended joke by the other characters. The affair is left offscreen and the characters remain mute about both their attraction for each other and their gayness. *Swingers* adopts the model of gay male friendship for its heterosexual characters problematizing rigid classifications of gay and straight, while *The Full Monty*, despite its gay characters, serves to reinforce the lines between gay and straight. When Guy and Lomper are judged to be gay, the other characters respond with ridicule and derision. Pointedly, these two gay characters are given no opportunity to counter these statements or to reintegrate into the group in a manner that would acknowledge their status as a sexual couple. *The Full Monty* therefore posits a more traditional view of the homosexual versus the homosocial, endorsing a clear division between the two.

The slippage of gay male friendship into mainstream culture follows from the larger assimilation of gay culture into dominant society. In *The Rise and Fall of Gay Culture*, Daniel Harris (1997) suggests that a process of cultural erosion has been taking place as gays have been absorbed into mainstream society. Charting features of gay culture—artifacts, fetishes, clothing, political rhetoric—from the early 1970s to the 1990s, Harris laments the manner through which commercial exploitation has diminished the distinctiveness of gay culture. Harris's analysis of film centers entirely on the ways through which gay pornography has become more mainstream over the last two decades, but the argument of gay cultural assimilation applies to film beyond the realm of the hard-core. Tracing the adoption of male homosocial bonding in cinema, a similar process of assimilation has occurred with gay male friendship.

The consequences of this assimilation are more difficult to assess. From the gay perspective, the adoption of the model of gay male friendship—including the elements of intimacy and the centrality of camp—within straight society does help to undo an important form of coding established within the gay world. As the codes become part of the larger social matrix, the sense of gay community may seem to be diminished. However, this process of cultural integration cannot be dismissed immediately. Considering just the aspect of camp within the gay male friendship, as Richard Dyer remarks, camp is always deeply ambiguous, harboring an inherent sexism and homophobia through, for example, the usage of female pronouns and nicknames as a form of address. With camp being "borrowed" by straight society through the model of gay male friendship, its transgressive power may be diminished.

As evidenced by *Swingers*, gay male friendship can shift the parameters of male bonding and can suggest that the division between homosocial and homosexual need not be as rigid as normally assumed. Rather than characterize this possibility negatively, I feel that the queer friendships of *Swingers* serve to broaden straight and gay definitions of male bonding, diluting the pressures of male socialization and stereotypes and thereby offering expanded possibilities for all, even for those in college fraternities.

63

notes

1. *Buddies* (1985) and *Parting Glances* (1986), two of the first independent films to address the impact of AIDS on the gay community, tellingly focus on caregiving friendships between a person with AIDS and another gay male.

2. Many of Barry Levinson's subsequent films engage the issue of homosocial bonding, albeit not in such a concentrated fashion as *Diner*. *Tin Men*

(1987) is structured around male rivalry dissolving the boundaries between commerce and personal relationships, *Good Morning, Vietnam* (1987) is bounded by its genre (war comedy) and the largely male cast, and *Rain Man* (1988) is reliant on a newly discovered fraternal relationship for much of its dramatic impact. *Sleepers* (1996) returns Levinson most directly to the line between the homosocial and homosexual. With its tale of four street kids, now adults, seeking revenge on a guard who sexually abused them, during their childhood incarceration, *Sleepers* resolutely presents gayness as other, aligning the homosexual with degradation, child molestation, and violence. The close friendship between the four male friends retains a homosocial, not homosexual, quality through fabricating gayness in utterly irredeemable terms.

3. In the curious scene which might be interpreted as homophobic, Trent taunts a deliveryman, as the script indicates, "by feigning homosexuality." Offscreen, Trent calls out to Mike, "Is he cute? Ask him if he wants to stay for a cocktail!" The gay-baiting immediately follows a scene with Trent and Sue wrestling on the floor, and Trent saying, "Admit it, you want to kiss me." One could interpret the gay-baiting as an obvious attempt to defuse any homosexual desire from Trent toward Sue.

4. Critic B. Ruby Rich (1992) heralded the "New Queer Cinema" as a media moment in the early 1990s, during which appeared several gay and lesbian films unapologetically queer in their political stance and aesthetic design. Films such as *Paris Is Burning*, *Poison*, *My Own Private Idaho*, and *Edward II* were labeled as part of the movement. Within the span of half a decade, the possibility of the New Queer Cinema was far from realized—undermined by increasingly "safe" projects and a spotty record of production and distribution for gay and lesbian features.

5. Doug Liman's next film, *Go* (1999) complicates the division between gay and straight, homosocial and homosexual even further. One of the three plotlines concerns two gay male lovers (Scott Wolf and Jay Mohr), actors in a daytime soap, who must shield their sexual identity from a sexually ambiguous cop. The entire story is centered on the limits of interpreting cues of sexuality from both gay and straight perspectives—in effect arguing that sexual coding of both gay and straight has become confused in the current era.

works cited

Babuscio, Jack. 1993. "Camp and the Gay Sensibility." In *Camp Grounds: Style and Homosexuality*, ed. David Bergman, 19–38. Amherst: University of Massachusetts Press.

D'Emilio, John. 1997. "Capitalism and Gay Identity." In *The Gender Sexuality Reader*, ed. Roger N. Lancaster and Micaela di Leonardo, 169–78. New York: Routledge.

Dyer, Richard. 1992. "It's Being So Camp as Keeps Us Going," *Only Entertainment*, 135–147. London: Routledge.

Farr, Kathryn Ann. 1988. "Dominance through the Good Old Boys Sociability Group," *Men's Lives*, ed. Michael S. Kimmel and Michael A. Messner, 403–18. New York: Macmillan Publishing Company.

"Going, Going, Vaughn." 1997. *Details* (January): 113–15.

Harris, Daniel. 1997. *The Rise and Fall of Gay Culture*. New York: Hyperion Books.

Levy, Shawn. 1998. *Rat Pack Confidential: Frank, Dean, Sammy, Peter, Joey and the Last Showbiz Party*. New York: Doubleday.

Marin, Rick. 1998. "A Man and His Cufflinks." *Newsweek* May 25, 64–65.

Nardi, Peter M. 1992. "That's What Friends Are For: Friends as Family in the Gay and Lesbian Community." In *Modern Homosexualities: Fragments of Lesbian and Gay Experience*, ed. Ken Plummer, 108–120. London: Routledge.

———. 1995. "The Politics of Gay Male Friendship." In *Men's Lives*, ed. Michael S. Kimmel and Michael A. Messner, 337–40. Needham Heights: Allyn & Bacon.

Rich, B. Ruby. 1992. "A Queer Sensation." *Village Voice*, March 24, 41–44.

Richmond-Abbott, Marie. 1992. *Masculine and Feminine: Gender Roles over the Life Cycle*. New York: McGraw-Hill.

Russo, Vito. 1987. *The Celluloid Closet*. New York: HarperCollins.

Sedgwick, Eve Kosofsky. 1985. *Between Men: English Literature and Male Homosocial Desire*. New York: Columbia University Press.

Tasker, Yvonne. 1993. *Spectacular Bodies: Gender, Genre, and the Action Cinema*. London: Routledge.

Vaughn, Vince, and Jon Favreau. 1996. "The Swingers Rules." *Swingers*. New York: Hyperion.

Weston, Kath, 1991. *Families We Choose: Lesbians, Gays, Kinship*. New York: Columbia University Press.

rape

fantasies

hollywood

and

homophobia

joe wlodarz

Although gay images have proliferated in contemporary Hollywood cinema in films such as *In and Out* (1997), *My Best Friend's Wedding* (1997), and *The Object of My Affection* (1998), the gay characters in these films are made to signify in very limited and easily assimilable ways. The primary missing element in these and most other mainstream representations of gay men is, of course, sex. This is certainly nothing new, but it does seem to exemplify Leo Bersani's claim in "Is the Rectum a Grave?" that dominant homophobia (at least in terms of gay men) is based on anxieties surrounding sex between men, particularly anal sex. According to Bersani, anal sex and its ties to the "suicidal ecstasy of being a woman" continues to be an uncontainable threat to straight masculinity and male subjectivity (1988, 212). Although Bersani has indeed moved to a more expansive view of the gay threat in recent work (*Homos*), given the persistence of phobias surrounding gay sex, it seems necessary to analyze just how pertinent his earlier claims about anal sex are to dominant cinema's representational strategies. Granted, homophobia in cinema can never directly reflect the intricacies of the operations of homophobia in our broader society, but the intensity of the gay sex phobia in Hollywood speaks to (but doesn't limit homophobia to) the overdetermined significance of gay sex in dominant society.

In order to clarify the potency and pertinence of this threat, I want to take a closer look at the rare occurrences in Hollywood film in which anal sex actually *is* represented. In a revealing twist on the visibility/invisibility double bind of gay representation, anal sex is indeed visible in film multiplexes across the country, but the catch is, it can be presented only as an act of rape. Cinema in the 1990s has been the site of the proliferation of the "children of *Deliverance*." Films such as *The Prince of Tides* (1991), *Pulp Fiction* (1994), *The Shawshank Redemption* (1994), *Sleepers* (1996), and, most recently, *Your Friends and Neighbors* (1998), and *American History X* (1998) have centered on a scenario in which boys or men are raped by other men. What is intriguing about this group of films is the way in which male rape becomes symbolically coded as homosexuality despite occasional narrative attempts to avoid this dangerous collapse of meanings.

This conflation, of course, is almost a necessity because as D. A. Miller has incisively noted, "straight men unabashedly *need* gay men, whom they forcibly recruit (as the object of their blows or, in better circles, just their jokes) to enter into a polarization that exorcises the 'woman' in man through assigning it to a class of man who may be considered no 'man' at all" (1991, 135). The frightening successes and yet significant weaknesses in the establishment of this polarization will occupy the bulk of my analysis in this study, which will focus primarily on Barry Levinson's *Sleepers* (1996) because its status as a male rape revenge film tends to concentrate issues that in other aforementioned films are more dispersed. Though gay men are nowhere to be seen in these representations of male rape (*Pulp Fiction* seems to be the exception) their presence haunts these scenarios in ways that blatantly reveal both straight male anxieties and psychic fantasies about anal sex between men. These films cannot be reduced to narratives about sadism or the trauma of rape in general because it is clearly the overdetermined anal violation and its associations with emasculation and homosexuality that is set apart by the films as the most damaging and avengeable trauma of all.

In order to effectively elaborate upon this trauma, which is generally coded as a form of extreme loss in *Sleepers*, it is necessary to detail the ways in which the film's pre-rape sequences work to conflate a notion of youthful innocence with an almost natural masculinity and, by extension, heterosexuality.[1] The opening credit sequence sets up this thematic with a voice-over by Jason Patric, as the lead character, Shakes, that speaks of "the children we *were*" while we are shown images of the four friends playing basketball in a gym. According to Shakes, this was the kind of friendship "that runs deeper than blood," and interestingly, the homoeroticism that these types of bonds tend to suggest is actually played up in several early scenes in the film that return us to this time of so-called "innocence," namely the summer of 1966 in Hell's Kitchen. The deep bond of the boys is visually suggested by the opening shot of the Hell's Kitchen sequence that fills the wide-screen frame with the bare sunbathing torsos of the pubescent lads lying side by side in a near fusion of flesh. This shot composition is repeated later in the film, and we're also treated to a scene of the boys diving off a small bridge clad only in their briefs. As we're informed about Hell's Kitchen, it was "a place of innocence ruled by corruption," but the corruption referred to is not of a sexual or erotic nature, rather it is simply the manly business of mob bosses. The innocence of this time is repeatedly signified throughout the film by an image of the boys frolicking in a gushing stream of water from an open fire hydrant. As the image suggests, it was a time of purity, of being perpetually cleansed by this holy water, free of any taint of sexual or psychic depravity.

This theme of youthful purity is inextricably bound up with a developing masculinity and is exemplified by the song that becomes the theme of their youth: "Walk Like a Man." Despite a few examples of masculinity gone wrong in the form of Shakes's wife-beating father and John's abusive stepfather, there is no shortage of unquestionably sound father figures. The most significant is Robert DeNiro's Father Bobby, a reformed juvenile delinquent who became the wise neighborhood priest and is the boys' key educator and defender. What is interesting about the presentation of the masculinity of the boys is that in many ways it is updated to a more '90s postfeminist "sensitive" masculinity. This is primarily done by distancing their form of masculinity from that of the abusive, misogynist fathers, but is also clearly conveyed by a scene in which Michael "throws" a game of street ball (by intentionally striking out) in order to please the wheelchair-bound sister of his opponent. This sequence in which Michael purposely "goes soft" immediately precedes a scene of Fat Mancho, another of the boys' male mentors, preaching the benefits of staying "hard and tough." He refers to one of the boys as "limp dick," and explains: "A guy smells it when you're weak—eats you up like salad. . . . Going soft is a habit. You have to keep yourself mean."

The boys are set apart from this type of base and crude masculinity, and this ultimately serves a number of functions. On one hand, it provides an out for masculinity/patriarchy itself by limiting the horrors of machismo and patriarchal sensibilities to a few bad seeds from an earlier generation. In addition, it also seems to be a way of interpellating

the film's spectators by presenting to them a more culturally acceptable form of masculine behavior with which to identify. Finally, this
"softer," less rigidly bounded masculinity can be seen as one that is less
threatened by certain forms of emotional expression, and even passivity, but is still just masculine enough to avoid being confused with the
ultimate form of passivity, namely homosexuality.[2] This distinction,
though, is complicated after the boys are sent to the Wilkinson Home
for Boys following a foolish prank that nearly kills a man.

Shakes's voice-over foreshadows the trauma that we're about to
witness in the detention center segment of the film when he states: "I
knew from the first day that I was neither tough nor strong." This vulnerability is conveyed by the film through a scene in which Nokes (one
of the guards, played by Kevin Bacon) peers into Shakes's cell omi-
nously and demands that he strip naked. Whereas an earlier scene in
the film clearly celebrates the covert erotic stares of the boys as they
peer through an outside window into a dressing room for women in an
Ice Capades show, this unlicensed look, which turns one of the boys
himself into an erotic, vulnerable spectacle, is clearly marked as
assaultive and thoroughly transgressive. Of course, it's not Shakes's status as erotic spectacle that is threatening—for the film itself is guilty
of that in its opening sunbathing shots—but rather his position as the
erotic object of a desiring *male* gaze.

The rape scene soon follows this ocular assault on Shakes as Nokes
and three other guards attack all four of the recently detained friends.
In a segment filmed in such a way as to highlight this descent into the
depths of human depravity, the director enters and exits the rape scene
with lengthy tracking shots down long, dark, ominous tunnels that
lead to the "lowest point" of the detention center, the basement.
Clearly, the parallels between these dark, ominous passageways and
the "forbidden passageway" of the male anatomy are made all too
apparent by this visual trope.[3] Moreover, this technique also suggests
the camera's (and, by extension, the cinema's) perilous descent to the
visualization of an act that has traditionally been unrepresentable. If
the boys and the guards are sinking to new depths of vileness, then so
is the film and so are its spectators.

Under a menacing, swaying overhead light, the boys are trapped in
a cluttered storage room that partially obstructs the view of the spectator, and the impending atrocity is introduced by the mere sound of a
zipper being undone. Immediately after Nokes demands a blow job of
Michael (Brad Renfro) and the other boys are clubbed into vulnerable
positions, the camera begins its retreat. As we quickly back up from
this horrific scene (it's almost as if the camera can't bring itself to look),
we're given aural evidence of the rape as increasingly loud groans of
agony tell the story that we apparently can't bear to witness. Once out

of the tunnel, Shakes's voice-over returns as the final verification of the atrocities just committed: "It was the end of my childhood."

The rapes are far from over after this initial gang rape. The guards merely split up and become solo "night visitors" to the individual rooms of each of the boys. At one point, Shakes, listening to John's agonized wailing through the wall, comments that "these were the cries that can change the course of a life ... ones that can never be erased." This particular pattern of individual abuse continues until the night before Shakes's release in which Nokes slips into his room and says: "I just wanna say goodbye. We all do." The return of the traveling shots down the tunnels tell us all we need to know, and it is only later in the film (in flashback) that we're shown Shakes being raped by Nokes's baton, presumably on this final night.

In order to further discuss the ways in which these rapes end up being coded as homosexuality, I want to address two key elements in the film. The first is the prison football game between the inmates and the guards that functions as the first instance of the boys' revenge. This is the game that they cannot throw, and they rely on the talents of a black inmate named Rizzo to assist in their efforts. As Shakes explains, the motivation behind the boys' intense investment in the game was "to make them feel what we feel just for a couple of hours." Much to the guards' dismay, the boys end up winning the game because, according to Shakes, they "took the game out of prison and brought it to the streets of Hell's Kitchen." In other words, they took this struggle of dominance and submission from the realm of improper masculinity to a more proper realm of "untainted" homosociality and aggressivity.[4] Still, despite the "rush" that this sequence provides, the fact that the game takes place within the prison walls guarantees that it is a futile victory. The boys are thrown into solitary confinement ("the hole"),[5] and Rizzo is beaten to death.

Rizzo's death is revealing because there is no suggestion in the film that he was raped. Furthermore, in another telling scene, Nokes's degradation of the boys (he makes them eat spilled food off of the floor) is thwarted by the protestations of a black guard who threateningly challenges Nokes: "No Nokes. You *fuck* with me. I'm asking you!" Intimidated, Nokes quickly backs away. Thus, in *Sleepers*, black men (and boys) are significantly distanced from the realm of specifically sexual victimization. And interestingly, with the sole exception of *Pulp Fiction*, the men and boys who are raped in all of these films are invariably white, and it is specifically white masculinity that is placed under assault.

The football sequence is also intriguing because of the way it foregrounds some of the tensions surrounding the revenge element of the male rape revenge films. Later, I will elaborate more on some of these tensions by contrasting this film with the female rape revenge genre, but for the moment I simply want to point out the fact that the shift from improper to proper realms of masculinity is necessary in the male rape revenge film in order to avoid a resexualization of the revenge itself. In other words, the boys *need* the football game here because *literally* "mak[ing] them feel what we feel for a couple of hours" would involve far too transgressive a reversal.

Another important element in the film is the insistent recuperation of religion as a holy, pure, and innocent institution that is enacted by a clear contrast to the series of blasphemies committed by the prison guards. Aside from the metaphorical good father/bad father binary constructed between Father Bobby and Nokes, Nokes is depicted as unwilling to acknowledge the significance of Shakes's Virgin Mary charm and makes him take it off during the voyeuristic strip scene. Later, during the final rape scene in which Shakes is raped by Nokes's baton, Shakes is shown clutching his rosary while Nokes implores him to "pray, pray real loud" as he rapes him with the baton. In contrast to this twofold violation (rape and blasphemy), Shakes is shown to be a willing altar boy during Father Bobby's sermons, and Father Bobby is the one who personally comforts him before he is sent to Wilkinson and who ultimately provides the necessary alibi for the boys in their criminal trial.[6] Moreover, the severity of the violation of the boys is expressed in the scene in which Shakes tells Father Bobby of the abuses to which he and the other boys were subjected. Using John as the prime example of a "fall from grace" (he's now a feared gang member), Shakes reminds Father Bobby that John "wanted to be a priest." This massive recuperation of Catholicism is interesting because of the ways that it redirects the crime of pedophilia. *Sleepers* basically functions as the antidote to the poisonous claims of *The Boys of St. Vincent* (1992) through its complete exoneration of pedophile priests. Of course, this erasure of pedophilia from its most likely candidate allows the charge to shift to its other most frequent (and far less substantiated) target, the homosexual man.

This potential shift in focus assists in the project of conflating the rape of boys with homosexuality in general, and it is this slippery, yet exceedingly dangerous conflation that demands attention. Certainly in part, this conflation is almost inevitable due to the overdetermined "violence" of the penetration of one man (or boy) by another. This is of course not to say that there isn't a clear difference between consensual sex and rape, but part of the reason for the slippage in these films from male rape to male homosexuality is due to the fact that in a patriarchal society, the penetration of a man is generally considered to be a fate worse than (or at least equal to) death. As Leo Bersani has succinctly claimed: "To be penetrated is to abdicate power" (1988, 212). But abdication of power is hardly the limit of the sacrifice, for as Bersani suggests, being penetrated is frequently coded as a form of suicide because it involves a "radical disintegration and humiliation of the self," a "shattering" process that is antithetical to the "hyperbolic sense of self" that is at the core of patriarchy and phallocentrism (Bersani 1988, 217–18). All of these anxieties about anal penetration as an act of suicide have of course been intensified by the AIDS crisis which has only solidified the social adhesion of gay men to fears surrounding the potential "violence" of sex.

One reason that anal sex between men *must* be represented as rape is that the absence of a form of consent not only opens the door for the narrative presentation of the recuperation of straight male subjectivity (they didn't *want* to be fucked, thus they can be "cured"), but it also encourages the expression of violent homophobia which is conveniently transformed into a classic revenge narrative that slyly masks its inherent prejudices. Thus, films like *Sleepers* ultimately, if indirectly, give license to the demoralization, prosecution, brutalization, and even murder of "fags."[7]

While some of the male rape films do deal with the rape of grown men, the specific use of adolescent boys in *Sleepers* seems to serve a strategic purpose in that it similarly allows for the masking of the homophobia that underlies the desire for revenge.[8] Granted, it does open up the possibility for a distinct separation between acts of child abuse and consensual homosexual sex, but given the aforementioned exoneration of pedophile priests as well as the pronounced conflation of pedophilia and homosexuality in the dominant media (witness the excessive coverage of the North American Man-Boy Love Association [NAMBLA] debates), it is unlikely that this separation is actually registered by mainstream viewers given the general absence of gay counterpoints within these films. In addition, while Nokes is never explicitly represented as homosexual, his clearly perverse or simply inadequate manhood (e.g., raping Shakes with his baton) isn't too far removed from stereotypes about gay men. Ultimately, the use of adolescent boys in *Sleepers* simply shores up support for the impending acts of revenge due to the boys' status as "innocent," "uncorrupted," and most important, "non-consenting" participants in an act of sexual violence. And as films like *A Time to Kill* (1996) and *An Eye for an Eye* (1996) clearly demonstrate, vigilantism can never be more justifiable than when it is in response to a victimized child. Unfortunately, due to the slippery, yet fairly unavoidable, conflation of pedophilia with homosexuality throughout *Sleepers*, Anita Bryant's hateful shrieks of "save our children" seem to be a key motivating force behind these condoned (and encouraged) brutal acts of vengeance.

The use of boys rather than women also enacts another shameful elision in that the film gives itself a way to avoid presenting potentially feminist critiques of rape in general that would indirectly implicate patriarchy in some way. In contrast to the female rape revenge films, which, as Carol Clover suggests, "repeatedly and explicitly articulate feminist politics," *Sleepers* makes no such effort (Clover 1992, 151). In addition, while the female rape revenge film is frequently critical of the potentially violent dynamic of "men in groups," *Sleepers* and other male rape films generally skirt this critique of the potential horrors of masculinity by concentrating on the apparently more horrifying instances of a perversion, corruption, or violation of that very masculinity (Clover 1992, 144).

A temporal leap forward (thirteen years) allows the revenge narrative of *Sleepers* to kick into high gear immediately following the presentation of the final gang rape at Wilkinson. It's almost as if the film simply can't wait to counter or at least ameliorate both its own cinematic transgressions (showing what shouldn't be shown) and the narrative atrocities that motivate the revenge narrative. By sheer coincidence, Nokes just happens to be eating at the very same bar that current gang leaders John and Tommy are shown entering, and Tommy's recognition of him initiates the first, and most significant, act of revenge of the film. After refreshing Nokes's mind about his abuses and giving him a few brief moments to contemplate his impending death, Tommy proceeds to shoot him in the crotch, and as Nokes moans in agony, Tommy asks: "Did that hurt, Nokes?" This question is followed by a barrage of bullets from the guns of both Tommy and John as we're visually "treated" to extended slow-motion close-ups of Nokes's agony as he's littered with gunshots.

There are certainly sadistic pleasures being exploited in this scene by Tommy and John as well as by the film's spectators, and the shooting of Nokes in the crotch is about as close an approximation as the revenge can come to "making [him] feel what we feel." Still, as mentioned earlier, this reversal of position can never be fully implemented in the male rape revenge because of the homophobic taboos placed on the act of anal penetration.[9] This is not to say that raping Nokes would in some way be the ultimate form of revenge; rather, I merely want to highlight the ways that the entire film is overdetermined by masculinist and homophobic notions of "proper" acts of male "penetration," and in this scenario, repeatedly shooting Nokes seems to be the most "proper" form. Later, the men will rely on both legal and street justice in order to enact revenge on the other three guards from Wilkinson. But, for the most part, the criminal indictment of Styler and the courtroom "outing" of the former sins of Ferguson hardly provide the vindictive "thrust" that the shooting of Nokes does. And yet, despite

74

the sexual connotations of the shooting of Nokes's crotch, *Sleepers* and the other male rape revenge films noticeably avoid an overt sexualization of the act of revenge. While a number of the female rape revenge films such as *I Spit on Your Grave* (1978), *Ms. 45* (1981), and *Sudden Impact* (1983) show their avenging heroines using sexual seduction to initiate the act of violent revenge, the male rape revenge films anxiously avoid this scenario both to guarantee the heterosexuality (and, by extension, masculinity) of the avengers and to ensure that homosexuality remains unspoken and hidden from direct view.

As Carol Clover claims, the key premises of the female rape revenge films are "that rape deserves full-scale revenge; that a rape-and-revenge story constitutes sufficient drama for a feature film and that having the victim survive to be her own avenger makes that drama even better; and (more directly politically) that we live in a 'rape culture' in which *all* males—husbands, boyfriends, lawyers, politicians—are directly or indirectly complicit and that men are thus not just individually but corporately liable" (Clover 1992, 138–39). As mentioned, male rape revenge films such as *Sleepers* have absolutely no stake in indicting patriarchy or masculinity, and thus the target of attack is shifted from their own bodies to those of gay men, who are conveniently situated "outside" of traditional masculinity and patriarchy. Again, while this redirected attack is generally made narratively invisible through either liberal lip service to tolerance or processes of disavowal (which is the case in *Sleepers*), the specter of homosexuality thoroughly haunts the proceedings, and thus tends to make clear the substantial violence that is being enacted by this narrative system.

Scenes of simmering homoeroticism near the end of *Sleepers* finally come to a boil in the last scene of the film in which the four friends are finally reunited. In an excessive bonding scene that feels as long as the interminable last hour of the film, Shakes, Michael, Tommy, and John do their best to recuperate "proper" male physical contact (and love). Then, in a rather stunning moment in the film, Carol (their childhood companion) arrives and calls them on the spectacle she witnesses with the simple question: "What is this, a gay bar?" Considering how coy the film has been about its ties to homosexuality, the line is quite surprising. And yet, in a convoluted way, the line seems to be merely another attempt to silence all of the gay whispering at the margins of the film. Like the nods to tolerance made in films such as *The Shawshank Redemption* and *The Prince of Tides*, Carol's comment functions as both a casual acknowledgment of the homosexual current that runs throughout the film and a convenient dismissal of the overriding significance of that very element.

John's response to Carol's gay bar inquiry—"It was until you showed up"—basically tells the story of Carol's entire role in the film, namely, she's there to defuse homoeroticism. Even in the final scene in which the gang unites in a group rendition of "Walk Like a Man" (a most ironic song considering that it's sung like a woman) and the four men specifically stress the line "forget about the girl," Carol is there in response, urging them: "don't forget about the girl." And finally, as we learn about the fates of the characters, Carol, now a single mother, is revealed (in the film's most sexist moment) to have committed the ultimate act of devotion by naming her first child John Thomas Michael Martinez, and nicknaming him Shakes, in honor of her long-time friends.

Carol is an essential element in *Sleepers* since, as D. A. Miller convincingly suggests, "only between the woman and the homosexual together may the normal male subject imagine himself covered front and back" (1991, 135). And yet, just how well "covered" are these men, especially considering that their past is overwhelmingly marked by a trauma of being anally "uncovered?" Despite the normalizing masculine futurity implied by the naming of Carol's child, what needs to be considered is just how effective *Sleepers* and other male rape films are in recuperating masculinity and patriarchy after subjecting them to this ultimate attack.[10] David Savran's recent study of white masculinity and masochism presents some interesting ways of looking at this phenomenon. In his study, Savran suggests that the cultural discourses surrounding "white victimization" that have been increasingly prevalent in the United States since the Vietnam War function primarily, if not always decisively, to reinforce and stabilize white male hegemony. Savran veers somewhat from both Leo Bersani's and Kaja Silverman's discussion of male masochism as a potentially "shattering" threat to male subjectivity and argues that "masochism functions precisely as a kind of decoy and that the cultural texts constructing masochistic masculinities characteristically conclude with an almost magical restoration of phallic power" (1998, 37).

As mentioned, *Sleepers* and most other male rape films do indeed attempt this "magical restoration" near their conclusions, and yet, perhaps it is because the male rape films come so precariously close to crossing the culturally instated barriers between homosexuality and normative masculinity that phallic power can never adequately or convincingly recover.[11] Considering that Shakes's voice-over at the end of *Sleepers* informs us that John drank himself to death, Tommy was shot and killed, and Michael never married and lives quietly alone in the country, one wonders just how effective the acts of revenge really were in reinstituting a coherent sense of identity and masculinity in these men. Might we extend Bersani's claims and suggest "once shattered, always shattered?" In the logic of this film, might there be no going back after being penetrated by the scourge that is homosexuality? After all, the director himself has referred to the film as an "American tragedy," and Peter Travers finds it a "powerfully unsettling movie" (Hoberman 1996, 45; Travers 1996, 75). Consequently, if the role that revenge indirectly plays in the film is to suggest that the most effective way of exorcising the "queerness" (aka: the "shattered, non-masculine subjectivity") from within the straight male subject is to kill the projected sources of that internal "violation," and the film itself hints that even this extreme a revenge is sometimes not enough, then perhaps what is ultimately (if unconsciously) being said is that internal "queerness" (as described above) is an endemic problem to straight masculinity that is necessarily but *insufficiently* countered by the process of projection and the violent attack on that projected Other.[12]

In light of this insufficiency, it may very well be more productive to consider the role that a film like *Sleepers* plays in terms of straight male spectatorship in allowing for both the "thrills" of a "descent" into perverse depths and an ameliorative act of revenge to settle spectators's "unsettled" experience. But, perhaps there is something that persistently remains "unsettled" in the spectator after a "descent" of this particular sort in the male rape films. Perhaps the traumas of male rape (and all of its implications) don't miraculously vanish once the credits roll. Lee Edelman's discussion of the "spectacle of sodomy," certainly supports this notion. As he suggests, "the spectacle or representation of the scene of sodomy between men is a threat to the epistemological security of the observer—whether a heterosexual male himself or merely heterosexual-male-identified—for whom the vision of the sodomitical encounter refutes the determinacy of positional distinctions, compelling him to confront his too clear implication in a spectacle that, from the perspective of castration, can only be *seen* as a 'catastrophe'" (1994, 191).

Furthermore, if we keep in mind that one of the driving forces behind the violent acts of revenge as well as the potential recuperation of manhood in *Sleepers* is the absence of the "consent" of the penetrated boys, then perhaps we want to think about the motivations of the straight male spectator who willingly pays eight dollars for two and one-half hours in the dark presumably identifying with the victim of a male rape. Might he be indirectly giving "consent" to be "fucked" by this representational system, or does his pleasure lie in the momentary lapse of power that is guaranteed to be followed by a brutal reinstatement of masculine subjectivity?

If this question cannot be definitively answered one way or another because of the multiplicity of spectatorial positioning and desire, it certainly needs to be reconsidered in light of the surprisingly extreme eroticization of the male rape scenarios in Neil LaBute's *Your Friends and Neighbors* and Tony Kaye's *American History X*. And yet, despite both films' rather complicated (and somewhat incoherent) investment in the erotic potential of male bodies *and*, more significantly, male rape, the demonizing link between anal rape and gay sex persists. Thus, while the female rape revenge films may be laden with disruptive feminist politics, the male rape revenge films continue to go out of their way to recuperate patriarchy and masculinity (as best as possible) through the incessant scapegoating of gay men. And although their success in the recuperation of masculinity is notably incomplete, the severity of the attack on homosexuality is in no way diminished. In *Sleepers* and most other male rape films, gay men end up being the whipping boys who both allow for the potential transgression of straight male subjectivity and provide the opportunity to recontain it (at least somewhat). Therefore, while these films may indeed provide an opportunity for straight male spectators to experience the thrills of getting "fucked," it is gay men who end up more directly violated by this system of representation.

notes

I would like to thank Douglas Crimp, Sharon Willis, and Peter Lehman for their helpful comments and suggestions during the various revisions of this essay.

1. This theme of youthful innocence is similarly elaborated in *The Prince of Tides*, including the complication of it by issues of domestic abuse. *The Shawshank Redemption* plays more upon a retroactive establishment of Andy's (Tim Robbins) innocence (of the crime of murder), which is meant to heighten our shock at the horrors that he is confronted with in prison as well as to increase our sympathy for him.

2. *The Prince of Tides* also partakes in this expansion of masculinity, particularly through Bernard's (Jason Gould) training to be both a football player and an accomplished violinist. In addition, Tom Wingo's (Nick Nolte) eventual ability to cry and grieve over the painful experiences of his "lost" youth allows him to move beyond his Southern upbringing that insisted that "boys don't cry."

3. The metaphoric anality of tunnels reaches its representational apotheosis near the end of *The Shawshank Redemption* in which Andy must crawl through a milelong sewage pipe in order to escape from the prison. As his buddy Red (Morgan Freeman) announces in voice-over: "Andy Dufresne, who crawled through a river of shit and came out clean on the other side." As if this weren't enough, Andy emerges from the pipe in the middle of a rain shower that cleanses the body that was so tainted within the prison walls.

4. *The Prince of Tides* utilizes football in a similar manner by allowing it to properly balance out the masculinity of Lowenstein's (Barbara Streisand) son Bernard. Over the course of the film, Bernard turns into a thoroughly skilled football player whose manhood is exemplified in lines such as: "it'll be great puttin' you on your ass coach." What's interesting about this transformation is how hard it works to recuperate the extra-

textual star discourse about Jason Gould himself that was circulating at the time of the film's production and provided a different spin on why Jason/Bernard couldn't quite catch that football initially.

5. Again we have the return of these metaphors of anality that suggest degradation.

6. Father Bobby swears on the Bible and then proceeds to willfully perjure himself in court in order to get the boys acquitted. And yet this "fall from grace" is in no way frowned upon by the film because it is done to ameliorate the far greater "fall from grace" that was forced upon the boys at Wilkinson.

7. While *Sleepers* doesn't exactly follow this pattern, a few of the other male rape films do try to counter this almost inevitable homophobia by giving rather disingenuous lip service to tolerance. For example, the use of the conveniently asexual gay neighbor in *The Prince of Tides* or the comment in *The Shawshank Redemption* that in order for the rapists to be homosexual, "they'd have to be human first." What I find most disturbing about these nods to tolerance is that they basically acknowledge the dangerous slippage that takes place in these films, and yet they fail to curb that very slippage.

8. The theme of revenge is also completely motivated in the films in which grown men are raped (*The Shawshank Redemption* and *Pulp Fiction*), and *Shawshank* even plays off a notion of "violated innocence." In *Pulp Fiction*, the sense of violation is intensified by the fact that for most of the film the raped man, Marsellus (Ving Rhames), is presented as the most powerful man in the narrative. Thus, his motivation is driven more by a loss of "power" than a loss of "innocence," and this motivation is clearly intensified by the presentation of the rapists as gay hillbillies into S/M.

9. Actual revenge rapes are also noticeably absent in the female rape revenge genre which only seems to emphasize the overwhelming significance of (and anxieties surrounding) the anal penetration of a man. As far as the low-budget female rape revenge films are willing to go in terms of an assault on the male body, they never come close to anything even resembling anal penetration. While castration is commonplace in these films, the taboos surrounding male penetration persist. Thus, as completely as the female rape revenge films complicate male sexuality, subjectivity, and spectatorship, they still refrain from crossing the homosexual/heterosexual divide that is so thoroughly troubled by scenes of men being raped. This, of course, makes the recent explosion in representations of male rape in mainstream cinema even more compelling.

10. Lee Edelman has recently written on the ideological function of the child in dominant culture and its role in perpetuating an ultimately unsustainable notion of "futurity" in relation to heterosexual normativity. Lee Edelman, "The Future Is Kid Stuff: Queer Theory, Disidentification, and the Death Drive," a paper presented at the University of Rochester in December 1997.

11. While Savran's impressive study covers a wide spectrum of cultural texts and historical moments, his film-related discussion of white victimization centers on films such as *First Blood* (1982) and *Falling Down* (1993). And although the claims he makes about these films seem more than accurate, I'm inclined to argue that these particular films don't challenge

white masculinity as thoroughly as the male rape films because they generally avoid the complicated issues surrounding the potential sexual victimization or traumatization of white men.

12. In discussing the female rape revenge genre, Peter Lehman has suggested that male spectators' desire to witness brutal, often sexualized, assaults on the male body is not exclusively masochistic, but may also reveal a repressed homosexual desire that manifests itself in violent homophobia. Thus, through identification with the female rape victim, the male spectator can experience a certain erotic pleasure in the attacks on the male rapists that at once reveal homoerotic desires and brutally deny them (1993, 114–16). As mentioned, a similar dynamic operates in the male rape revenge films, but the anxieties surrounding homosexuality are multiplied exponentially in these films due to the actual anal penetration of the male protagonists. Consequently, the acts of revenge need to be carefully shielded from the realm of eroticism that so many of the female rape revenge films exploit. And yet, the many layers of disavowal that function in a film like *Sleepers* ultimately accentuates the connections between the genre's masochistic elements and its relationship to homosexuality and homophobia. Thus, the male rape revenge films indirectly make the homosexual undercurrent that Lehman identifies in terms of the female rape revenge films even more explicit. And yet, the displacement of these complicated issues onto the body of the gay man that the films enact serves only to perpetuate the homophobia that is such a revealing component within them.

works cited

Bersani, Leo. 1988. "Is the Rectum a Grave?" In *AIDS: Cultural Analysis, Cultural Activism*, ed. Douglas Crimp, 197–222. Cambridge: MIT Press.

Clover, Carol J. 1992. *Men, Women, and Chain Saws: Gender in the Modern Horror Film.* Princeton: Princeton University Press.

Edelman, Lee. 1994. *Homographesis.* New York: Routledge.

———. 1997. "The Future is Kid Stuff: Queer Theory, Disidentification, and the Death Drive." Unpublished paper presented at the University of Rochester, December.

Hoberman, J. 1996. "Guyland." *Village Voice*, Oct. 29, 45.

Lehman, Peter. 1993. "'Don't Blame This on a Girl': Female Rape-Revenge Films." In *Screening the Male: Exploring Masculinities in Hollywood*, ed. Steven Cohan and Ina Rae Hark, 103–17. London: Routledge.

Miller, D. A. 1991. "Anal Rope." In *inside/out: Lesbian Theories, Gay Theories*, ed. Diana Fuss, 119–41. New York: Routledge.

Savran, David. 1998. *Taking it Like a Man: White Masculinity, Masochism, and Contemporary American Culture.* Princeton, NJ: Princeton University Press.

Travers, Peter. 1996. "Getting Away with Murder." *Rolling Stone*, Oct. 31, 75.

choosing

to be

six

"not a man"

masculine anxiety

in nouri bouzid's

rih essed/man of ashes

robert lang and maher ben moussa

In 1995, the Institut du Monde Arabe in Paris celebrated one hundred years of Tunisian cinema with a comprehensive film retrospective that lasted three months. The main essay in the printed program was titled, "Un cinéma sans tabou," and it suggested that the Tunisian cinema is unique (among the Arab countries, at any rate) in its willingness to confront the major taboos of contemporary society: sexuality, the status of women, the Jewish question, government power, Islamic fundamentalism, the cultural identity of the country, and so on.

Whether or not this characterization of Tunisian cinema is accurate, there has perhaps been no Arab film more daring on the subject of male (homo)sexuality than Nouri Bouzid's spectacularly accomplished debut feature, *Rih Essed*, which tells the story of Hachemi (Imad Maalal), a young wood-carver in the old city of Sfax, and the acute anxiety he experiences on the eve of his marriage. Hachemi's nightmare coincides with the public disclosure of his best friend Farfat (Khaled Ksouri) that he is "not a man," and Farfat's subsequent banishment by his father. In the ensuing scandal, Hachemi relives his past, as he attempts to come to terms with his reluctance to marry, and to weigh the significance of the time when he and Farfat, at age ten, were raped by Ameur (Mustafa Adouani), their supervisor at the wood-carving shop. Seeking refuge in friendship—only Touil the black-smith, Azaiez the baker, and Farfat remain (his Jewish friend Jacko having emigrated)—Hachemi struggles to become a man who is true to himself. Farfat reacts to his humiliation with rebellious defiance, while Hachemi becomes more withdrawn and unhappy about his approaching marriage and his friend's distress. During a bachelor party in a brothel, in which both young men have their first experiences with women, Farfat is overcome with humiliation and rage when Azaiez reminds him that "everyone knows" what happened between him and Ameur. Farfat runs to Ameur's house, and there, on the street, stabs him mortally in the groin. The next day, in an image that suggests he is free at last, Farfat kills himself.

At the time of the film's release, in an interview given to a Tunisian newspaper, Bouzid insisted that the idea for the film originated in his fascination with the "total rupture" between the world of children and the world of adults. In adulthood, "you put yourself in someone else's skin, in a completely new decor, and you get rid of the old, you throw away a large part of yourself, perhaps the most intimate part" (Bouzid 1986).[1] And with marriage, he said, "you are forced to break with your past and your childhood, to get rid of the child in you, at least to dis-tance yourself from it as much as possible." After circumcision, mar-riage is the most significant formal "rite of passage," and it often sepa-rates a man from his group of friends. Certainly, the "long and profound friendship [between Hachemi and Farfat] is threatened by this rupture." Bouzid indicated that he wished to tell a story in which these rites of passage would be seen as traumatic, with lasting consequences.

The film succeeds in this effort, but what emerges is a complex and contradictory discourse on what the Tunisian scholar Abdelwahab Bouhdiba has described as the Arab man's profound alienation from his own masculinity (1985, 239). While the film seems to wish to "explain" both Hachemi's revulsion at the prospect of marriage and Farfat's sui-cide as the unhappy consequences of their rape, it is also quite clearly an appeal, in Bouzid's own words, for "the freedom to be different, to choose your own life, to choose your solitude" (Bouzid 1986). The rape of the two boys is really only a device—a means of showing what hap-pens when a young man (for Hachemi and Farfat are two sides of the same character)[2] refuses the sexual role chosen for him by society. Why, Hachemi's mother wants to know, does her son refuse his "hap-piness"? The film is a radical critique of an entire sexual system that puts tremendous pressure on individuals to conform. Essentially authoritarian, Arabo-Muslim society is "castrating," according to Bouhdiba in *Sexuality in Islam* (1985), "not only from the sexual point of view, but also from the point of view of individual autonomy in the political, economic, ethical and cultural spheres" (210). Bouzid concurs. Ten years after making *Rih Essed*, he published an essay titled, "On Inspiration," in which he remarks on the significance of "the filial relationship" in his work:

> With us the problem of the father is associated not with the Oedipus complex but with the myth of Abraham, who was prepared to sacrifice his own son. The son submits to the father and serves him. In our society the individual is nothing; it's the family that counts, the group. Our cinema is trying to destroy the edifice of the family and liberate the individual. (1996, 54)

Rih Essed shows an individual whose family and society specifically reject his sexuality and will not let him "choose his own life." His society is one in which, above all, the sexes are radically separated. And as Bouhdiba asks, "To what extremities did the system of sexual division [in Arabo-Muslim societies] not drive one?" Where Bouhdiba implies that most homosexuality is caused by the Manichaeism of the sexes, Bouzid's film takes a less heterosexist position on the close bonds among men. *Rih Essed* makes it plain that Farfat's misery and suicide are caused by homophobia. The real trauma for the two young men is perhaps not their rape by Ameur but the fact that their love for each other, their friendship, will be ruptured by Hachemi's marriage; and if Farfat cannot overcome the stigma of the graffito on the wall that says he is "not a man," he can have no future. As the little boy Anis says to him at the dock, "Farfat, your boat has left without you."

There is a scene in the film that powerfully conveys the love Farfat and Hachemi have for each other. Bouzid shoots it in the manner of silent film, without dialogue, to suggest that the emotional bond between them does not need words. Farfat is in a noisy café, playing cards with several other, apparently older, men. He has been losing, and one of the players offers him the consoling remark that it's not his lucky day. Farfat looks up, and sees Hachemi shyly waiting for him just outside the café. He breaks into a smile and winks at his friend, who bashfully looks down and returns a radiant smile. Bouzid lingers on the repeated shots of the two men looking into each other's eyes, while on the soundtrack we hear the refrain of a song playing on the café radio: "Allah wa akkbar ... Allah wa akkbar," a common phrase in Arabo-Muslim culture, meaning "God the Almighty," expressing feelings of awe, admiration, and fascination—a kind of *jouissance*, even—

when one is moved by God's power, whether uttered spontaneously in response to a reading from the Koran, or during a song by a sensual/spiritual performer like the great Oum Kalthoum.

In the same interview in which Bouzid spoke, as of a tragedy, of the man who marries having to renounce the intimacy of his male friendships, he spoke of a "corollary problem" which also fascinates him: *virility*. The worst thing that can happen to a boy in a society described by Bouhdiba as "male-worshipping, in its essence and in its appearances, in its deep structures and in its superficial manifestations" (1985, 239)— is for the boy to have his sense of masculinity fundamentally compromised (Bouzid 1986). In the film, both boys discover that their society defines adult masculinity in terms of castration. Proper manhood is achieved through an internalization of the meaning of castration (as a male trauma harnessed for patriarchal purposes, bonding men), with the major moments in this process marked by the rite of circumcision, marriage, and the abandonment of intimacy in male friendship.

The pressure on young men to organize their affective impulses in exclusively heterosexual terms is, of course, a phenomenon not unique to Muslim societies. Consider the American critic Molly Haskell's famous remarks in her landmark study, *From Reverence to Rape: The Treatment of Women in the Movies* (1974), on the subject of "love in which men understand and support each other, speak the same language, and risk their lives to gain each other's respect": "But this is also a delusion. . . . This is the easiest of loves: a love that is adolescent, presexual, tacit, the love of one's *semblable*, one's mirror reflection" (24). Haskell's barely concealed contempt for the male homosocial love she describes comes, no doubt, from knowing how it is frequently implicated in a dialectic of misogyny. In *Rih Essed*, however, we are given no evidence that Hachemi and Farfat are misogynistic. If anything, Hachemi's disinclination to marry is a form of resistance to patriarchal structures that we know also subordinate women.

The precedent for Hachemi's despair at the prospect of losing his friends—of losing the special, intimate quality of his friendships with them, and with Farfat in particular—is the misery he felt when Jacko left Tunisia during a wave of Jewish emigration years before. "I've been around Jews all my life," Bouzid explains. "Hachemi has also lived amongst Jews, and is close to them. . . . He experiences a double crisis in his childhood: the rape, and the emotional trauma of the 'forced' departure of his friend 'Jacko'" (Bouzid 1986).

The movie opens on an image of castration: a wounded and bloody cockerel flapping about helplessly in the dust. This shot is immediately followed by images of a wedding feast in preparation. The symbolism of the juxtaposition is undeniable: marriage demands a sacrifice. As the story will be told from the point of view of a double character—

a young man who is about to marry, and a young man who, according to the definitions of conventional masculinity, feels he is "not a man"— the wounded bird[3] surely recalls a Muslim boy's first official rite of initiation into adulthood: circumcision. "There is a clear correspondence for the boy between circumcision and marriage," writes Bouhdiba. "The wedding night is the time when the man experiences and proves his virility" (1985, 185). Circumcision is "a passage to the world of adults and a preparation carried out in blood and pain, and therefore unforgettable, into an age of responsibilities" (182). Later in the film, when Hachemi is reminiscing with old Levy about his grandson, Levy remarks that Jacko is now married, "and is even a father." Hachemi smiles to himself, and in a flashback we see the three boys giggling as they show each other their penises, with Jacko saying, "Me too, I'm circumcised!" Though circumcision is more a practice of Muslims than a practice of Islam (Bouhdiba 1985, 182), it is performed nominally as a rite through which the boy accedes to Islam. But this does not explain the powerful sociological imperatives behind the rite; nor is it, of course, how the boy will remember it:

> As for the mutilated child, he could do nothing but cry
> out in pain and weep in shock at the violence done to
> his body. This wound in his flesh, these men and
> women torturing him, that gleaming razor, the stri-
> dent oohs and ahs of inquisitive, indiscreet old women,
> the jugs smashing on the floor, the cry of the cockerel,
> struggling and losing its blood, the din outside and
> finally the endless stream of people coming to congrat-
> ulate the patient on "his happy accession to Islam," that
> is what circumcision means to a child. (Bouhdiba
> 1985, 178)

In any event, it is clear that for Hachemi the "happiness" his mother refers to (and which all of society insists he seize as his masculine right) is not worth the price. Obviously, he had no choice in the matter of his circumcision, but he wonders if he dare refuse to marry. The film's ostensible explanation for Hachemi's unwillingness to take a bride is that he is suffering from a permanent loss of sexual confidence as a consequence of his having been raped as a child. And yet the film offers another, contradictory discourse that suggests this might not be so. Bouzid has said that when he was writing the script for the film, he asked himself, "What would happen if Hachemi said to society, 'Get stuffed, I'll do what I like.' Will he make it? But he can't do it, he's not the type of character who can do that. So I had to create his double, the other side of the coin, because the germ of the double existed in the first one" (1996, 50).

85

Quite simply, Hachemi is not interested in having heterosexual relations, and his refusal—seen in conjunction with Farfat's despairing, defiant writing on the wall that he is "not a man"—must be seen as courageous. The violent storm that destroys the wedding marquee is nothing less than a cosmic indication of his inner turmoil, and of the resources of will he has to draw on if he should decide not to go through with the marriage.[4] In resisting the extraordinary pressure on him to marry, Hachemi is showing bravery, not cowardice. He is indeed trying to say, "Get stuffed, I'll do what I like." His nightmares suggest that his fears have to do with entrapment, just as Farfat's dreams have to do with flight. But when Hachemi and Farfat are taken to the brothel by their friends in the hope, or on the assumption, that all they will need is a positive heterosexual experience to launch them into a life of heterosexual "happiness" (the 1956 Hollywood film *Tea and Sympathy* offers the same fraudulent conceit),[5] Bouzid leaves the question open as to whether he "believes" in this scene, just as the best Hollywood melodramas allow for ironic readings of their "happy endings." The scene is altogether extraordinary, especially when one considers how Bouzid conceives Farfat and Hachemi as two sides of the same subjective experience. For example, at the very moment Hachemi and the prostitute Amina are rolling about on the bed in a carnal embrace, Farfat is attacking Azaiez because he believes Azaiez was flirting with him (with the intention of humiliating him), and the two men roll about on the floor in the same manner as the couple having sex upstairs. Just after Hachemi has finished having sex with Amina, we get a shot of Hachemi's mother hysterically slashing the wedding *baclawa*, signifying, perhaps, that Hachemi will not marry, even after this "proof" that he is capable of having sex with a woman. Though Farfat also finally succeeds with his prostitute, Hasna, their coupling is brief, and he withdraws, saying to Azaiez as he leaves the brothel, "You don't deserve any more"—as if to say: "I'm doing this only to prove to you that I can do it—and that's enough!"

In a curiously revealing choice of words, Molly Haskell (1974) sums up the heterosexist point of view (one shared by the majority of society, which explains why Bouzid treads carefully, in this his first feature film): "The homophile impulse, like most decadent tropisms, like incest, is, or can be, a surrender, a sinking back into one's nature. Just as we have lost faith in narrative forms, we have lost our sexual confidence" (28). These remarks reveal that Haskell—like the society Hachemi and Farfat live in—believes that there is only one true narrative, the heterosexual narrative, and any other narrative is proof that "we have lost faith in narrative forms." Indeed, Hachemi's mother tells him: "On your wedding night, I shan't be able to sleep until I know you have consummated it" (i.e., until she knows that Hachemi has successfully followed the script of the conventional heterosexual trajectory to its proper conclusion).

There are several indications in the film that Hachemi is not sexually interested in women; but it is also important to point out that he is not necessarily afraid of them (his experience with the prostitute, Amina, for example, is apparently not traumatic); and we see that he has a relaxed and intimate friendship with Amna, a girl he has grown up with in the neighborhood (her name, like Amina, means "keeper of secrets," or "trustworthy confidante").

At one point in the film, we see Hachemi and Azaiez standing below a balcony on which a beautiful young woman is bending over as she washes a window. She pretends not to notice the two men, although Azaiez is staring longingly up her skirt and is caressing his bare chest in frustrated desire. Hachemi does not so much as glance at the girl. Rather, he is turned toward his friend and standing very close to him. As Azaiez murmurs appreciatively to Hachemi about the girl, it is as if Hachemi were putting himself in her place, shyly accepting his friend's declarations of desire.

The scene is followed by an even more blatant example of how Hachemi's desire is different from that of his friend, who urges him to value heterosexual love above the bonds of male friendship. Hachemi has come to Azaiez for some money for Farfat, who has resolved to leave Sfax and start a new life in Tunis. As he paces about the bakery, Azaiez grumbles about not being paid any more by his father since the motorcycle was stolen: "I steal from my father to get drunk.... [But] I respect my father. With his mustaches, you don't play the kid!" Hachemi responds violently: "Is that what you think it means to be a man! To have a mustache! ... Have you forgotten what [Farfat] did for you?" Azaiez tries to explain: "I'm in a tight spot. It was because of [Farfat] that we argued. Who would have believed that our friendship would be touched? You know, friendship ... even when it is reduced to ashes, burns whoever touches it." Azaiez urges Hachemi to stop feeling responsible for Farfat: "Think of yourself a little. Now, finally, you will know life, warmth.... Forget our misery, forget bachelorhood and the empty bed, the long nights ..." (Hachemi turns and leaves in disgust, as Azaiez continues, in a reverie): "Love's thirst, cold sheets ... You have found warmth! Don't think about others, we're of no account. Forget us, and taste life before it's too late! I've reached my age without knowing tenderness...."

Like his father, Azaiez wears a mustache, the ubiquitous symbol of virility in Arab culture. Hachemi's fair coloring and beardlessness—in a culture that fetishizes hair, and in which "the mere sight of pretty boys is regarded by the fiqh[6] as disturbing and terribly tempting" (Bouhdiba, 32)—signal his desirability (to men) rather than function as signs of his youth. To use an Islamic metaphor, we may see his beard-less beauty in terms of *fitna*, or revolt against God. As Bouhdiba puts it, "*Fitna* is both seduction and sedition, charm and revolt" (1985, 118). He quotes Al-Hassan Ibn Dhakwam, the fifth-century Cordovan *khadi* (judge), who cautioned: "Do not sit next to the sons of the rich and noble: they have faces like those of virgins and are even more tempting than women" (32–33). Bouhdiba then comments, "Thus we pass imperceptibly from a world based on the dichotomy of the sexes to a world based on the dichotomy of the ages, since youth is quite simply projected on to the feminine side—and duly repressed!" (33).

Near the beginning of the film, shortly after the flashback in which Hachemi remembers the happy days of his childhood, when he and Farfat and Jacko used to play together at the beach, Hachemi overhears one of the women in the house saying, "Hachemi has white skin; he should have been a girl." (In disgust, he glances at himself in the mirror on the wall.) "My father takes me for a child," he later tells his friend Touil, who comments, "You talk like Farfat. One would say you were twins!" And when a group of Hachemi's friends at a bar decide they should give him a bachelor party ["Enterrons sa vie de garçon"], one of them says, "Is it a celebration or an interment?"

There is a strong theme in the film of male childhood being under-stood as a feminine, or feminized period, and of a properly masculine adulthood being achieved primarily through a conscious rejection of the feminine. Certainly, more than once in *Rih Essed*, we see Hachemi as a little boy being embraced by his mother, in images that suggest an erotic element in the bond between mother and son; and in a key scene, we see him being bathed by her after he has spent the afternoon playing with Farfat and Jacko on the beach. "My son has grown up," she mur-murs, "I'm going to marry him." Hachemi's father, realizing that his son has been with the Jewish boy, angrily reminds Hachemi that he has expressly forbidden him to see Jacko. In this and earlier scenes, the father is associated with interdiction. He is unambiguously the Oedipal father who is jealous of the mother-son bond, and whom the boy fears, with good reason (and no doubt remembering the occasion of his cir-cumcision), as the one with the power to castrate. Love for the mother, in other words, and sensual pleasures (the feeling of the sun and the sea on his skin as he plays with Farfat and Jacko; his mother bathing him when he gets home) are threatened by the father. *Rih Essed* is unusual in suggesting that the world Hachemi inhabits (and that he is obviously reluctant to give up) may very well be far preferable to the "adult" (het-erosexual, patriarchal) world so valorized by his society.

As Lizbeth Malkmus and Roy Armes note in their book *Arab and African Film Making* (1991), *Rih Essed* is marked by "the delicate, tactile, sensual perceptions of the young carpenter hero," and the film is structured as a battle between the senses and the elements, in a way that "is fairly rare in Arab cinema, which is not awash with the sensuality supposed by nineteenth-century Orientalism" (118). The film in this way is entirely sympathetic with Hachemi's point of view, and expresses the filmmaker's desire. The "sensuality" of the mise-en-scène, as an index of Hachemi's psychic reality, contradicts the film's claim that he is a victim marked by a childhood trauma. If Bouzid is torn between these two ways of answering the film's central questions—Why is Hachemi reluctant to marry? And why does Farfat believe he is "not a man"?—it is because he wishes to tell the truth about the desire treated in the film, but must disguise that truth in order not to alienate his (potentially homophobic) audience. Bouzid has to find a way to get his cards on the table, and to make his audience take responsibility for his characters. In a sense, Bouzid has to trick his audience into acknowledging that homosexual desire is the issue, by pretending that the intertwined story of Hachemi and Farfat can be explained in terms of a childhood trauma. Françoise Vergès (1996) sheds some light on [Bouzid's] dilemma in her comments about why sodomy, or anal rape, comes to acquire such an overdetermined and intolerable emotional significance in representations of colonization in the work of Frantz Fanon:

> Fanon always privileged trauma over fantasy. "Fantasy" did not belong to his psychological vocabulary. With fantasy one admits that there is a psychic reality; there is a domain which resists total mastery and control, is heterogeneous and speaks in many voices. It is the construction of a narrative in which one's own desire is expressed. This domain cannot be assimilated to reality. With traumatism you are a victim: there is no conscious desire. One can attempt to find the source of the trauma which has wounded one's psyche and then find a cure. (139)

To suggest that Hachemi has a horror of heterosexuality because of a childhood trauma is a way of disowning responsibility for the complexity of sexuality—which is why Bouzid also offers a counterdiscourse (he wants to allow for the possibility that Hachemi and Farfat are gay), in telling the story from Hachemi's point of view.

One night, while saying goodbye to all his friends, Farfat becomes thoroughly drunk, and afterward makes his way to the atelier where Hachemi works. As it happens, Hachemi is there, and he tries to calm Farfat, whose maudlin shouts become increasingly despairing as he stumbles about chaotically. The scene is marked by eroticism, as Hachemi, bare chested, struggles to subdue his violently unhappy friend, who is also shirtless. The key to *Rih Essed*'s latent currents of desire can be found not only in Bouzid's blatantly associative, thematic editing, but in mise-en-scène such as this, in which the golden light and close-ups of the young men's naked torsos say what the characters themselves don't acknowledge in the narrative, namely that their friendship contains an element of suppressed physical desire.

This scene immediately follows one in which Hachemi, in obvious distress, has recalled his rape by Ameur, in just such a wood-carving workshop; and it is followed by an almost surreal scene showing Hachemi coming home to his overwrought family (his mother meets him at the front door—and with the complicity that is wont to enrage Hachemi's father—urgently whispers to him: "My darling. I've missed you. It's as if I'd just given birth to you all over again. But, you smell of wine? Your father will kill us! Come inside . . . he'll see us!"); and his then being prevented from leaving the house again by a family member standing in every doorway.

The memory of his molestation, the suppressed eroticism of the two half-naked friends wrestling with each other, followed by this powerful image of familial entrapment, as a cacophony of ringing bells dominates the soundtrack (Hachemi brings his hands to his ears in an attempt to block out this imaginary din), obliquely reveal that Hachemi's trauma is colored by fantasy.

The mix of fear and desire that characterizes oedipal yearning, and which in sexual contexts gives castration anxiety its uniquely conflicted quality, is in fact condensed in the poster for the film: a drawing, in close-up, of a man's bulging crotch, and his hand clutching at his bloodstained groin. The image is extraordinary because it announces that the film is about a wounded man, desire, and murder; or about a murderous desire; or perhaps about the victim of a (sexually motivated) attack. The drawing would seem to be of Hachemi, wearing chinos and a cotton shirt (Farfat wears dungarees, without a shirt, throughout most of the movie), although it is in fact of Ameur. As a wounded man ("un homme blessé," to echo the title of a 1984 French film about a young man's brutal awakening to his gay sexuality), Hachemi feels like a victim, despite his father's conviction that he is merely being perversely ungrateful for not taking up his hetero-patriarchal privileges in marriage. "We're like puppets in your hands!" his father shouts, when Hachemi gets home from comforting his distraught friend. "Do you want to turn the wedding feast into a funeral? The marriage is on Tuesday! It was decided, between men!"

Hachemi, at his wits' end, sobs: "You're all against me. Even my brother, the doctor! May God deliver me, and leave you in peace! I don't want this marriage. God didn't want it." Hachemi's father responds by beating him violently, lashing him repeatedly with a leather belt, as he crouches on the floor, and all the women wail in fright. Hachemi's invoking the name of God is a last resort, for even his brother, the doctor—the voice of modern science—has betrayed him; and the frighteningly ugly old woman his family brings in to exorcise his demons also fails. She moans and cries out to various saints to help deliver Hachemi of the fire consuming him, and to "return him to health." She even calls on the barber of the Prophet to help him. But, as Bouzid wants to make clear, Hachemi is what he is. The proposed marriage is society's way of containing and organizing his sexuality, for patriarchal purposes. And, if Hachemi is to remain true to himself, the institution of marriage must be revealed as precisely that: an institution (i.e., an *ideological* structure).

In "On Inspiration" (1996) Bouzid admits that as a filmmaker he has had to put some effort into "winning over a badly educated public" that was used to the ideologically retrograde Egyptian commercial cinema. He sees himself as one of a group of Tunisian filmmakers who sought "to challenge [Tunisian audiences] too, put forward something different and accustom them to seeing new things" (49). And in this new cinema, "You shouldn't try to explain everything, in my opinion" (51). But Bouzid in fact explains a great deal in the essay, and does so eloquently. For example, he explains what he means by "defeat as destiny," as one of "the six constants" of his cinema: "For me it's a feeling ... of helplessness faced with something we're being dragged into, something we haven't chosen" (52). Bouzid describes *Rih Essed* as a key film in his oeuvre for understanding what he means by this: "The true defeat is in one's education and the type of relations one has with individuals; the relations between the social structure and the individual, whether the state, the family, or the religious structure. This relationship is one that destroys the individual" (54). How the individual is destroyed in *Rih Essed* is obvious (Hachemi's fate remains undecided at the end of the film, but Farfat dies). The ambiguities of the film's ending, however, suggest that there is hope—for all those who might recognize something of themselves in Hachemi and Farfat. Bouzid edits the ending of the film in such a way that we understand that Farfat both dies *and* lives. Farfat is wearing a dark blue shirt and similarly dark pants when he fatally stabs Ameur. As Ameur falls forward—muttering the dying words, "You will always be my apprentices. I nevertheless initiated you ..."—Touil throws Farfat across his shoulder, and with Hachemi disappears into the nighttime safety of the narrow streets of the medina. The next day, we see Anis, Farfat's young companion, tip Farfat off that two men are after him. A chase ensues, throughout which Farfat is still wearing the dark pants and unbuttoned shirt of the night before. He laughs joyfully as he plays cat and mouse with his pursuers. Finally, having made his way to an open space traversed by a railroad track, he pauses. Anis, standing on the overpass above the track, whistles to Farfat and indicates that a train is approaching. Farfat stands beside the track, smiling, and the moment the train reaches him, he throws himself in front of it. As the train pulls away from the camera, and the two men run to the spot where Farfat's body would be, Anis—as if out of nowhere—steps onto the track in front of them. The boy is wearing denim dungarees, without a shirt, as we have seen Farfat wear throughout most of the movie. With his hands on his hips, he says to the men: "Let him be." Bouzid then cuts to a medium close-up of Anis, who, turning to face the departing train, looks into the camera, and with a smile, winks [at me; at Farfat]. In the shots that follow, we see Farfat running and jumping—in slow motion, with his arms outstretched, as if flying—across the rooftops of the city. He is again wearing his denim dungarees, without a shirt. In the very last shot of the film, we see Anis erase the graffito that announced to the world that "Farfat is not a man."

The film's message is clear: There will always be Farfats and Hachemis in the world, who courageously reject their society's definition of what it means to be a man. Farfat and Hachemi have seized their destiny. They have, in effect, found the courage to say: "Get stuffed. I'll do what I like."

In the concluding remarks of their book *Islamic Homosexualities* (1997), Stephen O. Murray and Will Roscoe note that egalitarian (or "gay") male homosexuality is largely, though not entirely, missing from historical Muslim societies and from contemporary ones, with minor exceptions in the capitals of the relatively secular states of Turkey and Pakistan (306). They acknowledge, however, that in many non-Western urban centers around the world we are beginning to see "men adopting the new terminology and self-conceptions of a gay identity under the influence of Western examples, while continuing to observe traditional distinctions of older/younger, active/passive, and even masculine/non-masculine in their personal relationships" (313). In *Rih Essed*, Bouzid shows his two young heroes caught precisely between their society's view of them and how they would see themselves—poised, perhaps, on the threshold of an identity that would permit them to love each other without forfeiting their sense of being masculine.

As "two sides of the same coin," Hachemi and Farfat are very similar, and yet different in significant ways; we can even see how—in relation to each other—some of the dichotomies that are said to mark men in traditional Muslim societies as masculine or not-masculine, are inscribed in the differences between their bodies. For Bouzid, "The body is really the heart of the matter.... [T]he most important vector of dramatic technique and conflicts, dramas, characters." Hachemi, for example, "needed to have a feminine beauty whose purpose is to bring out his drama still more," whereas "Farfat, his counterpart, needed to be volatile, androgynous.... Farfat needs fragility in his body" (1996, 55). The physical beauty of the two young men—which for Bouzid is crucial to the film's meanings, not least because they attract a male gaze—is acknowledged in the way they are photographed. Though Bouzid insists that (in general?) "the camera has to caress bodies to bring them closer to the viewer" (55), he rather confusingly remarks, "In all my films, and most of the scripts I've done, I've worked through pain. I make the character suffer in his internal dilemma. Pain, for me, is incompatible with pleasure. For example, I've never used the body for visual pleasure" (56). He admits, however, that "for the fundamentalists there has always been a confusion between sex and the body, but this confusion is in me too. But while the fundamentalists think that the whole body is sex, for me sex is part of the body, everything is body" (55). If *Rih Essed* oscillates between celebrating the beauty of the young male body, and on some level denying that there is an erotic element in looking at this body, it is perhaps because (as Murray and Roscoe observe) within Islamic cosmology, "Loving without touching (let alone penetrating) remains the ideal—even for men. Muslim men are expected to be aim-inhibited, noble martyrs to a male love kept pure from any physical contact, let alone consummation. Even permitted gazes tend to lead to the 'tasting of forbidden pleasures'..." (1997, 308).

As should be obvious by now, *Rih Essed* is not without its internal contradictions. But the film's critique of repressive patriarchal structures is consistent. The film begins with the question of whether or not Hachemi and Farfat will be able to achieve a satisfactory masculinity, and it asserts, finally—although the price each pays is exorbitant— that they do, in the sense that they remain true to themselves, and to the viewer. They do not foreclose on their desire. From a Western, "gay" point of view—if we can call it that—the hypocrisy at the heart of traditional Islamic homosexuality lies in its claim that "the pleasure of the man was and is the justification for Muslims to fuck boys, and the culturally appropriate basis for desiring boys is their beauty, not their incipient masculinity" (Murray and Roscoe 1997, 302). While Murray and Roscoe note that there is disagreement both within and between Islamic cultures about "whether sexual relationships with older boys or men is harmful to the development of the masculinity of those penetrated" (302), they go on to remark that, "Of all the societies in which age-stratified homosexuality has been described in some detail (including Greece, Melanesia, Japan, and Sudanic tribes), Islamic ones seem least to expect that the sexually used boy will grow up to be a man" (304). They acknowledge that "some pretty boys 'graduate' to being husbands and fathers, but in the native view others are fated to continue being penetrated by men" (305). In *Rih Essed*, Bouzid's young heroes go beyond the system that offers them only the options to "graduate" to respectable masculinity (confirmed by marriage and fatherhood) or to be relegated to a twilight zone of nonsubjectivity as "not a man." They insist, in the spirit of a Tunisian cinema *sans tabou*, on the "freedom to be different, to choose your own life."

notes

For their help and encouragement, the authors wish to thank Jeanne Mrad, director of the Centre d'Etudes Maghrébines à Tunis, and H'ssine Ben Azouna at the University of Tunis at Manouba.

1. Unpaginated document.
2. Bouzid makes this clear in his essay "On Inspiration."
3. Farfat's name, it should be pointed out, refers to flight.
4. This storm is suggested in the film's title, which is drawn from the Tunisian proverb, "Rih essed yeddi maa y'rude," which refers to a strong wind that sweeps away everything in its path. With this title, and through his main characters' rebellious actions, Bouzid would blow away "the edifice of the family" (and the homophobia which gives it support) to "liberate the individual" (Bouzid 1996, 54).
5. Cf. George F. Custen, "Strange Brew: Hollywood and the Fabrication of Homosexuality in *Tea and Sympathy*."
6. The interpretations of the Muslim scholars of the Sharià (Islamic laws) and the Sunna (the speeches of the Prophet).

works cited

Bouhdiba, Abdelwahab. 1985. *Sexuality in Islam*. Trans. Alan Sheridan. London: Routledge and Kegan Paul.

Bouzid, Nouri. 1986. "Note d'Intention: Extraits d'interview donnée par le réalisateur à des journaux tunisiens." In *Rih Essed* press kit. Clippings archive of the Museum of Modern Art Film Study Center, New York.

———. 1996. "On Inspiration." In *African Experiences of Cinema*, ed. Imruh Bakari and Mbye Cham, 48–59. London: British Film Institute.

Custen, George F. 1997. "Strange Brew: Hollywood and the Fabrication of Homosexuality in *Tea and Sympathy*." In *Queer Representations: Reading Lives, Reading Cultures*, ed. Martin Duberman, 166–38. New York: New York University Press.

Haskell, Molly. 1974. *From Reverence to Rape: The Treatment of Women in the Movies*. New York: Holt, Rinehart and Winston.

Khayati, Khémaïs. 1995. "Un Cinéma sans tabou." *Journal Programme: Cinéma* 4. ["La Saison Tunisienne" at the Institut du Monde Arabe, Paris.] (January-February-March): 1–2.

Malkmus, Lizbeth, and Roy Armes. 1991. *Arab and African Film Making*. London: Zed Books.

Murray, Stephen O., and Will Roscoe. 1997. *Islamic Homosexualities: Culture, History, and Literature*. New York: New York University Press.

Vergès, Françoise. 1996. "Dialogue." In *The Fact of Blackness: Frantz Fanon and Visual Representation*, ed. Alan Read, 132–41. London: Institute of Contemporary Arts/Seattle: Bay Press.

t(he)-men's room

seven

masculinity and space

in anthony mann's

t-men

s u s a n   w h i t e

[T]o a large degree, forties narrative is nothing so much as a vast meditation
on place and space, on the field in which action and meaning are constituted.

—Dana Polan, *Power and Paranoia* (1986, 252)

Anthony Mann's 1947 film *T-Men* confronts the problems of nationalism, gender boundaries, and space in a diegetic world whose actions
unfold almost uniquely between and among men. As Paul Willeman
put it in a seminal essay (1981), the structure of Mann's films "is piv-
oted on the look at the male figure: the male 'in context', as it were.
The viewer's experience is predicated on the pleasure of seeing the
male 'exist' (that is, walk, move, ride, fight) in or through cityscapes,
landscapes or, more abstractly, history." (16)

   T-Men, which distills to perfection the pleasures and threat of "looking at the male," is a complex treatment of what Eve Kosofsky Sedgwick
has termed, in her book on the English novel (1985), "male homosocial
desire." In this chapter, I will use close textual analysis and historical

contextualization to examine the social and political implications of this homosocial desire and its repression in Mann's film.

T-Men, directed by Mann for Eagle-Lion in 1947, was his first collaboration with cinematographer John Alton, and was one of two Mann films starring Dennis O'Keefe.[2] The modest but distinct critical and box-office success of *T-Men* drew the director-cinematographer team to the attention of MGM, where both men began work in 1949. Their first film for MGM was, in fact, a remake of *T-Men* shifted to the California-Mexico border.[3] Basinger (1979, 61) describes *T-Men* as Mann's first "fully realized project," technically and thematically speaking. The film falls in the tradition of what Frank Krutnik terms the "police procedural" (1991, 204), a category that includes *The Naked City* (1948) and *Panic in the Streets* (1950). The story of Treasury Department agents infiltrating a counterfeit money ring in Los Angeles, *T-Men* also obviously cites the anti-gangster film of the '30s in its title, reminiscent of *G-Men*, which attempted to recuperate Cagney's criminal cachet at the service of the FBI. The "semidocumentary aura" of *T-Men* and *Border Incident* lies in their "detailed foregrounding of the machinery of investigative procedure" (Krutnik 1991, 204), and in their framing of the crime story with voice-overs issuing from the world of the law. Indeed, *T-Men* splits its narrative space into three distinct parts. The prologue depicts the Treasury Department itself, shot for the most part in high-key lighting. The body of the film alternates between sequences taking place in the criminal underworld, which feature some of the most distinctive *noir* stylistics in the history of the *film noir* movement, and scenes depicting the activities of Treasury Department agents in more "official" settings.

This narrative split in *T-Men*, supported by the voice-over that explains and glorifies the actions of the government men (a device also used to good effect in *He Walked by Night* [1949]), seems designed to place an unassailable boundary between lawful and unlawful in a film in which such boundaries are often in flux. *T-Men* is initially very much concerned with establishing and maintaining a visible and audible distinction between criminal and government agent. Thus, in the tradition of certain films of the 1930s, in their effort to adapt themselves to the increased enforcement of the Production Code by presenting strong figures of the law as framing devices, *T-Men* features a soporific introduction by the former Chief Coordinator of the Law Enforcement Agencies of the Treasury Department, Elmer Lincoln Irey, in which he describes with deadpan seriousness the "six fingers" of the fist of the Treasury Department, including the Intelligence Unit, the Customs Agency Service (Border Patrol), the Narcotics Unit, the Secret Service, the Alcohol Tax Unit, and the Coast Guard. A statuette of Lincoln in the left foreground, an obvious pun on Irey's name, underscores his link to benevolent patriarchy. Still, the shadiness of the underworld infiltrates even this inviolable frame narrative: the very black shadow cast by the statue anticipates the darkness of the world the agents are about to enter, a darkness perhaps cast, in the final analysis, by the law itself.

Irey describes the Treasury Department case that forms the basis of the film as a composite of several real investigations. The "Shanghai paper case," as he terms it, involves seeking out the source of counterfeit money being distributed in the United States. The money, we learn, is printed on excellent paper but is photoengraved and thus technically inferior to U.S. government-issued currency. In an early scene of the film, an agent goes to meet an informant who had promised to turn over a "clean sample" of the paper being used by the counterfeit ring. The opening shots of the criminal investigation are still at pains to distinguish criminal from investigator, although this must and will become more difficult as the film continues. Thus, although shadows engulf both the underworld informant and the Treasury agent, the latter is wearing a light-colored trench coat and smoking a pipe, a reassuringly non-mobsterish vice. A mob assassin dressed like the informant, in dark colors, but without the latter's ratty moustache, steps into the harsh lamplight and blasts the informant before he can tell his story to the Treasury agent. The visible difference between mobster, agent, and informant has led to the latter's demise.

The very fact that the agent can be demarcated as agent causes him to be recognized and rendered useless to the investigation. Officials decide to take an indirect route to infiltrating the counterfeiting ring in Los Angeles. Two agents are sent to earn their criminal credentials with the Vantucci mob in Detroit, before moving on to the West Coast. These two agents, Dennis O'Brien and Tony Genaro (Dennis O'Keefe and Alfred Ryder), form what Krutnik (1991) has called the "'male couple' who are bonded together and tested in a context of ever-present danger." He continues: "The drama of allegiance and respect between the two-man detective team takes the place of the conventional heterosexual love story" (204). Indeed, the only trace of the traditional love story—a brief and chance encounter between Genaro and his wife in the Los Angeles Farmer's Market—will prove fatal to the married agent. Ironically, then, the real *femme fatale* in this film is the "good" woman who holds her man to the heterosexual contract under the eyes of the law. Although it is for that law and that contract that the T-men are ostensibly fighting, the fact that the good woman's breaching of the borders of the criminal underworld is fatal to her man reinforces the legitimacy of the homoerotic bond between the agents. With few exceptions, women cannot and must not traverse the boundary surrounding the criminal milieu the agents are investigating, for their investigation into the underworld is emphatically, as in so many other films by Anthony Mann, an exploration of what it means to be a man among men.

This exploration has its dangers and its rewards, among them the freedom to take on some of the characteristics of women within the context of a strongly ethnicized masculinity. The formation of the male couple is marked by theater. Genaro and O'Brien must disguise themselves as hoods, taking on the more colorful regalia of the Irish-Italian mob, the River Gang. In one of the scenes in which the men prepare for their role as mobsters, O'Brien, now Harrigan, makes it clear to his partner, Genaro, now Galvani, that their fancy suits are made for male delectation alone:

> TONY: My wife would like this outfit; she's always trying
>   to get me to dress up.
> DENNIS: Ah, ah, ah—don't forget, you're not married;
>   you've been divorced for reasons of duty.
> TONY: I hope Uncle appreciates it.

Tony refers to his suit as something his wife would like, but surely this flamboyant costume is not to the taste of the extraordinarily Anglo and middle-class woman to whom Tony is married, played by June Lockhart (although she might relish the naughtiness of the bad-boy disguise). The wide lapels and (presumably) colorful ties adopted by the agents have class and ethnic associations ordinarily perceived as dangerous by middle-class Anglo-Americans of the '40s. In the history of the gangster film we need only recall how the protagonist of *Scarface* (1932), another Italian Tony, dons silk dressing gowns, luxurious suits, and gorgeous jewelry as he machine-guns his way to the top of the gangster hierarchy. The "classy" woman to whom he aspires, the very blonde and elegant Poppy, is both fascinated and repelled by this attire, which she labels "effeminate."

In the mid-1940s, Latinos, African-Americans, and other non-Anglo ethnic groups in the United States militantly adopted the zoot suit as a marker of ethnic pride and masculine parade.[4] This refusal of what Flugel has termed the "Great Masculine Renunciation" of "sumptuous dress"[5] has long been a means of expressing difference from the Anglo-American male ethos and aesthetic. Miriam Hansen (1991) observes that this masculine renunciation of the eighteenth century made such displays of sartorial splendor "(once the mark of aristocratic status) the domain of women, channeling masculine exhibitionism into professional display behavior, scopophilia, or identification with woman-as-spectacle." Hansen describes the Anglo male's hostility toward Valentino, who "personified the Italian man's stereotypical penchant for fashion, by flaunting his spats, ties, custom-made suits and furs, his flamboyant suspenders and notorious slave bracelet" (259). Thus Genaro and O'Brien must emphasize that they are adopting this feminized and ethnically marked clothing for the sake of "Uncle," the regulator of appropriate male-male behavior in a context where erotic appeal is strategic, and female desire may figure only as a conduit for male-male interactions.

O'Brien and Galvani attempt the transition from government agent to the Detroit mob to the edges of the counterfeit ring in Los Angeles, beginning their sojourn in a number of spaces I have described in the title of this chapter as "masculine," including apparently all-male hotels, men's rooms, locker rooms, and, most dramatically, steam baths. It is, primarily, O'Brien's journey into these spaces that is recounted by the narrative of *T-Men.* As the two agents try to earn their criminal credentials in Detroit, they are holed up in a seedy hotel run by a small Italian man, Pasquale, operating at the margins of legality. A Treasury agent shows up with a phony warrant for O'Brien and Genaro's arrest, hoping that Pasquale will warn them that they are being hunted, and then introduce them into the Italian mob they want to infiltrate. This process of recognition and initiation into the criminal brotherhood takes place in a scene typically redolent of male physical threats, violence, and intimacy, as the two men attack Pasquale when he tries to warn them of a police shakedown.

O'Brien's physical domination of Pasquale on the hotel room bed anticipates a number of other scenes in the film in which male-male violence seems to have an erotic component: in several scenes a large man masters a smaller one through behavior that implies the threat of rape. But once this violent entry has been made into the protected boundary of the Italian mob, and Pasquale assures them that he is part of the criminal brotherhood, Tony initiates a strongly ethnicized interaction expressive of mutual affection and gratitude, speaking his thanks in fluent Italian.[6] The two agents are now "inside" the criminal world (just as the voice-over at the beginning of the film has promised to take the spectator inside a Treasury Department case) and must commit themselves physically to the purgation of criminal activity. Violence is a means of broaching the distance between men. It serves to unite the two agents in their confrontation with violence side by side, as it were, but it also makes possible an intensification of physical and psychic involvement with other men, men whose lives and spaces the agents must infiltrate. As Steve Neale notes, in an essay that inspired this one, violence may serve to mark the repression of the erotic content of one man's look at another: "The mutilation and sadism so often involved in Mann's films are marks both of the repression involved and of a means by which the male body may be disqualified, so to speak, as an object of erotic contemplation and desire" (1992, 281).

After passing an oral quiz given by Vantucci on how the various members of the River Gang met their demise, O'Brien and Genaro are taken to a locker room to put on coveralls. As O'Brien holds up an impossibly short and wide pair of coveralls, another member of the mob lets drop that these were once the property of "the Schemer." The "otherness" of the Schemer's body (played by Wallace Ford)—its failure to conform to the classical proportions of O'Brien's—brings it to O'Brien's attention. When he discovers that the Schemer is part of the operation working out on the West Coast, and is in bad standing with the Vantucci crowd, O'Brien steals the coveralls by wrapping them around his body. The Treasury Department lab analyzes them and looks up the Schemer's name in the nickname files. O'Brien is informed, as he reiterates, that the Schemer is "about fifty, fat, smokes strong cigars, chews Chinese dragon liver herb medicine, and has a scar on his shoulder, maybe."[7] This information permits O'Brien to go in search of the Schemer. Thus, Paul Willeman's description of the Mann hero or villain holds true for *T-Men*: he is "pursued by a name. A father's name, or the name the hero wants to make for himself, or merely the name that makes you a target."(16) Having himself taken on a false name, O'Brien launches his pursuit of a man whose nickname the government has in its files (as the voice-over informs us in awestruck tones)—a more benign version of Robespierre's black book, which is used as a tool for the purgation of political enemies in Mann's noir costume drama, *Reign of Terror* (1949). The frisson of paranoia one may detect in *T-Men*'s celebration of governmental omniscience is borne out by the revelation, at the end of the film, that the most treacherous criminals don't wear mob regalia, but are indistinguishable from ordinary citizens. Not incidentally, 1947 marks the year when the House Unamerican Activities committee began to focus its attention on Hollywood.

When O'Brien takes off for Los Angeles he leaves Genaro behind to take the heat. Once again, a scene of violence builds to a crescendo and ends with expressions of belonging and respect, as Tony is smacked around by Vantucci's boys under a harsh interrogation-style top-light. Tony resists telling why O'Brien has left town and wins Vantucci's plaudit: "You're okay, kid." Resisting physical torture and refusing to betray a male partnership are behaviors valued by men in the criminal world, just as they are by the military or in the halls of justice. Thus, even though O'Brien and Genaro are off on what Krutnik might term a "criminal adventure," perhaps acting out latent fantasies of criminality, there are certain masculine values that span both worlds and serve to reassure them and the spectator. But lawlessness has other implications for male-male interactions: the fantasy of escaping into the man's realm of action also entails the danger of pushing the boundaries of

susan white

100

homosociality into the homoerotic, a homoeroticism tinged with racial terror, as the first of two extensive montage sequences follows O'Brien's search is shown when for the Schemer in Los Angeles's Chinatown.

If one is familiar with the history of *film noir,* it is not surprising that the plot of *T-Men* contrives to make the first stop on the search for the Schemer in Chinatown. In *film noir,* the Orient often functions as an obsessive metonymy for corruption too unspeakable to describe in Western terms (almost always linked, in one way or another, to homosexuality). Recall, for example, the resonance of Hong Kong and Malta in *The Maltese Falcon,* the dope-tainted perversion expressed through Geiger's Chinese decor in *The Big Sleep,* and so forth.[8] O'Brien is looking for a man with certain physical characteristics and, especially, habits that single him out. The Schemer chews Chinese dragon liver—indeed, his body is a site of conflict between Eastern and Western medical practices. A Chinese herbalist who gives O'Brien his first real "clue" as to the Schemer's whereabouts expresses contempt for the latter's habit of taking steam baths. Westerners may be mildly appalled at the idea of eating dragon liver, however metaphorical this term may be. Thus, from both Western and Eastern points of view, the Schemer is caught in a cycle of purgation and pollution, of strengthening and weakening that render his masculinity problematic. O'Brien's job is to clean out the monetary system of his country—to purge it of counterfeit bills that pollute its clean and proper circulation. In his search for the Schemer, O'Brien places his own body on the line, allowing himself to be purged to the point of weakness as he begins his search of Los Angeles's men's bathhouses, which the Schemer is said to frequent.

It is not by chance, I believe, that *T-Men*'s notorious bathhouse sequence follows hard upon the montage of Chinese faces and shops. The metonymic link between the Orient and homoeroticism is, as I have mentioned, a staple of *film noir.* The threat represented by near-nude male bodies looming out of the steam in the latter sequence is tinged with the unease inspired by the relaxing of racial boundaries, the crossing over into Chinatown, of the former sequence. In his discussion of race and *film noir* in "The Whiteness of Film Noir" (1997), Eric Lott notes: "What such films appear to dread is the infiltration into the white home or self of unsanctioned behaviors reminiscent of the dark figures exemplified in the 1940s and 1950s imaginary by zoot suiters, pachucos, and Asian conspirators" (95).

But, Lott also claims, "*film noir* is a cinematic mode defined by its border crossings. In it people fall from (g)race into the deep shadows that the new film technologies had made possible" (86–87). Such border crossings are fraught with danger, but alluring since, according to Slavoj Žižek (cited by Lott), "unspeakable powers of enjoyment . . . are imagined to be the special privilege or province of racial Others and whose experience or return, therefore, threatens the white self girded by specifically racial negations" (88). Defining the relationship between race, gender, and forbidden pleasure in *T-Men* is no simple task. But even this preliminary analysis indicates that crossing the boundaries of the law for the sake of the law is, in this film, the occasion for crossing racial and ethnic barriers into realms that offer both threatening and alluring forms of male homosociality and homoeroticism. Certainly O'Brien has been marked by his experience in the steam baths. When he reports back to his chief's office on his findings, he greets another agent who has also been on a case. A close-up details O'Brien's placement of a counterfeit bill into the buttonhole of his jacket as he banters with his colleague:

> O'BRIEN: "I'd better get back on the Schemer's tail. I lost
>   eight pounds trying to find him.
> COLLEAGUE: "Worried?"
> O'BRIEN: "Have you ever spent ten nights in a Turkish
>   bath looking for a man? Well, don't."

When I first saw *T-Men* I was amazed by the bold homoeroticism of O'Brien's admission that he was "looking for a man." The comment's sexual overtones are reinforced by his stated determination to "get back on the Schemer's tail." Certainly a gay or bisexual spectator in 1947 would have been struck by this dialogue, even if s/he did not assign any intentionality on the part of the makers of the film to the remark's homosexual connotations.

The more I have read about sexual encounters between men in public places during the past century, the more strongly I feel that almost any adult spectator in the late 1940s would be aware that bathhouses had long been, as Allan Bérubé puts it in his "History of Gay Bathhouses" (1996), places to "steal" intimacy, along with YMCA rooms, certain streets and alleys, public rest rooms, parked autos, and so forth (189). Certainly there were many contemporary newspaper accounts of police infiltration into bathhouses where homosexual encounters were reputed to occur. The following is an account by a young man involved in one such raid in New York in 1929:

> At about ten-thirty I go up to the dormitory and look
> for a bed. Chance brings me together with a young racy
> Sicilian. Unfortunately, we hadn't noticed that there
> were eight detectives among the customers of the
> baths.... Various people were struck down, kicked,
> in short, the brutality of these officials was simply
> indescribable. (194)

T-Men is in part about the erotic curiosity driving the police infiltrators to enter into spaces defined as homoerotic, and often associated with human waste, and about the violence with which these detectives "abject" their own desire for erotic contact with men, scapegoating other men for embodying and acting out commonly felt but forbidden desires (Kristeva, 1982).

Even more important to this reading of *T-Men* than the preceding account from 1929 is a 1933 newspaper article discussed in detail by Bérubé:

> In 1933, a New York City weekly ran an account of a San Francisco bathhouse in the process of becoming primarily gay against the wishes of the owners. Seizing the opportunity to demean homosexuals in its pages, the weekly described an extremely dangerous situation in its baths …: "Many a pansy, caught in the act of approach, has been tossed from this place by a gang of wise-money boys who patronize the establishment in hours of relaxation from guiding the destinies of their rackets." (197)

The article goes on to mock the gay community's sense that such "pansies," some of whom died when their heads cracked open on the pavement, were martyrs to their sexual preference. Although this newspaper story precedes the making of *T-Men* by fourteen years, I contend that a significant segment of the audience would have recognized as a familiar *topos* the condensed violence of this ejection from an all-male space for having made a sexual advance. This *topos* is taken on and enacted, in particular, by O'Brien and by the Schemer during the course of the film. In *T-Men* the infiltrating cop can purify Uncle Sam's money system, protect it from the encroachment of Oriental and other foul influences, only if he himself allows himself to be sullied, to make an approach via Chinatown that is both monetary and homoerotic in its implications.

There are spaces within spaces in the scene where O'Brien makes his first approach to the Schemer, and the intensity of the male-male interactions begins to be amplified as the film moves toward its series of climaxes. Tipped off to the Schemer's habits, O'Brien enters a gambling den through a seedy hotel in Ocean Park. The den itself is crowded with men. Bluesy New Orleans jazz issues from behind the closed door as O'Brien tells the desk clerk about the guy ("Smith") who recommended the place. Hard toplighting over the gambling table etches out the exchanges between men on a backdrop of Rembrandtian gloom. O'Brien slips a "big bill" to the Schemer, who recognizes by touch that the bill is false. When the Schemer looks suspiciously at the money in his hand, O'Brien offers to change the large bill for smaller ones. He proceeds to the men's room, where he slips the counterfeit bill back into his lapel. Realizing that phony money is being passed at the table, the men rush into the restroom, push O'Brien dramatically against the wall, beat him, and throw him out the door. In the newspaper article cited earlier, the author of the piece fantasizes about the action whereby a "gang of wise-money boys" would eject a homosexual from their midst. The violent unleashing of energy is made intimate: it occurs in the men's room, where O'Brien has just tucked the now-sullied money into a small orifice—the lapel we'd seen earlier in close-up—in his gangster suit. It is the Schemer who is actually "passing" (as one man in the crowd puts it) queer money, but O'Brien takes the fall for him, and smiles with pleasure through his pain as he lies on the street outside the hotel.

The way that homosexuality is allegorized in this scene and in the film is complex: the male-dominated world of the mobsters is characterized as both hypermasculine and "queer" with respect to the mainstream of American culture (this hypermasculinity and this queerness are, of course, closely related). Thus, in a sense the two agents must "queer" themselves in order to pass as legitimate inhabitants of the underworld. On the other hand, a kind of chiasmatic structure reveals itself at certain moments, when the agents show themselves to be "more criminal" than is acceptable in this milieu (passing counterfeit money) or when they are suspected of being just what they are, Treasury agents. Any positionality that distinguishes a man from his fellows at a particular moment can make him subject to the scapegoating behavior of the other men, who wish to eject the "queer" from their midst.[9]

In "Character and Anal Eroticism," Freud discusses the connection between money and defecation, the circulation and hoarding of money and anal eroticism. In the scene of his "abjection" from the gambling den, O'Brien must be careful not to allow his money actually to pass to the Schemer: he has promised his superior not to let it pass into circulation—in a sense, he avoids "consummation" of the exchange. A series of displacements links scenes of eroticism and violence in the steam baths, hotel rooms, the gambling den, and this, the first of several climactic scenes taking place in men's rooms. The passing of "queer" money tips the scales of homosocial bonding and rivalry in the gambling den to overtly homoerotic, even homosexual interaction. Anality is seen for what it is, and O'Brien is ravished/ravaged in the men's room for making the nature of these men's interactions explicit. The placement of the counterfeit money into the hidden slit in his lapel may be regarded as O'Brien's "displacement upward" (in Freud's terms) of the bill's anal contamination.[10]

O'Brien's next move, as a man who understands the importance of the permutation of beatings in the vernacular of the underworld, is to

O'Brien on the verge of ejection from the men's room.

turn the violence he has undergone onto the Schemer. After throwing the smaller man against the wall in a hotel room, as he had been thrown against the wall in the men's room, O'Brien takes his part in an "I'll show you mine if you show me yours" transaction. In a very striking low-angle composition, the men take out the counterfeit bills secreted on their persons and compare them, deeming O'Brien's bill far superior in its engraving process, while the Schemer's paper is better. Their decision to strike a deal reiterates the Schemer's liminal position both inside and outside the counterfeiting mob. He is an entrepreneurial man, a focus of fascination because he defies the corporate mentality of both the mafioso and the Treasury Department suits: he avoids what has been called the "routinization" of everyday life and is oddly sympathetic in his role as symbol of the ever-

105

enterprising "small man" keeping intact the free market frontier mentality.[11] O'Brien's tactic with the Schemer is to resist his attempts to make a separate deal and to use him to connect to the top guy.

O'Brien trails the Schemer to an Ocean Park night spot, the Club Trinidad, where he observes and then imitates the Schemer's method for passing along counterfeit bills, and where he encounters one of two women involved in the criminal enterprise. Initially, O'Brien's entrance into the nightclub (one of what Sobchack has described as the "chronotopes" of *film noir* [1998, 146] seems to guarantee the prototypical erotic clash with a femme fatale. The club is laden with signifiers of feminine allure. An "exotic" female dancer (Cuca Martinez) performs to background cha-cha music, while O'Brien watches the floor from a telephone booth whose glass reflects the image of the club back to the spectator. A sultry blonde photographer (Evangeline, played by Mary Meade) approaches the Schemer, who slips her an oddly folded ten-dollar bill into which O'Brien's torn counterfeit bill is rolled. Moments later, O'Brien oozes charm as he debates the merits of having a picture taken by Evangeline. True to the image of the criminal type divorced from domesticity, he insists that he has "no folks, no home"—no one who would be interested in a photo of himself except perhaps his cousin in Leavenworth. The photo is taken, nonetheless, and O'Brien casually slips the photographer a bill folded, like the Schemer's, into two symmetrical points. The startled woman invokes the name of the law, interjecting that this is "no way to treat Uncle Sam's money." In a subsequent scene, Evangeline takes the bill to the engraver who works for the mob. The engraver admires the bill's artistry and speculates that the man who pushed it may be a treasury agent, a suspicion that is, of course, later borne out. Evangeline's role as an intermediary in these scenes is an important plot device, but this is the beginning and end of her part in the film. Nevertheless, and symptomatically, the film's production stills played up the importance of this, the one woman in the film who seems to conform to the moll type. The stills depict, for example, a scene of Evangeline's obviously dead body stretched out on a couch, while O'Brien kneels nearby. One imagines the publicity agents for the film desperately trying to make it conform to genre by exaggerating the woman's role.

An incident from later in *T-Men* also uses this bait-and-switch tactic to underline the film's insistence on the masculine context of criminal spaces. When O'Brien makes his way to the top of the counterfeit ring, he encounters a woman whom he initially takes to be the "big boss." O'Brien flatters and flirts with Diana, leading the spectator to wonder whether this conservatively dressed woman serves to incarnate another noir stereotype: the classy dame who either spells doom to the protagonist (Phyllis Dietrichson in *Double Indemnity,* Brigid O'Shaunessey in

The Maltese Falcon), or who may turn out to be wife material (Vivian Rutledge in *The Big Sleep*). Is corrupt femininity, as is so often the case, at the heart of this drama of interlocking masculine spaces? Will O'Brien be bailed out by the love of a good woman fallen into bad ways? As the scene unfolds, it becomes clear that Mann has included this woman only to disqualify her. Diana is just a mouthpiece for the guy at the top. Like Tony's wife, Evangeline and Diana represent the pull of spaces associated with competing forms of femininity—the wife in the home, the doll in the nightclub, the dangerous lady in a den of criminals. But those spaces and those women fade into insignificance in contrast with the potent physicality of the film's male-dominated scenes.[12]

The fact that O'Brien "shoved" a bill in the Club Trinidad does not go unnoticed by the mobsters. The Schemer, in a convincing but very brief display of toughness, invades O'Brien's hotel room and submits him to torture via the intermediary of Moxie (Charles McGraw), the biggest tough boy in the film. This torture, which includes finger-twisting and getting smacked in the ears, again has something of the erotic. It is "good" suffering in that it is suffering for the sake of Uncle. Agent O'Brien has artistic license to express his pain with moans, hard-boiled wisecracks, and contorted facial expressions: the tough guy's battle between pain and stoicism is theatricalized in the interest of building trust in the underworld. The Schemer begins to feel marginalized, as his cohorts take over and begin their physical abuse of O'Brien, and addresses Moxie as would a injured wife:

> MOXIE: "Beat it, fat man."
> SCHEMER: "You didn't used to talk to me that way."

The fat man out of his way, Moxie then instructs his sidekick, Brownie (Jack Overman), to "wake [O'Brien] up in the morning and put him to bed at night." If dialogue is one index of character relations, Brownie's includes playing a maternal—or at any rate intimate— role. ("I sleep on the bed," he announces rather grumpily to his new roommate.) O'Brien has literally moved in with the mob. It is, perhaps, the very intimacy of this cohabitation that produces the emotional explosions of the last part of the film.

Asked for a definition of his prototypical Western hero, Anthony Mann replied, "A man who could kill his own brother" (Willeman 1981, 16). The urge for such killing is cut from the same cloth as the fierce love binding the antagonists in Mann's Westerns. For example, in *Winchester 73* (1950), a man does, in fact, kill his own brother, and in *The Man from Laramie* (1955), Arthur Kennedy's "doubling" of Jimmy Stewart unleashes orgiastic violence and mutual mutilation.[13] Two deaths in *T-Men* fuse pain, emotion, and eroticism in the context of masculine space. The demise of the Schemer reiterates the theme of murderous

Moxie directs Brownie's torture of O'Brien.

brothers within this context. Tony and the Schemer visit the Farmer's Market, where Tony's wife's friend accidentally blows the latter's cover. Shortly thereafter, Moxie shows up in the steam bath where the Schemer is sweating away his anxieties. The mob has decided to eliminate the Schemer, who tries to save his own life by selling out Tony. The iconography of the murder figures it both as a rape and as an ironic purgation through steam. Moxie, clad only in a towel and sweating profusely, looms over the Schemer, who slowly realizes that he is about to die. "Tony propositioned me!" the Schemer yells, as Moxie backs him up against the wall, craning his neck to look down upon the smaller man, in the kind of two-shot normally reserved for intimate heterosexual moments. Soft light pours through the steam room window behind

Moxie's head. "Moxie, we've been friends; when I was up I used to help you," the Schemer pleads, reiterating the "brother against brother" perversity of the scene that serves both to distract the viewer from the scene's extraordinarily homoerotic overtones, and to reinforce the suggestion of homoeroticism. The Schemer is left to die, stewing in his own juices, closed in the steam room by the sadistically smiling Moxie.

Tony's poignant death scene follows soon thereafter. The baroque and spectacular quality of the Schemer's death is replaced by the quiet intensity of utter desperation and heroic male reserve. Again, Moxie is the hit man, as the gang enters Tony's hotel room in order to confront Tony with their knowledge that he is a Treasury agent. Tony remains in his tough-guy role to the end, hurling taunts at O'Brien in an effort simultaneously to throw the others off his partner's trail and to telegraph the whereabouts of a piece of vital information. The humorous theatricality of the men's "passing" now turns to tragedy, as O'Brien is forced to witness Moxie's execution of his partner.[14] Like a curtain falling over his face, the shadow of mourning follows the brim of O'Brien's hat as he lowers his head. Such heartrending depictions of a man's grief and love for another man are also a staple of Mann's Westerns, as if his works were in part a meditation on the melancholy state of men's relations to each other, in which love can be expressed only through and between bursts of rage and hails of bullets, and in which spectatorship is at the service of a sublime but instantly punished eroticism.

Moxie contemplates steaming the Schemer.

The film's final scenes bring the "men's room" thematic down to a hard focus in the small space of a bathroom where Moxie grooms himself, while O'Brien struggles to take one of the counterfeiting plates from its hiding place beneath the sink. Again, extreme low-angle shots of the sink and the harsh light of a single lightbulb produce an unbearably tense atmosphere, as O'Brien must transgress the codes of male solidarity and "make his move" under the probing gaze of a man who is engaged in the most quintessential of male behaviors, shaving. Although he successfully removes the plate, O'Brien is shanghaied (so to speak) by the mob boss and taken to a docked ship, the center of the counterfeiting activities. The Feds then carry out a raid using tear gas that, ironically, visually repeats the "steam" motif, now in the interest of purging the nest of men who wish to contaminate the money system with Orientalized and "queer" money.

The final images of the film, photographs of the principals of the case featured in *Look* magazine, show us how infested our society was and may still be. "The mysterious leader of the ring turned out to be Oscar Gaffney, masquerading as a dealer in rare antiques, posing as a philanthropist and civic leader," the voice-over informs us as a picture of an ordinary-looking older man is shown in close-up. Thus, the multitude of threats to the community is summarized in this final story of "passing," and visual tribute is paid to the T-men who sacrificed themselves in the interest of purifying society of contaminating entities that would otherwise "pass" unnoticed until the damage had been done. What are these threats? That false money can "pass" as real, that

Moxie shaves in the hotel bathroom as O'Brien looks on.

a gay man can look straight, that a racially "other" person could infiltrate white America surreptitiously, that our desire for clear racial/gender/sexual boundaries may finally be foiled. Entrepreneurialism itself, as the expression of an older form of capitalism, is linked to liminal characters like the Schemer, and threatens the ascendency of corporate America. The film's evident promotion of homosexual panic is both offset and intensified by the final indistinguishability of professional male bonds and the bonds of homoerotic love. In the name of their partnership, and under "Uncle's" watchful gaze, Tony and Dennis are willing to make the ultimate sacrifice—of home, heterosexuality, and high-key lighting. Despite this sacrifice, which acts as a ritual purification of the threatened body politic in *T-Men*, I wonder how many men have gone home from viewing the film and dreamed uneasily of gleaming male bodies and the consummation of a bullet.

notes

Thanks to Krin Gabbard, Jacqueline Reich, and the other members of the Columbia University Seminar on Cinema and Interdisciplinary Interpretation, to Barbara Hall and the staff of the Margaret Herrick Library at the Academy for Motion Picture Arts and Sciences, and to Jeanine Basinger, Jason Byrne, Doug Hodapp, Peter Lehman, and Michael Trosset, who helped me formulate the ideas and locate the materials used in this chapter.

1. In *Between Men: English Literature and Male Homosocial Desire*, Sedgwick posits, and I agree, that homosociality, which involves "social bonds between persons of the same sex" (1), exists on a *continuum* with homoeroticism (erotic but not necessarily sexually consummated relationships) and, ultimately, homosexuality (which may involve sexual consummation, identity politics, and so on), despite the fact that for most men (in both Britain and America during the past two centuries) homosociality *seems* to exist in radical rupture from erotic or sexual relationships. There is often a powerful cathexis of male sexuality and erotic bonding even in those relationships, perhaps especially in those relationships, which seem most to embrace homophobic defenses against male-male desire.

2. Mann made *Raw Deal* (released July 8, 1948), starring O'Keefe (as Joe) and Claire Trevor (as Pat), just after finishing *T-Men* (filming completed September 1947, released January 22, 1948).

3. For an overview of Mann's *noir* period, see Robert E. Smith, "Mann in the Dark: The *Films Noir* of Anthony Mann."

4. The Zoot Suit Riots took place in June, 1943. See James Naremore's discussion of the Sleepy Lagoon case of 1943 and the representation of Latinos and Latin America in the context of *film noir* in *More Than Night: Film Noir in Its Contexts*, 229–33.

5. Miriam Hansen, *Babel and Babylon: Spectatorship in American Silent Film*, 259, cites Kaja Silverman on the "Great Masculine Renunciation," a phrase introduced by J. C. Flugel in *The Psychology of Clothes*.

6. Thanks to Jacqueline Reich for pointing out to me that Genaro speaks with a regional (Sicilian) accent when he is acting the part of the gangster, while Pasquale speaks with a purer accent—perhaps implying that

he is more truly "Italian," less assimilated, than Tony (who is, after all, a nice college boy married to an Anglo woman).

7. Peter Lehman describes men's scars in cinema as being associated with a loss of phallic power in *Running Scared: Masculinity and the Representation of the Male Body*, 61–63, 66–69.

8. The paper that is being used by the counterfeiters, and which is frighteningly similar to official banknote paper, turns out (not surprisingly) to contain Egyptian cotton, rice paper, and a shrinking agent used by Chinese papermakers that "points to an Oriental source." I have written more extensively on Orientalism in *film noir* in "Male Bonding, Hollywood Orientalism, and the Repression of the Feminine in Kubrick's *Full Metal Jacket*." See also Naremore, *More Than Night*, 225–29, for his discussion of Asians in *film noir*. It is worth noting that Higgins's script for *T-Men* makes no mention in the montage sequence of (specifically) *Turkish* baths, while a bath with a Turkish or Arabic name (Abdul Hamid Turkish Baths) is the first one listed in the telephone directory in the film itself.

9. I was recently able to examine two versions of the script for *T-Men* at the Margaret Herrick Library at the Academy for Motion Picture Arts and Sciences in Los Angeles. John C. Higgins's final revision of the "T-Man" (sic) script is dated July 28, 1947. Numerous lines in this script were changed before the film was shot or during shooting. Among the most interesting eliminations from the final product is the word "queer," used several times in early versions of the script, but absent from the film. The script describes the gambling scene: "Schemer's dodge is simple—he is using five dollar 'queer' notes to bet with, making as much change as possible. . . . We know he has spotted Dennis' 'queer'. . . ." (47). Then, after Dennis runs into the men's room:

> ATTENDANT'S VOICE: —big tall guy. Shovin' queer inna game! (49)

Although the PCA files don't indicate that their office required these cuts, I suspect the word "queer" was eliminated because although it is "legitimate" slang for counterfeit money, the word's homosexual connotations were very well established by 1948 and probably seemed too obvious in the context of these male-male interactions. In *An American Dictionary of Slang and Colloquial Speech*, Joseph A. Weingarten gives the first meaning of "queer" as "counterfeit money" and the second meaning as "effeminate; having homosexual tendencies." "Queer shover" is defined as "a circulator of counterfeit money" (292). In *Wicked Words*, Hugh Rawson dates the first American appearance of "queer" as meaning "homosexual" to 1922 (318). I would also like to point out that "tearoom" is British-derived slang for public restrooms where male-male sex occurs (tea-urine). Although I doubt whether there was any conscious awareness that the term "T-Man" might be read as pertaining to the practices taking place in "tearooms," surely some viewers made this connection. See Laud Humphrey's well-known study of sex in public restrooms, *Tearoom Trade: Impersonal Sex in Public Places*.

10. Certainly the rectum has long been used as a hiding place for money, drugs (often referred to as "shit"), and other contraband. I make this comment by way of alluding to Sharon Willis's essay on men's rooms in Tarantino's films, "The Fathers Watch the Boys' Room," in which she catalogues the numerous activities inflecting male subject-formation and male bonding that occur in Tarantino's bathrooms. As in *T-Men*, the

men's room functions in Tarantino's films as a means of confronting an abjected femininity which has its source in the male psyche and male interactions. It is often a perceived femininity that is being abjected (as is also the case when Norman Bates cleans the bathroom after killing Marion in Psycho), but the connection between blood, excrement, anal sexuality (with its traditional connotations of passivity and femininity) and violent intimacy is, for both Mann and Tarantino, more fundamentally a masculine affair.

11. On this topic see Robert J. Corber, Homosexuality in Cold War America: Resistance and the Crisis of Masculinity.

12. In "Film Noir and Women," Elizabeth Cowie describes *Raw Deal*, which employs an "intensely personal and subjective" first-person narration by Pat, as conveying a "woman's story" (139). I find it extraordinarily interesting that Mann would turn from the obsessively masculine world of *T-Men* to the unusually "feminized" focalization on Pat in *Raw Deal*.

13. On masculinity and violence in Mann's Westerns, see Douglas Pye, "The Collapse of Fantasy: Masculinity in the Westerns of Anthony Mann," and for a compelling discussion of eroticism and masculinity in Mann's Westerns, see Amy Lawrence, "American Shame: *Rope*, James Stewart, and the Postwar Crisis in American Masculinity."

14. Both the spectacular quality and the forced impassivity of the agent found in the death scenes of the Schemer and Tony are reiterated in the death of the agent played by George Murphy in *Border Incident*.

works cited

Basinger, Jeanine. 1979. *Anthony Mann*. Boston: Twayne Publishers.

Bérubé, Allan. 1996. "Policing Sexuality: The History of Gay Bathhouses." In *Policing Public Sex: Queer Politics and the Future of AIDS Activism*, ed. Ephen Glenn Colter, 187–220. Boston, Mass.: South End Press.

Corber, Robert J. 1997. *Homosexuality in Cold War America: Resistance and the Crisis of Masculinity*. Durham, N.C. and London: Duke University Press.

Cowie, Elizabeth. 1993. "*Film Noir* and Women. In *Shades of Noir*, ed. Joan Copjec, 121–65. London: Verso.

Flugel, J. C. 1930. *The Psychology of Clothes*. London: Hogarth.

Freud, Sigmund. 1957. "Character and Anal Eroticism" (1908). In *The Standard Edition of the Complete Psychological Works*, Vol. 9, 173–74, ed. and trans. James Strachey. 24 vols. London: Hogarth Press.

Hansen, Miriam. 1991. *Babel and Babylon: Spectatorship in American Silent Film*. Cambridge, Mass.: Harvard University Press.

Higgins, John C. "T-Man." Unpublished script, 1947. The Margaret Herrick Library, Academy for Motion Picture Arts and Sciences, Los Angeles, California.

Humphrey, Laud. 1970. *Tearoom Trade: Impersonal Sex in Public Places*. Chicago: Aldine.

Kristeva, Julia. 1982. *Powers of Horror: An Essay on Abjection*. Trans. Leon S. Roudiez. New York: Columbia University Press.

Krutnik, Frank. 1991. *In a Lonely Street: Film Noir, Genre, Masculinity*. London: Routledge.

Lawrence, Amy. 1999. "American Shame: *Rope*, James Stewart, and the Postwar Crisis in American Masculinity." In *Hitchcock's America*, ed. Jonathan Freedman and Richard Millington, 55–76. New York and Oxford: Oxford University Press.

Lehman, Peter. 1993. *Running Scared: Masculinity and the Representation of the Male Body*. Philadelphia: Temple University Press.

Lott, Eric. 1997. "The Whiteness of Film Noir." In *Whiteness: A Critical Reader*, ed. Mike Hill, 81–101. New York: NYU Press.

Mann, Anthony, dir. *T-Men*. Exec. Prod. Edward Small. Prod Aubrey Schenck. Cinematog. John Alton. Asst. Dir. Howard W. Koch. Script by John C. Higgins. Original Story by Virginia Kellogg. Music Paul Sawtell. Perf. Dennis O'Keefe (Dennis O'Brien), Alfred Ryder (Anthony Genaro), Wallace Ford (the Schemer), Charles McGraw (Moxie), June Lockhart (Mary Genaro), Elmer Lincoln Irey (himself), John Wengraf (Shiv Triano), Jane Randolph (Diana), Mary Meade (Evangeline), Jack Overman (Brownie), Tito Vuolo (Pasquale), Art Smith (Gregg), William Yip (Chinese merchant), William Malten (Paul Miller), Cuca Martinez (dancer in club). Eagle-Lion/Reliance Films, 1947.

Naremore, James. 1998. *More Than Night: Film Noir in Its Contexts*. Berkeley and Los Angeles: U.C. Press.

Neale, Steve. 1992. "Masculinity as Spectacle." In *The Sexual Subject: A Screen Reader in Sexuality*, New York: Routledge, 277–87.

Polan, Dana. 1986. *Power and Paranoia: History, Narrative, and the American Cinema, 1940–1950*. New York: Columbia University Press.

Pye, Douglas. 1996. "The Collapse of Fantasy: Masculinity in the Westerns of Anthony Mann" in *The Book of Westerns*, ed. Ian Cameron and Douglas Pye, 167–73. New York: Continuum.

Rawson, Hugh. 1989. *Wicked Words*. New York: Crown Publishers.

Sedgwick, Eve Kosofsky. 1985. *Between Men: English Literature and Male Homosocial Desire*. New York: Columbia University Press.

Silverman, Kaja. 1986. "Fragments of a Fashionable Discourse." In *Studies in Entertainment: Critical Approaches to Mass Culture*, ed. Tania Modleski, 139–52. Bloomington: Indiana University Press.

Smith, Robert E. 1996. "Mann in the Dark: The *Films Noir* of Anthony Mann." In *The Film Noir Reader*, ed. Alain Silver and James Ursini, 189–201. New York: Limelight Editions.

Sobchack, Vivian. 1998. "Lounge Time: Post War Crises and the Chronotope of Film Noir." In *Refiguring American Film Genres: Theory and History*, ed. Nick Browne, 129–170, Berkeley and Los Angeles: UC Press.

Taubin, Amy. 1992. "The Men's Room." *Sight and Sound* 2, 8 (December): 2–4.

Weingarten, Joseph A. 1954. *An American Dictionary of Slang and Colloquial Speech*. New York: n.p.

White, Susan. 1991. "Male Bonding, Hollywood Orientalism, and the Repression of the Feminine in Kubrick's *Full Metal Jacket*." In *Inventing Vietnam: The War in Film and Television*, ed. Michael Anderegg, 204–30. Philadelphia: Temple University Press.

Willeman, Paul. "Anthony Mann: Looking at the Male." *Framework* 15, 17 (Summer 1981): 16–20.

Sharon Willis. 1993–94. "The Fathers Watch the Boys' Room." *Camera Obscura* 32 (September-January): 40–73.

Žižek, Slavoj. 1993. "Eastern Europe's Republics of Gilead." In *Tarrying with the Negative: Kant, Hegel, and the Critique of Ideology*, 201–214. Durham, N.C.: Duke University Press.

the

talented

poststructuralist

heteromasculinity,

gay artifice,

and class passing

chris straayer

One man kills a second man for his money. This familiar plot anchors both the film *Purple Noon* (Clément 1960) and the novel on which it is based, *The Talented Mr. Ripley* (Highsmith 1955). However, while the film concludes with Tom Ripley's impending capture by police, in the novel he gets away with murder. These divergent endings are the result of contradictory attitudes toward identity. This article analyzes the two texts in relation to masculinity, homosexuality, and class and argues that in these realms the novel, unlike the film, endorses a freedom from determination and fixity that is compatible with both existentialism of the 1950s and contemporary poststructuralism.

Tom Ripley's victim in *Purple Noon* and *The Talented Mr. Ripley* is Philippe/Dickie Greenleaf,[1] a rich American who has lived in Italy for several years supported by his trust fund. Back in the United States, Greenleaf's father locates a prior acquaintance of his son, Tom Ripley, and sponsors his trip to Italy for the purpose of influencing Greenleaf to return home. Very soon after meeting up with Greenleaf, Tom reveals his travel arrangement to him, and they get on with enjoying Italy. Although they had not been close friends in the United States, now Greenleaf is amused by Tom's displays of forgery and mimicry, and Tom savors Greenleaf's higher-class lifestyle. At first, Greenleaf's female companion, Marge, also an American living abroad,[2] is the only hindrance to the men's bonding. However, when Greenleaf does not write an encouraging, if insincere, letter to his father—as he promised Tom he would do—Tom's expense account is cut off. Tom, who covets upward class mobility more than anything, kills Greenleaf. At first Tom Ripley impersonates his wealthier victim, wearing his mono-grammed clothes, spending his family money, traveling in his style. To protect this acquired identity, he even commits a second murder when Freddie Miles, one of Greenleaf's old friends, pays an unexpected visit. The real Greenleaf, who is missing but presumed still alive, is blamed for the murder. At this point Tom forges Greenleaf's will to his own advantage and resumes using the name Tom Ripley. This summarizes that portion of the plot shared by film and novel. Before analyzing the texts individually, I must note several significant discrepancies, especially with regard to homosexuality and class. My general purpose in comparing the texts is not to measure the adaptation's accuracy, but rather to explore the consequences for identity of their different por-trayals of repressed homosexuality.

Both texts use homosexuality to provide depth to the story. Because homosexuality is not analyzed but rather connoted via literary tropes and cultural stereotypes, I cannot really describe this depth as properly psychological. Yet, I think this undercurrent of homosexuality offers mainstream viewers/readers an opportunity to utilize popularized psy-chology for their interpretive efforts in at least two areas: the associa-tion of repressed sexuality with violence, and the association of homosexuality with narcissism.

In the film *Purple Noon,* homosexuality remains subtextual, coded primarily (but not entirely) through triangles involving the two men and a woman. For example, early in the film Tom and Greenleaf are visiting Rome. During a game of pretending to be blind, Greenleaf induces a woman to join them. They take her on a buggy ride during which she is positioned between them as they both kiss and fondle her.[3] Eve Kosofsky Sedgwick (1985) has argued that such triangulation is an instance of "homosocial desire" in which the desire of two (assumed heterosexual) men for each other is exchanged through a woman.[4] Later in the film, when Greenleaf, Marge, and Tom are boat-ing together, Tom reacts jealously to Greenleaf and Marge's private lovemaking below deck. In light of the earlier scene in the buggy, one might understand this as Tom's jealousy of Greenleaf over Marge, of

Marge over Greenleaf, or of the couple together that excludes him (that is, as his desire to join them).

By contrast, in the novel *The Talented Mr. Ripley*, Tom would not tolerate any such triangulation. Women disgust him, as does any semblance of heterosexuality. This is attributable to a homosexuality that he resolutely resists and denies. He wants Greenleaf to leave Marge behind in Mongibello during their travels. He fantasizes a committed, idyllic bond between Greenleaf and himself that transcends sexuality. In other words, Tom adamantly seeks an exclusively male homosociality with Greenleaf. Traditionally understood as heterosexual male bonding in male-only social environments (such as sports, the military, etc.), the concept of *homosociality* precludes homosexuality. Homosociality assumes that men desire to emulate one another but do not desire to have one another sexually. Taking issue with this, Sedgwick's theorization of *homosocial desire* (1985) posits a continuum between homosociality and homosexuality, despite heterosexuality's pertinacious espousal of a distinct separation. This distinction maintains a normative masculinity regulated by heterosexuality.

In "On Narcissism," Freud assigned the ego ideal of heterosexuals to one's own sex and the object of desire to one's opposite sex. In accordance with this schema, homosociality reinforces manliness by providing manly role models as ego ideals. Against Tom's will, however, Greenleaf is both his ego ideal and the object of his (forbidden) desire. In such a location of both ego ideal and object of desire in a single sex, Freud finds a basis for homosexuality: narcissism. Michael Warner (1990) has astutely critiqued this equation of homosexuality with narcissism. Warner not only interrupts Freud's collapse of same sex into sameness, and sameness into self, but also reveals the arbitrariness of Freud's sex-specific scenarios, thus indicating the equal possibility of heterosexuals locating ego ideals in the same sex that they desire. In *The Talented Mr. Ripley*, Tom wants to become Greenleaf and also desires to couple with him. As Tom Ripley will learn, homosociality can precipitate homosexual panic in the repressed homosexual. And, as we will learn, murder is not the enactment of homosexual panic but the means by which Tom avoids it.

In the novel, Tom's passing as Greenleaf is absolutely convincing. In fact, I will argue later that Tom not only impersonates Greenleaf but becomes him. This transformation is made possible by Tom's total lack of allegiance to any former identity. By contrast, the film binds Tom to his working-class identity. When Tom claims to be a close friend from Greenleaf's past, Greenleaf not only denies it to Marge but uses class difference to disprove it. Correcting the way Tom holds his silverware, Greenleaf not only performs a classist infantilization but also implies that, because Tom is of the wrong class, they could not possibly have been close friends. Cutting both ways, Greenleaf also criticizes Tom's class passing by declaring that the sure sign of someone not being upper class is his effort to act that way. "If you're trying to look well bred, which is a sign of bad breeding, don't use the knife to cut fish, and don't hold the knife that way. Hold it this way. I'm telling you this for your own good." After Tom kills Greenleaf and is traveling under his name, film viewers (as opposed to diegetic characters) see Tom in his private luxurious space eating chicken from the baking pan instead of at a properly set table. This portrays Tom as ultimately unable to become upper class. While the film nods toward what the novel calls Tom's "talent," it ultimately denies his mutability through an essentialist discourse on class. Tom remains a common crook. According to *Purple Noon,* class is natural and unchangeable, located in certain people, not in their possessions. Even though Tom obtains Greenleaf's money, he can never assume his class. Hence the novel and film produce different discourses about both class identity and (repressed) homosexuality.

Despite its blazing sunlight and European holiday location, *Purple Noon* has a root in film noir.[5] Like the classic *femme fatale* but here a man, the film's central agency, Tom Ripley (Alain Delon), pursues upward mobility via charm and murder. He is an *homme fatal*: handsome, wanting, duplicitous, enticing, unknowable, and fatal. His soon-to-be victim, Greenleaf (Maurice Ronet), although aware of Tom's plan, is irresistibly drawn to him. This attraction is Greenleaf's downfall. After Greenleaf invites Tom to join him and Marge (Marie Laforet) on his yacht, Tom plants in Greenleaf's pocket an earring taken from the woman they kissed together in the buggy in Rome. Just as he hopes, Marge finds the earring, and it causes a rift between her and Greenleaf. Less explainable is why, rather than trying to make up with Marge, Greenleaf then thoroughly ruptures the relationship by throwing her book manuscript overboard during their argument. Marge asks to be put ashore, and both men seem helpless and unwilling to change her mind.

In collaboration, Tom and Greenleaf have arranged for the two of them to be alone. And, without a female intermediary, they proceed toward physical contact. Prior to eliminating Marge from their company, Greenleaf had discovered some of his bank statements among Tom's clothes. He even asked Tom if he had felt like killing him, and Tom did not deny it. So, why did Greenleaf not put Tom ashore instead of Marge? Alone now on the yacht, Greenleaf and Tom sit at a small table playing poker. Against Tom's watch, his most precious possession, Greenleaf bets $2,500, one-half the reward that his father would pay Tom for bringing him home. They pretend to be joking as they continue discussing the murder scheme. When Greenleaf declares his love for Marge, Tom averts his eyes. Then, in a shot reverse-shot pattern, the camera alternates between the men as they smile at one another and look intensely into each other's eyes. Camera positioning and focal length bring the two faces even nearer to each other. Then Greenleaf cheats so that Tom can win, but Tom catches him cheating. A discarded card lies on the floor between their feet. Tom tells Greenleaf that he cannot be bought, not for $2500, not even for $5000 now. As Greenleaf bends to get his card from the floor, Tom nimbly swings a dagger off the bench at his hips and stabs Greenleaf in the chest. More than a psychological cliché calls for reading this scene as sexual desire displaced onto violence: Greenleaf's attraction to Tom, his active complicity in Tom's attempt to rid them of Marge, the hypocritic foreplay in their card playing, the final penetration. Did Greenleaf think he could buy Tom as if he were trade?

Tom's life ambitions exceed those of a working-class thief. He cannot settle for money when the opportunity for upward mobility is facing him. He lusts for the kind of class that comes complete with identity, with being, with family, with blood. Thus, Tom kills Greenleaf and exceeds his formerly inept class passing by assuming Greenleaf's identity. Later, when suspicions about Philippe Greenleaf's disappearance begin to impinge on Tom's confidence, he forges a will, leaving Greenleaf's money to Marge, whom Tom then seduces. Here we find another triangle in *Purple Noon*. Greenleaf's money passes through Marge to her new partner, Tom. By replacing Greenleaf in the heterosexual couple, Tom *inherits* Greenleaf's money. In this transaction, Tom makes himself the recipient of homosocial desire and achieves his ego ideal. Tom becomes Greenleaf's "family."

Unfortunately for Tom, the film's discourse on class ultimately will not abide such status-shaking success. In retrospect, the ominous ending of *Purple Noon,* in which Tom sips a cool drink on the beach unaware that at that very moment Greenleaf's body has been found nearby in circumstances that incriminate him, seems foreshadowed by an earlier scene in which Tom is apprehended wearing Greenleaf's clothes. Greenleaf has expelled Tom from the living room, where he and Marge are embracing each other after Greenleaf's return from vacationing with Tom. Upon entering Greenleaf's bedroom, Tom begins trying on Greenleaf's clothes before a full-length mirror. Even Greenleaf's shoes fit him as he reclines on the floor, pulling them on and tilting his feet in the air in a quite feminine gesture. Tom recombs his hair in Greenleaf's style as the film cuts to a closer image of him. Finally Tom leans into the mirror, pointing his finger at the image and murmuring: "My Marge. Marge, my love. My little Marge knows I love her and that I won't go with that nasty Tom to San Francisco." Tom kisses the image before him. "My love for Marge is blind."

Alain Delon as Tom Ripley in *Purple Noon* (Plein Soleil, René Clément, France, 1960).

Obviously this scene offers a third instance of triangulation in the film: Marge serves as intermediary in an otherwise same-sex kiss. Yet the scene is quite complex and encourages numerous simultaneous readings, including: Tom is kissing Marge; Greenleaf is kissing Marge; Tom is kissing Greenleaf (via Marge); Greenleaf is kissing Tom (via Marge). At the level of pure image, however, we cannot help but see Tom kissing Tom. In relation to the film's understanding of homosexuality, I contend that this image of a man kissing his mirror reflection is the most powerful moment in the film. It fixes viewers' memories and effectively manages the film's homosexual subtext. First, the audio indexing of Marge is inconsequential next to the visual semiotics of this shot. In a sense, the audiovisual construction of this scene ejects Marge, just as Greenleaf and Tom later evacuate her from the yacht. If we privilege the central image—an isolation the film executes by cutting to medium close-up and then tracking closer—it contains only one person, regardless of whether or not we find Tom's impersonation convincing, who kisses his mirror image. Hence we move inward from a *scene* that contained both Tom dressing up as Greenleaf and then kissing him in the mirror, to the *image* of a person kissing his own image. While we might understand Tom's donning of Greenleaf's clothes as a feigning of his ego ideal and his subsequent kissing that image of Greenleaf as expressing desire for Greenleaf via Marge, the dominance of the scene by his mirrored image privileges a reading of homo-narcissism.

This accusation of homo-narcissism, which locks Tom within his own identity, is amplified when Greenleaf walks into the room, interrupting our gaze at the mirror and causing Tom to stop.

Let's compare the above scene, which I have related as the modification of a triangle of homosocial desire toward homo-narcissism, to its rendering in *The Talented Mr. Ripley*. To contextualize the written scene, it must be noted that Greenleaf's heterosexuality is subdued in the novel, so much so that it remains in question. That Greenleaf is very private about his (hetero)sexuality, that he is latently homosexual, and that he is nearly asexual are all plausible conclusions. In Mongibello, Marge and Greenleaf rent separate houses but are very friendly neighbors, sharing their privileged life almost on a daily basis. In the novel, the mirror scene quoted below occurs after Tom, standing outside Marge's window, has surreptitiously observed Greenleaf in a rare moment embracing her and kissing her cheeks. Shocked, Tom runs back to Greenleaf's house.

> He wondered when Dickie was coming back? Or was he going to stay and make an afternoon of it, really take her to bed with him? He jerked Dickie's closet door open and looked in. There was a freshly pressed, new-looking grey flannel suit that he had never seen Dickie wearing. Tom took it out. He took off his knee-length shorts and put on the grey flannel trousers. He put on a pair of Dickie's shoes. Then he opened the bottom drawer of the chest and took out a clean blue-and-white striped shirt.
>
> He chose a dark-blue silk tie and knotted it carefully. The suit fitted him. Tom re-parted his hair and put the part a little more to one side, the way Dickie wore his.
>
> "Marge, you must understand that I don't *love* you," Tom said into the mirror in Dickie's voice, with Dickie's higher pitch on the emphasized words, with the little growl in his throat at the end of the phrase that could be pleasant or unpleasant, intimate or cool, according to Dickie's mood. "Marge, stop it!" Tom turned suddenly and made a grab in the air as if he were seizing Marge's throat. He shook her, twisted her, while she sank lower and lower, until at last he left her, limp, on the floor. He was panting. He wiped his forehead the way Dickie did, reached for a handkerchief and, not finding any, got one from Dickie's top drawer, then resumed in front of the mirror. Even his parted lips looked like Dickie's lips when he was out of breath from swimming, drawn down a little from his lower teeth.

121

"You know why I had to do that," he said, still breathlessly, addressing Marge, though he watched himself in
the mirror. "You were interfering between Tom and
me—No, not that! But there is a bond between us!"
(78–79)

Three points drastically distinguish this scene from its articulation
in the film and point us to significant qualities of the novel. First, Tom
does not kiss the mirror but instead uses it to appraise his impersonation
of Greenleaf. Tom is never reduced to an image as he is in the
film, but rather retains a looking agency. This, along with his frequent
movements, maintain his presence in three-dimensional space. Second,
Tom exhibits complete competence in transforming himself into
Greenleaf. Not only do Greenleaf's clothes fit him physically, but they
fit his taste. His body can stand in for Greenleaf's, naturally performing
his gestures and expressions. Tom's automatic movements in locating
Greenleaf's clothes suggest that he would know just how to handle
and arrange such a wardrobe, that his own preferences and instincts
about personal space are *simpatico* with Greenleaf's. His attention to
detail, appreciation of nice materials, and quick decisions suggest a natural
affiliation with the finery of this class. Tom is not a clumsy
"wannabe" as in *Purple Noon,* but a fully malleable person. To a degree
impossible with the visually denotative language of film, readers are
able to receive Tom as Greenleaf here. By the time he talks to Marge,
Tom *is* Greenleaf. When Tom looks in the mirror and sees Greenleaf's
likeness, he reaps another benefit from his impersonation. Rather than
being reduced to homo-narcissism, he has produced Greenleaf and
himself as a *couple.* Tom populates this couple as both himself and
Greenleaf. Or, in other words, Tom has succeeded in both being and
having Greenleaf. When he speaks as Greenleaf and looks at Greenleaf,
it is as if they were standing right next to each other, Greenleaf defending
him against Marge. And not only that: Tom in this configuration
has ascended to Greenleaf's class. He has obtained an identity that
would warrant Greenleaf's acceptance and desire.[6]

The third significant difference between this scene and its rendering
in the film is that Tom strangles Marge instead of kissing her. There is
no homosocial triangulation that safely conducts desire between the
two men without exposing it as such. Instead, Tom imagines an outright
accusation of homosexuality from Marge. As it happens (one
page later), Greenleaf does tell Tom that Marge thinks he is queer. But
here, Tom (speaking as Greenleaf to the imaginary Marge) denies any
homosexuality between the men while nevertheless claiming (without
elaboration) a primary bond between them.[7] More important, he says
this to Marge after supposedly killing her. His non-comprehension of

death in this imaginary scenario foreshadows his later reaction to Greenleaf's death.

It is because Tom is rebuffed by Greenleaf that he murders him. During their last trip together, Greenleaf says that next time he wants to travel alone with Marge.[8] On the train he seems bored, distant, only politely cheerful like a "host who has loathed his guest and is afraid the guest realizes it, and who tries to make it up at the last minute" (96). Later when Tom points out a group of young male acrobats on the beach (wearing yellow G-strings),[9] Greenleaf makes a sour remark that fills Tom with shame. He remembers Marge thinking he was queer and his aunt calling him a sissy when he was a boy. When Greenleaf attempts to leave him there, Tom's hurt turns to anger. "Damn him anyway, Tom thought. Did he have to act so damned aloof and superior all the time? You'd think he'd never seen a pansy! Obvious what was the matter with Dickie [Greenleaf], all right! Why didn't he break down, just for once? What did he have that was so important to lose?" (99). The suddenness of this shift from inward guilt to outward anger is typical of Tom. Soon after the incident with the acrobats, Tom quickly proceeds from fantasizing to enacting murder. In San Remo, he suggests they take out a motorboat and, when they have reached a secluded spot, he beats Greenleaf to death with the oar and throws him overboard.

This murder was not fate. Things could have happened differently. Upon reaching the decisive moment in which Tom hits Greenleaf, the text abruptly tells us that Tom could have "sprung on him, or kissed him, or thrown him overboard" (103). Russell Harrison has written about the influence of French existentialism on Patricia Highsmith's work in the 1950s. This postwar philosophy insisted on the necessity of choice even when no choice can be transcendentally justified or meaningful. Even when choice is absurd, it is unavoidable. Harrison argues that Highsmith took a positive stance toward irrationality and even motiveless behavior (1997, 3–7). Although I have repeatedly characterized Tom Ripley as desiring upward mobility, the kiss-or-kill moment described above complicates any assumption that this is *the* reason he kills Greenleaf. Indeed, it acknowledges an equally forceful alternate desire and the necessity to choose between these two desires. Tom makes the decision instantly. This is an integral part of his "talent." Combined with his practical play-acting skills, extensively rendered in the novel, Tom's ability to react quickly to situations, to seize immediate opportunities, to take advantage of the present is what makes him successful. Adaptability, not deliberation, makes a con man.[10] This talent of Tom's springs into action in the absence of any essential identity. Tom's refusal of any past formation grants him freedom. As Harrison states, "Reacting against the literature of the 1930s, especially that which depicted people as overwhelmingly determined by their circumstances, Highsmith's fiction pushed 'choice' to a solipsistic extreme" (1997, 6).

Was Tom panicked when he killed Greenleaf? Certainly at that moment he closely resembles the profile for the *psychiatric* understanding of acute homosexual panic during the 1950s: he is severely defensive if not actually repressed about his homosexuality; he is horrified by heterosexuality; he senses an impending separation from a same-sex friend to whom he is emotionally attached; he feels an outsider (Marge) is trying to negatively influence his life; and he is self-derogative. Numerous times throughout the novel Tom succumbs to severe depression and hopelessness when made to face up to what he judges as his own inadequacy. Shortly before their trip to San Remo, Tom and Greenleaf have an argument. Greenleaf disapproves of a scheme for making money in which Tom wants to involve them. Greenleaf says that Tom is being taken in by a dirty crook. Tom resents Greenleaf's smug attitude. Suddenly Tom feels an unbearable estrangement and inferiority.

> Tom felt a painful wrench in his breast, and he covered his face with his hands. It was as if Dickie had been suddenly snatched away from him. They were not friends. They didn't know each other. It struck Tom like a horrible truth, true for all time, true for the people he had known in the past and for those he would know in the future: each had stood and would stand before him, and he would know time and time again that he would never know them, and the worst was that there would always be the illusion, for a time, that he did know them, and that he and they were completely in harmony and alike. For an instant the wordless shock of his realization seemed more than he could bear. He felt the grip of a fit, as if he would fall to the ground. It was too much: the foreignness around him, the different language, his failure, and the fact that Dickie hated him. (89)

124

Tom has become gravely dependent on Greenleaf's attention. For Greenleaf to rebuff Tom is to threaten his stability. Certainly Tom is panicked before he kills Greenleaf.

Gary David Comstock (1992) convincingly demonstrates the critical differences between the psychiatric category of homosexual panic and its misappropriation by the courts as a legal defense.[11] The latter, homosexual panic defense, is more familiar to a contemporary public. A strategy to defend men who have murdered homosexuals, it presents the following narrative: a (latently gay) heterosexual-identified man responds to a sexual solicitation from a homosexual with a violent psychotic reaction. The argument presented is that the defendant was temporarily unable to distinguish right from wrong, and so should be absolved of responsibility. As Comstock makes clear, this narrative and argument severely distort the psychiatric theory (and actual cases) on which its authority depends. In psychiatric homosexual panic, the patient has uncontrollable homosexual urges that compete against his socially accepted goals. These homosexual urges are precipitated or strengthened by same-sex environments or the loss of a same-sex friend to whom the patient has become attached. In addition, the patient intensely fears heterosexuality. Already, the illogic of the homosexual panic defense is obvious: practicing heterosexuals do not demonstrate sufficient fear of heterosexuality. Furthermore, in order to gain sympathy from jurors, lawyers generally downplay or deny any latent homosexuality in the defendants. Most important to disputing the homosexual panic defense, however, is the total absence of outward violence in its psychiatric basis. Patients are not aggressive, but rather self-punishing, sometimes to the point of suicide. So, we see that although Tom does seem a likely candidate for homosexual panic before the murder, by murdering he actually avoids it. Instead, he enacts an equally psychotic scenario: acute aggressive panic. By killing Greenleaf, Tom saves himself. But not simply himself.

In his murder and subsequent impersonation of Greenleaf, Tom consummates a corporeal union and reproduction that simultaneously rids him of the Tom he so detests, transforms him into Greenleaf, makes him worthy of Greenleaf's approval, and produces them as a couple. Surely Greenleaf had become the ego ideal beside which Tom's ego was deficient. But Tom did not kill Greenleaf to save his ego. As the quote above illustrates so pitiably, Tom could not have survived with himself alone. Homosexual panic would have destroyed him. Instead, he survives psychologically by abandoning rather than reprimanding his ego, by becoming his ego ideal.

Impersonating Greenleaf, Tom is exceedingly happy. He travels about the country, staying at expensive hotels, eating the foods that he knows Greenleaf liked, wearing the rings he often admired on Greenleaf's hands. He buys two Gucci suitcases that Greenleaf would surely have liked: "one large, soft suitcase of antelope hide, the other a neat tan canvas with brown leather straps. Both bore Dickie's initials" (138–39). Competent in his new identity, he telephones Greenleaf's family and friends. He almost forgets how to talk like Tom. "It was impossible ever to be lonely or bored, he thought, so long as he was Dickie Greenleaf" (122). And he *is* Greenleaf. And yet he also is always *with* Greenleaf. Tom feels no remorse about killing Greenleaf, because

Greenleaf still lives for Tom. And Tom lives for Greenleaf. He sings in the shower "in Dickie's loud baritone that he had never heard, but he felt sure that Dickie would have been pleased with" (180). Tom's living as Greenleaf creates him. Tom relishes life with Greenleaf in harmonious unity. Celebrating his good fortune, he goes to a Roman nightclub and orders a superb dinner "which he ate in elegant solitude at a candlelit table for two" (133). Tom is psychotic.

One of the paramount benefits Tom gained by killing Greenleaf is heterosexuality. In the novel, despite Greenleaf's ability to shame him, Tom is proficient at passing. *The Talented Mr. Ripley* never states whether Tom is homosexual. Highsmith's reliance on gay stereotypes and codes produces a text that, in its opacity, resembles Tom's personality. Such a gay stereotype links Tom's performative ability to his proclivity for artifice. The affectation and affection for style that are often described as effeminacy in the gay male subject are simply attributed to class in the wealthy heterosexual male. Thus one can argue that Tom's homosexuality actually assists his class passing. His fondness for jewelry and exquisite clothing suits the upper-class masculinity of Greenleaf. Ironically, once achieved, this upper-class masculinity then smooths Tom's passing as straight. It was only his desire for Greenleaf that ever interrupted Tom's heterosexual attitude and cracked his facade. By killing Greenleaf, he eliminated that vulnerability. Now, he *has* Greenleaf. And he has Greenleaf's heterosexuality. Together they form his ideal homosocial *couple*, two heterosexual men (with the woman excluded).

As long as Tom is Greenleaf, he does not have to worry about being called a sissy. But when Freddie unexpectedly shows up at his door one day and Tom has to revert to the unsanctioned friend, paranoia returns. How did Freddie know his address? From an Italian fellow, Freddie says, a young kid whom he met at the Greco. Freddie asks if Tom is living here. No. Tom tries to send Freddie off to a restaurant where he claims Greenleaf is having lunch. Even though Freddie has already seen too much—Greenleaf's shoes and jewelry on Tom's person—Tom reckons he can pack hastily and disappear before Freddie returns. On his way out of the building, however, Freddie asks the landlady about Greenleaf's apartment and, upon hearing "only Signor Greenleaf," returns up the stairs. Again Tom murders without forethought. He clubs Freddie over the head with an ashtray, pours gin down him, carries his slouching body to the car, and dumps it along the Appian Way.

It seems logical that Tom kills Freddie because Freddie has discovered his fraud. Perhaps Tom killed too quickly and carelessly, but Freddie was on the verge of realizing that Tom had killed Greenleaf. But what really happened to make Tom kill? The following thoughts, which run through Tom's head as he stands over Freddie's body, scream out another reason.

> [H]ow sad, stupid, clumsy, dangerous and unnecessary his death had been, and how brutally unfair to Freddie. Of course one could loathe Freddie, too. A selfish, stupid bastard who had sneered at one of his best friends— Dickie [Greenleaf] certainly was one of his best friends—just because he suspected him of sexual deviation. Tom laughed at that phrase "sexual deviation." Where was the sex? Where was the deviation? He looked at Freddie and said low and bitterly: "Freddie Miles, you're a victim of your own dirty mind." (146–47)

Tom has been caught wearing Greenleaf's identification bracelet and tie clip. *Why* do men exchange jewelry? Freddie's reference to the Italian kid shamed Tom. What was Freddie insinuating when he asked if Tom lived here too? What does he suspect Tom and Greenleaf of *doing*? One of two things was going to happen if Freddie had been allowed to go on. He would either discover that Tom was passing as Greenleaf, or that Tom and Greenleaf had been passing as straight. Freddie's discovery would explode Tom's beautiful union of ego ideal and lover—"Freddie and his stinking, filthy suspicions" (146). Tom kills Freddie because Freddie sees his homosexuality. But Tom's incarnation is so replete that he feels Freddie arraigning Greenleaf as well. Tom kills Freddie for sneering at the man Tom recently killed. Tom is a psychopath.

Robert J. Corber describes the discursive construction of the homosexual in postwar U.S. culture as "an extended ideological struggle among competing political interests" (1993, 67). Homosexuals were considered to have both a fundamental identity different from heterosexuals and an unstable identity (or no identity at all). They were both recognizable via an established paradigm of gender inversion and, contradictorily, unidentifiable due to a lack of physical markers. Because of their ability to pass, homosexuals were considered national security risks. The Kinsey studies, which divulged that a large percentage of heterosexuals had engaged in homosexual behaviors, contributed to a perception of sexual identity as precarious. This indicated that both homosexuals and heterosexuals required surveillance and regulation, and exacerbated an already emergent heterosexual panic (Corber 1993, 63). Homosexuals were denied government jobs not only because they were susceptible to blackmail but because heterosexuals were susceptible to their sexual advances. Rather than offer clarification or redress, psychology depoliticized and personalized the "problem" of homosexuality. "Psychoanalysis was itself one of the major tropes of the postwar period" (Corber 1993, 10). As theories and diagnoses proliferated and contributed to the popular imagination, passing homosexuals became more "dangerous," their subversiveness presumed.

No wonder Tom Ripley would want to be heterosexual. As for Patricia Highsmith: "Barbara Grier [of Naiad Press, which republished Highsmith's *The Price of Salt*], who never met her in person but corresponded with her frequently, says Highsmith suffered acutely from 'internalized homophobia,' which was not surprising, she adds, considering the era in which she was raised. Highsmith's own attitude is put rather succinctly in a postscript to *The Price of Salt,* in which she states, 'I like to avoid labels'" (Peters 1995, 150). We would be wrong to seek a clear discourse on or picture of homosexuality in *The Talented Mr. Ripley.* What we can find is a shameless exploitation of cultural perplexity, in which, with existential absurdity, I choose to see a poststructural disobedience with regard to identity.

When it becomes necessary for Tom to retreat from his impersonation of Greenleaf, there is no return to a former self. Tom's second murder of Greenleaf is nothing but a name change. True, he can no longer lay claim to his life as Greenleaf. The suitcases he bought belong to Greenleaf (160). But then, so does the guilt of Freddie's murder (194). Fortunately, while Tom was Greenleaf, he forged a will leaving everything to Tom. This means that Tom, unsuccessfully interpellated by the U.S. work ethic, will continue in his travels—a rich man's "pleasant, rewarding, life's work" (289). It is not this fortune, however, that qualifies Tom for his elite station in life. Rather it is his poststructuralist recognition of artifice, which the novel indulges. Whereas in *Purple Noon* Greenleaf's body resurfaces to ensnare Tom, in *The Talented Mr. Ripley* surface evidence is an unreliable signifier. When police retrieve Greenleaf's suitcases, the fingerprints they reveal match those of Freddie's murderer: Greenleaf. Whereas the *homme fatal* must meet his fate at the end of the film, the poststructuralist of the novel has learned how to survive by being Greenleaf. "If you want to be cheerful, or melancholic, or wistful, or thoughtful, or courteous, you simply had to *act* those things with every gesture" (193).

I have argued that *Purple Noon* maintains a notion of fixed identity in relation to both class and sexual orientation while *The Talented Mr. Ripley* asserts identity as artificial and flexible. What in the film is class passing is a matter of becoming in the novel. In *Purple Noon,* Tom and Greenleaf are first separated by a triangular structure that inserts a woman between them and then collapsed into the oneness of narcissism. Although Sedgwick would recognize homosocial desire in the first, and Freud would recognize homosexual psychology in the second, both figurations disallow homosexual coupling. Despite the desires that bring Tom and Greenleaf together briefly on the boat, violence not only displaces sex but also reduces their number, once again, to one. By contrast, in *The Talented Mr. Ripley,* murder produces the perfect poststructuralist twosome. Tom not only becomes rich and heterosexual but also couples with Greenleaf. For Patricia Highsmith, this is possible because homosexuality and heterosexuality, like being, are not things.

Now Tom can love himself the way he loves Greenleaf. And Greenleaf will love him back. For the couple lives on. "It was his! Dickie's money and his freedom. And the freedom, like everything else, seemed combined, his and Dickie's combined" (294).[12]

notes

1. Philippe Greenleaf in the film, Dickie Greenleaf in the novel. Throughout the rest of this article I will refer to this character as Greenleaf. This has the disadvantage of formalizing him in relation to those characters referred to by first names. I must ask the reader to this overlook this unfortunate repercussion and bear in mind that my intent is simply to avoid confusion.

2. This European setting is not inconsequential. Pierre Bourdieu has noted how, from a U.S. perspective, Europe's cultural difference reads as class distinction. To U.S. homosexuals of the 1950s it also offered a respite from the oppression of Cold War labeling. Patricia Highsmith was also an American who lived much of her life in Europe. Although she did not come out publicly as homosexual until after the gay liberation movement, her lesbian novel *The Price of Salt* was published under the pseudonym Claire Morgan in 1952 (republished as *Carol* in 1984 under the name Patricia Highsmith).

3. A corresponding scene occurs in the novel but without the kissing when the two men escort a woman home in a taxi. "Dickie and Tom sat very properly on the jump seats with their arms folded like a couple of footmen" (p. 67). After dropping her off, Tom conjectures that other Americans would have raped her.

4. Although Sedgwick is describing a triangulation in mid-eighteenth to mid-nineteenth century English novels, I believe her model and arguments offer insight here. In chapter 2 of *Deviant Eyes, Deviant Bodies*, while discussing what I call the hypothetical lesbian heroine, I investigate a triangle formed by a man between two women. I argue that this male intermediary separates the women and prohibits homosexuality even as he connects them and eroticizes their relationship. I see this contradictory function of the intermediary operating in *Purple Noon*, not so much within specific triangulations but in their contrast to the murder scene, which seems to require Marge's absence for the men to achieve direct physical contact.

5. The original French title for the film was *Plein Soleil.* The English translation of the title in 1960 was *Broad Daylight* (*Variety*, March 23, 1960). *Purple Noon* is the title given the film upon its U.S. rerelease by Miramax in 1996. Whereas *Broad Daylight* rings of Tom's getting away with crime in the novel, the darkening that occurs in the change of the title to *Purple Noon* might appropriately suggest the noir element I attribute to the film.

6. Mirror images that substantiate my reading of this scene are abundant in the novel. As if disassociated from himself, Tom frequently surveys himself in mirrors. After Greenleaf's father first talks with him in a bar: "Slowly [Tom] took off his jacket and untied his tie, watching every move he made as if it were somebody else's movements" (10). During his visit to Greenleaf's father's Park Avenue home near the beginning of the novel: "Several times Tom got up with his drink and strolled to the fireplace and back, and when he looked into the mirror he saw that his mouth was turned down at the corners." Also, Tom observes he and Greenleaf as mirror images when they are together. During their trip to Rome: "They sat slumped in the carrozza, each with a sandalled foot propped on a knee, and it seemed to Tom that he was looking in a mirror when he looked at Dickie's leg and his propped foot beside him. They were the same height, and very much the same weight, Dickie perhaps a bit heavier, and they wore the same size bathrobe, socks, and probably shirts" (67).

7. In the novel, Tom's belief in this primary bond early on is explicitly bound with the homosocial. "[Marge] seemed to know that Dickie [Greenleaf] had formed a closer bond with [Tom] in twenty-four hours, just because he was another man, than she could ever have with Dickie, whether he loved her or not, and he didn't (70).

8. In the novel. soon after the scene in which Greenleaf catches Tom wearing his clothes before the mirror, Tom explicitly asks Greenleaf if he is in love with Marge. He answers, "No, but I feel sorry for her. I care about her. She's been very nice to me. We've had some good times together. You don't seem to understand that. . . . I haven't been to bed with her and I don't intend to, but I do intend to keep her friendship" (82). So Tom was correct when, in his fantasy before the mirror, he/Greenleaf tells Marge that he doesn't love her. However, by now Tom is (possibly) fantasizing more than actually exists between Greenleaf and Marge. This is not outlandish since Greenleaf is buying perfume to take back to Marge. Late in the novel, Tom looks back on this as one of his imaginary fears, "which, a couple of weeks later, he was ashamed that he *could* have believed. Such as that Marge and Dickie were having an affair in Mongibello, or were even on the brink of having an affair" (247).

9. Much earlier, when first arriving in Mongibello, Tom had bought himself a black and yellow bathing suit "hardly bigger than a G-string" (44).

10. In the novel, when Greenleaf asks Tom what kind of work he does, the answer seems to be anything but holding down a job. "'Oh, I can do a number of things—valeting, baby-sitting, accounting — I've got an unfortunate talent for figures. No matter how drunk I get, I can always tell when a waiter's cheating me on a bill. I can forge a signature, fly a helicopter, handle dice, impersonate practically anybody, cook—and do a one-man show in a nightclub in case the regular entertainer's sick. Shall I go on?' Tom was leaning forward counting them on his fingers. He could have gone on" (58). Tom then springs up and, with one hand on his hip, one foot extended, impersonates Lady Assburden, which enchants Greenleaf. But, of course, Tom's "talents" are more sophisticated when it comes to murdering and impersonating Greenleaf and murdering Freddie.

11. For a history of the psychiatric category acute homosexual panic, Comstock draws heavily on the work of Burton S. Glick, MD, in the 1950s. Interesting to my discussion here, Glick (1959) observes already in the 1950s many variegated descriptions of homosexual panic in the psychiatric discussions although not among case studies. (Homosexual panic as a psychiatric disorder was introduced in 1920.)

12. Another movie based on Highsmith's novel was recently made: *The Talented Mr. Ripley* (Anthony Minghella, 1999). Unfortunately it had not been released when I was writing this essay. Therefore I can only add a few brief remarks here. In some ways, the 1999 film creatively echoes my reading of the novel. For example, Tom's desire to *become* Greenleaf/heterosexual is suggested by his willingness to accept Greenleaf's responsibility for impregnating a woman. And, the scene in which Tom-as-Greenleaf celebrates Christmas by giving presents to "himself" suggests a couple. However, to a much greater degree, this film, like *Purple Noon* before it, prefers fixed identity, despite Tom's saying he'd rather be a fake somebody than a real nobody. Identity is deeply psychological here, and homosexuality is highly visible. Homosexuality is rendered through a somewhat confused combination of pre-Stonewall sexological discourse on gender inversion and post-Stonewall (retroactive) discourse on "the closet." The closet figures as a dominant motif in the film both visually via shots of doors, etc. and verbally via Tom's remarks about secrets in the basement of his self. Gender inversion allows for some identity play, for example, in the film's use of the song "My Funny Valentine," as does the film's proliferation of mirror/reflection scenes. Ultimately, the film offers a "gay" visibility that corresponds more to 1990s representation than to 1950s culture, along with contemporary mainstream assumptions about the psychological damage caused by closeted homosexuality in less enlightened days. In other words, the 1999 film *The Talented Mr. Ripley* exceeds the framework I have found useful in discussing Highsmith's novel and the film *Purple Noon*. It seems to me that the postmodern fluidity I discuss in relation to Ripley's character has been relocated onto the (1999) film itself, thus giving "homosexuality" a historically fluid status.

works cited

Bourdieu, Pierre. 1984. *Distinction*. Cambridge: Harvard University Press.

Comstock, Gary David. 1992. "Dismantling the Homosexual Panic Defense." *Law and Sexuality* 2.81: 81–102.

Corber, Robert J. 1993. *In the Name of National Security: Hitchcock, Homophobia, and the Political Construction of Gender in Postwar America*. Durham, NC: Duke University Press.

Freud, Sigmund. 1953–1974. "On Narcissism." In *The Standard Edition of the Complete Psychological Works of Sigmund Freud,* 24 vols., ed. James Strachey, 14–88. London: Hogarth Press.

Glick, Burton S., MD. 1959. "Homosexual Panic: Clinical and Theoretical Considerations." 129 *Journal of Nervous and Mental Disease* 20: 20–27.

Harrison, Russell. 1997. *Patricia Highsmith*. New York: Twayne Publishers.

Highsmith, Patricia. 1992 [1955]. *The Talented Mr. Ripley*. New York: Vintage Books.

Peters, Brooks. 1995. "Stranger than Fiction." *Out* (June): 70, 72, 150.

Purple Noon (*Plein Soleil,* René Clément, France 1960).

Sedgwick, Eve Kosofsky. 1985. *Between Men: English Literature and Male Homosocial Desire.* New York: Columbia University Press.

Straayer, Chris. 1996. *Deviant Eyes, Deviant Bodies: Sexual Re-Orientations in Film and Video.* New York: Columbia University Press.

Warner, Michael. 1990. "Homo-Narcissism; or Heterosexuality." In *Engendering Men: The Question of Male Feminist Criticism,* ed. Joseph A. Boone and Michael Cadder. New York: Routledge.

chris straayer

"emotional constipation" and the power of dammed masculinity

nine

deliverance

and the paradoxes

of male liberation

s a l l y   r o b i n s o n

John Boorman's 1972 film *Deliverance* is, inevitably, most often remembered for the humiliating scene of male rape at its center, with Bobby
Trippe (Ned Beatty) forced to "squeal like a pig" as he is sodomized by a
hillbilly who embodies a middle-class nightmare vision of "white
trash." This scene alone would be enough to qualify *Deliverance* as a film
about white, middle-class masculinity in crisis, but the larger crisis the
film explores has little to do with the rape. Indeed, as Linda Ruth
Williams (1994) points out, a "collective disavowal" rules both the film
and its critical reception, as the rape must be buried along with the male
bodies that keep piling up in its wake.[1] The imperative to disavow
knowledge of the rape is emblematic of the film's larger concern with
the perils of emotional, sexual, and "natural" expression and its concern, as well, with the equally perilous repression of emotional, sexual,

This essay is based on chapters 4 and 5 of *Marked Men: White Masculinity in Crisis*,
published by Columbia University Press, 2000.

and "natural" impulses. The film, Williams speculates parenthetically, "could be seen almost as a treatise on the many forms of repression" (9), and, we might add, their inadequacy. Damned if they do, and damned if they don't,[2] the men in Boorman's film are caught between two competing, but oddly complementary, truths structuring masculinity and male experience: male power is secured by inexpressivity, even as inexpressivity damages the male psyche and the male body.

These contradictory imperatives, to express or repress, are evidenced throughout the history of American masculinity, but came to the surface with particular force in the mid- to late 1970s, when questions about the future of straight, white masculinity became urgent following a full-scale critique of white and male privilege mounted by the liberation movements of that era. While the suppression of men's impulses has occasionally been understood as a necessary evil, if not a positive good, in the liberationist 1970s, blockage becomes synonymous with oppression, and a discourse on men's liberation begins to anatomize the "hazards of being male," as the title of Herb Goldberg's 1976 men's liberationist guidebook has it. The key term in Goldberg's diagnosis of the crisis in masculinity is "blockage," a trope he uses repeatedly to describe the condition of straight white professional men. Because men "have introjected the voices of their feminist accusers," they have accepted prohibitions against expressing a "heavily repressed male rage" (17). Self-control and control of others is not the route toward social power; it is, instead, a certain path toward ulcers, cancer, mental breakdown, and pain. The rhetoric of crisis that marks calls for "male liberation" evokes images of white male minds and bodies at risk, even as it springs from a recognition of white and male privilege. In order to negotiate between the privileges of patriarchal power and the guilt induced by the feminist critique of that power, the men's liberationists rely on a rhetoric of blockage and release that resurrects a bodily explanation for sexual difference and, subtly and ironically, works to naturalize the very power that is wounding men. Further, in constructing masculinity as dangerously blocked, the men's liberationists compete with an increasingly visible, post–women's liberation understanding of masculinity as dangerously *expressive* of violent emotions and sexuality. "Every man is a potential rapist," writes Marilyn French in *The Woman's Room* (1977), a diagnosis that ratifies the construction of masculinity as always on the verge of explosion, even as it argues *for* the blockage of male emotional and sexual energies. Against feminist analyses of male privilege, the male liberationists represent white, middle-class heterosexual men as both literally and metaphorically wounded. The affective and somatic go hand in hand in accounts of male (in)expressivity, as men's inability to express emotional and psychic distress produces bodily symptoms that point toward a representation of the male body as hysterical. The language in which male inexpressivity and men's liberation is articulated emphasizes the therapeutic value of male release and, as we will see, provides an important context for *Deliverance*'s representation of the "damming"— and, indeed, the *damning*—of masculinity. Stephen Farber (1972), reviewing the film for the *New York Times*, hinted at this context when he enjoined his readers to appreciate the film as a "major work, important for the artistic vision it brings to the urgent question of understanding and redefining masculinity" (300).

Nowhere was this question more urgent than in a body of texts concerned with diagnosing the "disease" of a "toxic" masculinity. In line with the shift from the political to the personal, these texts intent on liberating men from rigid gender prescriptions take the notion of disease quite literally. In *The Liberated Man* (1974), for instance, Warren Farrell uses a bodily metaphor to describe an emotional blockage and to argue that men's "emotional constipation" is a psychophysical condition that actually produces ulcers and other somatic symptoms:

> In [the standard workplace] atmosphere, men cannot help but be either emotionally incompetent (unable to handle emotions expressed by others) or emotionally constipated (unable to express their own emotions) or both. His emotional constipation leaves no outlet for his stomach but ulcers. One wonders if there is such a thing as a liberated top executive, or does the trip through the bureaucracy maim them all? (71)

Farrell means "liberation" literally, as well as figuratively, and the dominant trope of his and other studies of "constipated" masculinity is *flow*: if masculinity and men are to be liberated from the "harness" of the male role, emotional energies must be released. The bodily rhetoric marshaled to construct a masculinity in crisis assimilates the political to the personal, and thus depoliticizes the very language of "liberation" or revolution in which the male libbers stake their claims. Like the more recent men's movement encapsulated by Robert Bly's mythopoesis, male liberation in the '70s relied on anatomizing the male wounds caused by various forms of repression or blocked possibilities, coupled with a therapeutic program for male expression.

The idea that men are emotionally blocked owes its sense and its dominance to a particular construction of male heterosexuality and the male body: male sexual energies are constantly flowing, sexual arousal "automatic" and uncontrollable, and any blockage of these energies, and the substance through which those energies are expressed, leads either to psychological and physical damage or to violent explosions. "Emotional discharge," in Goldberg's terms, is

135

meaningful only in analogy to sexual discharge, and the blockage of male sexual and emotional energies becomes identically dangerous. Sexuality, like emotion, is framed as always potentially violent and explosive, a "natural" force that, according to Goldberg (1976), is endangered by the feminist tinkering with elemental impulses. Drawing on a social Darwinist conceptualization of biological imperatives, Goldberg joins popular sexologists in naturalizing, and depoliticizing, a particular construction of male heterosexuality. Kenneth Purvis, author of *The Male Sexual Machine: An Owner's Manual*, positions women and feminism against an entire evolutionary history when he argues that women are requiring men to go against nature in demanding that their lovers "suppress" the "primitive reflex" of speedy ejaculation; Purvis notes, "in our modern, sexually emancipated society, men are under increasing pressure to overcome this reflex, which has taken nature millions of years to evolve" (1992, 77).[3] In this frame, sensitivity to female sexual needs equates with repression of natural male impulses and evolutionary needs, and like the sexologist who touts a naturalized male release, Goldberg's analysis subtly constructs true, unrepressed masculinity as the antithesis of the sensitive male—invitations to cry notwithstanding. In doing so, he cements the analogy between violence, sexuality, and male "liberation"; sexual energies and violent impulses are psychophysical essences that naturally seek an outlet. If men continue to control their natural impulses, Goldberg warns, "emotional starvation" will eventually produce "drinking binges, wild driving, a blatantly destructive affair, or a violent outburst, among other [problems]. All are spoutings of the inner, hidden volcano" (1976, 69). The language of bodily trauma and natural explosions ratifies the construction of masculinity and the male body as dangerously blocked and works to construct an hysterical male body through which substantial male energies circulate without proper outlet.

The seemingly unimpeachable assumption that emotional and sexual forces *must* be set flowing constructs a blocked masculinity in order to legitimize various forms of release and, thus, to recuperate a masculinity that has suffered from the feminist critique of male power and privilege. The biologistic slant of men's liberation discourse, echoed by popular sexologies intent upon negotiating the feminist challenges to a particular construction of male heterosexuality, has the effect of naturalizing both a set of social relations and a narrowly conceived construction of the male body and the male psyche. Men's liberation discourse conflates emotional, sexual and violent "release" and suggests that men will suffer psychic and physiological wounds if no "outlet" can be found. Implicitly, if not explicitly, contemporary masculinity is diagnosed as hysterical, and the male body the canvas on which repressed trauma is written. The body "speaks" men's discontent, much as the feminist analysis of hysteria has suggested that the female body "speaks" the woman's oppression under patriarchy. The intertwining of the sexual with the emotional furthers such a diagnosis, as the men's liberationists represent men as torn between a "natural" imperative toward sexuality and a social imperative toward restraint. A disturbance in the field of sexuality, thus, codes a political trauma that the men's liberationists are loath to admit. The reluctance to blame women or feminism for men's disempowerment, then, can be read as a reluctance to trace the crisis of masculinity to the political. In this sense, male hysteria itself becomes both subject of, and subject to, repression in the discourse of male liberation.

The political realignments of this era form the more or less invisible backdrop to James Dickey's 1970 novel and, like the liberationist guide-books with which the novel shares a context, *Deliverance* is intent upon psychologizing the trauma its protagonists endure, and prescribing a personal, rather than social, "cure." The narrative follows pretty closely the men's liberation narrative, offering a diagnosis of blocked masculinity and a prescription for release. Critics of the novel have liberally used the language of repression and expression, blockage and release, to describe the narrative's treatment of male violence and the encounter with the "primitive" elements of human nature. James Griffith notes the major motif of "constipation, choking, and block-ing" in the novel, and Michael Glenday points to the novel's represen-tation of its narrator Ed as seeking "release from the alienation of his business life" (1984, 151) and from the "disabling stresses of city life" (153). The novel cloaks the contemporary crisis of white masculinity in an atavistic, ahistorical language of elemental impulses and their blockage, and the struggle over the meanings of dominant masculinity takes place not on a social stage, but rather as a battle between primi-tivism and civilization. For Dickey, the route toward remasculinization flows through the body, as the novel attempts to recover a biologistic essence of maleness that has been tamped down, or blocked, by civil society. Ed gets revitalized and remasculinized in the woods, having incorporated the experience of violence into his own body. The wounds he suffers during the trip are key to his remasculinization, as his earlier blockage gives way to an orgy of "release" that conflates the violent with the sexual, and frames his killing of the mountain man as a sexual and remasculinizing experience.

The novel draws heavily on what Gail Bederman (1995) has identi-fied as a nineteenth-century narrative invested in "remaking man-hood," a narrative that leans on a racialized discourse of "civilization" to reconstruct a white manhood widely understood as enervated and lacking the passion and virility that marks "primitive" masculinity. "Manliness," long thought to be contingent upon control, an iron will,

137

and, most of all, self-restraint, was the basis of civilization, white supremacy, and male power; but as the economy moved toward consumerism, and immigrant, African-American and working-class men became more visible as the embodiment of a powerful, physical masculinity, middle- and upper-class white men began to be anxious about that "manliness." Educators, medical men, and politicians undertook to solve what Bederman refers to as the "neurasthenic paradox" haunting middle-class white men:

> Only civilized white men had the manly strength to restrain their powerful masculine passions. But what if civilized, manly self-restraint was not a source of power, but merely a symptom of nerve-exhaustion and effeminacy? What if civilized advancement led merely to delicacy and weakness? Then the male body becomes not a strong storage battery, highly charged with tightly leashed masculine sexuality, but a decadent wreck, an undercharged battery with a dangerous scarcity of nerve force. (88)

This paradox was never "solved" in any final sense, and Bederman suggests that the conflict between manly self-restraint and a masculine expression of primitivism or savagery remains the hallmark of manhood in the Progressive Era. Indeed, as *Deliverance* suggests, this conflict still structures masculinity.[4]

The paradox of blockage and release that animates men's liberation discourse of the '70s replays the neurasthenic paradox in strikingly similar terms. Dickey's *Deliverance* follows its Victorian progenitors' attempts to negotiate this paradox by invoking Darwinism, natural selection, and a racialized discourse of male power.[5] The novel also suggests that the genetically flawed mountain men, unlike Ed, remain stuck in an earlier evolutionary phase, overwhelmed by, and not capable of schooling, their primitive impulses. The novel is resolutely ahistorical, framed as a timeless narrative that transcends any political moment. Dickey represents the male body as the source of power, an elemental force that must be recaptured and channeled if middle-class white men are to regain virility. Lewis, the virile survivalist, is the prototype of that powerful, white male body, and the novel offers a frank appreciation of it. It's important to stress the importance of the "damming" of that masculine, bodily power, though; for, the mountain men represent an inadequate solution to the problem of the primitive, a purely bodily expressiveness that threatens civilization and, not incidentally, white masculinity. Like the "savages" who people the pages of Victorian writings on the relationship between manly civilization and masculine primitivism, the mountain men have not evolved into a state where they can *use* their power, channel it and increase it. The revitalization Ed feels stems not only from the experience of whitewater rafting; it comes, as well, from his experience of violence controlled. The novel ends with the now dammed river running through Ed's veins, making of his body a living testament to the power of a released masculinity, and one made even more powerful for its "damming." The release of his male energies has also enabled him to release his creative energies; no longer involved only in the business aspects of his advertising firm, Ed rediscovers the aesthetic sense he had lost in the "feminizing" stream of white-collar work.[6]

While the men's liberationists and Dickey's novel are primarily interested in mapping out a new route to men's psychological health, Boorman's film offers a darkly pessimistic view of the therapeutic powers of male release and, instead, leaves its protagonists hysterically torn between repression and expression. Bobby never talks about the rape, Drew (Ronny Cox) must die because he cannot come to terms with the decision to suppress evidence of the hillbilly's death, and Lewis's (Burt Reynolds's) body literally implodes with the force of his unexpressed male energies, a bone hideously protruding from his leg and his entire body attempting to keep a lid on his agony. Ed's (Jon Voight's) face, as the camera plays over it, seethes with storm after storm of unexpressed emotion, as the violence escalates and the imperative to keep silent becomes more pressing. In the film, in contrast to the novel, Ed remains blocked and haunted, the most vivid image of his state remembered in the moment when he failed to shoot the arrow that would have easily killed the advancing mountain man, desperately whispering/shouting "Release!"[7]

The film registers the importance of popular ideas about evolution to this story, but ends up demonstrating the bankruptcy of the myth of masculinity that the novel embraces. The myth of the saving power of a primitive but restrained masculinity, the film suggests, is based on certain premises that are no longer tenable. In this respect, it's interesting to note that the film both exaggerates and ironizes Lewis as the figure of that myth. Lewis likens their trip to the "first explorers" discovering virgin territory and, thus, at least implicitly, positions the "rednecks" as the "redskins" of American frontier legend. Lewis speaks for evolutionary fitness, racial superiority, and male power, as he looks forward to a time when "the machines are gonna fail, the system's gonna fail. And then ... Survival. Who's going to survive. That's the name of the game." The visibility of the genetically deformed hillbillies functions to underline Lewis's credo as a version of early twentieth-century solutions to the problem of "race suicide" in the eugenics movement. Although Dickey's novel represents Lewis as far more sympathetic with the "natives" of this strange and foreign land, Boorman's

139

film emphasizes the difference between Lewis's strong, bounded, and powerful body, and the deformed and decadent bodies of the hillbillies. Yet, it is Lewis who suffers the most visible wound, and Lewis's body that comes to signify the failure of the myth of masculinity. Boorman uses Lewis to elaborate on the key contradictions structuring masculinity: Is masculinity secured by manly restraint of primitive impulses, or the expression of those impulses? In Boorman's treatment, the male body becomes, not the source of male power, but the text on which is written the emotional, physical, and social traumas of contemporary masculinity.

The film meditates on male inexpressivity, and represents emotion as a psychophysical force that gets trapped in, and thus endangers the stability of, the male body. Throughout the film, the body "speaks" the psychological and emotional condition of the group, and the wounds the men suffer offer visual evidence of the costs of male repression. Bobby's rape is the occasion for repression, and it sets in motion a representation of the hysterical male body.[8] Lewis's body, more than any other, registers the trauma of Bobby's rape, as the imperative to "forget" that trauma causes that previously hard and bounded body to implode, and a horrifyingly phallic projection of bone and tissue becomes visible on its surface. Prior to the rape, Burt Reynolds's body is represented as solid, impermeable, unpenetratable, bounded by the wet suit that sheathes him. The camera dwells lovingly on this body, eroticizing and objectifying it, as his bulging arms signify a physicality always on the verge of the excessive. A human phallus, Reynolds/Medlock is the very figure of the power of a "dammed" masculinity: stony-faced and emotionally inexpressive, Lewis's bottled-up power is quite literally written on his body. As if in reaction to the repression instituted almost immediately after the rape, Lewis's body appears to produce its own phallic wound from the inside, a kind of penetration imposed by his own body to mirror the penetration suffered by Bobby. Drew, too, appears to be penetrated (by a bullet), but the film's representation of his corpse as horribly mangled evokes nothing so much as an image of a masculinity strangling itself. But, as I noted at the beginning of this essay, the rape is merely the precipitating event; what truly traumatizes these men is the imperative to repress itself. The crisis figured in the film, thus, is produced by the conflict between a socially conditioned requirement that men not speak of a "feminizing" trauma and a naturalized, even biological impulse toward the expression of male rage that would align the protagonists with the "primitive" mountain men. That conflict might best be described as the conflict between nature and culture, biology and the social, and it is written on the hystericized bodies of the film's main characters in an exploration of what film theorists have recently suggested is a surprising prevalence of male hysteria (and masochism) in Hollywood film.

Paul Smith, in particular, has argued that male action and adventure films produce the male body as hysterical by following a three-stage narrative whose closure always fails to rein in the anxieties provoked by images of eroticized or wounded male bodies. These films, according to Smith (1989), frame the male body in a narrative that moves from objectification/eroticization, through a temporary destruction that "masochizes" the male body, and ends in a regeneration of that body and a reemergence of the phallic masculinity that was damaged by the second, and even the first, stage of the narrative (96–98). Questioning the critical impulse to see male masochism as subversive of traditional constructions of masculinity, Smith notes that such masochism appears almost always as a merely temporary violation of phallic norms, submitted to a narrative pull that inevitably works to rephallicize masculinity, in part by erasing or "forgetting" the (vulnerable) male body (102).[9] The hysteria produced by a never fully successful repression of the body and its wounds becomes the *subject*, not just the effect, of these films. These films are *about* the necessary repression of the male body, just as hysteria is an acknowledgment of the impossibility of "forgetting" the trauma of a visualized and masochized male body. The "hysterical moment" Smith isolates marks the inevitable return of the repressed body *and* the difficulty of representing the male body. The male body has to be repressed, its representation "blocked," even as this repression and this blockage perpetuates the hysteria and the physical and psychic trauma it is meant to manage. Male hysteria, thus, is the perfect vehicle to figure the particular dynamics of wounded white masculinity in the era I'm discussing: like the men's liberationists' somatization of the social and political symptoms of a decentered white masculinity, the hysterical male body registers, in personal and bodily terms, the trauma of the social.

In Boorman's *Deliverance*, Ed's facial expressions register emotional trauma and voicelessness, and his body bears the wounds of his repression as well.[10] While the rape precipitates the crisis that necessitates the repression that produces hysteria, it is in the process of killing or burying the mountain men's bodies that Ed gets wounded. Thus, the film literalizes the fact that the male body is "that which has to be repressed" (Smith 1989, 103): the efforts to literally *bury* the male body, and the impossibility of doing so, preoccupy the second half of the film. While Dickey's novel might be the story of "a modern mind in search of a body" (Beaton 1978, 294), Boorman's film is characterized by a futile attempt to escape the male body, a concern emblematized by the men's frantic efforts to hide the male bodies that keep piling up as they progress down the river. When Ed wrestles the man he has killed down the side of the cliff and into the water, the futility of getting rid of these bodies/the body becomes clear, as Ed and the corpse become entangled underwater. It is telling that the final image in the film is the return of the repressed, the inadequately buried body emerging from the now placid and still water of the man-made lake.

Deliverance is so intent on hystericizing the male body and, thus, exploring the dangers of male repression, that it breaks out of the action-adventure paradigm Smith analyses and, thus, might be seen to critique that paradigm. The film does, indeed, follow the first two stages of this narrative, distributing objectification and masochization among its four main characters, but most directly narrativized through Lewis. But, whereas the action films that Smith analyses "forget" the male body, its display and subsequent wounding, *Deliverance* deprives its characters and its audience of the transcendence of remasculinization and triumph over the body. If the film does nod to what Smith suggests is the father of all such narratives, by having Ed bear vaguely stigmata-like wounds to his chest and arms, no resurrection follows that wounding and no "deliverance" is, in fact, offered. Although there are any number of places where we might identify the dissolution of this narrative, and point to the male trouble caused by the transition from novel/original screenplay to film, one scene will serve nicely. That scene, important to both the screenplay and the film, takes place at the end of the journey, when Ed returns from getting his wounds dressed to find Bobby at the dinner table with the group of locals who are hosting them.

This scene *should*, according to Hollywood convention, herald the regeneration stage of the male action narrative, a healing of the wounds exposed in the earlier stages. Indeed, Dickey's screenplay uses this scene to literally register the "beefing up" of Ed's manhood, as he nourishes himself on a dinner presented as a well-deserved reward for having survived his ordeal. The point of the scene as Dickey writes it is to signify Ed's deep-down bodily *pleasure*: "Food begins to come at him from all sides. Shyly he takes a little of this and a little of that, and then he is eating madly, trying to thank the various people who are passing him things. He begins to wolf things down, in one of the best moments of his life" (Dickey 1972, 132). Even the sheriff, who greets the survivors' story with some skepticism, reads Ed as heroic and ratifies the "best moments of his life" view of the ending. "You done good," the sheriff tells him. "You'uz hurt bad, but if it wudn't for you, you'd all be in the river with your other man" (144).

The film, in contrast, makes this a far edgier scene, not least by the suggestion that these quite ordinary inhabitants of Aintry seem ridiculously removed from the inbred, redneck townspeople Lewis argued would hang the city boys for murder with not so much as a trial. But the tension that really animates the scene comes from the subtly but undeniably changed relationship between Ed and Bobby. Bobby, despite having arguably experienced the worst horrors of all on the river, appears protective of and anxious about a palpably vulnerable and quasi-hysterical Ed. For his part, Ed begins eating tentatively, as if his mouth is sore or his stomach unstable, only to burst into wracking sobs. This outburst is quite brief, and therein lies its pathos. Ed "releases" his pent-up emotions—once again, written on his expressively contorted face—but only for the briefest of spurts. We are left with the image of a man who desperately needs to be purged, but will remain emotionally constipated. The film thus joins the men's liberationists in representing the dangers of male repression as *bodily* dangers, as both the narrative and the camera construct the male body as a simmering cauldron of warring impulses that, lacking a proper outlet, are doomed to endlessly recirculate, poisoning the male body and the male psyche. But, unlike the men's liberationists and Dickey's novel, Boorman's film suggests that a therapeutic release of stunted male energies is no longer socially or personally tenable. Male *expression* is as dangerous as male repression, and the film resists romanticizing violent, sexual, or emotional "release."

The film may be best remembered, with a collective male shudder, for the demasculinization inherent in the "squeal like a pig" scene—a demasculinization that mirrors that threatened by the damming of the river—but I want to end by suggesting that the film's residual damage to constructions of masculinity be sought elsewhere. The film uses the mountain men to demonize the kind of release-oriented, "expressive" masculinity that underwrites the violence the film explores. It is significant that Lewis speaks of the damming of the Cuwalahassee as a "rape," and this point of view is reinforced by the images of destruction that Boorman juxtaposes with this dialogue in the opening frames of the film. The explosion that destroys the natural beauty of the landscape is, thus, paralleled to the explosion of primitive male energies evident in the mountain man's rape of Bobby. *Both* the "system" that Lewis excoriates *and* the savagery that Dickey's novel embraces are linked to a masculinity out of control, and, thus, Boorman's film offers no safe or positive alternative masculinity. The seeming opposition between the machine-driven forces of civilization and the machine-ignorant forces of primitivism falls apart, leaving the four protagonists with no route for the recuperation at the end of Dickey's narrative. Since release has been demonized, blockage becomes a mode for managing, although never curing, the trauma experienced by the men in the film. Not at all marked by sentimentality or nostalgia for a

143

time when men were men, the film's tone is more of a sad acknowledgment that the crisis in masculinity it chronicles has become incurable, indeed, the norm of a masculinity that can never find health through violence. All that is left is an image of an hysterical male body, torn between the competing, and mutually unsatisfying, imperatives to repress and express.

notes

1. Williams's point is nicely illustrated by a phenomenon reported by Jerry Bledsoe in a 1973 *Esquire* article, in which it becomes clear that audiences were willing to "forget" the trauma at the heart of the film. The release of *Deliverance* spurred a renewed interest in whitewater rafting in the South, as young men took to the water to experience firsthand the "adventure" experienced by Boorman's canoers. Bledsoe reports on the number of drownings produced by what law enforcement and rescue workers called the "*Deliverance* Syndrome," a syndrome marked by the absolute repression of the rape at the movie's center. As one enthusiast, a professor of microbiology at Emory University, described it, "'it's the last ultimate challenge.... This is the rites of passage, man. I mean, for some of us old guys it still is, I guess'" (230).

2. "Damned if You Do, and Damned If You Don't" is the title of James Griffith's 1986 essay on *Deliverance*, in which he argues that critics who complain that Boorman "missed the point" of Dickey's novel themselves miss the point that Boorman had his own agenda, his own story to tell. For Griffith, while Dickey focuses on how a previously "bored and rudderless" Ed "draws strength from nature and is restored to creativity and vitality," Boorman creates a different protagonist, one that "may be as easily found in suburban living: one whose unexamined comforts keep him away from any personal doubts" (47). While this reading seems partially right, it also seems too vague and lacks an argument about why, and to what effect, Dickey's story of "creative growth" diverges from Boorman's story of "self-betrayal" (58). In my view, as will become clear, the answer lies in what the two texts see as the future of a masculinity recently come under attack.

3. Like most post–women's liberation sexologists, Purvis undertakes to reassure men that liberated female sexuality need not mean the death of male sexuality. As this quotation suggests, however, the experts often seem to be trying to convince themselves. In general, recent sexologists hold two contradictory views: they directly reassure men that feminism and the rise of female sexual agency will "liberate" men from sole sexual responsibility and the performance ethos, while indirectly suggesting that this new model of sexuality is doomed to failure, since it goes against the "natural," "instinctual," and "biological" dispositions of male sexuality. The tactic of reassuring men, and in contradictory terms, dates back to postwar sexologists who, as Peter Lehman notes, reassure men that penis size doesn't matter, even as they themselves get "caught up in a phallic discourse" (146).

4. See, also, David Rosen for a discussion of how "muscular Christianity" negotiated this conflict; and David Leverenz for an analysis of its persistence into the present.

5. See Ronald T. Curran for a reading of the novel's use of evolutionary ideas.

6. Although Dickey does not explicitly identify the agents of Ed's blockage, his emotional flatness is linked to women and the feminizing effects of white-collar work. Ed sees women as "represent[ing] normalcy" that produces male boredom (29). Returning to work after the lunch at which Lewis introduces the idea of the canoe trip, Dickey's Ed comments on the suffocating feminization of his world. Entering the stream of returning secretaries with "barren, gum-chewing faces," Ed acknowledges that "I was of them, sure enough" (17). The feminized stream of secretaries flowing toward work provides the context against which the masculinized river can flow toward a recuperation of the male body and male psyche that has been endangered by the requirements of the social.

7. Critics who hail Dickey's novel as everything from a reworking of the masculine myth of regeneration through violence (Butterworth 1996 and others) to a meditation on Hobbesian political theory (Redenius 1986) have been almost unanimously hostile toward John Boorman's film. Dickey himself was unhappy with what Boorman did with his screenplay, lamenting that what gets lost in the translation is the "psychological orientation—the *being*—of the characters, their interrelations, their talk with each other, the true dramatic progression" (1972, 156–57). Literary critics excoriate Boorman for "bowdlerizing" Dickey's novel and the film for "perjur[ing] itself by falsifying the story material on which it is based" (Samuels 1972–73, 152; Beaton 1978, 306). What is "falsified" in the film is, precisely, the myth of masculinity at the heart of the novel. Similarly, what Dickey sees as the film's erasure of the "psychological orientation" of the characters and their stories is, in actuality, a critique of the psychological truths at the center of Dickey's novel. Critical discomfort with the film, I would suggest, has less to do with aesthetics and more to do with the fact that, while the novel follows a narrative trajectory tending toward the recuperation of masculinity, the film goes in exactly the opposite direction.

8. Joan Mellen (1977) argues that what the film must disavow is not just the rape, but the fact that the rape materializes the homosexual desires circulating among the characters; the "violence of these strangers allows the sexuality trembling between the men to surface" (318). In concluding that the film ultimately endorses the sublimation of these natural impulses, I think Mellen misses the import of Ed's continued trauma.

9. Smith holds Kaja Silverman, Gaylyn Studlar, and Leo Bersani among the writers who theorize masochism as subversive. His point is, in part, that all three theorize masochism outside of its narrative contexts and, thus, fail to track the twists and turns (toward subversion or recuperation) such narratives can take. This seems a valid critique, and one that might be extended to ask: why is it when masculinity becomes the object of study, that so many theorists (including Smith himself) look toward hysteria and/or masochism as the site of a nonphallic or alternative masculinity? What lies behind these narratives of wounding? I take up these questions in the introduction to my book, *Marked Men: White Masculinity in Crisis*. For other discussions of male hysteria, see Knee (1993); Kirby (1993); Fischer (1993); and Creed (1990).

10. See Adam Knee's (1993) reading of Clint Eastwood's *Play Misty for Me* for an argument that parallels mine here.

works cited

Beaton, James. 1978. "Dickey Down the River." In *The Modern American Novel and the Movies*, ed. Gerald Peary and Roger Shatzkin, 293–306. New York: Ungar.

Bederman, Gail. 1995. *Manliness and Civilization: A Cultural History of Gender and Race in the United States, 1880–1917*. Chicago and London: University of Chicago Press.

Bledsoe, Jerry. 1973. "What Will Save Us From Boredom?" *Esquire* 80, December, 227–33.

Butterworth, Ken. 1996. "The Savage Mind: James Dickey's *Deliverance*." *Southern Literary Journal* 28, 2 (spring): 69–78.

Cohan, Steven, and Ina Rae Hark, eds. 1993. *Screening the Male: Exploring Masculinities in Hollywood Cinema*. New York and London: Routledge.

Creed, Barbara. 1990. "Phallic Panic: Male Hysteria and *Dead Ringers*." *Screen* 31, 2 (summer): 125–46.

Dickey, James. 1970. *Deliverance*. New York: Dell.

———. *Deliverance*. [1972] 1982. (Screenplay). Carbondale and Edwardsville: Southern Illinois University Press.

Farber, Stephen. 1972. "'Deliverance'—How It Delivers." *New York Times*, August 20, II, reprinted in *New York Times Film Review Annual 1972*, 299–300.

Farrell, Warren. 1974. *The Liberated Man: Beyond Masculinity: Freeing Men and Their Relationships with Women*. New York: Random House.

Fischer, Lucy. 1993. "Mama's Boy: Filial Hysteria in *White Heat*." In *Screening the Male*, ed. Steven Cohan and Ina Rae Hark, 70–84. New York: Routledge.

Glenday, Michael K. 1984. "*Deliverance* and the Aesthetics of Survival." *American Literature* 56, 2 (May): 149–61.

Goldberg, Herb. 1976. *The Hazards of Being Male: Surviving the Myth of Masculine Privilege*. New York: Nash Publishing.

Griffith, James. 1986. "Damned If You Do, and Damned If You Don't: James Dickey's *Deliverance*." *Post Script* 5, 3 (spring/summer): 47–59.

Kirby, Lynne. 1993. "Male Hysteria and Early Cinema." In *Male Trouble*, ed. Constance Penley and Sharon Willis, 67–86. Minneapolis: University of Minnesota Press.

Knee, Adam. 1993. "The Dialectic of Female Power and Male Hysteria in *Play Misty for Me*." In *Screening the Male*, ed. Steven Cohan and Ina Rae Hark, 87–102. New York: Routledge.

Lehman, Peter. 1993. *Running Scared: Masculinity and the Representation of the Male Body*. Philadelphia: Temple University Press.

Leverenz, David. 1991. "The Last Real Man in America: From Natty Bumppo to Batman." *American Literary History* 3 (winter 1991): 753–81.

Mellen, Joan. 1997. *Big Bad Wolves: Masculinity in the American Film*. New York: Pantheon.

Purvis, Kenneth. 1992. *The Male Sexual Machine: An Owner's Manuel*. New York: St. Martin's Press.

Redenius, Charles M. 1986. "Recreating the Social Contract: James Dickey's *Deliverance*." *Canadian Review of American Studies* 17, 3 (fall): 285–99.

Robinson, Sally. 2000. *Marked Men: White Masculinity in Crisis*. New York: Columbia University Press.

Rosen, David. 1994. "The Volcano and the Cathedral: Muscular Christianity and the Origins of Primal Manliness." In *Muscular Christianity: Embodying the Victorian Age*, ed. Donald E. Hall, 17–44. Cambridge: Cambridge University Press.

Samuels, Charles Thomas. 1972–73. "How Not to Film a Novel." *American Scholar* 42, 1 (winter): 148–54.

Silverman, Kaja. 1992. *Male Subjectivity at the Margins*. New York and London: Routledge.

Smith, Paul. 1989. "Action Movie Hysteria, or Eastwood Bound." *differences* 1, 3 (fall): 88–107.

Studlar, Gaylyn. 1988. *In the Realm of Pleasure: Von Sternberg, Dietrich, and the Masochistic Aesthetic*. Urbana and Chicago: University of Illinois Press.

Williams, Linda Ruth. 1994. "Blood Brothers." *Sight and Sound* 4, 9 (September): 16–19.

"as a

mother

cuddles

a child"

sexuality and masculinity

in world war II

combat films

robert eberwein

Anthony Easthope, commenting on *The Deer Hunter* (Michael Cimino, 1978), observes:

> In the dominant versions of men at war, men are permitted to behave towards each other in ways that would not be allowed elsewhere, caressing and holding each other, comforting and weeping together, admitting their love. The pain of war is the price paid for the way it expresses the male bond. War's suffering is a kind of punishment for the release of homosexual desire and male femininity that only the war allows. In this special form the male bond is fully legitimated. (1990, 66)

Mark Simpson expands on Easthope's argument, calling "the war film ... perhaps the richest of all texts of masculinity" (1994, 212). In *Memphis Belle* (Michael Caton-Jones, 1990) and *A Midnight Clear* (Keith Gordon, 1992), he says,

> The war film not only offers a text on masculinity and
> how to take one's place in patriarchy, it also offers a
> vision of a world in which the privileges of heterosexual
> manhood can be combined with boyish homoeroti-
> cism—a purely masculine world awash with feminin-
> ity.... The lesson that the buddy film has to teach boys
> (and remind men) is that "war" is a place where queer
> love can not only be expressed but *endorsed*—but only
> when married to death. Death justifies and romanti-
> cizes the signs but not the practice of queer love. (1994,
> 214–15)[1]

Easthope and Simpson offer a totalizing reading of displays of the
feminine and of affection in the war film. In effect, they see representations of behavior readable as feminine and/or homosexual as validated
by suffering and death. But examination of the combat films made
during World War II suggests that their arguments need qualifying.
Although their readings may be appropriate for certain contemporary
films, they ignore the complexities of the earlier films' relation to their
sociocultural-historical framework.

If we look at a variety of discourses—training, documentary, and
Hollywood Films; academic and popular writing; advertisements—we
find that two issues pertaining to male sexuality were discussed:
venereal disease and homosexuality. Neither could be addressed in
commercial Hollywood films because of the restrictions of the Production Code Administration. Venereal disease was treated with varying
degrees of specificity in training and documentary films and in professional and academic journals as well as popular magazines. Although
homosexuality received much less attention, two topics in particular
got scrutiny: the effectiveness of the preinduction physical to screen
recruits and the possible effects of military life on sexuality.

Examinations of the discourses mentioned above reveal the extent
to which concerns about homosexuality are present as a kind of structuring absence in representations of male sexuality. One of the most
complex signifying practices that occurs during World War II involves
showing males in ways that connect them to the feminine or that present scenes of non-aggressive close physical contact. When this happens at the level of the mise-en-scène or the image, the implications
are negotiated by the narrative or by dialogue and commentary.

As I have indicated elsewhere, training films made for soldiers displayed graphically the results of male sexuality by showing enactments
of interactions with prostitutes and contagious women and by revealing the effects of venereal disease on genitals. Such films were part of a
larger campaign involving public service documentaries as well as pro-

fessional and popular literature dealing with the threats posed by venereal disease (Eberwein 1999a, 63–101).

The campaign against venereal disease was one part of the government's efforts to protect servicemen while acknowledging their sexual
needs. In 1941, Joel T. Boone, the captain of the Naval Medical Corps,
spoke at a conference on hygiene. Rather than deny the sexual needs
of men, he urged his auditors to recognize that "armies and navies use
men. Men of the very essence of masculinity. Men in the prime of
life.... [Soldiers'] education befits nature, induces sexual aggression,
and makes them the stern dynamic type we associate with men of an
armed force. The sexual aggressiveness cannot be stifled" (116). He
argued: "We cannot legislate morals, and the passing of absurd laws
will not bury instincts upon which the very fabric of our race is spun.
We can only hope to control and educate"—tasks he saw being accomplished by training films and instruction (117).

Writing in *The American Mercury* in 1941, Irwin Ross observed that
"the sex life of its 1,500,000 charges is one of the biggest headaches of the
U.S. Army. The problem is to keep the men both happy and clean"
(667). Although Ross did not advocate encouraging prostitution (a
suggestion that had been made by others), he thought that by denying
men such an outlet and only offering sublimating activities like sports
and recreation, the military risked "turn[ing] the Army camp into a
penal institution." Moreover, he was concerned about the effects of
"enforced abstention" on the mental health of the men and the possibility that this "may encourage homosexuality" (668).

The concern about homosexuality appeared in a number of venues.
For example, a report in *Time* magazine on the preinduction physical
describes the conditions under which the examination is conducted:
"Recruits come before the psychiatrist when they are worn out from
physical tests, completely naked, identified only by a mercurochrome
number on their chests." These short psychiatric examinations were
designed to identify those who couldn't make it in battle, among them
"'The Mama Boys' who in peacetime (when there is no selective service) choose invariably the Navy and find that, though the sea may be
'Mama,' the Navy is definitely 'Papa,' and blow up promptly in the
training stations with the shock of this discovery" ("In Uniform &
Their Right Minds," 37). This report came out *before* the publication
later in 1942 of what would become the more commonly cited source
of the expression "Mama's boy," Philip Wylie's vitriolic and disturbing
screed *Generation of Vipers* (184–204).[2]

Although neither the *Time* report nor Wylie directly connects the
"Mama's boy" to homosexuality, the suggestion of effeminacy is
clearly implicit. It is such behavior that C. L. Wittson, a Naval psychiatrist, discusses in an article in *American Journal of Psychiatry* written shortly

before World War II began. Describing "The Neuropsychiatric Selection of Recruits," he explains that after the physical, the recruit is in "an ideal condition in which to be examined from a naval psychiatric viewpoint. He is naked and stripped of his individuality" (1943, 639). "The psychiatric examination takes place in a private room immediately following the physical examination while the recruit is undressed and usually still tense" (642). "The recruit who mincingly enters the office immediately arouses a suspicion of homosexuality, either overt or sublimated" (643).[3]

In addition, *Psychology for the Fighting Man* (1943), a book published in the *Infantry Journal* and circulated among soldiers, openly acknowledged the possibility of encountering homosexual behavior. The collective authors, a committee of the National Research Council, included such notable figures as G. W. Allport of Harvard and S. A. Stouffer of the Special Services Division of the War Department. The authors note that the preinduction screening mentioned above may fail: "Although medical officers at the induction centers try to keep them out of the Army, a sexually abnormal man who finds satisfaction only with other men may get in" (340). They discuss the possibility of what would later be called situational homosexual activity and advance a position that seems to anticipate the current argument of "don't tell, don't ask" (340). But homosexuality is clearly considered considered a negative form of sexual behavior.[4]

To see how those in the period negotiated their concerns about male sexuality, let me begin with a film, an essay, and a photograph. In *Thirty Seconds over Tokyo* (Mervyn LeRoy, 1944), after Ted Lawson (Van Johnson) and his crew participate in the surprise bombing of the Japanese capital, they try but fail to return to their base. Nearly out of fuel, Lawson attempts to land the plane but crashes into the water. The survivors drag themselves to the shore. Hugging and supporting each other, the men cry out in pain and anguish as they are pelted by rain. The dazed Lawson is at the center of a triangular formation including Thatcher (Robert Walker), McClure (Don DeFore), who rests his head on Lawson's shoulder, and Davenport (Tim Murdock), whose head rests on Lawson's thigh. The camera dollies in to Lawson's face and the image dissolves to his memory of a scene we saw earlier as his pregnant wife Ellen (Phyllis Thaxter) reassured him: "Ted, Look at me. The baby and I won't ever need anything. The baby is why I know you're coming home." Lawson rises, apparently coming out of his daze, and stumbles away from the men as one of them calls out his name.

The face of Captain Eddie Rickenbacker appears on the cover of the January 25, 1943, issue of *Life* magazine, the first of three issues containing installments of his "Pacific Mission" in which he recounts a remarkable story of heroism and survival. Rickenbacker was at that time the most decorated and successful pilot in American history. When his plane ran out of fuel in October 1942, he and the seven other men of the crew ditched in the Pacific Ocean and, in two rafts, drifted for twenty-one days before being rescued. After exhausting their meager food supply—four oranges, which they divided among themselves in the first few days—they lived on raw fish, a gull, and rain water collected during squalls. One of the men, Sgt. Alexander Kacmarczyk, weakened before the flight, became ill and did not survive the ordeal. Here is Rickenbacker describing how he tried to help: "I asked . . . to change rafts with Sergeant Alex, thinking that Alex might rest better. It took the combined strength of Bartek, DeAngelis and myself to move him. I stretched him on the lee side of the bottom of the boat and put my arm around him, as a mother cuddles a child, hoping in that way to transfer the heat of my body to him during the night. In an hour or so his shivering stopped and sleep came—a shallow sleep in which Alex mumbled intermittently in Polish—phrases about his mother and his girl 'Snooks.' I kept Alex there all night, the next day and night, and the twelfth day. . . . I knew he couldn't last many hours longer. . . . We had to lift him like a baby" (99–100). The essay includes a drawing of Rickenbacker cuddling the doomed sergeant (99).

In the same year that Rickenbacker's report was published, Edward Steichen, the famous photographer who had directed the Army photographic unit in World War I and who now had a commission in the Navy (even though, at 62, he was well over the age limit), became chief of Naval photography. In November he was assigned to the USS *Lexington*, an aircraft carrier in the Pacific. One of the pictures he took within his first few weeks on board is "Sailors Sleeping" (see figure 1). Three men are intertwined: one lies face down on the deck; a second rests his head on the former's back; a third rests his head on the second's stomach. A fourth man, awake, sits facing them a few feet away, looking off to his left.

In *The Blue Ghost* Steichen comments on this and similar photographs of sailors at rest: "There are not many methods of taking things easy on a carrier, but we try all of them. Reading, studying, sleeping, poker, and in secluded corners maybe a nice little crap game" (1947, 54). "The men, in small groups, are sprawled around the deck; some choose the hot sun on the open deck, others park themselves in the shade of a plane's wing; they pillow up for each other in a fine earthly fellowship, reminiscent of colts resting under a tree or alongside the fence of a pasture, the head of one colt is draped over the neck of another, or again, something in the manner of a litter of puppies, are curled up over, under, and about each other" (58). Steichen's caption for the photograph is: "Here we sprawl like pups in a kennel—pillow up together" (59).

The film, the account, and the commentary share the negotiating

Sailors sleeping on flight deck of the USS *Lexington* (80–G–471182). Courtesy National Archives and Records Administration.

tendency I see manifested in representations of sexuality during World War II. *Thirty Seconds* establishes a mise-en-scène consisting of a grouping of intertwined, weeping men and then counteracts any possible sexual implications of the bond by cutting to the leader's memory of his wife whose comment on their unborn baby is followed by his breaking away from the men. Rickenbacher's account of the cuddling with the doomed sergeant qualifies the description of maternal intimacy not only by virtue of the exigencies of survival but also by recounting how the man called out for his girlfriend. Steichen's description of the men in his photograph explains the bonding figuratively in terms of the men's similarity to animals. The various kinds of qualifications illustrate a phenomenon found throughout films and other kinds of wartime discourses in which the heterosexuality of the men in reaffirmed.

All three are expressions of people in the period responding to manifestations of behavior that foreground the potentialities of male sexuality outside its traditional heterosexual framework. In fact, there seems almost to be a curious compulsion to show something in the mise-en-scène and images that *requires* its own containment and inoculation through negotiation.[5]

Extensive examples of the kinds of qualifications of representations of feminine and maternal behavior and of affectionate and supportive physical contact appear in the combat film and in other manifestations of contemporary culture, such as magazine advertisements. First, in films we find men shown positively or sympathetically enacting behavior associated with the feminine. For example, in *Bataan* (Tay Garnett, 1943), as the malaria-delirious Rameriz (Desi Arnez) succumbs, his medic stands watch over him, offering him water. Rameriz momentarily confuses him with his "mother," for whom he calls out. In addition, when Purckett (Robert Walker) is unable to bind his own wounds, he is assisted by Todd (Lloyd Nolan). As Todd applies a tourniquet, Purckett looks at him like a child lovingly admiring his mother, and Todd responds negatively by tightening the cloth roughly. The second scene in particular plays it both ways: showing a male acting in a maternal function and then rejecting the appreciative response this evokes in the soldier he helps.

In *Destination Tokyo* (Delmer Davies, 1943), Cary Grant as Captain Cassidy is tough and assured. When one of the sailors (Robert Hutton) on the submarine needs an emergency appendectomy, Cassidy participates in the operation by administering ether to the young boy who, as he would at home, says his prayers before going to "sleep" under the anesthetic. Framed with his hands clasped around a towel over the face of the boy, Cassidy displays maternal tenderness. As the kid comes out of the anesthetic after the successful surgery, Cassidy's head is practically resting on the boy's in order to hear what he is saying: the continuation of his prayers. Earlier, though, before news of the emergency reaches him, Cassidy has been seen tenderly recounting a story about taking his young son to the barbershop. The highlight of his year, he claims, was hearing his son declare that Cassidy was his dad. Thus Cassidy's maternal capacities are complemented by a monologue about his paternal role.

An advertisement sponsored by Nash Kelvinator that is reminiscent of the scene I mentioned in *Bataan* appeared in *Time* (May 29, 1944: inside cover). It shows a wounded and apparently dying soldier being ministered to by a medic. The top caption "MOM . . . " is followed by the supposed commentary of the medic:

> It was damned hard to just lie there . . . and grind our teeth together and tighten our guts because each time he cried "Mom" . . . it tore out our insides. . . . I put a syrette into his arm and then another, and he relaxed and his head fell back and his eyes were still wide but I could tell he thought his mother was there by his side.

Here the medic who is perceived as a mother accedes to the role assigned him by the wounded man in a manner that reinforces his masculinity, underscored by the language ("damned hard," "grind our teeth," "tighten our guts").

Any discussion of sexuality has to deal with behavior associated with the feminine that is not medically related. This is manifested most overtly in musical scenes in which men dance with one another. Although not a combat film as such, *This Is the Army* (Michael Curtiz, 1943) with its numerous drag numbers is relevant. Significantly, the film was Warner Brothers' most successful film of the decade and the highest grossing film made during the war. As I have indicated more fully elsewhere, *This Is the Army* negotiates the problematic of white military men in drag by using a number of strategies (Eberwein 1999b). Some of them are obvious, such as overstated disavowals of femininity by one character who objects to dressing up like a woman or by having the men's hairy chests very much in evidence.[6]

Equally relevant here are numerous scenes in films showing men who are not in drag dancing together. One such moment occurs in *The Story of a Transport*, which documents how the Wakefield, a Coast Guard ship, is used as a transport vehicle for the Army (1944). One sequence displays how the Coast Guard personnel entertain the troops by playing music for them. As a small band plays, two soldiers dance to the lively music ("One O'Clock Jump"). They are joined shortly by two Coast Guard sailors. This activity is presented as perfectly routine, and is followed by shots indicating that dancing is one among many common elements of shipboard life, such as boxing and exercising.

In *V.D. Control: The Story of D.E. 733*, a training film on venereal disease made by Paramount for the Navy (1945), the depiction of shipboard life includes one scene in which two sailors dance to "Bell Bottom Trousers." The ship's pharmacist sees them and asks: "What's the matter with you guys? Can't you wait?" One of the dancers responds: "Just practicing."

The most interesting example of male dancing occurs in *Guadalcanal Diary* (Lewis Seiler, 1943). In one scene on board ship, two Marines (one shirtless) dance to "Chattanooga Choo-Choo," which is being played on a harmonica. They are clearly presented as entertaining their fellow troops, who are watching appreciatively. Taxi Potts (William Bendix) enters (holding the group's mascot dog) and talks about a conversation he had with a woman who was rejecting his advances. The dance continues, off camera, and then is seen again as Malone (Lloyd Nolan) announces lights out and "quit your skylarking." The dance concludes as the shirtless man jumps into the arms of his partner. Shortly after, another scene below deck begins as we see Taxi dressed in semi-drag as an Hawaiian "woman" dancing a hula. The ship's chaplain Father Donnelly (Preston Foster) enters and watches Taxi, who, in mild embarrassment takes off some of his makeshift costume. The music changes from the Hawaiian melody to an Irish tune, and Taxi and Father Donnelly dance a jig, concluded with an arm-in-arm spin.

Thus the dancing in these examples is qualified in a way that assuages any problematic issues of sexuality. In *Transport*, it is entertainment and part of the usual physical exercise routine; in *D.E. 733*, it is in preparation for a later date; in *Diary*, it is entertainment presented in a context in which heterosexuality is confirmed through conversation and inoculated by the folk dancing.

Numerous scenes of close physical bonding that are qualified also appear in the combat films. For example, in *Wake Island* (John Farrow, 1942), as Smacksie (William Bendix) and Joe (Robert Preston) prepare for a final and deadly assault by their Japanese attackers, the former puts his hand briefly and tenderly on Joe's thigh. In the same scene, the doomed Smacksie and Joe joke about what they're going to miss because of their imminent deaths: "How many blondes are there that we didn't get to?" Thus, the sign of affection is qualified by the testimonial to heterosexuality.

The sharing and exchange of cigarettes serves as a significant way of demonstrating bonding among men in combat films. Virtually every new recruit into the armed services had to watch John Ford's *Sex Hygiene* (1941), a training film about venereal disease. Included in that film is a clear warning about sharing cigarettes. Later training films did not include this caveat, but, to the extent that sharing had at some point been presented as a potential risk, it is interesting to see how often the exchange of cigarettes signals the depth of a bond and of trust among soldiers. For example, *Immortal Sergeant* (John Stahl, 1943) contains one of the most remarkable smoking scenes in film. Out of supplies, four men led by Colin Spence (Henry Fonda) share a final cigarette. Spence begins with a couple of drags and then passes it around to the men who silently puff and observe the others, until the camera pans down to show it being extinguished. The prolonged scene suggests the intense intimacy that binds the men together, even though there has been personal friction among them earlier.

Spence, the person who initiates the sharing, has become increasingly aggressive and courageous up to this point in the narrative, especially after the death of his mentor, Sergeant Kelly (Thomas Mitchell). As we watch him turning into a tough soldier, flashbacks show the development of love between him and Val (Maureen O'Hara). In the penultimate scene, now a wounded hero, he lies in a hospital bed ordering Benedict, a somewhat unmanly reporter (Reginald Denny) who has been an apparent rival for Val's affections, to wire her a proposal of marriage. Spence threatens him if he doesn't do it: "You see

I'm not the man you may have thought you knew. I'm another man altogether now, and a good one. That's not a bad thing for a man to find out, or a nation."

Guadalcanal Diary contains two remarkable scenes demonstrating male affection. The film opens with a shipboard service led by Father Donnelly and then shows the men relaxing. Most are shirtless and closely linked physically. Taxi Potts forms the apex of an extended triangular group of figures. He cradles the head of a shirtless Sosse (Anthony Quinn), on whose arm another Marine's head rests; the head of a shirtless Chicken Anderson (Richard Jaeckel) rests on Taxi's stomach, close to the groin, and Taxi's hand is on Chicken's bare chest. In the second scene, shortly afterward, as the men hear their orders, Sosse rests his hand on Chicken's chest.

The physical intimacy in these scenes displayed in the mise-en-scène is qualified by the conversations that occur. In the first Sosse contemplates which of his two girlfriends he would be dating were he home and opts for both; Taxi talks about baseball. In the second, the bonding between Chicken and Sosse takes place as they hear orders that will send them into dangerous circumstances.

There are other examples worth noting, specifically one with John Wayne. In *They Were Expendable* (John Ford, 1945), playing Rusty Ryan, he puts his hand briefly and tenderly on the shoulder of John Brinkley (Robert Montgomery) as their plane prepares to leave Bataan. Wayne's behavior is qualified by the fact that he has been shown to be clearly in love with Lt. Sandy Davyss (Donna Reed). In his review of the film, Bosley Crowther calls Wayne "magnificently robust," and obviously did not read that sign of tenderness toward Montgomery as problematical in terms of Wayne's sexuality because his masculinity has already been established so forcefully (25).[7]

Some scenes in which male sexuality is affirmed and inoculated occur in war films that refer humorously to homosexuality. For example, in *Gung Ho!* (Ray Enright, 1943), one of the soldiers on a troop ship asks Transport (Sam Levene): "Got any pictures of pin-ups?" After Transport answers that he doesn't have pin-up pictures, the soldier says "I got a picture of me in a bathing suit. Want me to autograph it?" A voice (unidentified) asks: "Where is it?" and produces a comic double take from Levene.

In *Wing and a Prayer* (Henry Hathaway, 1944), one husky character lying on his bunk who is swatted on the behind by another walking through the cabin says: "Do it again! I love it." But that moment is qualified by a major scene in the film in which a large group of men watch *Tin Pan Alley,* with Betty Grable and Alice Faye. They hoot appreciatively at the display of the dancers' bodies and the stars, and become irate when the film breaks.[8]

In some cases, potentially problematic behavior is so exaggerated that it needs only humor to qualify it. For example, in *Immortal Sergeant*, one soldier rips off a towel from another man, leaving him naked (but unseen by the camera), producing a brief comic moment. In *Objective Burma* (Raoul Walsh, 1945), we see Gabby (George Tobias) washing out his socks in a pond. Ordered to get moving, he responds in a purposely inflected feminine tone: "I'm washing out my last pair of nylons." Another character asks for a hand with his gear: "Give me a hand with my bustle," and is told: "Very fine, sweetheart. If it doesn't work, you can bring it back." These moments did not deter the *New York Times* reviewer of the film from speaking of the "hard bitten story of a group of tough, tight-lipped paratroopers" (Review 15).

Commenting not on these films but on various defensive strategies used by servicemen in general to deal with their sexual drives and potential homosexual impulses, Allan Bérubé (1991, 37) and John D'Emilio (1983,25) both draw on the work of psychiatrist William C. Menninger. In *Psychiatry in a Troubled World* (1948), Menninger suggests that, among the ways servicemen found to accommodate the absence of women, "The physical substitutes were varied. . . . There were numerous psychological substitutes used: possession of 'pin-up girl' photographs; an increased interest in 'dirty' stories, in profanity, and in homosexual buffoonery" (224).

But such buffoonery needs to be understood in the larger context of representations of sexuality and masculinity within American culture during World War II. Although Bérubé in particular cites popular magazine advertisements and articles that can be read as having a potential homosexual appeal (1991, 298, 341), he fails to see that the very presence of such representations in the widely read magazines demonstrates the extent to which films and advertisements were constantly reassuring their audiences that there was nothing about which they should be concerned because male heterosexuality was validated by emphasizing masculinity.

For example, three advertisements worth noting that Bérubé does not mention involve a play on masculinity apparently being undermined by femininity. First, one for Monsanto Chemicals in *Newsweek* shows the drawing of a shirtless soldier holding a slip in one hand and a lady's undergarment in another, with the caption: "Hey! What goes on here? *Yes, we know—this couldn't actually happen!* You'll never encounter any lady whatcha-ma-callits in Army laundry." The ad copy goes on to argue that the detergent will work for the troops, no matter the quality of the water they have to use; hence it will be fine for "Mrs. Housewife" as well (December 7, 1942: back cover).

An advertisement for the Bead Chain Manufacturing Company in *Newsweek* shows a drawing of a tough-looking soldier with the caption:

"Yeah, I wear a necklace—but brother, I ain't no sissy. Every mother's son of us ... and daughter, too ... in the Army, Navy, Marine Corps and Coast Guard wears identification tags around his neck" (August 9, 1943, 2).

B. F. Goodrich touts its newest contribution to protecting sailors on ship decks, a helmet with special rubber lining, by displaying a sailor in uniform standing before a mirror. He adjusts his helmet in a pose that suggests a woman before a mirror. The caption reads, "Latest fashion for ocean cruises," and the copy explains: "Because of dive bombers, it's healthier for exposed gunners on ship decks to wear steel helmets. But for real protection a helmet has to fit"—hence the advantages of their new process (*Time*, July 27, 1942, 1).

In different ways all three ads confirm not only that the servicemen are still clearly male but also that their toughness and masculinity are in no way compromised by being linked to the feminine. The representations of the feminine are of the same order as Gabby's "washing out [his] last pair of nylons"—something understood as strictly performative. Displays of overtly and stereotypical feminine behavior or images of apparent confusion about gender identity are instantly qualified in the ads by the valorization of masculinity (the tough soldier, the guy who's not a sissy, the sailor on his way to battle), hence reassuring readers about the males' heterosexuality.

I want to conclude by talking about something that viewers never saw in commercial combat films. The PCA restrictions precluded any display of the naked male body. Such controls obviously did not apply to training films, in which numerous graphic shots of genitals were presented to show men the physical effects of venereal disease, and in which naked servicemen were not uncommonly shown in showers. But the American public did occasionally see photographs of naked soldiers in *Life* and drawings of them in certain advertisements.[9] I'm interested in the extent to which the display of naked, bathing men is accompanied by qualifying material similar to what we have already seen. *Life* showed the naked male body in a state of sexual innocence, a theme that was constantly inflected in war films, mainly through the raw recruit or kid.[10]

Life's extended coverage of the assault on Guadalcanal included two full-page photographs of naked and semi-naked troops. The "Picture of the Week" for February 8, 1943, shows more than two dozen men bathing and relaxing in a river; frontal nudity is shadowed out, but not that from behind. The explanatory caption is:

> The gray American transports steamed in near to the
> beaches of Guadalcanal. Over the sides into landing
> boats went thousands of American troops, hot and
> bearded and dirty from weeks at sea with no fresh water

to wash in. As soon as their boats crunched up on the same and their tents were pitched and their foxholes dug, the troops wandered over to a nearby river, gratefully pulled off their clothes, plunged into the cool fresh water. (24)

The caption on the photograph itself repeats the notion of their gratitude for the relief afforded by the refreshing water. Three weeks later, *Life* ran a photograph of naked and partially clothed soldiers washing their clothes, again with dorsal but not frontal nudity ("Guadalcanal," 68).

This display of naked males relaxing and washing themselves or clothing in *Life* was followed by a remarkable series of six ads run by the Cannon towel company on the inside covers of the same magazine from August 1943 to June 1944 in which naked or partially clothed servicemen were shown bathing in comic scenes. These "true towel tales" were credited to various sources such as "a doctor in the medical corps" (August 16, 1943) or "a sergeant in the tank corps" (January 3, 1944). Some reveal the kind of "homosexual buffoonery" referred to earlier. In the ad for the October 4, 1944, issue a flier throws a bucket of water on a man emerging from a galvanized washing tub, thus sending his towel flying. This is reminiscent of the scene mentioned in *Immortal Sergeant* when a soldier rips off a man's towel. The "Buna Bathtub" ad, the last in the series (June 26, 1944), shows a naked soldier posed seductively with a palm frond over his genitals. (In its coverage of Buna Village, *Life* had run another photograph of naked soldiers bathing ["Battle of Buna," 21]). Each of the ads contains a small inserted drawing of a different woman discreetly covered by a towel with the same accompanying caption alerting readers that they may encounter less of a selection in towels because "Millions of Cannon Towels are now going to the Armed Forces." The presence of the woman not only evokes the typical Cannon Towel ads which, prior to and after the true towel campaign, featured typical cheesecake illustrations in which women were the objects of visual pleasure (for example, one in the October 2, 1944 issue). It also inserts an image that negotiates the problematic of male sexuality by reminding viewers that women, not men, are the traditional objects of sexual desire for these tough men.[10]

The significance of this display of nakedness to a mass audience needs comment. According to George Roeder: "By late 1942 *Life* was claiming that tens of millions of civilians and two out of three Americans in the military read the magazine" (1993, 4−5). Such a public display should be understood in the larger context of how sexuality was negotiated in war films. Photographs of naked soldiers washing and at play in *Life* provide testimony that affirms these men *can* be observed;

161

that is, the very act of representing their nakedness serves as an assurance that their sexuality is *representable*. The naked men shown to the American public must be heterosexual. If nakedness can be shown in airbrushed photographs, then the sexuality of those shown in the photographs is not in question.

Although commercial combat films could not show a naked male body, they could and did show males performing feminine roles, a hand resting casually on a bare chest, men performing in drag and dancing together, a young man looking lovingly at an older man who has just performed a maternal function, a man joking about a pin-up of himself, and horseplay that evoked the potential range of male sexuality. But these were consistently qualified, in a way demonstrating that what was potentially signified at one level needed to be understood at another. The very fact that any of these scenes were shown signified at some level that they *could* be presented—that males' sexuality was contained and inoculated by their masculinity.

The Easthope-Simpson argument that explains such displays as signifiers of homoeroticism sanctioned by the inevitability of death does not take into account the complex logic of representation discussed in this essay. In addition, many of the scenes mentioned here might even be considered as anticipations of an expansive conception of masculinity that escapes stereotypical constraints, rather like what Jillian Sandell identifies in the films of John Woo: "While it is possible to read [the films'] friendships in terms of homoerotic tensions and desires (and many reviewers and critics have done so), relegating male intimacy to the realm of homosexuality ... offers little to challenge contemporary stereotypes about gender and sexuality" (1996, 24). What distinguishes the films treated here from those of Woo is, of course, the high level of self-consciousness about representation in the latter. Nonetheless, combat films and other discourses produced during World War II can be seen to have provided some indication of an as yet unarticulated conception of sexuality and masculinity developing in the American consciousness.

notes

1. Both Easthope and Simpson address psychoanalytic elements in their arguments. Easthope sees "four crucial moments" in representations of war:

   > "defeat, combat, victory, and comradeship.... [A]ssociated with all the others, there is the moment of comradeship, the picture of the soldier weeping for his wounded buddy. For psychoanalysis these moments are to be explained in terms of the fear of castration, the triumph of the masculine ego, fathers and sons, and the sublimated intimacies of the male bond." (1990, 63)

Having considered both Freudian and post-Freudian views of castration, Simpson suggests that the buddy war film presents "something of an *escape* from the Oedipus complex," (1994, 214) given its focus on friendship rather than on conflict with the father. Lynne Segal also explores the connection between war and homoeroticism (1990, 142). Steve Neale calls "the war film . . . quite clearly a form of 'masculine romance'" (1991, 53). Bernard Dick notes: "Howard Hawks claimed some of his films were male love stories. William Wellman could have said the same of *The Story of G.I. Joe*" (1985, 141). Clayton R. Koppes and Gregory D. Black claim this same film's scene of mourning for a dead soldier "came as close as the movies dared to speaking of male love" (1990, 307−8).

2. Wylie assumes that "Mom's boy" will go through the usual Oedipal progression and marry: "With her captive son or sons in a state of automatic adoration of herself (and just enough dubiety of their wives to keep them limp or querulous at home), mom has ushered in the new form of American marriage: eternal ricochet" (1942, 196). "The mealy look of men today is the result of momism" (197).

3. In a study of "The Sexual Psychopath in the Military Service," Lt. Col. Lewis H. Loeser (1945) offers four "etiological factors" to account for homosexuality, one of which manifests itself in a "group with normal endocrine status, [that] presents histories of severe dislocation in the psychological field in early childhood. They include the male children brought up as females by mothers; the only son in a large company of females; the Oedipus complex with a strong dislike of the father; and other sub-mechanisms. Throughout this sub-group one can trace the influence of abnormal environment during the formative years of the child—the end result being a distortion of the sexual drive and failure of normal heterosexual development" (98). Here again the dominance of the mother is presented as a threat to normal sexual development.

4. See Allan Bérubé (1991, 49, 51) for commentary on the work. He sees a level of tolerance in the authors' position (51). Steven Cohan (1997) suggests: "The manual's cautious advice about the likelihood of homosexual encounters in the army's all-male environment is . . . quite striking, given the homophobia which erupted in periodic purges of effeminate men during the war and which, more perniciously, came to dominate military policy after the war ended" (86). For additional valuable historical treatments of gays in the military during World War II, see also John Costello (1985) and John D'Emilio (1983). *Time*'s article about the release of the report did not mention that it talked about sexual matters but stressed what it said about morale and dealing with fear ("Why Men Fight and Fear").

5. In this regard I am grateful to Krin Gabbard for suggesting the relevance of Roland Barthes. In *Image—Music—Text*, Barthes introduces the concept of "anchorage" in captions. The caption delimits the potential range of meanings in the photograph it explains: "the anchorage may be ideological and indeed this is its principal function; the text *directs* the reader through the signifieds of the image, causing him to avoid some and receive others; by means of an often subtle *dispatching*, it remote-controls him towards a meaning chosen in advance. . . . Anchorage is the most frequent function of the linguistic message and is commonly found in press photographs and advertisements" (1977, 40−41).

6. In fact the *Time* reviewer spoke of "the horsing and singing of the wool-

bearing *Ladies of the Chorus,* who have taken almost excruciating care to be mistaken neither for transvestite chorusmen nor for the quite convincing young ladies they dared to be on Broadway" ("New Picture: *This Is the Army,*" 93—94).

7. It is helpful to contextualize the moment in *Expendable* by looking at the way Wayne was conceived of in terms of masculinity in the popular press. For example, the anonymous reviewer in *Time* of *The Flying Tigers* (David Miller, 1942) says that Wayne and others in the film "play their parts manfully. John Wayne is a rudimentary actor, but he has the look and bearing, unusual in his trade, of a capable human male. . . . He is able to make his habitual inarticulateness suggest the uncommunicative competence that men expect in their leaders" ("New Picture: *Flying Tigers,*" 96). The *Newsweek* reviewer of the same film speaks approvingly of Wayne as "the tight-lipped squadron leader" ("Tribute to Tigers," 72).

8. As Thomas Doherty has explained, servicemen overseas were regularly afforded opportunities to watch Hollywood films (1999, 75—78). An article in *Time* ("Second Chain") on domestic camp movie theaters indicated that the most popular films among soldiers were "musicals with girls" (96).

9. Doherty notes: "In the combat reports, GI backsides were exposed during scenes of jungle bathing" (1999, 56).

10. For important arguments about showing males naked, see Peter Lehman's *Running Scared: Masculinity and the Representation of the Male Body* (1993), especially the introduction (1—36) and chapter 8 (147—68).

11. The drawing of naked soldiers bathing in the first True towel ad was repeated in a much smaller ad for Strathmore Letterhead Papers (owned by Cannon). This ad did not have the insert of the woman although it offers the qualifying commentary that stresses the need for the refreshment offered by the water (*Time,* April 17, 1944, 93). The caption reads: "Cannon towels get a mighty hand from the boys at the front. A cooling dip . . . a brisk rubdown with a sturdy, durable Cannon towel . . . that's tops after grilling marches or hours of combat under blazing skies and in steaming jungles." D'Emilio refers to a paper by Bérubé, "Marching to a Different Drummer: Coming Out During World War II," given at the American Historical Association Meeting (Los Angeles, 1981), as the source of his information about some of the Cannon towel ads. D'Emilio refers to two in *Life* and one in *The Saturday Evening Post.* I have not seen the ad in the *Post* but assume it reproduced what was in *Life.* D'Emilio does not indicate that the Cannon towel ads include a drawing of a woman.

works cited

Barthes, Roland. 1977. *Image—Music—Text.* Trans. Stephen Heath. New York: Hill and Wang.

"Battle of Buna." 1943. *Life,* Feb. 15, 17—29.

Bérubé, Allan. 1991. *Coming Out under Fire: The History of Gay Men and Women in World War Two.* New York: Plume.

Boone, Joel T. 1941. "The Sexual Aspects of Military Personnel." *Journal of Social Hygiene* 27 (March): 113—24.

Cohan, Steven. 1997. *Masked Men: Masculinity and the Movies in the Fifties.* Bloomington: Indiana University Press.

Costello, John. 1985. *Virtue under Fire: How World War II Changed Our Social and Sexual Attitudes.* Boston: Little, Brown.

Crowther, Bosley. 1945. "'They Were Expendable,' Seen at Capital, Called Stirring Picture of Small but Vital Aspect of War Just Ended." *New York Times,* Dec. 21, 25.

D' Emilio, John. 1983. *Sexual Politics, Sexual Communities: The Making of a Homosexual Minority in the United States, 1940–1970.* Chicago: University of Chicago Press.

Dick, Bernard F. 1985. *The Star-Spangled Screen: The American World War II Film.* Lexington: University of Kentucky Press.

Doherty, Thomas. 1999. *Projections of War: Hollywood, American Culture, and World War II.* rev. ed. New York: Columbia University Press.

Easthope, Anthony. 1990. *What a Man's Gotta Do: The Masculine Myth in Popular Culture.* Boston: Unwin Hyman.

Eberwein, Robert. 1999a. *Sex Ed: Film, Video, and the Framework of Desire.* Piscataway, N.J.: Rutgers University Press.

———. 1999b. "Representing Masculinity in a World War II Film." Florida State University Conference on Literature and Film, January.

"Guadalcanal." 1943. *Life,* March 1: 68–71.

"In Uniform & Their Right Minds." 1942, *Time,* June 1: 37–38.

Koppes, Clayton R., and Gregory D. Black. 1990. *Hollywood Goes to War: How Politics, Profits and Propaganda Shaped World War II Movies.* Berkeley: University of California Press.

Lehman, Peter. 1993. *Running Scared: Masculinity and the Representation of the Male Body.* Philadelphia: Temple University Press.

Loeser, Lewis H. 1945. "The Sexual Psychopath in the Military Service (A Study of 270 Cases)." *American Journal of Psychiatry* 102 (July): 92–101.

Menninger, William. 1948. *Psychiatry in a Troubled World: Yesterday's War and Today's Challenge.* New York: Macmillan, 1948.

National Research Council. 1943. *Psychology for the Fighting Man: What You Should Know about Yourself and Others.* Washington, D.C.: Infantry Journal.

Neale, Steve. 1991. "Aspects of Ideology and Narrative Form in the American War Film." *Screen* 32, 1 (Spring): 35–57.

"New Picture." [Rev. of *Flying Tigers*] 1942. *Time,* Oct. 12, 96, 98.

"New Picture." [Rev. of *This Is the Army*] 1943. *Time,* Aug. 16, 93–94.

Rev. of *Objective Burma.* 1945. New York Times, Jan. 27, 15.

"Picture of the Week." 1943. *Life,* Feb. 8, 24–25.

Rickenbacker, Eddie. 1943. "Pacific Mission [Part I]. *Life,* Jan. 25, 20–27, 90, 92, 94–96, 99–100.

Roeder, George H., Jr. 1993. *The Censored War: American Visual Experience of World War Two.* New Haven, Conn.: Yale University Press.

Ross, Irwin. 1941. "Sex in the Army." *American Mercury* 53 (December): 661–69.

Sandell, Jillian. 1996. "Reinventing Masculinity: The Spectacle of Male Intimacy in the Films of John Woo." *Film Quarterly* 49, 4 (Summer): 23–34.

"Second Chain." 1943. *Time,* July 5, 96.

Segal, Lynne. 1990. *Slow Motion: Changing Masculinities, Changing Men.* New Brunswick, N.J.: Rutgers University Press.

Simpson, Mark. 1994. *Male Impersonators: Men Performing Masculinity.* New York: Routledge.

Steichen, Edward. 1947. *The Blue Ghost.* New York: Harcourt Brace.

"Tribute to Tigers." 1942. *Newsweek*, Oct. 5, 72.

"Why Men Fight and Fear." 1943. *Time*, Jan. 11, 48, 50.

Wittson, C. L., H. I. Harris, W. A. Hunt, P. S. Solomon, and M. M. Jackson. 1943. "The Neuropsychiatric Selection of Recruits." *American Journal of Psychiatry* 99 (March): 639–50.

Wylie, Philip. 1942. *Generation of Vipers.* New York: Farrar and Reinhart.

robert eberwein

the nation

and

the nude

colonial masculinity

and the spectacle

of the male body in recent

canadian cinema(s)

l e e   p a r p a r t

In order to take narrative cinema's powerfully ideal male body seriously,
we must not see its literal truth.

—Peter Lehman, *Running Scared* (172)

In the seven years since Peter Lehman published *Running Scared: Masculinity and the Representation of the Male Body*, a book that did a great deal to shatter what he termed "the silence surrounding the representation of the male body" (1993, 4), male nudity has gradually become a more accepted part of films from many different genres and countries. With a widespread rediscovery of the male body's erotic potential underway in a variety of commercial and cultural contexts, from queer cinema to Calvin Klein ads, more mainstream directors than ever before seem to be finding it possible to flirt with male sexual representation, in some cases even tackling the previously taboo spectacle of full frontal nudity.[1] Exposures of the nude male body continue to be powerfully regulated by cultural norms which tend to uphold phallic authority within patriarchal societies by keeping the penis out of sight, but it has become easier in recent years to point to films where such restrictions are relaxed, and where the male body is permitted a degree of exposure not generally found in mainstream cinema before the mid-1990s.[2]

Lehman pointed to various narrative and generic contexts for recent cinematic exposures of the male body, such as heightened and hyperbolic representations of the "melodramatic penis" and the "dead penis" (1998; this volume). While he grants that recent Hollywood cinema has shown a greater willingness to toy with explicit male sexual representation, he finds that dominant narrative cinema still tends to position and unveil the nude male body in ways that reinforce the patriarchal assumption that "penises cannot simply be shown as penises in ordinary contexts," since to do so would "threaten the awe and mystique resulting from keeping [the penis] hidden and fall outside the various cultural discourses such as pornography, art, medicine, and humor that attempt to give it special significance" (1998, 7).

Throughout his work, Lehman has tended to allow for certain differences in the way male nudity is handled within Hollywood cinema and in other traditions, such as the European art cinema. But his emphasis on crosscultural and transgeneric patterns marking male sexual representation in different cinemas suggests that he finds the continuities more meaningful than the contrasts (1993, 218).[3] One example discussed in *Running Scared* is the recurring image (found in films as diverse as Paul Verhoeven's *Turkish Delight* [1974], Jonathan Demme's *Silence of the Lambs* [1991] and the porn movie *Kinky Business 2* [1989]) of a male character masquerading before the camera with his genitals tucked between his thighs. For Lehman, the appearance of the same image within the European art cinema, Hollywood film, and hard-core pornography suggests that the idea of an invisible or temporarily absent penis holds "a particular fascination for men," and that this fascination may be rooted in a contradictory desire to be rid of the penis-phallus and the fear of such an occurrence (217–18).

For all its usefulness as a way of foregrounding transcultural patterns within male sexual representation, an overemphasis on shared characteristics and universal principles may tend to obscure important distinctions in the way such images have been dealt with in different genres and national cinemas. My starting point here is that male sexual representation (like the practice of masculinities in general) varies considerably across time and place, and that to some extent the job of trying to grasp what form such imagery takes becomes a matter of unraveling the conditions of visibility in particular social, cultural, and political contexts. Specifically, I want to explore the question of whether nondominant cinemas and cinemas of different nations can be seen to generate their own narrative, aesthetic, and ideological contexts for managing the freighted spectacle of the nude male body.

Recent Canadian cinema, with its unique institutional constraints and combined debt to European art cinema, British "cinema of quality," and American independent film, offers a rich vein for taking up such questions. On a simple empirical level, even accounting for the widespread "desublimation of the penis" that Lawrence R. Schehr (1997) argues has been under way in Western societies since the mid-1990s, Canadian cinema is still curiously full of images of the nude male body (18).[4] In films ranging from *Kissed* (Lynne Stopkewich, 1996) and *Post-Mortem* (Louis Bélanger, 1999) to *Beefcake* (Thom Fitzgerald, 1999), *Full Blast* (Rodrigue Jean, 1999), *Live Bait* and *Dirty* (both Bruce Sweeney, 1995 and 1997, respectively), *Paris, France* (Jerry Ciccoritti, 1993), *Lilies, Urinal, Zero Patience* and *Uncut* (John Greyson, 1996, 1988, 1993 and 1997), *Mustard Bath* (Darrell Wasyk, 1992), *The Adjuster* (Atom Egoyan, 1991), *I Love a Man in Uniform* (Peter Wellington, 1993), *Margaret's Museum* (Mort Ransen, 1995), *Bubbles Galore* (Cynthia Roberts, 1996), Gregory Wild's puppet musical *Highway of Heartache* (1994), virtually all of Bruce La Bruce's art-porn corpus (*Super 8 1/2* [1994], *No Skin off My Ass* [1991], *White Hustler*, various shorts by experimental film and video artists Mike Hoolboom (including *Justify My Love*, 1994) and Steve Reinke (*Lonely Boy*, 1993) and Karethe Linaae's minor but memorable short *Off Key* (1994), the male body undergoes a degree of exposure not often seen outside the confines of gay porn, experimental film or the generally more permissive arena of European art cinema. Even Canadian animation pays special attention to the male nude, with cartoon images of the penis taking center stage in Alison Snowden and David Fine's Oscar-winning short *Bob's Birthday* (1995), one episode of the TV spinoff *Bob & Margaret* (1998–99) and Marv Newland's compilation film *Pink Komkommer* (1991).[5]

The fact that some of these films and videos (notably those by John Greyson and Bruce LaBruce) borrow from the narrative and stylistic conventions of gay pornography and experimental cinema clearly helps to account for their attention to the nude male body as a source of erotic imagery and social critique.[6] But what may surprise outside observers is that even the most conventional narrative films mentioned so far (such as *Live Bait, Dirty, Full Blast, Margaret's Museum* and *I Love a Man in Uniform*) have found it possible, and even, at times, crucial, to make a spectacle of the nude male body. Moreover, some of them have done so in ways that seem to contradict the assumption that "penises cannot simply be shown as penises in ordinary contexts" (Lehman 1998, 7).

An unusually clear example of this deviation from the usual pattern shows up in British Columbian director Bruce Sweeney's debut feature, *Live Bait.* In this low-budget, bittersweet comedy of errors from

Vancouver's semi-independent film scene, the lead character, a sexually insecure college student named Trevor (Tom Scholte) is glimpsed briefly in the nude as he pulls himself out of the lake near his family's cottage, where he has been reading a book of philosophy about the concept of 'between' and working out some conflicts with his father and his more sexually mature older brother. No particular dramatic importance seems to be attached to this instance of nudity, although the narrative context might justify a reading of the image of Trevor/Scholte's limp and retracted penis as a kind of physical manifestation of his growing sense of incompetence in sexual matters and the rage he feels about having witnessed his father's infidelity days earlier. Even so, there is something unusually matter-of-fact, or at least narratively and aesthetically understated, about the nudity in this scene, which is handled more as a simple moment between brothers than as the focal point of a vulnerable male character's cringing inadequacies or sexual crisis. Trevor climbs naked from the lake onto a dock in the nude and faces the camera for several seconds, his older brother tosses him a towel, and they both walk out of frame. Despite the wider narrative context, with its focus on a young man's frustrating sexual inexperience, and the brevity of this moment of nudity, it is tempting to argue that *Live Bait* offers one of a few cases where, for a brief moment at least, the penis is just a penis—not a focal point of phallic power, shame, hysterical action, violence or melodrama, but an ordinary organ that happens to be undergoing normal levels of shrinkage after exposure to cold water. Whereas Lehman has argued persuasively that most images of the nude male body in Western culture "[continue] to assert that showing the penis must be of some special, if bizarre, significance," (1998, 7) *Live Bait* supplies a partial alternative to this pattern, and comes close to meeting Lehman's model of one version of a healthy approach to male sexual representation: the nonchalant, nonjudgmental, non-joking presentation of the penis *as* a penis, rather than a symbolic register of phallic authority. The fact that Trevor goes on to have sex with a much older woman—a charismatic sculptor played by veteran Canadian stage actress Micki Maunsell, who appears to be in her late 60s—does not, in my opinion, raise the stakes of this scene and turn it into a revelation of the "melodramatic penis." The couple's *Harold and Maude* (1971) style encounter is handled with such simplicity, sweetness, and lack of censure that we are encouraged to believe Trevor when he is able to move on from the experience without regret. No one is punished or left in ruins, and the penis avoids becoming either a site of shame or of exaggerated sexual prowess.

A different pattern prevails in two Atlantic Canadian films, *Full Blast* and *Margaret's Museum*, where the sight of the male sexual organ seems to coincide with a playing out of cultural norms and expectations related to regional inequality and to form part of an analysis of working class masculinity on the periphery of the nation.[7] As I have argued elsewhere, the sight of coal miners showering and undressing in the company locker room in *Margaret's Museum* tends to call attention to the masculinist ideals of solidarity at work in mining communities, hint at the homosocial closeness of the "men of the deeps," and render visible and literal, for a brief moment, the vulnerability of the politically and economically marginalized neocolonial male (1999a: 75–76). The regional and class elements of this analysis are stressed by the fact that the nude bodies of several anonymous coal miners begin to weave in and out of frame just as Margaret's Uncle Angus (Kenneth Welsh) learns he will not be able to send his nephew off to a better life in Toronto because his wife has been to the company store to buy shoes for his own children and his pay envelope now contains only three cents. When Angus complains about his predicament to anyone who will listen, he is scolded by one of his coworkers who tells him he has only himself to blame for failing to support the union. A similar relay of class, labor, and regional considerations marks the representation of the male body in *Full Blast*, where the brief spectacle of a man's penis during a shower scene at the local pulp mill dovetails with the news of a strike vote and the use of pressure tactics by one group of workers (union supporters, we are led to believe) against another group. (Instead of allowing pro-union toughs to beat him up, one of the

Trevor MacIntosh (Tom Scholte, right) and Brain MacIntosh (David Lovgren) share a brotherly moment in *Live Bait*.

victims takes his cigarette and burns the arm of his companion, in a kind of sacrificial gesture and concession to labor politics that is written directly on the male body). Moreover, while *Margaret's Museum* uses the spectacle of the male body to draw attention to the homosocial closeness of men working side by side under dangerous conditions in an industry that tends to symbolize Cape Breton's history of neocolonial servitude relative to Central Canada, *Full Blast* pushes the suggestion of homosexual intimacy to the surface with its handling of an on-again, off-again affair between the son of a company boss and another (male) pulp mill employee. The visual handling of their encounters includes a relatively graphic scene of anal sex—an image that has become something of a motif in Canadian narrative film, with other representations of forced and consensual sex between men in *Being at Home with Claude* (Jean Beaudin, 1991), *Eclipse* (Jeremy Podeswa, 1994), *Fortune and Men's Eyes* (Harvey Hart, 1971), and *Un Zoo, la nuit* (Jean-Claude Lauzon, 1987).

Many other examples of non-normative treatment of male nudity could suggest themselves here, but my point is that far from shying away from revealing the nude male body, recent Canadian cinema has made its explicit sexual representation something of a specialty, and has done so within narrative and aesthetic contexts that are often best read in relation to cultural, historical, and institutional conditions "on the ground."

On the institutional side, one obvious reply to our question of "why men's bodies, why here and why now?" has to do with factors (such as state funding, modest production budgets, and limited domestic distribution) tending to align Canadian narrative cinema more closely with European and Third World cinemas than with dominant cinema from either Hollywood or the increasingly formula-driven and commodified U.S. independent sector. Even a cursory look at the films of Peter Greenaway, Fassbinder, Derek Jarman, Rosa von Praunheim, and Lars von Trier suggests that the European art film has tended to enjoy a greater comfort level with displays of the nude male body than is generally found in Hollywood film. The pattern also extends to recent European films that are closer to mainstream narrative traditions, such as *Ridicule* (1996), *Angels and Insects* (1995), and (within the horror genre) Alex de la Iglesia's *Day of the Beast* (1995). The opening frames of *Ridicule*, for example, offer the spectacle of a bitter aristocrat urinating on his old enemy from the court of Louis XIV. Viewed in extreme close-up, the penis in this costume drama becomes a kind of physical corollary to the masculinist, penetrating, "rapier" wit that courtiers relied on to establish and maintain strict social hierarchies in pre-revolutionary Paris. Britain's *Angels and Insects* is one of several recent films to evoke Lehman's category of the "melodramatic penis"—a heightened, hyperbolic moment of male sexual representation, in this case coinciding with a man's discovery of his wife's incestuous relationship with her brother. And in the smart, heretical horror comedy *The Day of the Beast*, de la Iglesia repeatedly turns a static and seemingly nonchalant camera on the spectacle of a nude and nearly comatose old man—the grandfather of a heavy metal fan who has teamed up with a renegade priest to try and stop the Antichrist from rising to destroy the world on Christmas Eve. Though the spectacle of the penis functions differently in each of these films, the mere fact that it can be represented signals a comfort level with revealing the male body that is not as easily observed in Hollywood film. Canadian tendencies in this area may need to be viewed, first of all, in the context of European-style state-funding mechanisms that allow a degree of freedom from commercial imperatives and liberty to experiment with narrative alternatives to empowered masculinity and unorthodox representations of the male body. It may be easier to make a spectacle of the nude male body within a state-subsidized "cinema of quality" where profits are not the only engine driving narrative and aesthetic decisions—or, perhaps, where male nudity is viewed as a source of profit in itself, within the progressive, oppositional, (largely) gay-friendly and self-consciously bohemian political and aesthetic contexts driving the production and reception of art cinema.

On a more abstract level, I believe we also need to look to at least two other related factors influencing male sexual representation: the effect of a particular version of "colonial masculinity" that has been part of the discourse of nationhood in Canada for many years, and what has often been described as the fractured, heterogeneous nature of Canadian social and political life. In thinking through what it is about Canada as an imagined community or Canadian cinema as an institutional site that offers fertile ground for exposures of the male body, my sense is that we can begin to talk about a kind of structural alliance or resonance between this kind of sociopolitical and institutional heterogeneity (or, at a minimum, a discursive insistence on such heterogeneity),[8] the experience of colonial masculinity, and a willingness to reveal the nude male body in contexts that either tend to interrogate phallic power or express anxiety about its loss.

Readers familiar with recent debates on "colonial masculinity" may be surprised to find the term applied outside of a discussion of the colonial histories of Africa, India, and the West Indies, since much of the work on colonial masculinity to date has centered on a critique of the gendered assumptions operating within anticolonial nationalisms and the writings of Frantz Fanon. As bell hooks argues in her contribution to Alan Read's 1996 anthology, *The Fact of Blackness*, an important and long-overlooked part of Fanon's legacy has been to construct the notion of colonial injury as a matter pertaining exclusively to men: "The blackness/darkness of the colonised body that marks it as other to the white coloniser is always framed within a gendered context wherein the metaphors of emasculation and castration symbolically articulate the psychic wounds of the colonised. That pain then is inscribed always as the pain of men inflicted upon them by other men. Healing, as Fanon envisions it, takes place only as this conflict between men is resolved" (82). In any attempt to introduce Commonwealth countries into this debate, it is crucial to distinguish between white and nonwhite experience. As Linda Hutcheon points out, "the primarily white Canadian historical *experience* of colonialism, and therefore of post-colonialism, cannot be equated with that of the West Indies or Africa or India" without trivializing the latter or exaggerating the former (1991, 74). Without wanting to conflate the two basic varieties of colonialism pointed to by her analysis, I start from the assumption that many English Canadians and Quebeckers (white and nonwhite) do experience themselves as colonized on some level, either in relation to central Canada, Britain, France, the United States, or all of the above, and that this subject position works its way, forcefully at times, into discourses on masculinity as well as representations of the male body. What interests me here is how we can begin to understand the various manifestations of colonial experience in Canada as inflected by conditions of socioeconomic heterogeneity, and how both factors might be helping to lay the foundation for a range of approaches to male sexual representation in Canadian movies.

As a complex federation or "mosaic" (rather than "melting pot") fractured by powerful regional identities and divided not only along historic French-English lines but among ten relatively autonomous provinces and dozens of minority groups whose separateness is encouraged by "official multiculturalism," Canada has, according to Hutcheon, Carol Ann Howells, and other commentators, developed into an unusually heterogeneous society, defining itself more in terms of its divisions than in relation to a metanarrative of national unity.[9] However accurately or inaccurately this describes the Canadian scene, something of a parallel can be found in Canada's film system, which has tended to support an array of micro-cinemas (all more or less fledgling) rather than a single overarching body of work on film. Whereas in American cinema the key distinctions tend to be between Hollywood and independent work, with certain important but rarely mentioned regional differences (between, for example, Boston and New York independents), Canadian cinema can hardly be said to exist apart from the regional, subcultural, aesthetic, and institutional divisions that correspond to the country's social, geographical, and political arrangements.

Despite the presence of a national funding body in Telefilm Canada and the centralizing influence of the National Film Board, Canadian cinema continues to be starkly divided between the "two solitudes" of English Canada and Québec, with each stream attracting separate provincial funding and generating different production, distributional, and exhibition patterns.[10] Moreover, the French-English split is only the beginning. One also finds dramatic regional distinctions, such as an emerging French-language Acadian cinema (represented by the recent *Full Blast*), an established English-language cinema from Atlantic Canada (*Margaret's Museum, Understanding Bliss* [1990], *Life Classes* [1987], *The Hanging Garden* [1997], *New Waterford Girl* [1999] and the originary text of Atlantic Canadian disaffection: *Goin' Down the Road* [1970]); a not-so-new Ontario Wave dominated by Atom Egoyan (*Exotica* [1994], *The Adjuster* [1991], *The Sweet Hereafter* [1997]), David Cronenberg (*Videodrome* [1983], *The Fly* [1986], *Dead Ringers* [1988], *Crash* [1996]), Peter Wellington (*I Love a Man in Uniform*), Jeremy Podeswa (*Eclipse* [1994], *The Five Senses* [1999]) and a few other Central Canadian auteurs; a related but distinct Vancouver-based cinema (*Kissed, Live Bait, Dirty* [1998], *The Grocer's Wife* [1991], *off Key* [1994]), a Prairie cinema (*Kitchen Party* [1997], *The Suburbanators* [1995]), and a famously offbeat Winnipeg school led by Guy Maddin and John Paisz (*Tales of Gimli Hospital* [1988], *Crime Wave* [1985]).

Alongside these subnational distinctions, queer cinema and feminist film directors tend to occupy a kind of vaguely institutionalized middle ground between the truly independent sector and various levels of the state-funded Canadian "mainstream." Film and video artists such as John Greyson (*Urinal, Zero Patience, Lilies*) and art porn director Bruce La Bruce (*No Skin off My Ass, Super 8½, Hustler White*) tend to receive some federal and provincial funding for their work, although the theatrical potential for their films and videos has generally been limited to festivals (in the case of La Bruce) and a few screenings in metropolitan markets.[11] Meanwhile, relatively mainstream gay filmmakers such as Robert LePage (*Le Confessional* [1995], *Le Polygraphe* [1996]) and well-known lesbian and/or feminist directors such as Patricia Rozema (*I've Heard the Mermaids Singing* [1987], *White Room* [1990], *When Night is Falling* [1995], *Mansfield Park* [1999]), Léa Pool (*La Femme de l'hotel* [1984], *Emporte-Moi* [1999]), and Anne Wheeler (*Bye Bye Blues* [1989], *Loyalties* [1986]) have consistently attracted moderate to large sums of money for their projects (much of it, as well, from government sources) and been able to secure domestic and in many cases international theatrical release, video deals, and television broadcasts. As Tom Waugh points out, queer cinema in Canada enjoys the status of a genuine alternative canon, serving as a "corrective, antidote, and *salon des refusés*" (18) relative to the official canon as it has been reflected in Canadian film studies syllabi and on Canadian postage stamps. While Waugh points to the silencing and exclusion of queer cinemas within critical and theoretical work on Canadian cinema, his comments also suggest that in Canada gay self-representation has occupied a privileged space of alterity: "The queer canon, with its resilient iconography of community formation, troubled relationships, unrequited passion, self-hatred, camp bravado, internal prejudice, martyrdom, and, yes, positive images, is both a therapeutic communal history and an indispensable political resource" (19).[12]

Within this complex field of sociocultural divisions and the "proliferating diversity of Canadian cinemas" (Waugh, 18) it has tended to support, there has, according to some recent commentators, been little room for smug metanarratives of empowered nationhood or its frequent corollary, dominant masculinity. Canadians, it has often been argued, experience themselves as colonized, at least historically speaking, in relation to Britain and France, and as systematically dominated (or neocolonized) by the United States on political, cultural, and economic grounds. Whether we are talking about split-run magazines, NATO military policies, fishing disputes, or the overwhelming dominance of American movies, magazines, and television in Canadian culture, large numbers of Canadians appear to view themselves as dominated on some level by the United States, while also, by some accounts, holding onto residual feelings of cultural superiority. Pierre Trudeau famously likened Canada to a mouse sleeping next to an elephant, and Canadians who have internalized this notion (or simply looked around them) seem to instinctively grasp their precarious position relative to the United States, while at the same time priding themselves on having produced a kinder, gentler society and nursing the idea that a chronic fear of being crushed under foot has transformed Canadians into superior observers and great comedians. Connecting this observation to work on masculinity, it seems plausible that the same conditions—chronic political and economic uncertainty and exposure to heterogeneous influences from within—may have contributed to a spectrum of masculine/Canadian performative styles that are in some cases milder, more respectful of marginality and less invested in symbolic shows of phallic authority than those in other parts of the world. As Québec feminist Madeleine Gagnon once put it, "the men here are softer than elsewhere" due to their experience of colonialism (1997, 113). Where softness and pliability are allowable (or perhaps just inescapable) features within a range of national and sub-national gender identities, male sexual representation is bound to take interesting forms.

All of this generalizing about the Canadian zeitgeist would be of little help to us here if not for the fact that in the early 1970s, Canadian cultural nationalists began to conflate questions of gender and nation in ways that explicitly pointed to the problem of weak masculine role models in Canadian cinema and attempted to explain it as an out-growth of the country's colonial relationships with Britain and the United States. The film studies side of this debate began with a 1973 essay by Robert Fothergill, "Coward, Bully or Clown: The Dream-Life of a Younger Brother," which argued that Canadian cinema was rife with "the depiction, through many different scenarios, of the radical inadequacy of the male protagonist—his moral failure, especially, and most visibly, in his relationships with women" (235). Fothergill explained the pattern in terms of a now famous psychological analogy that figured Canada as a permanent "little brother" to its domineering southern neighbor, the United States:

> Aware of his more powerful brother as a feature in the landscape, in a way that has never been reciprocated, the younger brother has grown up with a painfully confined sense of his own capacity for self-realization. An abiding sense of himself as inescapably diminished, secondary, immature, has become second nature, has indeed shaped his nature and bred into it a self-thwarting knowledge of personal inadequacy. (243)

Although Fothergill appears to have left this work behind, magazines and the popular press continue to rehash his thesis in less subtle form with perennial "think pieces" about the inadequacy (and fundamental effeminacy) of male characters in Canadian cinema.[13] Built into these popularized accounts of imperiled Canadian masculinity is the deeply problematic assumption that hegemonic masculinities, or those that adhere to the ideal of an omnipotent, empowered, and stable core of subjectivity, are desirable and a credit to the nation, while nonhegemonic, or subordinate, masculinities (those tinged by effeminacy, dissolution or disempowerment) constitute a threat to the maturity and stability of the nation. It was partially this problematic bundle of assumptions that Christine Ramsay unpacked in her 1993 essay "Canadian Narrative Cinema From the Margins: 'The Nation' and Masculinity in *Goin' Down the Road*," which brought on something of a paradigm change in the way masculinities are understood to operate within English Canadian film. Arguing that dominant masculine gender identity and the modern nation are both "product[s] of imagination" (rather than essences) that are linked by a common metaphoric impulse to power and mastery, Ramsay points out that English Canadian films have tended to imagine both "the nation" and the ideal of omnipotent, empowered masculinity from the position of the margins. In keeping with a general, postmodern revaluing of peripheral experiences and identities, Ramsay argues that "minority discourse[s]" around masculinity and nation (of the kind she suggests are on offer in

Don Shebib's *Goin' Down the Road*) carve out a "performative space" for the representation of English Canada's social self. Such work, she writes, should be

> celebrated and studied ... for what it offers as a lived text that makes intelligible to us, as English Canadians, from the position of the margins, the unique way we have historically faced the problems of social and personal identity through the Western concepts of "the nation" and omnipotent masculinity. (47)

Tom Waugh has recently called for a recasting of the terms of the debate on masculinity in Canadian cinema, on the grounds that both Fothergill and his critics (myself included) have tended to define the problem in ways that privilege "the conventional canon of Toronto straight-male, middle-class, baby-boomer, art-movie angst" represented by auteurs such as Egoyan and Cronenberg, while consistently putting Canada's queer cinematic traditions at risk of erasure. Waugh's advice is for everyone to simply stop using the national pronoun "we" and opt, instead, to "bracket the national-sexual that has prematurely and problematically been the animus of Canadian film studies" (22). While I want to take this recommendation seriously, I also need to deal with the fact that the exclusionary debates and canonizing moves that have been carried out in connection with Canadian masculinities have taken on a life of their own, and that like all discourses, they have become a part of the fabric that defines the imaginative possibilities for representation within their reach. I don't want to uphold (*or* bracket) the national-sexual so much as try to grasp how the conflation of those terms might have contributed to imaginative possibilities for representing the male body. What narrative contexts and conditions of visibility are suggested by a discourse that assumes the health of the nation is directly dependent on its ability to mount empowered scripts of masculinity? Alternatively, what imaginative possibilities for representing the male body might flow out of a careful separation of these terms and an attempt to defuse the loaded fraternal metaphor underlying worried and anxiety-ridden conceptions of colonial masculinity? How might the nude male body be represented (or read) in texts that position themselves alongside discourses privileging marginality, heterogeneity, difference, flexibility, and "softness" over authority, autonomy, inviolability, and phallic power?

Since representation is rarely as much of an either-or proposition, as this framing suggests, it makes little sense to look for a strictly dichotomous model for reading images of the colonial male body (as, for example, either hopelessly compromised by their embeddedness in the fraternal metaphor or as liberatory by virtue of their embrace of difference). The most that can be said, perhaps, is that texts tend to arrange themselves along a spectrum of approaches to the colonial male body, and that individual moments of male nudity may register (with different spectators at different times) as comparatively anxiety-ridden or affirmative of difference and marginality.

A dramatic example of the first tendency can be found in the late Québécois director Jean-Claude Lauzon's first feature, *Un Zoo, la nuit (Night Zoo)*. Lurching between its generic roots and looking at times like a hybrid of *Action Cop* and *Oklahoma!* (1955), *Un Zoo* tells the story of a young Québec man's imprisonment for narcotics trafficking, his revenge on the corrupt police officers who provided him with the drugs, and his reconciliation with his dying father. In keeping with stark fissures in the narrative that position this film between the two poles of slick urban phallic masculinity and pastoral romanticism, the son is a drug-dealing, motorcycle-riding street tough who tends to function as an emblem of modern, citified Québec, while his father, played by the late Roger Lebel, fishes and hunts for moose and generally stands as a kind of representative of Québec's mythical, pre-lapsarian past, before contact with the colonizing, English Canadian Other. I have argued elsewhere that this film, which was written directly after Québec's first failed attempt to win political independence from Canada and released six years after the referendum defeat, can be read as a kind of limit text or hyperbolic expression of the links between

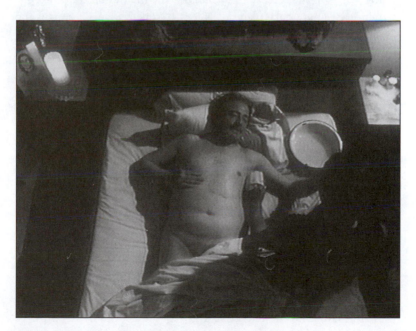

Albert (Roger Lebel) is given a sponge bath in *Un Zoo, la nuit (Night Zoo)*.

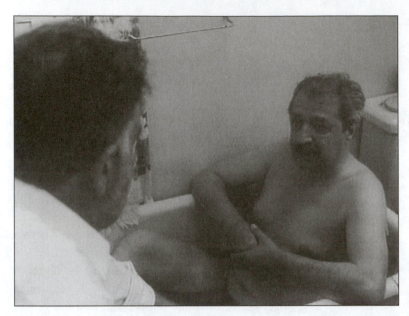

Albert (Lebel) speaks to his landlord, Tony.

colonial frustration and male sexual representation at a certain moment within post-referendum Québec. As an extreme example of what Chantal Nadeau has described as a post-referendum cycle of films geared to "consolidating the centrality of the male subject in the construction of a national [Québécois] identity" (1992, 8), *Un Zoo* maps the disappointments of a failed political project on the suffering colonial male body by way of a dizzying relay of references to impalement, unwanted penetrations and intrusions, coy games of hide-and-seek with the penis, and a palpable undercurrent of what Cynthia Fuchs (1993) has termed "homoerotic homophobia (209)."[14]

The fresh wounds of a stalled anticolonial project are visible in almost every frame of *Un Zoo* and profoundly affect the way male bodies are arranged and represented on screen. At the core of this circuit of abjection is Marcel Brisebois, played with smouldering and sometimes ridiculous intensity by Québec actor Gilles Maheu. An artist and musician who has just served two years in prison for selling drugs provided to him by the police, Marcel is a walking victim of the *prison sans barreaux* that serves as a frequent metaphor for life in Québec — although he has also experienced a prison *with* bars — and his body becomes the front line in a series of invasions and violent expulsions that structure the film. The initial, all-important moment of penetration that launches the narrative and sets off a series of attempts to cleanse the neocolonial male body of abject matter is a prison rape — a "singing [i.e., sodomizing] telegram" sent to Marcel during his final

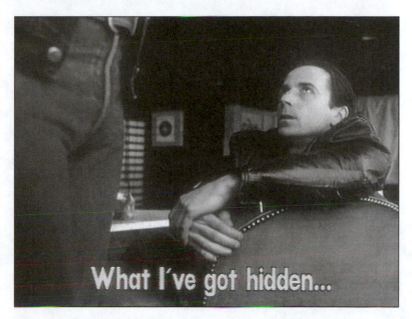

What I've got hidden...

Marcel (Gilles Maheu) speaks to one of the corrupt police officers who supplied him with drugs in *Un Zoo*.

days in jail. The rapist's visit is arranged by Marcel's former drug suppliers on the police force, Charlie (Germain Houde) and his new Anglo-Canadian partner, George (Lorne Brass), as a bid to secure Marcel's silence and remind him that he still owes the police money from their last deal together. The attack functions as more than a plot point, however. As a hyperliteral instance of defilement by the Other, it launches a series of cleansing rituals that take the form of brutal acts of homophobic revenge, culminating in an elaborate set-up to entrap and kill both policemen, one of whom (George) is gay. As the key event in the narrative that motivates Marcel's intensifying homophobia in later scenes, the rape is used to justify a steady stream of bitter jokes, references to the penis and acts of anti-gay violence, culminating in the murder of both police officers at a sleazy "sex motel" punningly called the Bangkok Paradise.

The remainder of the film is geared to exploring Marcel's conflicts with his father, Albert, and gradually bringing about a deathbed reconciliation between the two men. Marked as one in a long line of ineffectual fathers in Québec cinema,[17] Albert is the sweet but bumbling tenant in an apartment attached to a pizza parlor and is about to be evicted to make way for another dining room. As an unemployed manual laborer, neocolonial subject and an older, rural-identified "French Canadian" who has been left behind by the galloping pace of urbanization in Québec, Albert is a relic whose masculinity is at stake, and the extent to which this is a problem is frequently

181

Marcel (Maheu) being raped in prison.

written on his body. As the film delves into his uneasy relationship with his Italian landlord, Tony, and follows the elderly Québécois man's declining status among the overtly macho crowd of hunters and construction workers who populate the restaurant, Albert's lack of authority is often conveyed through partial nudity and barely concealed references to castration. Rarely dressed, he is often seen taking baths (accompanied in the bathroom by his pet parakeet, Florida), lying partially nude in bed, wearing only an undershirt or being given a sponge bath by Marcel during the film's final moments. In one early scene, Albert and Florida have retreated to the bathroom to escape the construction noise when Tony walks in and sits down next to the tub. Although the landlord is enough of a friend to earn the affectionate, if flatly stereotyping, nickname "Spaghet," there is a problem here: the immigrant, who spoke not a word of French when he first went to work with Albert at the plant years earlier, but whom Albert befriended anyway, has now surpassed him. Not only has Tony managed to keep his family intact (unlike Albert, whose wife has abandoned him for the last time), but he has succeeded well enough financially to be expanding his business—an expansion that could put Albert on the street. On a personal level, then, Albert is far from fulfilling the 1960s Quiet Revolution rallying cry of "Maître chez nous." Not only is he not the master of his house, but the house is owned by Italians, whose invasion will be complete, the film seems to suggest, when they oust Albert in order to "sell lasagne."

This relationship may have held special resonance for Québécois audiences recalling statistics popularized by sociologist Marcel Rioux after the first Canadian Royal Commission on Bilingualism and Biculturalism. In his classic sovereigntist text *La question du Québec*, Rioux reported that in 1961, Italians living in Québec were the only group to perform worse economically than the French-speaking Québécois. He wondered in print whether the gap might already have closed (1978, 99). At a certain period in Québec's history, then, the position of Italian immigrants seems to have served as a kind of low watermark for the aspirations of some French-speaking Québécois. In the bathroom scene of *Un Zoo, la nuit*, the watermark has literally shifted to a place right around Albert's seemingly missing loins,[16] while his friend looks down from on high, fully clothed, in a two-shot geared to exaggerating their unequal exposure and Albert's resulting vulnerability.

Power relations between men are not always written this overtly on the body, however. In fact, because *Un Zoo, la nuit* has so much to do with locating the phallus that it sees as having gone missing in post-referendum, neocolonial Québec, the film actually has quite a lot invested in *not* revealing too much of the male body. Since the phallus as understood by psychoanalysis is specifically *not* the penis but rather the "non-thing" that symbolizes and constantly surpasses the penis (i.e., the "[symbolic] ideal that offers an impossible and originary measure for the genitals to approximate" [Butler, 617]) *Un Zoo, la nuit*'s anxiety-filled search for the phallus predictably entails a steady stream of substitutes for the penis, while somewhat hysterically avoiding the object of desire. This helps to explain the film's litany of references to smoked meat, pool sticks, crossbows, fishing rods, and other phallic substitutions, as well as the various innuendo-laden nicknames (such as "poignard," meaning knife, and "Whizzer") referring to Marcel's stunted psychosexual development, overcompensations, or actual anatomy. In such an anxiety-ridden narrative, it comes as no surprise that all of *Un Zoo, la nuit*'s manic flirtation with the penis produces no clear view of the actual organ, since it would be impossible to reveal the object of such frantic attention in a narrative so single-mindedly dedicated to reclaiming a nostalgically defined lost phallic authority.

It is not as easy to point to examples of truly margin-affirming works, but clearly a different sensibility is at work in projects as far-ranging as Greyson's *Urinal* (a campy, experimental docudrama geared to studying gay washroom sex and defending it as a queer sexual practice) and Wellington's *I Love a Man in Uniform* (an action picture that dissects the genre). Though they represent radically different streams within Canadian cinema, both films can be read as making room for representations of the nude male body by way of an analysis of products of colonial identity that tends, in very different ways, to break down normative conceptions of phallic authority.

Urinal's narrative centers on a playfully didactic time-travel premise about a group of gay and lesbian artistic and literary figures—Frida Kahlo, Langston Hughes, Sergei Eisenstein, Florence Wyle, Francis Loring, and Yukio Mishima—who are brought together to study the provincial Canadian attitudes and institutions that led to a crackdown on gay washroom sex during the 1980s. Tricked into attending a nonexistent conference, all of them wind up converging on a house somewhere in Ontario on Gay Pride Day, 1987, where they are put to work on a historical study and sociological critique of the bathroom raids. While affirming the marginal practices that allow gay men in small Canadian communities to meet and enjoy fleeting sexual encounters in public places, Greyson's film also draws attention to the repression and colonial residue in such communities by opening them up to scrutiny by these worldly representatives of the artistic and sexual avant-gardes. As the visiting luminaries deliver the results of their research, the film alternates between fictional set pieces and documentary material, including a brief social history of the public washroom (one that makes use of several images of men masturbating on toilets), official police pronouncements on homosexual depravity, and interviews with several men arrested in the raids.

While all this is going on, the film returns repeatedly to the image of a nude young Asian man whose portrait is being painted by Frida Kahlo. The painting, we are told, is a reference to Oscar Wilde's *The Picture of Dorian Gray*, and the subject in this case is an undercover police officer who may (or may not) have agreed to the sitting in order to infiltrate the group and expose its agenda. Within *Urinal*'s fractured narrative, we can read the presence of this Wildean figure as a repository of conflicted and colliding meanings around colonial and masculine gender identity, the role of the law, and the male body as a source of erotic spectacle. In keeping with the plot of Wilde's novel, Kahlo's portrait of Dorian Gray changes throughout the film, as a computer paint program adds layer upon layer of random, multicolored lines to his nude body, eventually covering his chest and legs and finally obscuring his penis. Though it suffers from a touch of coyness, this device is interesting in terms of the way it rewrites and reimagines an already ambiguously colonial/canonical text,[17] primarily by filtering one of its core motifs through a post-colonial instance of sexual and racial difference. By choosing a widely known novel by a gay author and transforming the text's basic features—dragging its (perhaps) sublimated queer content to the surface, for example, and casting an Asian Canadian actor (Lance Eng) to play a conflicted Royal Candian Mounted Police officer who is not sure whether he wants to join the fun or report the artists to the proper authorities—*Urinal* tends to draw attention to *Dorian Gray* as a coded and closeted queer text that, for all its manifest content as a Gothic/fantastic model of the moral contradictions pervading late Victorian society, has at least as much to say about male sexual looking and homosocial or homosexual longing, and about the way the law treats such instances of desire.[18] By queering what has been interpreted by some critics as Wilde's latent meaning and turning his protagonist into a conflicted authority figure, Greyson opens up new avenues for imagining the role of colonial and canonical texts, their normalizing functions and their availability to resistant readings in a postcolonial setting. In and around these multiple subversions of textual and sexual practices and national identities, Greyson is frequently able to represent the penis "as a penis," rather than a symbol of any desire to mount new symbolic structures of phallic authority in place of the colonial and canonical ones that are among this satirical film's targets. More is at stake here, in other words, than a filmmaker choosing to represent the penis for erotic reasons. Eng's/Dorian Gray's full frontal nudity and the film's other images of male genitals form part of an imaginative landscape geared to a general valuing of sexual margins and racial/sexual difference within a critique of colonially inflected literary and sexual mores.

While I do not wish to go into as much detail here about *I Love a Man in Uniform*, I would argue that it is not simply the work of a poet of homosocial anxiety, to again quote Waugh, and that one indication (among many) that more is going on in the film stems from Wellington's handling of male nudity. The narrative revolves around a dissatisfied bank teller and part-time actor (Tom McCamus) who begins to sink a little too deeply into his first major television role as a sadistic police officer on a cheap, American-style cop show, eventually believing that he is a real member of the force. As he gradually loses his hold on reality, we see him walking around his apartment in the nude, pacing from room to room like a caged animal, swinging his nightstick at imaginary offenders and rehearsing the body movements and overall habitus of an empowered male authority figure. While parts of the film certainly smack of an anxiety-ridden response to the requirements of phallic masculinity (McCamus's character is not living up to his role in the business world; he's a failure with women, and his bank is robbed by a man dressed as Marilyn Monroe, who forces him to kneel down and "fellate" his gun), I would agree with Christine Ramsay's argument that the film does more to analyze anxiety-ridden masculinity than embody or reflect it.[19] Through its painstaking, step-by-step chronicling of the lead character's loss of control, *I Love a Man in Uniform* suggests that the empowered masculine role he takes on is both insane and artificial: far from natural, it has to be built up through an accretion of phallic symbols (guns and night sticks), outright lies ("Shut up, I'm a cop"), and aggressive speech acts ("Scum like you make my trigger finger itch"). By foregrounding the shaky architecture of that campaign, Wellington reveals what is at stake for the male subject who would try to take on these phallic attributes: uncontrolled violence and a radical loss of connection to the world. Furthermore, Wellington seems to be trying to evoke some of the effects of Canada's neocolonial relationship to the United States through a dissection of the stylistic conventions and narrative contexts of reality-based police shows. By borrowing some of those conventions and altering them (unlike most protagonists of the police genre in American film or television, the lead character here is a creepy antihero who loses the girl and blows his head off in the final frames while watching himself on video), *I Love a Man in Uniform* is clearly trying to situate its study of phallic masculinity within a complicit critique of American popular culture. Far from being a simple expression of a threatened filmmaker's wish for superior masculine identity, *I Love a Man in Uniform* can be read as a mediated and self-aware commentary on that very wish, while Wellington's (not to mention McCamus's) willingness to put the nude male body on display is just one indicator of the film's commitment to questioning naturalized definitions of empowered masculinity. McCamus's character may be wielding a night stick in some of these scenes, but with a flaccid penis in plain view, there can be no mistaking the swag of flesh for a symbol of unfettered phallic authority and control.

conclusion

As the recent example of *Eyes Wide Shut*'s (1999) censored North American version tends to suggest, mores regarding sexual representation and the spectacle of the nude male body vary, sometimes substantially, between cultures and over time. While all viewers of Stanley Kubrick's final film were permitted to gaze at a dozen or more fully nude female characters, audiences who watched the censored North American version were prevented from seeing parts of the orgy scene, which reportedly included instances of full frontal male nudity. Whether or not the North American version was censored due to the presence of graphic sex scenes in general or specifically in order to block out the offending view of the penis may always be a matter of speculation. However it seems safe to say that Hollywood cinema (along with some independent work from the United States) has had more trouble with the spectacle of the nude male body—and in particular the sight of male genitals—than other cultures.

Even when the penis has been revealed in recent American cinema, there is usually something mediating that exposure. In the case of Paul

Anderson's *Boogie Nights* (1997), for example, the publicity machines were working overtime to make sure audiences knew that the enormous, limp penis Mark Whalberg's character (washed-up porn star Dirk Diggler) reveals to a mirror near the end of the film was a 10-inch prosthetic rather than his own organ. Something similar happens in *The Election* (1999), which calls attention to the artificiality of its only image of the penis by pulling back to reveal that the limp (but large) genitals in question belong to a museum replica of prehistoric man. *Fight Club* (1999) deviates from this pattern by flashing what appears to be an image of a real, semi-erect penis, but the image is so brief—two or three frames, at most—that most viewers are unlikely to notice it unless they know about the subliminal plant in advance and choose to pause the film on video.[20] In three recent cases, then, rubber devices, industrial strategies, and extreme brevity are used to drive a wedge between the viewer's experience of the film and the spectacle of the nude male body, which is still in many ways considered unrepresentable. As Lehman's work indicates, Hollywood and its semi-independent outskirts may *think* they are ready to embrace new scripts of masculinity by exposing the penis in ways that signal a rejection or distancing from patriarchal concepts of phallic power, but often the organ in question turns out to be a safe, plastic, or barely visible substitute— a fleeting copy of a copy, rather than an image carrying any kind of potentially de-phallicizing, indexical relation to a bodily real.[21]

In its difference from such models, recent Canadian cinema points to the possibility that social and political conditions, national, substate national, regional and subcultural identities, along with localized discourses on cultural and political life, all have the potential to influence cinematic representations of the male body, giving rise to culturally specific (but never fixed or homogeneous) patterns in the handling of male nudity. Recent sociological and ethnographic work on masculine gender identity (Kandiyoti 1994) has stressed the need to "situate masculinities—however fragmented and variegated they may appear—in historically and culturally specific institutional contexts, (212)" and I have tried to show that the same observation (and the same methodological need) holds for analyses of male sexual representation in the cinema. As my example of recent Canadian film tends to show, not all national cinemas hysterically avoid or regulate the spectacle of the nude male body—although both patterns can be detected in Canadian films from regions and time periods where (I argue) threatening aspects of colonial masculinity hover closer to the surface and generate anxiety-ridden narrative and visual approaches to the colonial male body. Through attention to such distinctions, part of what this study illustrates is that the category of "nation" or "national cinema" obscures as much as it reveals, particularly in a complex heterogeneous society such as Canada's, where, as Carol Ann Howells argues, "the problem of identity is not the problem of having no identity but of having multiple identities, so that any single national self image is perceived as reductive and always open to revision" (1991, 318).

I have been arguing that this heterogeneity and the experience of colonialism should be viewed as conditions that have influenced the imaginative possibilities for representing the male body in Canadian cinema. This approach could, of course, be applied to other national cinemas, where we might begin by asking: What does it mean to take nation into account in thinking about how male bodies are represented on screen? How does the category of nation help to generate (or obstruct) narrative and aesthetic possibilities and imaginative contexts for representing the male body? What other conditions (substate, subcultural or institutional, for example) help shape these narrative contexts and imaginative possibilities, and how might they influence decisions about whether (and how; within what formal and narrative contexts) the male body is covered up, exposed, de-phallicized, demystified or put forth as inviolable vessels for ideal masculinity?

Since all attempts to define national identity (or to designate a national cinema) involve what Andrew Higson (1989) describes as "a homogonising, mythologising process" (37) geared to producing and assigning particular meanings and containing or preventing the proliferation of other meanings, it is worth remembering that there may be any number of other ways to define the social and identificatory practices underlying male sexual representation, and a wide range of possible approaches to the social starting points and significance of moments of male nudity in other national cinemas. In keeping with Higson's recommendations for an "inward-looking" means to defining national cinema, the search for cultural conditions influencing the sexual representation of the male body should lead us to inquire how the narrative and aesthetic contexts and manifest content of such representations "[insert themselves] alongside other cultural practices" (42) and draw on existing cultural histories and cultural traditions of the producing nation, reformulating them in cinematic terms.

notes

I would like to thank Perter Harcourt, Peter Lehman, and Brenda Longfellow for their comments on an earlier draft of this essay.

1. On this rediscovery see Mark Simpson, *Male Impersonators: Men Performing Masculinity* (New York and London: Routledge, 1994).
2. In the past six years, for example, audiences have been treated to the previously taboo spectacle of full frontal male nudity in films such as *American History X* (1998), *Angels and Insects* (1995), *Ridicule* (1996), *The Election* (1999), *Cobb* (1994), *The Day of the Beast* (1995), *Seven* (1995), *Shallow Grave* (1994), and *Fight Club* (1999) to name only a handful of titles.

lee parpart

3. In the context of a discussion of feral child narratives, for example, Lehman argues that "the sexually explicit male body has always posed a problem for the cinema, including the European Art Cinema" (1993, 44).

4. The pattern dates back to the mid-1960s and can be traced to at least two early examples: David Secter's *Winter Kept Us Warm* (1965), with its subtle narrative of unconsummated love between two young men at the University of Toronto, and experimental director John Hofsess's dual-projector compilation film, *Palace of Pleasure* (1966–67), which included strobelike images of a disembodied penis, followed by shots of a young man lounging nude on a day bed. Neither film ventured so far as to reveal the penis "attached" to the male body (the would-be lovers in *Winter Kept Us Warm* are glimpsed from behind as they shower together in a college changing room, and the *Palace of Pleasure* scene is carefully choreographed to keep the man's genitals out of sight), but the seeds were being sown for a full-blown cinematic investigation of the nude male beginning in the late 1980s and continuing into the 1990s.

5. In *Bob's Birthday*, an unhappy dentist signals his midlife crisis by stripping down to his shirt and tie and swinging a bunch of bananas in front of his exposed penis. In one episode of *Bob & Margaret,* Bob dreams of being flushed down a toilet in the nude. *Pink Komkommer*, a compilation film to which Fine and Snowden contributed a segment, alternates between cheerfully lewd dream sequences (several of them including images of transmogrifying penislike objects) and images of an elderly woman snoozing next to a parrot.

6. Both directors have consistently felt free to reveal the penis, both as a source of erotic imagery and, to borrow Silverman's phrase, seemingly as a way of saying "no" to patriarchal and heteronormative varieties of phallic power and authority. Silverman (1992) ascribed this effect to Fassbinder's cinema—a queer corpus that she argues does everything possible, including staging insistent exposures of the nude male body, to interrupt mainstream, bourgeois, heterosexual society's classic insistence on the "commensurability of the penis and the phallus," or its assumption that the symbolic power and privilege associated with the phallus should or does adhere automatically to those subjects possessing its representative, the penis (15–16).

7. While British Columbia may qualify as a periphery in geographical terms, its residents and film industry are financially healthy in comparison to average income or film budgets in Cape Breton or New Brunswick, the locations for these Atlantic Canadian films.

8. Ian Balfour has drawn my attention to the gap between empirically defensible claims of sociopolitical heterogeneity and the discursive tendency to make such claims about whatever culture one happens to be a part of. While there is some empirical evidence to suggest that Canada may be more heterogeneous than other nations—statistically, for example, Toronto is considered the most multicultural city in the world—it may be of equal or greater importance to note the pervasiveness of *claims* to the effect that Canada is a fractured mosaic. Whether or not Canada is actually more heterogeneous as a society than the United States, for example, may be less important than the widespread acceptance of such claims. This is especially true when it comes to the effect discourses can have on representation, since representation is embedded

in imaginative aspects of community, rather than transparently reflecting a pre-existing "real."

9. Carol Ann Howells notes: "Whereas the Americans have a meta-narrative of nationhood spelled out in their Constitution and by nineteenth century Transcendentalist writers ... Canadians by contrast and by their history have told a different New World narrative about national identity, focussing not on unity but on disunity, highlighting individual difference through regionalism, bilingualism, multiculturalism." Carol Ann Howells, "No Transcendental Image: Canadianness in Contemporary Women's Fictions in English." In *Canada on the Threshold of the 21st Century*, ed., C. H. W. Remie and J. M. Lacroix. Amsterdam: John Benjamin Publishing Company, 1991, 318.

10. Faced with greater competition from the U.S. market and a greater degree of assimilation with American culture, English Canadian films famously occupy less than 2 percent of total screen time in Canadian theaters, while domestically produced French-language films occupy closer to 16 percent of the total screen time within Québec.

11. Before we make too much of the fact that Greyson's fairly explicit gay-themed work is shown in theaters at all in Canada, it is worth noting that police tried to shut down one of his screenings of *Zero Patience* at Toronto's Carlton Cinema.

12. Thomas Haig has argued that Canada might even be considered a kind of "queer nation"—a marginal site that shares many of the qualities and predicaments of gays and lesbians. Thomas Haig, "Not Just Some Sexless Queen: A Note on 'Kids in the Hall' and the Queerness of Canada," *semiotext(e) canadas*, No. 17, Vol. VI, Issue 2 (New York and Peterborough, Ontario, Marginal Editions, 1994): 227–29.

13. See, for example, Anthony Anderson, "Gawking at Geeks," *Take One* 7 (winter 1995): 37.

14. For a longer and more detailed reading of *Un Zoo, la nuit*, see my "Nostalgic Nationalisms and the Spectacle of the Male Body in Canadian and Québécois Cinema," unpublished master's thesis, York University, Toronto, August 1997.

15. See *Le Confessional* (1995), *Les Bons débarras* (1980), *Jacques et novembre* (1984), *Piwi* (1982), *Léolo* (1992), *Bonheur d'occasion* (1983), and *La Petite Aurore l'enfant martyre* (1951).

16. While Lebel's penis is not glimpsed in this scene, the framing reveals so much of his pubic area that it could lead viewers to question how it was shot *without* revealing the penis.

17. One written by a gay Irish man, first commissioned in novella form by a Philadelphia magazine, then republished in London and gradually, after much initial resistance, incorporated into the British canon. See Michael Patrick Gillespie, *The Picture of Dorian Gray: "What in the World Thinks Me"* (New York: Twayne Publishers, 1995), 21–28.

18. For a discussion of queer content/intent in *Dorian Gray*, see Ed Cohen, "Writing Gone Wilde: Homoerotic Desire in the Closet of Repression," *PMLA* 102 (October 1987): 801–13.

19. Ramsay reads the film as critically probing "the affective psychic depths of [the] dominant North American phallic world of male narcissism, omnipotence, and violence" (26). Christine Ramsay, "Social Surfaces and

Psychic Depths in David Wellington's I Love a Man in Uniform," *Canadian Journal of Film Studies* 4, 1 (Spring 1995): 3–26.

20. In *Fight Club* (1999), Brad Pitt's character inserts subliminal images of "nice big cocks" into family films as part of a wider terrorist campaign to destroy consumer culture and upset bourgeois values—a rare example of hypermasculinity being placed in the service of social critique, within the (perhaps limiting) context of a major box office hit.

21. As added proof that dominant U.S. culture has had trouble with sexual representations of the male body, it is worth noting two censorship decisions from the mid-1990s. Several scenes depicting Catholic priests molesting little boys were removed from the American broadcast version of the Canadian mini-series *The Boys of St. Vincent,* and U.S. censors removed part of a male masturbation scene from the American video version of Atom Egoyan's film *The Adjuster.* The offending footage included a brief view of a Peeping Tom's erect penis, glimpsed through a sliding glass door. Telephone interview with Egoyan, Oct. 7, 1995.

works cited

Cohen, Ed. 1987. "Writing Gone Wilde: Homoerotic Desire in the Closet of Repression," *PMLA* 102 (October): 801–13.

Fuchs, Cynthia J. 1993. "The Buddy Politics." In *Screening the Male: Exploring Masculinities in Hollywood Cinema*, ed., Steven Cohan and Ina Rae Hark, 194–212. London and New York: Routledge.

Gillespie, Michael Patrick. 1995. *The Picture of Dorian Gray: "What in the World Thinks Me."* New York: Twayne Publishers.

Gould, Karen. 1985. "Madeleine Gagnon's Po(e)litical Vision: Portrait of an Artist and an Era." In *Traditionalism, Nationalism and Feminism: Women Writers of Québec*, ed., Paula Gilbert Lewis. Westport, Connecticut and London: Greenwood Press.

Haig, Thomas. 1994. "Not Just Some Sexless Queen: A Note on "Kids in the Hall" and the Queerness of Canada," *semiotext(e) canadas*, 17, VI, 2: 227–29. New York and Peterborough, Ontario: Marginal Editions.

Higson, Andrew. 1989. "The Concept of National Cinema," *Screen*, Autumn, 36–46.

hooks, bell. 1996. "Feminism as a Persistent Critique of History: What's Love Got to Do With It." In *The Fact of Blackness: Frantz Fanon and Visual Representation*, ed., 76–85. Alan Read. London and Seattle: Institute of Contemporary Arts and Bay Press.

Howells, Carroll Ann. 1991. "No Transcendental Image: Canadianness in Contemporary Women's Fictions in English." In *Canada on the Threshold of the 21st Century*, ed. C.H.W. Remie and J. M. Lacroix, 317–23. Amsterdam: John Benjamin Publishing.

Hutcheon, Linda. 1988. *The Canadian Postmodern: A Study of Contemporary English-Canadian Fiction.* Toronto, New York, Oxford: Oxford University Press.

———. 1991. *Splitting Images: Contemporary Canadian Ironies.* Toronto, Oxford, New York: Oxford University Press.

Kandiyoti, Deniz. 1994. "The Paradoxes of Masculinity: Some Thoughts on Segregated Societies." In *Dislocating Masculinity: Comparative Ethnographies*, ed. Andrea Cornwall and Nancy Lindisfarne, 197–213. London: Routledge.

Lehman, Peter. 1993. *Running Scared: Masculinity and the Representation of the Male Body*. Philadelphia: Temple University Press.

———. 1998. "The Act of Seeing the Dead Penis with One's Own Eyes." Paper delivered at the Society for Cinema Studies Conference, San Diego, April 4, 1998.

Nadeau, Chantal. 1992. "Women in French-Québec Cinema: The Space of Socio-Sexual (In)difference." *CineACTION* 28: 4–15.

Parpart, Lee. 1999a. "Pit(iful) Male Bodies: Colonial Masculinity, Class and Folk Innocence in *Margaret's Museum*." *Canadian Journal of Film Studies*, 8, 1: 63–86.

———. 1999b. "Cowards, Bullies and Cadavers: Feminist Re-Mappings of the Passive Male Body in English-Canadian Cinema." In *Gendering the Nation*, ed., Kay Armatage, Kass Banning, Brenda Longfellow, and Janine Marchessault. Toronto: University of Toronto Press, 2nd ed.

Ramsay, Christine. 1993. "Canadian Narrative Cinema from the Margins: "The Nation" and Masculinity. In *Goin' Down the Road*," *Canadian Journal of Film Studies* 2, 2–3: 27–50.

———. 1995. "Social Surfaces and Psychic Depths in David Wellington's I Love a Man in Uniform." *Canadian Journal of Film Studies* 4, 1 (spring): 3–26.

Rioux, Marcel. 1978. *Québec in Question*. Trans. by James Boake (Toronto: James Lorimer & Co.). First published as *La Question du Québec* (Paris: Éditions Seghers, 1969).

Schehr, Lawrence R. 1997. *Parts of an Andrology: On Representations of Men's Bodies*. Stanford: Stanford University Press.

Silverman, Kaja. 1992. *Male Subjectivity at the Margins*. New York: Routledge.

Simpson, Mark. 1994. *Male Impersonators: Men Performing Masculinity*. New York and London: Routledge.

lynching photography and the "black beast rapist" in the southern white masculine imagination

twelve

amy louise wood

I.

I can't say that I remember the day I saw the photograph, or even the book I saw it in. All I remember precisely is the image, a man strung to a tree, limp and yet not dead-looking, dressed in the clothes Christ wore in his last earthly moments. And then below, the white men who surrounded the spectacle in the spectacle: a child on the shoulders of one, a blur beneath the hat of another, still another with a Hitler moustache, pointing ambiguously. I remember, too, the shudder that went through me, that changed the way I looked at everything from that moment on.

—Jacquie Jones, "How Come Nobody Told Me about the Lynching?" 153.

The image of black men hanging from Southern trees, like "strange fruit" as Billie Holiday sang,[1] is a visual memory both haunting and obscure, unforgettable but misremembered. These images are every-where around us, in books, in museums, in magazines, and on television, evoked in verbal imagery or reprinted in pictorial representation, yet little is known about them. For African-American writer Jacquie Jones, the photograph she witnessed above (see Figure 1), represented racism itself—the image of a white mob casually surrounding an almost otherworldly black man lynched from a tree was more explicit and immediate than any other expression of racial violence and oppression. "It devastated," she writes, "because it made concrete in one moment the brutal history, the living legacy of human bondage and racial tyranny that Americans, both black and white, would prefer to forget" (Jones 1994, 157).

Photographs like the one Jones describes, have by and large created the very conceptual images of lynching that at once intrude into public discourse as the events they represent fade from public memory. My concern here is to examine lynching photographs because of the ways that these images, in the depiction of one frozen moment, can contain and express the meanings and implications of the violence represented, not only for Americans like Jones today, but for the white Southerners who originally made and collected them. Indeed, these photographs, for the most part taken by lynchers themselves, were invested with very particular racial significations—significations that, I will argue, were dynamically integrated with popular notions of Southern

Figure 1. Lynching of Thomas Shipp and Abram Smith, August 7, 1930 in Marion, Indiana. Courtesy, Allen/Littlefield Collection, Special Collections Department, Robert W. Woodruff Library, Emory University.

masculinity, both black and white. And the public display of these images at the time ensured that these meanings were visually remembered. In this way, lynching photography—both the act of taking a picture and the subsequent image itself—functioned as an integral part of the lynching (as "spectacle within the spectacle"), reinforcing the violence for the perpetrators, and perpetuating the racial and sexual ideologies embedded in the lynching act itself.

Between 1880 and 1930, more than twenty-five hundred African Americans were lynched in the South.[2] Lynching in America dates back to the eighteenth-century frontier, where mob vigilante violence substituted for legal and police institutions. By the 1880s, however, lynching was no longer a frontier, nonracial form of discipline, but instead a Southern racial phenomenon. With the collapse of Reconstruction, white Southerners sought to reassert their political and cultural dominance through institutionalized oppression, namely Jim Crow laws, and through brutal violence, such as lynching. Amid the economic uncertainty and social transformation of this period, African-American men were figured as "black beasts" whose purported desire for white women and white power threatened the moral and social order of the traditional, patriarchal South.

The practice of lynching increased not only in numbers in the post-Reconstruction period, but also in intensity. Many lynchings were no longer enacted as frenzied renegade outbursts or swift, corporal punishments; rather, they became elaborate, highly ritualized tortures, entailing not only hangings, but beatings, mutilations, shootings, and burnings. Thus, the process of violence itself, as well as its subsequent representation on the lynched body, became more significant than the lynching's intended result (that is, death to punish). Most significantly, they became more "spectacular." That is, many lynchings were public events, performed and watched by diverse sectors of the white community. They were advertised and publicized; souvenirs were collected and sold. Through the ritualized spectacle of a lynching, white Southern men enacted and inscribed their ideologies of race and sex onto the bodies of African-American men.

Central to these public spectacles, photographs were taken, printed, and circulated long after the event had taken place. Indeed, photography served to render the lynching a "spectacle," as recording the violence on film enhanced the cultural work of the lynching by making the social and racial meanings enacted through the violence visible. (These images, in this sense, even transformed smaller, "private" lynchings into public spectacles.[3]) For one, photography simulated the effects of lynching *as a ritual*, becoming a pivotal step in that ritual which affirmed and made manifest white solidarity and supremacy. The act of photography also changed the nature of that spectacle itself, so that the event was no longer viewed only in ritualized movement. The photograph both extended the violence beyond the frame of the actual event, and held the moment of violence in one static image.

The visual representation of photography therefore transformed the lynching ritual into symbolic form, of the white man's superiority and the black man's "brutishness." Though there were cases in which black women were lynched, most victims were black men. Likewise, while white women sometimes watched (see figure 1) and participated in lynchings, by and large it was white men who enacted these tortures. Moreover, the discourse surrounding lynching focused on masculinity as much as race, for notions of black depravity rested on both the black man's emasculation and the white man's hypermasculine honor. Within this rhetoric, the condemned black man's savage sexuality could be controlled only through white male torturous displays of power (Hall 1993, 144–57; Brundage 1993, 65–66).[4] The lynchers, through their torture, took the black man's body apart piece by piece to obliterate his human identity and to make him into the "black beast" that their racial/sexual ideology purported him to be. The lynching victim in this way was himself a "representation"—a signifier of black inferiority and depravity, and in turn, white (male) power and supremacy. To take a photograph of the victim in this state of debasement was an integral step therefore in this process of representation, as it froze the moment of representation in time. The visual representation of the violence was thus inextricable from the violence itself, becoming a sort of visual discourse that substantiated white supremacy and legitimized the supposed social need for lynching.

These anonymous photographers were, as far as we know, amateurs. In fact, the accessibility and popularity of amateur photography emerged at the same time that racialized lynchings in the South increased. In this sense, the intense spectacle enacted in lynching was intricately coupled with the social practice of photography. In the late nineteenth century, for the first time, these kinds of community rituals, and acts of violence, could be visually documented by the participants themselves. George Eastman's invention of the Kodak camera and roll film system in the mid-1880s revolutionized photography by making it possible for anyone who could afford a camera to take pictures. These first cameras cost twenty-five dollars, or a month's wages for the average American laborer. By 1900, however, Eastman had introduced the popular Brownie camera, which cost only one dollar. Exposed film could then be sent off to the Kodak Company or developed by a local studio (Jenkins 1995, 12–16; Conniff 1988, 114).

Most probably, the hundreds of lynching photographs that exist today, scattered across the country in libraries, archives, and private homes, were taken by the lynchers themselves. In fact, newspapers in this period rarely published photographs of lynchings, although they often included extremely graphic details of the event.[5] There is also evidence that when outsiders, including journalists, attempted to photograph these killings, they were thwarted. A reporter for the St. Joseph, Missouri, *News-Press* had his camera ripped way from him, and his film destroyed, when he tried to take pictures of a lynching in 1931. He had photographed the mob as it was dragging its victim to the lynching site to burn him, when the men angrily seized his camera. Once the burning had begun, however, several other photographers, not journalists, proceeded to take photographs (Raper 1933, 419−20). The lynchers clearly wanted control of the photographing. This control not only allowed them to govern what images could be recorded and remembered, but it assured that the photographing was integrated within the ritual ceremony itself.

II.

Men were sent into town for kerosene oil and chains, and finally the Negroes were bound to an old stump, fagots were heaped around them, and each was drenched with oil. Then the crowd stood back accommodatingly, while a photographer, standing there in the bright sunshine, took pictures of the chained Negroes. Citizens crowded up behind the stump and got their faces into the photograph. When the fagots were lighted, the crowd yelled wildly.... They threw knots and sticks at the writhing creatures, but always left room for the photographer to take more pictures.

—Ray Stannard Baker, *Following the Color Line*, 186−87.

Although lynchings were committed by large groups, sometimes by mass mobs, they were nevertheless tightly controlled and organized rituals, as is clear from journalist Ray Baker's account above of the double lynching of Paul Reid and Will Cato, accused of murdering a white family in Statesboro, Georgia, in 1904 (R. Baker 1908, 186−87). These rituals of violence were enacted as performances—public spectacles in which the white community dramatized its beliefs in racial superiority (Harris 1984, 11−19; Fouss 1999, 1−5). Not infrequently, they were advertised, and scheduled, so that as many people as possible could come to town, to both participate in and witness the drama. For the 1899 lynching of Sam Holt—a black man accused of murdering his white employer and raping that employer's wife—special trains brought people from Atlanta to nearby Newnan, Georgia. Approximately two thousand people watched and cheered as Holt was hideously tortured and then burned alive at the stake (*AC*, April 24, 1899, 1−2; Ginzberg 1988, 10−20).

While Holt's lynching was, to be sure, exceptionally spectacular, lynchings across the South were similarly ceremonious and elaborately ritualized. Indeed, the uniformity of ritual found in diverse types of lynchings across the South is remarkable (Brundage 1993, 39). Lynchings were rituals in the sense that they were set apart from everyday life, they followed particular rules and procedures, and they were enacted as self-conscious performances.[6] Most notably, the ritual of lynching encouraged a level of violence intolerable in everyday society. But when contained within the group, this otherwise individually deviant and atrocious behavior not only became socially acceptable but served to create cohesion among the mob. Ritual, in this sense, acted out white Southerners' desire and need for lynching in the first place. If lynching was publicly justified as a means to protect a unified conception of white honor and integrity against the threat of black insurgency, the ordered, synchronized mob replicated that fantasy. Such displays of unity furthermore countered the chaos and discord that otherwise pervaded the white South at this time.

A full generation after Reconstruction, as the planter elite were trying to reassert their cultural and political hegemony, more and more yeoman farmers were finding themselves pushed into tenancy and poverty. Meanwhile, the advance of commercial capitalism in the South, the growth of towns and cities, and the development of industry at this time disrupted traditional community life, and gave rise to new classes—an industrial working class (made up of farmers no longer able to survive on the land alone), and their bourgeois counterparts. The white community in the South was by no means monolithic, let alone a unified fellowship.

Yet, in lynching, a mob of enraged individuals performed together as an ordered, united group. As the Atlanta *Constitution* reported at Holt's lynching, "the crowd was cool and went about its work carefully and with a system . . . the whole male community seemed to be a unit" (*AC*, April 24, 1899, 1). Members of all social and economic classes committed and participated in lynchings, as is evidenced in the variety of dress and composure in some of the photographs. Newspaper reports at the time often pointed out that the mobs included the community's best and most influential citizens (a fact that surely further legitimized the lynching in readers' minds). And while, to be sure, there were many white detractors of lynching across the South whose critique of lynching was based in class assumptions,[7] there were just as many defenders of lynching from these same upper classes.

Historians have traditionally understood the class solidarity evidenced in lynching, and other racially oppressive institutions and practices, as a sort of "herrenvolk democracy" (Frederickson 1987, 60–64), in which white poor and middling classes in the South bonded with the elite classes, subjugating African Americans in order to uplift themselves. However, as historian Barbara Fields (1982) argues, "white supremacy" and the supposed unity of yeomen and planter whites to disenfranchise, subjugate, and murder African Americans was no great triumph of racial unity. Rather, because of the different economic circumstances of poor whites, yeoman and planter elites, their racial beliefs would have actually been quite dissimilar as well. "White supremacy," Fields points out, is not a unifying ideology, but a political slogan that serves to unite, on the surface, people with otherwise different, or even opposing, interests. And so white supremacy in the South not only effected the brutal subjugation of African Americans, but it also ultimately enacted the white elite's dominance over other whites (156–58).

The ritual performance of a lynching, therefore, was not so much a reflection of undisputed white solidarity, but an action that displayed and constructed a particular kind of racial solidarity—a racial solidarity that required constant replenishing and constant reenvisioning. That is, it needed to be performed and witnessed. White supremacy was, in this sense, a spectacle extraordinaire.

Photography, therefore, played a crucial role in this performative ritual and the social roles it produced. The photographing itself was carefully integrated into the ritual, acting as another step in the process of torture. It appears that the "shooting" of the lynching victim with a camera was highly standardized, coming right before the final desecration of the body. Most lynching photographs depicted the victim just after he was hanged, usually with the lynchers posing beside the body. None of the aftereffects of a lynching, such as bulging eyes, burst blood vessels, and bloating, are yet noticeable, suggesting that the hanging had just taken place. Moreover, these bodies may have been cut down to be burned, or riddled with bullets after the hanging. For instance, Charlie Hale was "shot full of holes" after his body was strung up on a telephone pole (*AC,* April 8, 1911, 1). Yet in the photograph of this lynching, his body was still in intact (figure 2). The lynching was presumably paused for the picture to be taken, and so the ceremony becomes prolonged and extended by the act of photographing it (Bourdieu 1990, 26).

Indeed, in many lynchings, the final killing was prolonged as long as possible. Hanging the victim not only allowed the entire crowd to see the body as it was shot, but it allowed the mob to kill the victim more than once. The mob that killed Claude Neal in Marietta, Florida, in 1934, for instance, pulled him up to be hanged and nearly choked him to death before they let him down only to start all over again (McGovern 1982, 80). In this way, lynchings were often reenacted repeat-

Figure 2. The lynching of Charlie Hale in Lawrenceville, Georgia, April 7, 1911. Accused of assaulting a local white woman, Hale was strung up on a telephone pole in the courthouse square. This particular photograph was made into a postcard. Courtesy, Georgia Department of Archives and History.

edly within the very process itself. The ceremonies surrounding the act—the declarations toward the accused, the extracted confessions, the sequence of torture and death—all served to extend the violence. Photography likewise required an interruption in the process, especially as at this time early in the technology, cameras required long shutter speeds to record the image. That is, cameras could not record the action as it was happening—they required still images. In this sense, both the image and the act of creating the image froze time.

These requirements of photography further promoted the representation of group solidarity that the lynching enacted. In the photographs, the lynchers gather as one, pushing their bodies together, leaning forward, heads peering over shoulders so all are in view. The introduction of both amateur photography and portable cameras in the late nineteenth century created new social roles and behaviors, as being the object of a photograph changed from posing for a professional photographer in a studio to posing at family gatherings, outdoor ceremonies, and other more private events (Moeller 1983, 3). Many of the same conventions from the photographer's studios nevertheless persisted. For example, the notion of posing without movement endured well after photographic technology required that people sit still for long exposures. This kind of frozen, affected posturing served to act as yet another ritual of social cohesion. Thus the social conventions attached to amateur photography enhanced the cultural work of lynching as a ritual performance.

Amateur photography also gave rise to new socially determined conventions regarding the time and place for picture taking: most people take out the camera at "special" family and social gatherings as a sign of social harmony and unity. Photographing then becomes a ritual within a ritual that acts as a sign of the celebration (we know it's a celebration because it is being specially recorded as such), and then comes to be the visual representation of the cohesiveness of the group (so we pose together as a group). As Bourdieu asserts, "the ceremony may be photographed because it is outside of the daily routine, and must be photographed because it realizes the image that the group seeks to give itself as a group" (1990, 19–31). The act of photographing a lynching, therefore, functioned not only as an integral part of the white community's ritualized violence, but its product—the image itself—became the representation of that ritual, and the white community's sense of its own solidarity and supremacy. The visual focus of the photograph is thus not so much on the lynched victim, who is often to the side of the frame (see figures 1 and 2), but the white men surrounding him.

III

Skinny Slaton said they wasn't no sense in lettin' him burn up all the way. So he pulled Shine offn the fire and put a rope around his neck and him and one or two others tied him up against a tree. Well, said Skinny Slaton, shore as I'm born I'm gonna borrer me a kodak tomorrer and I'm comin' back here and I'm gonna take me some pitchers of that. Don't look human, does it?

—Anonymous account in Nedra Tyre, *Red Wine First*, 120–21

The image of lynchers posed next to their victim's hanging bodies strongly resembles another photographic convention, that is, the hunter posed with his prey—the confident postures, the proprietary gestures (see figure 3). Hunting in the South was an intensely significant masculine ritual, distinctly segregated from feminine domesticity and virtue, indeed often marking a boy's initiation into manhood. For many Southern men, hunting was a ritualized performance, a ceremonial dance of power between man and animal and an outlet for masculine self-assertion and self-indulgence (Ownby 1990, 21–37; Wyatt-Brown 1982, 195–97).

In a culture that conceptualized black men as "beasts" and "brutes," it was not coincidental that lynching often reenacted the hunt-and-kill ritual, adopting its methods and discourse. A "manhunt" would be formed to search out and surround the "beast." Hunting dogs were frequently sent out to track the prey down (see figure 2—in this case, dogs from the county convict camp were used). Once caught, the black man was often dragged through town, as a trophy, before he was hanged or burned. Finally, the snapshot of hunter with his prey captured in memorial this triumphant moment. The word "snapshot" itself was a British hunting term denoting a shot that had gone off too quickly, a term photographers began using in the 1850s (Conniff 1988, 107).

Framing a lynching as a hunt not only underscored the dehumanization of the black man that the torture and killing itself enacted, but it additionally served to reaffirm the heroic masculinity of the lynchers. As many historians have pointed out, sexuality, gender, and lynching were inextricably tied together. Though most lynchings were instigated by crimes other than rape, namely murder or theft, the justification cited by proponents and defenders of lynching was invariably sexual assault upon white women. The protection of virtuous white womanhood became the rallying cry for white men across the South. Every black man was a potential beast who sought to violate the purity of white womanhood, and so it was every white man's chivalric obligation to protect that purity by avenging its violation. Moreover, within

Figure 3. Hunters with deer, Jenkins County, Georgia. Courtesy, Georgia Department of Archives and History.

Southern conceptions of honor, a man's masculine reputation was signified by his wife's (or daughter's, or sister's) virtue—to protect her purity was to assert his own masculinity.

While these notions of honor and sexuality had a long tradition in the South, the idea that the black man was a brutish danger to that honor was particularly specific to the post-Reconstruction period. It is significant that this powerful stereotype arose as the first generation of African Americans born out of slavery came of age (Williamson 1984, 183). Coupled with the economic uncertainty and social dislocations of the 1880s and 1890s, white Southerners felt intensely that traditional social structures and roles in the South had been disrupted. Indeed, scholars have documented that lynchings were more likely to occur in those areas of high socioeconomic stress. But Southerners did not conceptualize lynchings in economic terms; rather, by positing black men as the real threat to their traditional way of life, signified in the purity of white womanhood, white men could reassert both traditional racial and sexual hierarchies and white patriarchal power (Williamson 1984, 301). Thus, the image of the "black beast rapist" and the pure exalted woman were not merely justifications for the violence of lynching; they were codependent images, political weapons to ensure white, masculinist supremacy (Hall 1993, xxv). The photographic image further substantiated and re-created these ideological roles: white man as masculine hunter, black man as regenerate beast.

In a lynching, the white community felt compelled to desecrate the bodies of those they believed had desecrated their communal bodies. The lynching thus came to reenact the alleged rape (Harris 1984, 22). The black man was often stripped nude, or at least partly undressed, and every part of his body was touched, dismembered, or molested in some way. The lynchers slowly wreaked destruction on the victim's body, taking it apart piece by piece, occasionally even removing organs, before they completed their act. On the one hand, the body needed to be a human body in order to avenge and re-stage the crime against the white community. Newspaper reports, in this way, often detailed the victim's demeanor, his confessions, and cries, or alternatively, his quiet stoicism. But to perform the lynching was to dehumanize him, to gut him like a hunted animal. The "black beast rapist" was thus both inhuman brute ("beast") and hypersexual man ("rapist"). To transform him into an animal was to deflate the sexual threat he represented, while at the same time inflating the white man's human masculinity.

Genital dismemberment was and remains such a powerful symbol of lynching for these reasons. (Across the South, mobs castrated or cut off the penis of one in three lynching victims, reserving this practice for the very worst crimes and assaults [Brundage 1993, 66]. But nevertheless, genital mutilation, for obvious reasons, has affected the cultural memories of both blacks and whites, more than any other aspect of lynching). Through emasculating their victims, lynchers rendered the black man a negation of themselves, against which they, as white men, could define themselves as both white and male. By cutting off the black man's genitals, the white man could possess them himself—he could own that very sexual power he so feared. In addition, castration was performed routinely on farm animals, so for these rural Southerners, this kind of act would have been commonplace in association with animals (McGovern 1982, 81).

Significantly, however, photographs of lynchings almost never reveal the black man's genitalia, whether mutilated or not. Indeed, in some instances, it is clear that the lynching victim has been re-covered for the photograph—burlap sacks tied around their waists, pants clumsily pulled up. If the black man was imagined primarily through his penis, that member, in its supposed savage virility and size, signified at once his moral weakness, intellectual inferiority and animal nature (Fanon 1968, 165, 170). As an abstruse symbol, the imaginary signifier of black "beastliness," bolstering every defense of the lynching performance, it can never actually be revealed in a photograph for what it actually is. Even when, during the lynching, the penis was uncovered, molested, or cut off, there was evidently something forbidden about showing it in fixed detail within the powerful image of a photograph.

Indeed, the power ascribed to photography in this period was central to the racial ideologies enacted in the photograph. In the late nineteenth century, as photography became a "craze," many Americans also felt a keen discomfort with the camera, regarding photographers, as the *New York Tribune* asserted in 1892, "to be in league with evil spirits" (see Mensel 1991, 28–29). Because it was believed that they could so accurately capture reality and, even more powerfully, reveal moral character through an image or expression, cameras were considered "deadly weapons" and "instruments of torture" that threatened Victorian notions of privacy and self–presentation (Mensel 1991, 29–30).[8]

Historically, therefore, a photograph might imply even more intensely than today a violation or defilement. To photograph the black victim was further to violate, objectify, and appropriate him. Alternately, if a photograph revealed a true expression of moral character, retaining in a filmic image a person's social identity, then the lynching photograph—pictures of the lynchers' triumph in victory, the condemned's utter desecration—imparted and secured the very racial and social meanings the lynching itself enacted. Such visual display allowed these white Southerners to witness firsthand the black man's depravity, providing that ocular proof that justified the lynching in the first place (Fouss 1999, 17).

IV.

The Spectacle is not a collection of images, but a social relation among people, mediated by images.

—Guy Debord, *Society of the Spectacle*, 2

Unlike even the most detailed verbal account, photographs provide a chilling certainty and verification of the event. A photograph allows the viewer to know that the lynching actually took place, because someone—the photographer, the people in the picture, the victim even—was there to witness it. While today we are more likely to be skeptically attuned to the possibilities of manipulation and deception in photography, to nineteenth- and early-twentieth-century viewers, as noted above, a photograph presented a simulation of reality, a means

205

to perceive and authenticate a past event that had not existed previously (Barthes 1981, 76–85; Sontag 1977, 5).

That existential link between the photograph and the lynching therefore embodied an act of authenticity that was crucial to the lynching itself, as it substantiated for the white community the violence they committed. This is all the more reason why lynchers felt compelled to photograph their actions, and prevent outsiders from taking pictures as well. In the photograph of Charlie Hale (figure 2), the lynchers are clearly visible, staring intently and directly into the camera. Yet no photograph accompanied the report of Hale's lynching in the Atlanta *Constitution*, which moreover stated that "no member of the mob was recognized, and no arrests have been made" (*AC*, April 8, 1911,1). In this case, the certainty or proof that a photograph imputes clearly wanted to be avoided, at least outside the community (not that "proof" would have necessarily incriminated the lynchers, for very few lynchings were ever prosecuted). Nevertheless, for the image of the lynching to be presented in a wider context would have been to take the lynching and the purported heroism of the lynchers out of the community's domain.

However, many photographs, including the one of Charlie Hale's lynching, were made into postcards, sold in local establishments and sent to family and friends. In this sense, the community was broadened to include sympathizers in other towns and regions. The broad circulation of these images furthermore transformed even "private" lynchings into rather public spectacles, produced for collective consumption (Fouss 1999, 24). Small posses that quickly lynched their victims outside of town, but took long enough to snap a picture, nevertheless intended their actions to be witnessed, and in this way the violence was still symbolic and performative (Hale 1998, 357, n.7).

Moreover, these postcards were often popular commodities, their prices varying according to supply and demand. Commodifying the image further served to substantiate, and in turn, celebrate the triumph of the lynchers. "This is the barbeque we had last Saturday," wrote one young man to his parents on the back of a postcard. He then pointed himself out, standing proudly among the gathered crowd. The lynching was substantiated for this young man because he could visually testify his participation to his parents. At the same time, he showed apathetic detachment to the horror of his action and the humanity of his victim. This traumatic image, then, coupled with such casual text, stands as a vicious emblem to the transformations of the New South at the turn of the century. It evokes at once grisly racism, commodity display, and leisurely recreation.

The violation embedded in the lynching image thus persisted even after the photo was taken out of its original context, particularly as a fully lived (and in this case, suffered) experience was reduced to a static image (Sontag 1977, 9). As Roland Barthes eloquently noted, every photograph resembles death, as it represents time arrested on a particular, otherwise lost, moment (1981, 14–15). By stopping time in a photograph, the object is brought back to life, in memory at least, so that it becomes "the living image of a dead thing" (79). In a lynching photograph, significantly, an actual death has been frozen in time.

In this way, the black "criminal" was not ritually expunged from the community. Indeed, rather than exorcising the black "beast," and the threat his blackness represented to the white community, the rituals surrounding the lynching ensured that the (now dis-integrated) black body was integrated back into that community, if only to substantiate the superiority of the white (male) body. For instance, lynched corpses were often not buried for hours, sometimes days, after they were hanged. Steps were taken to protect the lynching site, particularly from the victim's family seeking to bury the body. Spectators would often turn parts of the body into souvenirs, stealing and then preserving pieces of bone, ears, fingers, toes. The photograph thus became yet another souvenir, guaranteeing that the victim—his black depravity and beastliness—would be remembered in his lynchers' mind. (For this very reason then, most lynching photographs do not depict the mutilated, and in some cases, burned body of the victim. The black man's body must still be recognizable as a body). The photograph re-dramatized and thus perpetuated the lynching, seeping it into each viewer's visual memory. The body of the lynching victim was brought back to life through the image, only to be killed once more by the viewer.

Scholars studying both the popular rhetoric surrounding lynching and the material culture that developed from it (including ballads, postcards, stories, and photographs) have understood them as a sort of "folk pornography," spreading from town to town, generation to generation (Hall 1993, 150; Fauss 1999, 25). Jacquelyn Hall, who coined the term, uses it to refer to the stories and rumors of rape that circulated the South, inflaming white Southern passions and ultimately justifying more racial violence. The supposed violation of the white woman stood at the center of these narratives, and in this way, they depended on women's participation (as witnesses and accusers). But, Hall suggests, the stories took on another purpose as lurid titillation embedded in violence and violation, of both the white woman and the black man. In this sense, the photographs were "pornographic" as well; the viewer could experience secondhand, or re-live, the danger, depravity, and sheer masculine power embedded in the image (Fouss 1999, 17). They thus became visual objects/evidence through which white men could confront and acknowledge their own masculinity. The spectacle in the images could both substantiate their own virility in relation to the black man's alleged sexual power, and act as an intermediary bond in their (class-based) connections with other white men.

On the other hand, although it is true that these materials circulated, and that circulation may have indeed provoked further violence,[9] the term "pornography" does not adequately imply the social acceptability of these "remembrances." While there is a lot more to be known on the circulation and private use of these photographs, we do know that at least some of these were sold openly in local stores, sent through the mail (child to parent as in figure 4), and presumably displayed openly in the home (figure 1).

It was only until much more recently, we can presume, that these photographs were hidden away, when lynching became obscured in public historical memory. As historian Bruce Baker has shown, while memories of lynchings remain within the private discourse of black communities and, to a lesser extent, in certain white communities, discussion of these events is purposely omitted in the public discourse of these same communities (B. Baker, forthcoming, 5–6). For, "by controlling public discourse—the newspapers, the courts, the books, . . . — whites had the luxury of remembering or forgetting the past as they chose in order to form a usable history" (31). As one white woman who was shown a photograph of a lynching that took place in her community seventy-five years earlier remarked, "Why do you keep that awful thing around? Who would want to remember this?" (8).

But it is only through bringing these memories from private discourse back into public discourse that old wrongs may be acknowledged (B. Baker, forthcoming, 35). While resurrecting these images from forgotten history is, to be sure, to risk once again reengaging in this process of violence and symbolic representation, we can hope that by recontextualizing these photographs, we can transform the ideological message embedded in the image. Indeed, both then and today, activists and artists have reappropriated these images, removing them from their original, oppressive contexts, to let them stand as a different kind of souvenir—reminders of racial terrorism and white brutality.[10] The photographs in these contexts transfigure a visual commemoration into visual memorial, the proof embedded in the image standing not as evidence of white superiority, but rather white culpability.

notes

1. "Southern trees bear strange fruit" sings Holiday in her 1956 lament against lynching. "Strange Fruit" was written by Danny Mendelsohn and Lewis Allan, Polygram Records, 1956.

2. It is difficult to ascertain exact numbers of lynchings. I have taken this figure from Tolnay and Beck 1995 (ix, 260), who in their sociological account of lynching have carefully compiled and confirmed the most well-known

lynching inventories collected by the NAACP, Tuskegee University, and the Chicago *Tribune*. According to Tolnay and Beck, between 1882 and 1930, 288 whites were lynched in the South, compared with 2,462 blacks. Though lynchings peaked in the 1890s, they continued to be an everyday occurrence across the South until the 1930s. By the 1940s, lynching were no longer mass, public events (see also Brundage 1993, 7–8).

3. Historian Fitzhugh Brundage, whose *Lynching in the New South* (1993) is the best and most comprehensive study of lynching in recent years, has catalogued mob violence against African Americans into four categories: posses, terrorist mobs, private mobs, and mass mobs. Mass mobs have received the most attention, from observers at the time and from scholars today, because of their size and spectacular quality. While Brundage reminds us that this attention to mass mob lynchings can be sensationalistic (17–48), his categories of lynchings, as Grace Hale points out, may be too rigid, and do not take into account how even private lynchings became spectacles through these kinds of visual practices (1998, 357, n.7).

4. Most lynchings victims were not accused of rape, yet the rhetoric surrounding lynching focused on this supposed outrage to white womanhood (Brundage 1993, 66; White 1969, 56).

5. This changed over time; by the 1920s and 30s, when extralegal lynchings were becoming less common, lynching photographs began to appear, albeit infrequently, in newspapers and magazines, often within the context of antilynching arguments.

6. These characteristics of secular rituals are delineated in Bell 1992, 138–69.

7. Early white critics of lynchings contended that lynchings plagued economically disadvantaged communities. The liberal Committee on Interracial Cooperation also argued that lynching allowed those in the community without social power to act as judges, executioners, and protectors of Southern women. See Committee on Interracial Cooperation, 43.

8. Both Alan Trachtenberg 1989 (26–32) and Robert Mensel indicate that, while the notion that photographs exposed moral character began with early photographic portraiture, it persisted into the early twentieth century. Mensel also notes that, as photography became more accessible and popular toward the end of the nineteenth century, middle-class Americans began to fear that snapshots taken out of context could be used to defame characters and impugn reputations.

9. In its 1931 report, the Georgia Committee on Interracial Cooperation deemed lynchings "contagious" in their spread from community to community (24).

10. In 1917, the Chicago *Defender* printed a photo of the severed head of Ells Persons, who was burned to death in Memphis for murdering a white teenager (Ginzberg 1988, 112). *Jet* magazine published a photograph of the body of Emmett Till (murdered in Mississippi in 1955 for allegedly "wolf-whistling" at a white woman. His mother allowed Jet to print the photograph because she "wanted 'all the world' to witness the atrocity" (*Jet*, September 22, 1955). The New York *Amsterdam News* (November 3, 1934) published a photo of Claude Neal's lynched body, which had been on sale as a postcard after the lynching in Marietta, Florida. More recently, in 1986, photographer/artist Pat Ward Williams used a lynching photograph taken in Duck Hill, Mississippi, in 1937 in a conceptual piece that interrogated the ethics of exhibiting lynching photography.

works cited

Primary Sources

Vanishing Georgia, Photo Collection, Georgia Department of Archives and History, Atlanta

Lynching Photographs, Special Collections, Robert W. Woodruff Library, Emory University

The Atlanta *Constitution* (AC)

The Chicago *Defender*

Jet Magazine (Jet)

The New York *Amsterdam News*

Secondary Sources

Baker, Bruce E. Forthcoming. "Lynching and Memory in Laurens County, South Carolina." In *No Deed but Memory: Essays on History and Memory in the American South*, ed. W. Fitzhugh Brundage. Chapel Hill: University of North Carolina Press.

Baker, Ray Stannard. 1908. *Following the Color Line*. New York: Harper and Row. .

Barthes, Roland. 1981. *Camera Lucida: Reflections on Photography*. Trans. Richard Howard. New York: Hill & Wang, Farrar, Straus and Giroux.

Bell, Catherine. 1992. *Ritual Theory, Ritual Practice.* New York: Oxford University Press.

Bourdieu, Pierre. 1990. *Photography*. Stanford, Calif.: Stanford University Press.

Brundage, W. Fitzhugh. 1993. *Lynching in the New South: Georgia and Virginia, 1880–1930*. Chicago: University of Illinois Press.

Committee on Interracial Cooperation. 1931. *Lynchings and What They Mean*. Atlanta, Ga.: The Commission.

Conniff, Richard. 1988. "When 'Fiends' Pressed the Button, There Was Nowhere to Hide." *Smithsonian* 19, 3: 106–17.

Debord, Guy. 1983. *Society of the Spectacle*. Detroit: Black and Red.

Fanon, Frantz. 1968. *Black Skins, White Masks*. New York: Grove Press.

Fields, Barbara. 1982. "Ideology and Race in American History." In *Region, Race and Reconstruction*, ed. J. Morgan Kousser and James M. McPherson. New York: Oxford University Press.

Fouss, Kirk W. 1999. "Lynching Performances, Theatres of Violence." *Text and Performance Quarterly* 19, 1 (January): 1–37.

Frederickson, George. 1987. *The Black Image in the White Mind: The Debated on Afro-American Character and Destiny, 1817–1914*. Middletown, Conn.: Wesleyan University Press.

Ginzberg, Ralph. 1988. *One Hundred Years of Lynching*. Baltimore, Md.: Black Classic Press.

Hale, Grace Elizabeth. 1998. *Making Whiteness: The Culture of Segregation in the South, 1890–1940*. New York: Pantheon Books.

Hall, Jacquelyn Dowd. 1993. *Revolt against Chivalry: Jesse Daniel Ames and the Woman's Campaign against Lynching*. New York: Columbia University Press, revised edition.

Harris, Trudier. 1984. *Exorcising Blackness: Historical and Literary Lynching and Burning Rituals*. Bloomington: University of Indiana Press.

Jenkins, Reese V. 1975. "Technology and the Market: George Eastman and the Origins of Mass Amateur Photography." *Technology and Culture* 16 (January): 1–19.

Jones, Jacquie. 1994. "How Come Nobody Told Me about the Lynching?" in *Picturing Us: African American Identity and Photography*, ed. Deborah Willis. New York: New Press.

McGovern, James R. 1982. *Anatomy of a Lynching: The Killing of Claude Neal.* Baton Rouge: Louisiana State University Press.

Mensel, Robert E. 1991. "'Kodakers Lying in Wait': Amateur Photography and the Right of Privacy in New York, 1885–1915." *American Quarterly* 43, 1 (March): 24–43.

Moeller, Madelyn. 1983. "Photography and History: Using Photographs in Interpreting our Cultural Past." *Journal of American Culture* 6: 3–17.

Ownby, Ted. 1990. *Subduing Satan: Religion, Recreation, and Manhood in the Rural South, 1865–1920.* Chapel Hill: University of North Carolina Press.

Raper, Arthur. 1933. *The Tragedy of Lynching.* Chapel Hill: University of North Carolina Press.

Sontag, Susan. 1977. *On Photography.* New York: Anchor Books, Doubleday.

Tolnay, Stewart E., and E. M. Beck. 1995. *A Festival of Violence: An Analysis of Southern Lynchings, 1882–1930.* Chicago: University of Illinois Press.

Trachtenberg, Alan. 1989. *Reading American Photographs: Images as History, Mathew Brady to Walker Evans.* New York: Noonday Press.

Tyre, Nedra. 1947. *Red Wine First.* New York: Simon and Schuster.

White, Walter. 1969. *Rope and Faggot.* New York: Arno Press.

Whitfield, Stephen J. 1988. *A Death in the Delta: The Story of Emmett Till.* New York: Free Press, Macmillan.

Williamson, Joel. 1984. *A Crucible of Race: Black-White Relations in the American South since Emancipation.* New York: Oxford University Press.

Wyatt-Brown, Bertram. 1982. *Southern Honor: Ethics and Behavior in the Old South.* New York: Oxford University Press.

screening the

italian-american

male

a a r o n   b a k e r   a n d   j u l i a n n   v i t u l l o

Six films released between 1972 and 1980—*The Godfather; Mean Streets; The Godfather, Part II; Rocky; Rocky II;* and *Raging Bull*—have found critical and/or monetary success by emphasizing a masculinized version of Italian-American identity.[1] All these films represent Italian Americans as a distinct urban group whose ethnicity is created and maintained by working-class men who learn everything they need to survive on the streets of their neighborhood. Ironically, this image of Italian-Americanness calcified at a time when most Italian Americans had already moved into middle-class suburban spaces, and sent their children to learn survival skills at universities rather than through fist-fights and gunplay.[2] Whereas these films depict Italian-American ethnicity as a timeless identity characterized by a seemingly stable form of masculinity, several films from the 1990s such as *A Bronx Tale, Mac, Household Saints,* and *Kiss Me Guido* represent both ethnicity and mas-culinity as part of a complex web of social identities that is constantly changing. In order to understand the ways in which the more recent movies revise canonical representations of Italian Americans, we will first analyze the connection created between urban, working-class men and white ethnicity in the earlier films.

In the 1970s movies about Italian Americans were part of a wave of both scholarly and popular interest in the cultural roots of the so-called "white ethnics" (Di Leonardo 1998, 82). The even broader appeal of *The Godfather* and *Rocky* resulted from how they also fit into what Micaela Di Leonardo describes as the larger society's post-counterculture ideas about identity. In contrast to stereotypes of WASPs as "too cold," bloodless, repressed, and selfish, and of blacks as "too hot," wild, primitive, and overly dependent, the Italian Americans in these movies appeared—like baby bear's porridge—"just right": expressive, physical and connected, yet strong and self-determining (Di Leonardo 1994, 176–77). The other four films upset this balance by showing how, through the process of assimilation, whiteness and individualism come to constitute Italian-American identity. Despite such differences, the stories in these six films eventually all return to a longing for "pure" ethnicity, an identity drawn from what Donald Tricarico calls "the world of our fathers" (1989, 26). They wind up therefore depicting those characters who try to move beyond an insular notion of Italian-Americanness defined within the space of the neighborhood as "sinners," regardless of their social and material success.

These six movies also represent Italian Americans as urban people, forging their identities within well-defined residential spaces of strong family and community values. Central to these urban communities are conservative characterizations of Italian-American women devoted to home and family, revered and protected for their support and self-sacrifice. Talia Shire established her career playing this kind of woman in *The Godfather* and *Rocky* films; even a brief rebellion against her brother Michael in *The Godfather* series is motivated not by self-interest but rather by her belief that he has violated the bonds of family. So important are such selfless women to these Italian-American men that the loss, real or imagined, of their support becomes a major narrative complication for the male protagonists in *Mean Streets*, *Rocky II*, and *Raging Bull*.

In addition to their reliance on strong women, the Italian-American men in these movies start off with close ties to other males in the community. Such alliances provide strength for the violent confrontations with outsiders by which the men often define themselves, yet the intensity of their homosocial relationships combined with their inclination to violence often explode in fratricidal conflict. *Godfather* screenwriter Mario Puzo opposed Francis Ford Coppola's idea that Michael Corleone kill his brother Freddo as an *infamia* that would never occur in an Italian-American family. Yet when one considers the extreme violence these films show between brothers or close male companions—

from Charlie dodging Johnny Boy's gunshots in *Mean Streets*, to Paulie's menacing Rocky with a baseball bat, and Jake LaMotta putting Joey's head through a glass door—that murder becomes less surprising.

Such fratricidal violence betrays a fundamental masculine anxiety in these Italian-American movies. While the relations with other men are a source of strength, they also recall the ties to community and family that restrict the protagonists as they seek to prove themselves by the standards of the larger society. The narrative impetus in all these films is away from the compromises and responsibilities of an Italian-American space toward a more individualized identity outside ethnicity. Part of this move also involves clarifying racial ambiguity, the perception of Italian Americans as somewhere between black and white. The male protagonists discard that hybridity as if it were a stigma and value a whiter identity because they view it as giving them greater access to economic opportunity and social position by which they seek to define themselves.

Robert Orsi (1992) describes such racial inbetweenness as having played an important role in defining the identity of Italian Americans from the time of their first arrival in the United States. Immigrants from the *Mezzogiorno* had already experienced racist categorization by Northern Italians, and after coming to this country they again faced discourses like those directed at blacks to position them as "lazy, criminal, sexually irresponsible, and emotionally volatile" (314–15). Such labeling as less-than-white, combined with their arrival in northern cities coincident with the migration of southern African Americans, African Caribbeans, and soon afterward, Puerto Ricans and Mexicans, created the determination among many Italians to make their experience in this country better and gain access to opportunity by "differentiating themselves from the dark-skinned other" (317).

In *Do the Right Thing* Spike Lee presents two contemporary Italian-American characters, pizzeria owner Sal and his son Pino, for whom this differentiation has retained such importance, and who struggle with the frustration created by others not recognizing their efforts at racial distinction. In front of a poster of the Roman Coliseum that symbolizes Italian-American assertion of a role in white cultural heritage, Lee's character Mookie asks Pino to identify his favorite professional basketball, movie, and music stars. Pino admits to liking Magic Johnson, Eddie Murphy, and Prince, but he strongly denies Mookie's conclusion that his cultural tastes, dark skin, and kinky hair suggest an affinity with blacks. Pino sees himself, his brother, and father as more industrious and therefore superior to the blacks who buy their pizza, and he explains that these stars are his favorites because "they're more than black." While the very presence of their pizzeria in a predominantly African-American and Latino part of Brooklyn is a painful reminder to Pino of his connection to nonwhites, his (and his father's) insistence on asserting the superiority of their Italian-American masculinity plays a major role in sparking the violent confrontation that destroys their business. As in the six films mentioned earlier, the whiteness pursued by the Italian Americans in *Do the Right Thing* is primarily a masculine identity. Certain of its qualities may be attributed to, or adopted by, Italian-American women, but whiteness in these films is an identity that men pursue and fight over.

Coppola's *Godfather* films also make the pursuit of whiteness a central concern. The first two movies advance the argument that exclusion from legitimate opportunities motivated the involvement of some Italian immigrants in organized crime, and that their unlawful activities employed the same might-makes-right logic used by political and corporate elites. As a result, despite the wealth and influence that he acquires, patriarch Vito Corleone can never move beyond a criminalized, in-between status. We see Vito as a young man positioned within the disadvantaged community of Little Italy, and when older, in the Corleone home, at the family olive oil business offices, and the hospital, spaces that represent his inability to achieve a white identity predicated on self-determination.

His son Michael's move toward business legitimacy therefore must literally destroy the Italian-American family and community as they demand cooperation and compromise. Michael regards his WASP wife Kay as part of his ascendance toward racial legitimacy; conversely she expects connectedness and intimacy, but instead finds a husband going the other way, toward the ethos of self-reliance in which she grew up. The violence that ultimately consumes the family is for the most part caused by Vito's and Michael's unwillingness to share wealth and influence, summed up in the father's aspirations for his son. "I never wanted this for you," he tells Michael. "I thought that . . . when it was your turn you would be the one to hold the strings, Senator Corleone, Governor Corleone." The main narrative theme of the first two films is the pursuit of "legitimate" power through the family's move away from illegal gambling and union racketeering; Vito's and Michael's disdain for the prostitution and drug businesses run by the other New York families comes from their concern about the white elite's displeasure with how these involvements call attention to widespread alienation and disenfranchisement. By *The Godfather, Part III* Michael has even left behind the legal gambling of the Las Vegas casinos for the eminently respectable domain of international finance.

All three *Godfather* films visualize the move toward individualism begun by Vito and completed by Michael through a transition from the noir spaces of in-betweenness (Little Italy, the Corleone family compound, New York in general) to those of dazzling whiteness: the

216

"frontiers" of Nevada, Havana, and Sicily where economic inequality and historical patterns of control over nonwhites are concealed by a rhetoric that describes them as locations of opportunity. All three films end with Michael in the domestic space within which he tried to preserve the identities of the past, yet we see him in compositions that emphasize his superiority over or isolation from others, unaware of or powerless against the contradictions between his ambitions and the family and community relationships he thought he was protecting.

Rocky as well uses a noir style in its early scenes to visualize the space of structural disadvantage that limits the title character to racial inbetweenness and restricts his access to the American dream. The film initially shows Rocky's neighborhood in South Philadelphia as a bleak urban landscape of empty, garbage-filled streets, rundown businesses, and dirty tenements. The story soon leaves that dark world behind, or rather, through the use of an implausible melodramatic turn, pits Rocky against it directly in the form of a match with the African-American heavyweight champion, Apollo Creed. Stallone wrote the part of Creed with Muhammad Ali in mind, portraying him like the real-life champion as a talented fighter, intelligent and articulate, but representative of the "misguided" cynicism of African Americans who can't see that America is the land of opportunity for all. Creed presents his choice of an unknown club fighter to meet him for the heavyweight title on the first day of the bicentennial as a celebration of how "in America, everyone has a chance to make it"; the film, however, shows us that, unlike Rocky, Creed himself doesn't really hold such patriotic beliefs, and that for him the matchup is just a public relations stunt. By highlighting Creed's social position and wealth, the movie suggests that his cynicism is without basis. What Stallone chose to ignore in his script is that Creed's historical referent, Ali, never denied the good fortune of his own life. Ali instead protested that such opportunity was not available for most African Americans, and he put his career on the line by rejecting claims that they should fight and die in the Vietnam War against other colonized people when the majority of blacks still lacked the full rights of citizenship at home.

Rocky II begins with a replay of the title character's heroic effort in the first fight with Creed, celebrating Balboa's symbolic if not literal defeat of the black champion. Rocky himself marks his success by acquiring more of the signs of whiteness: a clean, light-filled townhouse to replace his dirty, dark apartment, and marriage to his girlfriend, Adrian, which gives him the sanction of responsible sexuality. Yet Rocky continues to struggle against the limitations resulting from the parts of his identity that tie him to inbetweenness: his lack of formal education, his overdeveloped body, and his manner of speaking. Although Rocky communicates effectively, even with understated wit,

screening the italian-american male

217

his inability to speak standard English limits his access to the white-collar job he covets for its social position and economic return without having, as he puts it to one interviewer, to get "punched in the face five hundred times a night."

In order to move him fully beyond this racial inbetweenness, *Rocky II* matches Rocky with Creed again, and this time he beats the black fighter. Besides the distinction of victory, the second film puts greater emphasis on Rocky's Catholicism. Richard Dyer (1997) has noted that for centuries people who regarded themselves as white have used Christianity and their assumed possession of spirituality to establish superiority over nonwhites. While, as Dyer points out, the drawback of possessing divine spirit is its evocation of disembodiment and death, Rocky's bodily force in the victory over Creed allays any fears that whiteness here involves the loss of presence and strength. Dyer in fact sees the training scenes in these films as constructing Rocky's body within white ideas of physical restraint and discipline. He describes Rocky as showing "the signs of hard, planned labour, the spirit reigning over the flesh" (155).

As much as any of the male protagonists in these films, Jake LaMotta in *Raging Bull* represents this obsession with self-determination and control. However, as the nickname in the title implies, the aggression that made him a success in prizefighting extended beyond the ring. *Raging Bull* graphically presents how LaMotta's social dysfunction, his inability to negotiate with others or control his temper, results in rejection and isolation rather than independence and respect.

Using the logic of inbetweenness that Orsi describes, *Raging Bull* depicts LaMotta's frustrating battle for self-determination as a struggle against blackness. Throughout the film LaMotta obsesses about autonomy and control, which he believes can be achieved by mastering his appetites, demonstrating his dominance in the ring (in particular over the African-American fighter Sugar Ray Robinson), and moving from the Italian-American neighborhood where he grew up to bourgeois spaces on Pelham Parkway and in Miami. Yet as the film represents these battles through expressionist imagery and a heavy reliance on shots from LaMotta's point of view, it suggests that his dark vision of the world comes from a distorted understanding of what is holding him back. For example, in the scene of his fourth bout against Sugar Ray Robinson, we see through LaMotta's eyes the African-American fighter loom menacingly just before finishing off the title character with a fierce beating that goes unopposed. Through its visual style, this scene externalizes both LaMotta's failure to achieve the whiteness he desires and his insistence on pain and punishment as penitence for his inability to fully control his own identity.

While Jake LaMotta, like many of the protagonists of canonical Italian-American films, pays a high price for his desire to transgress the boundaries of working-class, urban ethnicity, several more recent movies about Italian Americans move away from the earlier emphasis on white ethnicity and leaving the residential spaces of community and family. Films such as *A Bronx Tale*, *Mac*, *Household Saints*, and *Kiss Me Guido* expand the canon of Italian-American cinema by concerning themselves more with dialogical characters who foreground other aspects of ethnic identity, especially race, gender, and sexuality. They follow the change in ethnic definition that Tricarico describes whereby, in contrast to traditional sociological theory that measures ethnicity by its adherence to Old World cultures, ethnic groups are now seen as "capable of altering boundaries and identity frameworks, cultural styles and forms of expression" (1989, 25). In the process, these later films revalorize Italian-American spaces, while still viewing them with a critical eye.

Even in the 1990s, when most Italian Americans live in middle-class suburbs, films continue to represent them within an urban, working-class landscape. But while the *Godfather* and *Rocky* contrast the physicality and determination of urban, ethnic men with overcivilized white men and cynical African Americans like Apollo Creed, recent films question those oppositions by adopting more complex and relational notions of identity. In both Orsi's work on Italian Americans in Harlem and Di Leonardo's on Italian Americans in California, their subjects define white ethnicity in close relation to people they regard as nonwhite. Italian-American neighborhoods were always more porous than those represented in the 1970s and early 1980s films; Italian Americans had frequent contact with people from other ethnic and racial groups through public institutions like schools, yet this everyday interaction and its importance in constituting white ethnicity is curiously absent from the earlier films.

Robert DeNiro's *A Bronx Tale* revises such depictions of the "old neighborhood." The film tells a coming-of-age story about a young man named Calogero, growing up in the Bronx during the 1960s. Although it follows the model of earlier films by portraying male street culture as a significant part of his maturation, *A Bronx Tale* also shows that Calogero creates an adult identity through his awareness about, and interaction with, African Americans.

A Bronx Tale represents the attraction of Calogero and his friends to African-American culture, as well as their attempt to distance themselves from non-whites as they move toward whiteness. Sporting the same leather car coats and porkpie hats worn by the African-American youth of the adjoining neighborhood, and listening to black or black-influenced popular music, the young Italian-American men in the story paradoxically engage in racial violence intended to deny their inbetweenness and to protect the neighborhood's ethnic purity.

A Bronx Tale also portrays Calogero's father Lorenzo, a bus driver, listening to jazz as he transports people from different ethnic and racial groups through the streets that connect their communities. The movie depicts him as embodying the traditional qualities associated with white ethnicity; Lorenzo is a hardworking family man who encourages his son to assimilate through sports and education. Despite this conventional portrayal of the father (who is juxtaposed with Sonny, the neighborhood mafioso in search of immediate gratification), Lorenzo expresses disappointment when he discovers that his son has fallen in love with a young African-American woman whom Calogero first saw on the bus. While his father advises him to stay within "our own," Calogero's other paternal figure, Sonny, encourages him to pursue the relationship. The contrast between the encouragement to move toward whiteness given by the hardworking father and the advice from the mafioso to transgress the traditional ethnic/racial boundaries of the neighborhood questions the nostalgic notion of a once pure and undivided Italian-American community that transmits a stable, coherent set of values to its young people. In addition, the scene between Lorenzo and his son illustrates the danger of defining one's ethnic character as industrious and family-centered when it suggests that others cannot possess the same qualities. This exchange also implies that the father's pursuit of whiteness might be tied to his work in a liminal space where the boundaries of his neighborhood and ethnic identity are continually confused. Although he encourages his son to listen to the jazz he plays on the bus, Lorenzo discourages Calogero from associating with members of the community that has played the greatest role in defining that musical form. In his everyday life, Lorenzo experiences movement both of people and culture between neighborhoods, and the film forces us to question what price his child (and African-American children) must pay to reinforce his faith in the value of pure ethnicity.

While *A Bronx Tale* depicts how Italian Americans' in-between status encourages them to contrast white ethnicity with those they regarded as nonwhites, *Kiss Me Guido* attempts to celebrate another form of inbetweenness by transforming the "old neighborhood" into a queer space. The film's main character, Frankie, longs to move from his working-class Italian-American neighborhood in the Bronx to Manhattan and leave behind his job in a pizzeria for an acting career. *Kiss Me Guido* emphasizes the performative aspect of being an Italian-American male, white ethnic male, or specifically a "Guido," by showing Frankie repeatedly imitating actors such as Al Pacino and Robert De Niro. Frankie's brother Pino also reinforces the constructedness of ethnic identity; his stylized and exaggerated gestures emphasize the hyper-masculinity of the Guido persona.[3]

At the same time that the movie represents the showmanship and machismo of Guidos, it highlights similarities between their culture and queerness. When Frankie moves to Manhattan he ends up in "Little Italy," which has transformed into a gay community. In an early sequence that establishes the film's version of Guido-ness, Pino, his hair slicked back and jacket open to show his gold chains, drives a Cadillac aggressively through Little Italy, sneering at gay men. Despite his homophobia, the same sequence juxtaposes gay men sharing a kiss in front of a coffeeshop with Pino's Italian-American friends back in the Bronx greeting each other in a similarly affectionate manner. By drawing such parallels between these two social groups, *Kiss Me Guido* implies that Italian-American inbetweenness extends also to gender and sexuality.

In several of the earlier films that helped create popular notions about their masculinity, Italian-American men fail to be accepted by the white community as truly virile because of their association with physicality and style. For instance, in *Godfather II* a U.S. senator from Nevada sneers at Michael's silk suit and "oily" hair, and in *Saturday Night Fever* Tony Manero from Brooklyn is defined by his sexualized dancing and blow dryer; the woman he desires compares him unfavorably to "real" men in Manhattan known less by how they look than what they do. The emphasis on personal style in both films suggests that working-class and ethnic men cannot embody an ideal masculinity of position and achievement, but represent instead a type of sexual inbetweenness. As a result, Tony Manero and his friends fight to distinguish themselves from both Puerto Ricans and gay men. While *Saturday Night Fever* and *The Godfather* films portray ethnic men who try to overcome the anxiety about their ambiguous status through violence, *Kiss Me Guido* celebrates that inbetweenness.

Mac and *Household Saints* also treat the nostalgic idea of an at once stable and pure urban Italian-American identity in an ironic fashion by questioning the traditional dichotomy between working-class ethnics and middle-class suburbanites. Set in the 1950s, *Mac* tells the story of the three Vitelli brothers who pull themselves up by their proverbial bootstraps building single-family homes on what were then the outer fringes of Queens. As the brothers slave away in order to realize the American dream by escaping the cramped, dark space of the family apartment for the suburban frontier, their partnership deteriorates to the point of violence.

The movie's first sequence depicts the brothers mourning their father's death at his wake: in a series of flashbacks each brother remembers his childhood relationship with the father, himself a builder. All three sons's recall him as valuing his work so much that he elevated it to the level of art, but also as an authoritarian patriarch whose favorite expression was "There are only two ways to do something: my way and the right way, and they're the same thing." In these sequences the father's code-switching between Italian and accented English, formulaic sayings, and disregard for American efficiency suggest that the identity he teaches his sons has originated in the old country.

While this portrayal of ethnicity initially seems to repeat conventional formulas by defining Italian Americans in terms of hard work, family values, physicality, and hypermasculinity, the movie then problematizes that depiction by showing the oldest brother, Mac, the new family patriarch, re-creating the same identity in the new suburban space of whiteness. The Vitelli Brothers construction company falls apart after its initial success, brought down by Mac's unbridled aggression in his push to become a financial success. Although the movie depicts Mac as like his father, an artisan who works hard and takes pride in his craft, his authoritarian behavior and refusal to think about anything except his job alienate him from both his friends and family. What this movie suggests then is that patriarchal hierarchies and the alienation they require find a home not only in precapitalist ethnic cultures but also in middle-class suburbia.

In a similar fashion, *Household Saints* collapses the opposition between urban ethnicity and middle-class suburban whiteness by suggesting that in both spaces the feminine ideal is defined by domesticity. The film analyzes the relationship between local religious practices of New York's Little Italy and the growing belief in the gospel of postwar American consumer culture centered in the home. By paralleling these two forms of piety, *Household Saints* questions whether the Americanization and consumerism that had infiltrated Italian-American life helped to liberate women from the "superstitions" of ethnic culture or rather reproduced the same contradictions. Especially through the character of Teresa, who sees a vision of Christ while ironing, *Household Saints* shows religious devotion that takes the form of an obsession with domesticity; the excessive desire that fuels both mysticism and consumerism undermines the "normality" of the traditional female domestic role.

The endings of *Mac* and *Household Saints* depict family elders passing on the virtues of traditional Italian-American culture. In *Mac*, the obsessive title character shows his young son the homes that he and his brothers built to illustrate the values associated with white ethnicity: hard work and family unity. Yet, he neglects to tell his son that the construction of those houses had torn the brothers apart instead of keeping them together. In a similar fashion, at the end of *Household Saints* we see three generations of an Italian-American family listening to a grandfather tell the tale of a girl from the "old neighborhood," Teresa, who became a saint after she saw Christ at the ironing board. In that scene, each generation interprets the story in a different way, with the storyteller's daughter questioning the hagiographic spin that the grandfather puts on it by saying: "I could name a list of women as long as my arm who went crazy cooking and cleaning and trying to please everybody." The self-reflexive endings of both movies, then, allow us to see what has been left out of the nostalgic tales about the old neighborhood. In addition, the conclusion of *Household Saints* suggests that many of the values associated with Italian-American mothers such as self-sacrifice could describe women both inside and outside the idealized urban space of ethnicity.

The earlier cycle of Italian-American movies tends to contrast urban, working-class, ethnic communities with middle-class suburbia. This opposition presents the Little Italies of yesteryear in a contradictory fashion as communities whose values the male protagonists fight to maintain, and at the same time a space that these men want to escape as they move toward whiteness. The later cycle of films problematizes such canonical depictions of Italian Americans by analyzing in an explicit way how other social identities help construct white ethnicity, and also by questioning whether the values of the "old neighborhood" and of middle-class suburbs are really so different.

update: analyze these

While *A Bronx Tale*, *Household Saints*, *Mac*, and *Kiss Me Guido* are small projects made on modest budgets for viewers interested in an independent film aesthetic, even those recent media representations of Italian Americans with the ambition of a mass audience, such as *Analyze This*, or looking for major critical acclaim, such as the HBO series *The Sopranos*, have begun to adopt similar revisionist ideas of ethnic identity. Both *Analyze This* and *The Sopranos* center on tough mob bosses who reveal fears and unconscious displeasure with their lives in analysis sessions to which we are privy, but that they conceal from their friends and opponents for fear it will make them appear weak and vulnerable. In these sessions Tony Soprano (James Gandolfini) and Paul Vitti (Robert DeNiro) express their misgivings about the pressures and costs of an individualized, hypercompetitive white masculinity like that pursued in the earlier cycle of Italian-American films.

In addition to questioning the construction of masculinity on which so many films about Italian Americans have been built, *Analyze This* and *The Sopranos* extend the revisionist idea that "authentic" ethnicity exists beyond the confines of urban communities. A *New York Times* story about a trend toward more positive representations of New Jersey in the media recognized this relocation of Italian Americaness when it commented about *The Sopranos*:

> The series, which is shot on location in areas well known to its creator David Chase [born Cesare] and James Gandolfini, both from New Jersey, is the highest-rated drama on cable. In its 13 weeks, it has touched off the kind of enthusiasm among hip audiences that "Twin Peaks" did nine years ago. If that cult show was a Pacific Northwest riddle wrapped in a mystery inside an enigma, "The Sopranos" is a *suburban* comedy wrapped in a mob drama inside a cannoli. (De Caro, April 5, 1999, B9) [Emphasis ours]

Likewise, in *Analyze This* a central device of its comic premise is that the soldiers for Paul Vitti track down his psychiatrist in the suburban spaces of the doctor's life (at his home office, at Seaworld, even at his wedding) for impromptu sessions with their boss.

Spike Lee's 1999 film *Summer of Sam* also looks critically at a more traditional version of Italian-American masculinity, showing it as involving not just racist positioning of the nonwhite other as in *Do the Right Thing*, but also unhealthy doses of repression. The film's main character Vinny and his neighborhood friend Richie both refuse to acknowledge sexual desire (in Vinny's case beyond the confines of marriage, for Richie homoerotic) that doesn't fit the conception of Italian-American masculinity and family they have grown up with in their Bronx neighborhood. Lee limits his definition of Italian Americans to those from an urban neighborhood, but his stubborn insistence on this locale also allows him to comment on representations of masculinity in the first cycle of Italian-American films.

In their analyses of *Raging Bull*, film scholars Robin Wood and Pam Cook both emphasize that movie's use of repression to explain the self-destructive behavior of its title character. Wood (1986) argues that Jake LaMotta, much like the Richie character in *Summer of Sam*, suffers from his denial of homoerotic desire. In Wood's view only once Jake acknowledges this attraction in a scene late in the film with his brother Joey does he gain greater control of his life, without the displacement of that desire into violence directed not just against opponents in the ring, but also neighbors, friends, and family. Cook (1982) analyzes Jake's repression of oedipal desire set up through the maternal associations with LaMotta's wife, Vicky, and his suspicions of her relations with other men. Cook views this oedipal desire as displaced into Jake's expressions of homoeroticism, and she notes as an example his comment about an upcoming opponent whom Vicky has described as attractive: "I got a problem if I should fuck 'em or fight 'em."

The repression of sexual desire emphasized in Wood's and Cook's writing on *Raging Bull* links those two analyses to the construction of Italian-American masculinity both in *Summer of Sam* and in the other early cycle films analysed in this essay. The Italian-American men in these films avoid homoerotic desire not only because it doesn't fit the models of white masculinity to which they aspire, but also because it questions the motivations behind their close relationships with other Italian-American men. Moreover, they regard homosexuality as a threat to their patriarchal power derived from a version of family founded on heterosexual relationships in which women are loyal to male authority. In *Analyze This* and *The Sopranos*, the selfish extramarital affairs of the main male characters, as well as references to the type of oedipal tensions Cook emphasizes, show how these recent texts question such notions of masculinity and family that had been central to Italian-American stories. Like marital infidelity, the oedipal narrative reveals the contradictions created by traditional constructions of the family, but it also suggests that relations between Italian-American men, both in urban and suburban spaces, often function less in the cause of ethnic unity than as brutal contests for authority.

notes

1. Most of the films we analyze in this essay fit Robert Casillo's definition of Italian/American cinema as "works by Italian-American directors who treat Italian-American subjects" (1991, 374). However, what matters most for us about these films is how they represent Italian Americans, not who made them. Therefore, even when these movies involve the contributions of non–Italian Americans, we still regard them as important texts, since ethnic identity is always defined not just by those within the group in question but through the perceptions and representations of those outside it. Regarding the earnings and/or critical reception of these films, *Rocky*, *The Godfather*, and *Godfather, Part II* have been blockbuster hits, each taking in more than $100 million worldwide. *Rocky II* made less than the first film, *Rocky III* (1982), or *Rocky IV* (1985), but nonetheless has taken in more than $40 million in rentals alone. *Raging Bull* and *Mean Streets* have earned far less money than the other four films, but have received critical acclaim. For example, film critic Roger Ebert put them both (along with *The Godfather*) on his list of "The Great Movies."

2. For a description of this demographic change, see Tricarico 1989, 24 and 1984, 77.

3. For an extended discussion of Guido subculture, see Tricarico 1991.

works cited

Casillo, Robert. 1991. "Moments in Italian-American Cinema: From *Little Caesar* to Coppola and Scorsese." In *From the Margin: Writings in Italian Americana*, ed. Anthony Julian Tamburri, Paolo A. Giordano, Fred L. Gardaphe. West Lafayette, Ind.: Purdue University Press.

Cook, Pam. 1982. "Masculinity in Crisis?" *Screen* 23, 3—4: 39—46.

DeCaro, Frank. 1999. "No Longer the Punch-Line State." *New York Times*, April 5, B1, B9.

Di Leonardo, Micaela. 1984. *The Varieties of Ethnic Experience: Kinship, Class, and Gender Among California Italian-Americans*. Ithaca, N.Y.: Cornell University Press.

———. 1994. White Ethnicities, Identity Politics, and Baby Bear's Chair," *Social Text* 41: 165—91.

———. 1998. *Exotics at Home. Anthropologies, Others, American Modernity*. Chicago: University of Chicago Press.

Dyer, Richard. 1997. *White*. New York: Routledge.

Orsi, Robert. 1992. "The Religious Boundaries of Inbetween People: Street Feste and the Problem of the Dark-Skinned Other in Italian Harlem, 1920—1990," *American Quarterly* 44, 3 (September): 313—47.

Tricarico, Donald. 1984. "The 'New' Italian-American Ethnicity," *Journal of Ethnic Studies* 12, 3: 75—93.

———. 1989. "In a New Light: Italian-American Ethnicity in the Mainstream." In *The Ethnic Enigma*, ed. Peter Kivisto, 24—46. Philadelphia: The Balch Institute Press.

———. 1991. "Guido: Fashioning an Italian-American Youth Style," *The Journal of Ethnic Studies* 19, 1: 41—66.

Wood, Robin. 1986. "Two Films by Martin Scorsese." *Hollywood from Vietnam to Reagan*, 243—48. New York: Columbia University Press.

"studs

have feelings

fourteen **too"**

warren beatty

and the question

of star discourse

and gender

l u c i a   b o z z o l a

"Hey, I'm a star, I'm a star."

—George Roundy

I think that everybody should see *Shampoo* if only to decide on the basis of
first-hand evidence whether Warren Beatty is God's gift to women or
merely an imaginative con man with a flair for self-promotion.

—Andrew Sarris, *Village Voice,* March 13, 1975

Warren Beatty is an actor who was famous before his first film was
released through, among other things, his highly publicized affair with
Joan Collins. The discourse of his personal life preceded that of movie
actor (Parker 1993, 37, 49–50). Warren Beatty as a star is just as famous
for never talking about his personal life; the power over his cinematic
image exercised as producer/writer/director extends to his private
activities. The knowledge to be gained about his exploits (but not from
him) further presents Beatty as a man in near-mythic control of his
desirability to women. The "truth" behind his sex symbol status for

those audience members who want to know might be gleaned from the interplay between movies and press stories but never from the source. Yet the sex symbol meaning of that offscreen private life combined with Beatty's onscreen penchant for playing men not in control render him a desired and acted-upon object, questioning the assumed relationship between "masculinity" and power, particularly in the realm of sexuality. The interplay between movies and metatext, especially in the films that (allegedly) intersect directly with Beatty's "private" life like *Shampoo* and *Love Affair*, underlines Beatty's image as a gender category breaker, in terms of his star persona and the posited audience relationship to that persona. The usual binary arrangement of sexual roles is broken down and redefined, revealing the binary's constructedness and the need to approach this type of male star from a different direction.

The representation of sexuality and desire in Hollywood film often rests on normative assumptions of what is "masculine" and what is "feminine" and how bodies, particularly star bodies, are treated accordingly.[1] With subjectivity assumed to be "male" and objectivity "female," the male star and his visibility have long been taken to exist in a dysfunctional relationship, with the male body often treated "as an object hiding in plain sight" as Dennis Bingham writes (1994b, 149). Steve Neale, for instance, states that Rock Hudson's objectification in Douglas Sirk's films is recuperated through his "feminization" at those moments (1993, 18); Steven Cohan asserts that William Holden's 1950s paratext of "normal" manhood could sufficiently offset the potential threat presented by Holden's objectified body in *Picnic* (1993, 223). Even Warren Beatty, whose body often seems to be front and center, literally as well as figuratively, manages, in Bingham's analysis, to avoid objectification. The paradoxical nature of this conclusion, and the nature of Beatty's star image as he himself addresses it, put into question the presumed gendered categories of subject and object that are used to maintain that this male body can hide "in plain sight." Indeed, it is the intersection of two star discourses in Beatty's image that destabilizes these assumed gender qualities, manifesting their mutability: the male star who is presented to be looked at expressly as a sexually desirable figure yet must maintain an idea of manhood, and the star in the post-studio era who has a large degree of agency over the formation of his image yet presents himself as an object for desire. The divide between "active" and "passive" and their gendered associations regarding sex and desire begins to collapse.[2] The categories of "male" and "female" vis-à-vis notions of desire need to be mapped out as the star discourse constructs them, rather than assuming that the star discourse inevitably conforms one way or the other.

The means for recuperating Holden's masculinity brings to the fore the strategy of reading a particular actor's films as one aspect of a larger discursive field, the "images in media texts" constituting the star (Dyer 1979, 10). The extratextual discourse constructs the star's sexuality through revealing the private life of the star, and therefore, according to Richard deCordova's use of Michel Foucault, the "secret" truth of the person and the connection of that truth to the star's films (1990, 140–41); a "truth" that is aimed at making the star conform to acceptable contemporary "norms" of heterosexuality, and is thus as much of a construct as the overall star image. The notion of a star's sexuality as a product of a network of discourses in turn invokes Foucault's model of the discursive production of "sexuality," and how it functions as a mechanism of power.[3] The sexualized body is paradoxically the subject of discourse "ad infinitum," while posited as *the* secret (35); knowing the secret of the body shifts the relationship of power. Returning to deCordova's notion of the star discourse locating the secret of the star's identity in the star's most private of lives, then, the dense intersection of relationships of sexuality, knowledge, and power are worked out across the site of the star's body, literally and figuratively. If a star "works" according to modes of masculinity or femininity that are considered "normative," then the star image abides by "strategic unities" constructing this norm, in or outside the films.[4] What is key here in the network of sexuality, knowledge, and power vis-à-vis the star is the instability inherent in that discursive construct. A star construct may abide by certain rules, but this does not mean that there will not be other star constructs that could break, and therefore alter, the rules.

The power/knowledge relationship figured by deCordova as the audience seeking to find out the star's secret points to the fact that in constructing a star's sexuality, the discursive network also constructs a receiver, mandating for whom the discourse exists, as well as who may appropriate that position. The question then becomes what investment does this audience have in this "truth": why, and ultimately *if,* they want to know. This issue regarding audience investment is raised in Bingham's essay (1994b) on Warren Beatty, as he concludes that Beatty offers a subjectivity that can only cause unease for the male spectator (174). If this is the case, then it must be asked who is *not* supposed to be caused unease by this construction; the answer in a hetero-norm culture is, of course, the elusive female spectator.

My aim here is not to try to theorize the female spectator, but to point out that the "man for woman's eyes" is a figure who foregrounds the notion of sexuality as a construction by destabilizing the accepted terminology.[5] Warren Beatty is quite the exemplar of the disruptive star body. Bingham is on the mark in his assertion that Beatty is a star who does not obey the accepted gender categories because the film texts and his own metatext do not seem to match in terms of a "mastery of the gaze," even though each is heavily invested in the other

(1994b, 154). Rather than presume then that Beatty is a figure of "incoherence" because of mismatched gazes, however, I want to take as the issue the categories themselves and examine how they are constructed or reconstructed in his body (of work). As Peter Lehman asserts, "Our rigid notions of male-female difference are over-simplified," and the positions available for identification are "multiple, fluid and contradictory" in discourses involving the sexualized male body (1993, 8). The intersection of the texts in the discursive field that is "Warren Beatty" seem to announce that *this* is what women want, but in so doing, the construction of femininity invested therein comes under question. The problematization of the categories and the reliance on textual intersection to create meaning necessitate a "mapping" of the discursive fields that construct sexuality in Beatty's film *Shampoo*, with a few thoughts about his 1994 film *Love Affair* and its aftermath.

"george roundy" = warren beatty?

While Beatty's extratextual discursive life has almost always managed to intersect with his films, the one film that provokes particular speculation about its closeness is *Shampoo*, featuring Beatty as a randy Beverly Hills hairdresser. Different publications note the snug fit, and attempt to draw Beatty out on the parallel. A gossip writer for the *New York Post* asked Beatty if he was "type-casting himself as the lady-killer" and then notes that Beatty "modestly" evades the answer (Winsten 1975, 22). An interview in *Viva* begins, "Although he'd be the last to admit it, Warren Beatty's new movie is alive with resonances from his own life" (Adler 1975, 40). The *Village Voice* also gets in on the act, with Tag Gallagher asking Beatty, "'I get the idea there was an autobiographical element.' WB: 'Are you talking about sex?' TG: 'Yes.'" Beatty then proceeds to say that his answer would be "boring," since it is not a good question (1975, 60). Several of the reviews make reference to the parallels between the sex life of Beatty's character George Roundy, and Beatty's sex life as it had been documented in the media. The most critical reference is Jay Cocks's assertion in *Time* (1975, 4) that the film, produced and co-written by Beatty as well, could have been called "Advertisements for Myself."[6] Besides Beatty's narcissism, this highlights the control that Beatty exercised over the film and his representation in it. The difference between the quip in *Time* and Beatty's various ways of avoiding the question in interviews makes apparent the slippery nature of the question itself as a means for reaching the "truth" of the matter. The person who wants to know if this film is Beatty advertising himself would have to see the film, read the articles and decide, since Beatty has *not* denied that reading.

Beatty's character in *Shampoo*, along with the multiple relationships that circulate around him further the question of sex and the construction of sexuality; issues given particular real-life contemporary political currency as the 1960s and '70s women's movement sought to break down the constrictive ideas of what traditionally constituted "male" and "female" (Chafe 1977, 133). Along with this political context of instability, Beatty's assertion that he and cowriter Robert Towne wanted to explore a Don Juan, "hoping not to make the classical ... Freudian analysis of Don Juan that requires that Don Juan has ... hostile feelings towards women" (Gallagher 1975, 62) recalls Foucault's description of Don Juan as the ultimate sexual rule-breaker (1990). As a man whose life "overturned" the "two great systems conceived by the West for governing sex: the law of marriage and the order of desire," Don Juan epitomizes the disruptive potential of the Great Lover type (39–40). George is unquestionably a "stud," as Andrew Sarris noted, but he is a stud who lives up to the benign description, used in a 1961 profile on Beatty, of "catnip for the opposite sex," rather than a stud who wields his powers of attraction as a weapon (Muir, 100). In his pursuit of physical gratification, George sleeps with Felicia (the wife of a businessman, Lester, who may back a salon for George), Lorna (Lester and Felicia's teenage daughter), and Jackie (his ex-girlfriend and Lester's mistress). His own girlfriend, Jill, who is Jackie's best friend, rightfully complains that she is always last in line for his favors. Without setting out to, George manages to render starkly what a farce the only marriage in the film is. The order of desire that would favor the under-30 Jill as the proper mate for George, and ratify her wish to be with him only, is jettisoned as George moves from woman to woman, regardless of age or other relationships. As he admits, he "fucked 'em all," but not out of hostility toward them, or toward Lester for that matter.

The benign nature of George as stud and the rethinking of male and female roles continue in the figuring of the women around him as decidedly not passive, and George's own status as an object for their desires. Beatty exercises his subjectivity to play George, and as George, Beatty chooses to objectify himself, authoring his "amorphousness" and disrupting the traditional order of desire (active male and passive female, subject and object). To borrow Lehman's reworking of Laura Mulvey, "he not only [carries] the 'burden of sexual objectification,' but indeed wants to carry it" (1993, 6). Beatty himself draws attention to the problematic nature of the blanket assertion of passivity as female in the *Viva* interview when he states: "First of all, I don't think females are necessarily people who would lie on their backs and let things be done to them; it says a lot about the sex life of a man who thinks they are" (Adler 1975, 42). In *Shampoo,* each woman asserts power in her own way over George, offsetting the power of George's ability to seduce. Felicia asserts herself physically by pulling George into the ladies' room at the

231

Nixon dinner; she is fiscally assertive in suggesting that George go to her husband to get money for a salon. Lorna and Jackie likewise state their demands with a clarity that leaves George speechless. George dodges Lorna's questions about whether he is "making it" with her mother, but when she asks, "You wanna fuck?" he pauses to consider. When Jackie announces to a table of Nixon supporters that what she really wants is to "suck [George's] cock," George is unable to talk her out of climbing under the table. Felicia's, Lorna's and Jackie's different means for demanding that George perform, or be performed on, reorder desire in terms of pursuer and pursued. Yet it is not a direct mirror/reversal that would seem to uphold the rules, since each woman has her own motives outside of George for demanding sex. He also initiates sexual encounters with Felicia and Jackie as well as being a willing participant all around. The relationships of power expressed through sex are not fixed in any of the circumstances.

Jackie's announcement at this election night dinner for Nixon supporters not only accentuates her position within a sex/power network, but also underscores the contemporary circumstances shaping that network. *Shampoo* is pointedly set on Election Day in 1968, a date that has extra resonance because of Nixon's resignation the summer before the film's release, and because of Beatty's own publicized involvement with George McGovern's presidential campaign (Parker 1993, 189–92). Jackie's raw, direct expression of sexual desire at a Nixon campaign VIP dinner encapsulates issues of sexual freedom at stake in the '70s women's movement, and the more general implications of the election (Chafe 1977, 121–22). Her demand evokes the clash of values inherent in an election contest between the conservative Nixon and Hubert Humphrey, who in Nixon's campaign rhetoric (regardless of what Humphrey's actual views may have been), "had a 'personal attitude of indulgence and permissiveness toward the lawless'" (Schell 1975, 21). Along with his status as a successful businessman and an active, albeit pragmatic, Nixon supporter, Lester uses the term "anti-establishment" as he tries to make sense of George's actions late in the film, aligning himself with the conservative order that consists of, among other things, fixed traditional gender roles. A 1975 view on 1968, however, doubly attests to the actual fluidity of those roles in a political matrix of power that is itself hardly fixed.

This flexibility of power and sex carries over into the relationship between George and Lester. While they correspond to opposing sides of the political spectrum (even though George never expresses what would be considered a political opinion), each has an aspect of power within the male/female relationship that the other does not, and each asks to share that power. George clearly possesses the physical power of attraction that the older Lester does not, but he also has the power of knowing what women think in general because of what he hears at the salon all day, and what the women around Lester think in particular. Lester listens attentively as George shares his own acquired wisdom— "We're always trying to nail 'em, and they know it. They know it, and they don't like it"—since Lester has no idea what Jackie and Felicia would "have against" him. He expresses genuine surprise when George informs him that Lorna hates her mother; the dynamics of their relationship never occurred to him, let alone what women think at all. What Lester does have, however, is the power of money. Lester uses his potential investment in George's salon to scold him with, "That's a helluva way to treat a business partner"; George loses Jackie to Lester because she likes to wake up "with the rent paid." George may know how women feel, but he loses out to Lester's power of security. This ending resonates with the 1968 Nixon victory, but the film's post-Watergate production and post-resignation release, as well as Lester's own ambivalence about his candidate, render this reversal of power in favor of Lester more complex than it might seem, undermining Lester's model of masculine power and privilege even as he succeeds. With this ending, however, the film also paradoxically asserts that what women do not want is the sort of man that Beatty is extratextually structured to be. *Shampoo* ultimately rejects the promiscuity inherent in the list of affairs that appears or is referred to in just about every Beatty article, along with the "mobility" described in a 1968 *Life* profile (Thompson, 86). He must be theirs alone and show the responsibility that commitment requires. Jill has the power to say no to him once she definitively knows that he spreads his favors around; Jackie leaves with Lester since she has no basis for believing that George will really take care of her.

"warren really is a sex symbol": beatty's body and the gaze

This intermingling of "subject" and "object" roles present in Jackie and Jill asserting their subjectivity to find a man who will take care of them or George as the seducer and seduced carries over into the physical presence of each in *Shampoo*. The use of the actors' bodies plays out the shifting roles of power in the construction of masculine and feminine as sexual entities that invite or evade a desiring look. While the women are "put on display" in certain ways, this display is usually offset by its conditions, evoking Neale's formulation of how the man avoids being seen as spectacle *only* through context (1993, 16–18). Goldie Hawn as Jill is always shown in either short nighties or mini dresses, but the camera never lingers on parts of her body. Lee Grant as the voracious Felicia is shown once in the opening scene without her top, but in a very dimly lit room; in the rest of the film she is fully covered or clothed, even during her sex scenes with George. Like Goldie Hawn, Julie Christie as

233

Jackie wears revealing outfits, but the circumstances argue against an interpretation of exhibition to the viewer for its own sake. The dress she wears to the Nixon party has a high neck and long sleeves, but no back; the various reactions to the view of her body are emphasized over the view itself. When Jackie turns so that Felicia can see the full effect, the camera is positioned at a medium long distance from the characters, so that the shot shows Jackie from the side, George helpless in the middle and Felicia glaring at the view. At the orgy after the Nixon dinner, George and Jackie are shot in conversation from the front, so that she is covered while George in his unbuttoned shirt is teasingly visible, and there to be investigated.

This arrangement of bodies that reveals George more than Jackie is part of the overall organization of the film. George's central position in the web of sexual relationships is echoed by the order of which body is meant to be seen; his tight jeans and perpetually open shirts set off his body throughout the film. When he does Jackie's hair, she is in a towel, but George's upper body is as revealed by his tank top. His placement in the frame favors the view of his muscular arms, chest and back as he cuts her hair; when he stops to show her the results in the mirror, he is framed so that his head is not visible. There is no choice but to look at his body, as he is center-frame with Jackie. A scene in the salon of George straddling a client while he dries her hair with her head bent toward his groin keeps the action that is supposed to displace the exhibition of the male body overtly sexual. Finally, the only well-lighted displays of nudity among the principals are reserved for George in both of his sex scenes with Jackie; he is positioned both times so that his body covers hers as his own is made available for the viewer.

This discourse designed to enlighten the audience about Beatty's physical attributes—since, of course, it is Beatty on display—is also part of his press. A 1974 article in *Women's Wear Daily* describes Beatty's physical impact as he walks around the set of *Shampoo*: "He moves across the set in well-fitted blue jeans, a blue silk shirt unbuttoned low, a bright green scarf tied at the neck and loads of Indian jewelry. Female crew members stare. 'There's a lot of grabbing around here because Warren really is a sex symbol,' someone explains. 'He puts everybody in the mood to kiss everybody else'" (Winner, 12). Beatty does not efface the effect of his body on- or offscreen in order to preserve his status as a "man," questioning the assumed necessity of the strategy to maintain a semblance of heterosexuality. Despite the display of Beatty's body during sex with Jackie, the "manliness" of the act is verified by the more "normal" Lester's approving statement, "That's what I call fucking." Lester, who bears all of the accoutrements of male privilege including a Rolls, a big house, a mistress, and a body that avoids the gaze, believes George is a "fairy" because of his job and appearance;

once he sees George in the act, however, Lester knows otherwise. The confirmed heterosexuality of this desirable male body on screen is echoed by the observation in the article that it is the female crewmembers who stare. It must be noted that what is not seen of Beatty is any full frontal nudity; if the representation of "phallic masculinity . . . depend[s] on keeping the male body and the genitals out of the critical spotlight," as Lehman (1993) suggests, then Beatty not only defies tradition by showing his body, but also retains his "manhood" by not revealing the physical sign (28). The knowledge that the female spectator, the female who would stare as Beatty walks across a set or read his non-answers about his sexual powers, can gain from the text of *Shampoo* is seeing that body in a very private moment, as well as watching him seduce and submit, but without the potentially disruptive revelation of the ultimate "truth." Seeing his body in the act is truth enough.[7]

Beatty's star image as something for women is reinforced by who does and does not understand why George is a "star" in his work. By writing George as a hairdresser, Beatty and Towne place George in a woman-oriented profession that exists to make women beautiful (objects). Yet at the same time, his attention is focused on fulfilling women's desires to be, somehow, better. Jill tells Jackie about how George woke her up in the middle of the night to do her hair and make her "the grooviest chick in town." Jill's response—"if you love me then I *am* the grooviest chick in town"—attests to the dual nature of George's talents. When George tells Felicia that he could have his own salon because "Hey, I'm a star, I'm a star," Felicia agrees that he would be a great "investment," since she also knows the appeal. The male loan officer at the bank, on the other hand, only wants to hear about financial references, not how many "heads" George cuts. Lester also expresses skepticism about George's "unusual trade," and accuses him of being "anti-establishment" because of his promiscuous life. Like Bingham's male spectator, the men are not "reassured" by George's presence, whereas the women all agree that "he's a great hairdresser," among other things.

The agency given to women by the presentation of a male body that is available for and will submit to their desire, as well as perform an act of improvement, is used against that male at the end of the film. In choosing to say no, Jill and Jackie have the final say in their relationships with George. The film closes with an image of George that differs from the rest of the film. He is alone, motionless, watching Jackie leave with Lester; Beatty is shot from behind and from the waist up, with his face and body position essentially denying one last look. It is at a moment of impotence that Beatty paradoxically obeys the order of the male not to be looked at. This end that denies the discourse of Beatty as "irresistible to women," and emphasizes George as being one more of a line of Beatty "schmucks" that includes Clyde and McCabe would seem to deny certain aspects of Beatty's metatext (Bingham 1994b, 165), but that would mean that the viewer would have to forget the rest of the film that devoted so much time to the display of George as an active symbol of sex and the breakdown of what "normally" constitutes "male" and "female." He is at his most powerful as a subject who has some agency when he is positioned as an object of female desire.

With this end, Jackie would seem to be placing herself as an object of male power and privilege, but it is her decision to do so based on a pragmatic assessment of the options. Beatty himself echoes this formulation of female as rational and male as sexual in another *Women's Wear Daily* article that asks, "Is Warren Beatty really a closet feminist?" because he asserts, "'Well, I think I've always treated women as equals.... But I think men are more controlled by their libidos'" (Collins 1975, 16). In explicating the "male libido and its absurdities" as well as its attractions, Beatty presents a body that can be investigated and possessed without a complete loss of power for him or the female investigator; the relationship is fluid. Beatty makes himself available, while simultaneously controlling access to himself and hinting through his film texts that he cannot be the Powerful Male in spite of his career control. The woman can get a glimpse of the "secret" that Beatty withholds in interviews (though it is always brought up)— "You're asking me to talk about my sex life and I never have and I never will talk publicly about it"—seeing in the process that she has the power to turn it down if she chooses (Beatty qtd. in Collins 1975, 16). The rules are subject to change.

don juan's love affair

The discourse of Beatty as sex symbol remains constant, even now, as an unavoidable part of his history as a star, despite his marriage and his turning sixty. But with the changes one must ask whether an audience still wants to know the secret as it has been altered to accommodate age, marriage, and family. The publicity surrounding the release of *Love Affair*, with Beatty co-starring with his wife, Annette Bening, in another remake of the Classical Hollywood romance *Love Affair* (1939)/*An Affair to Remember* (1957), not only relied on audience awareness of this history; it also reiterated it in various ways to sell the film through the proximity of film and life texts, in a manner similar to *Shampoo*. Among the requisite series of courtship shots in the film's trailer is the intentional mismatch of two scenes that alludes to audience knowledge about Beatty's life, as well as its knowledge that Bening also would have known before he married her in 1992. In the first, Beatty, lit softly in the style of Classical Hollywood "glamour" lighting, turns to Bening on an airplane and informs her that he has a reputation for rampant womanizing. The trailer cuts to Bening in reverse shot, but in an entirely different location, "replying" sarcastically, "I am *shocked* and *amazed*." This vignette also appeared frequently in the shorter television ads, emphasizing that part of the film's appeal was potentially "knowing" the "secret" of how a figure famous for his love life decided to settle down.

A joint appearance by the couple on Oprah Winfrey's talk show (for an overwhelmingly female studio audience) continued this mode of winking at the audience about Beatty's private life. Winfrey asked Bening if she ever thought, "So many women wanted Warren, but I got him," to which Bening sensibly replied, "No, of course not." Winfrey also asked both of them what "romantic things Warren does for Annette," as if this would contain the answer to the studio audience's prayers; a question he modestly tried to evade (he brings her flowers). With questions like this, a big entrance for Beatty twenty minutes after Bening that involved a standing ovation, and Winfrey addressing him as "Mr. Beatty" whereas Bening was simply "Annette," the program supported the discourse of Beatty as a big romantic star of long standing. This discourse was part of Dominick Dunne's profile in *Vanity Fair* that described Beatty as an "old-fashioned" movie star: "Think of Clark Gable, Gary Cooper, Cary Grant, those icons of another era ... who were still kissing Marilyn Monroe and Audrey Hepburn and Doris Day long past kissing time and you begin to get the idea about Warren Beatty" (1994, 143). Among the descriptions of Beatty's life-changing reaction to meeting Bening, and Beatty's fatherly love for his daughter, Dunne still includes references to Beatty's romantic history, a dance with Kim Novak at a party in the 1960s that created palpable sexual tension, and the fact that Beatty's body is still trim (144, 203, 202). Beatty inadvertently raises the specter of his sexual appeal when, as he is listing the roles he did not originally see himself in, like Clyde, he says, "In *Shampoo*, I never thought of anyone but myself" (203). The appeal of seeing *Love Affair*, the publicity implies, is not only that of seeing a great romantic idol in an old-fashioned love story with his beautiful wife, but also of seeing the powerful seducer seduced, and maybe knowing the "secret" of the seduction. The constant that remains, along with Beatty's address to a female audience, is the woman who still has the power to resist his powers of seduction if she chooses, with a sarcastic quip in the case of the film trailer; a woman who entrances Beatty equally.

The tease of the publicity is verified by the opening of the film itself, through the establishment of the reputation of Beatty's character, Mike Gambril, a promiscuous sports figure whose profession recalls Beatty's prematurely dead quarterback from *Heaven Can Wait*, not to mention Beatty's own personal history as a high school jock. As Mike

237

and his fiancée are celebrities, the news of his engagement is treated in a manner similar to the news of Beatty's engagement to Bening. A report on the TV tabloid program *Hard Copy* within the film shows actual paparazzi shots of Beatty with old girlfriends, doctored so that the women are not quite recognizable, to announce that one of the world's most durable bachelors has finally settled down. As if the various entertainment news reports reiterating Mike's reputation were not enough, he and his agent are stopped on their way out to Mike's car by a young pretty editing assistant who brings Mike his watch. As she tells Mike he forgot it in the editing room, she gives him a meaningful glance that is duly noted by his agent, who then asks him not to mess up his engagement. The line between Mike Gambril and Warren Beatty is blurred from the outset.

Even with this beginning that parades Beatty's sexual past one more time, the overtly sexual appeal of Beatty is displaced to overt romanticism in the film as well as in the publicity, in keeping with the extratextual events of marriage, age and the pre- and post-AIDS sexual and political climates of 1975 and 1994.[8] This difference in climate is acknowledged by Beatty himself in a New York *Newsday* interview, as he "muses aloud ... 'Could *Love Affair* have been made fifteen, twenty years ago? ... During the period of sexual and drug mayhem, the picture might have been a little less appealing'" (Pacheco 1994, 25). In a 1996 *Esquire* piece about the purported end of Hollywood's rapacious sexual culture, one of the professed reasons that "Don Juan" is "in turnaround" is simply "Warren Beatty is married," and no longer a purveyor of such hedonism (Hedley, 122). Whereas *Shampoo* features George/Beatty *in flagrante* several times, *Love Affair* shows that the relationship has been consummated through the strategic use of a dissolve from Beatty and Bening deciding to stay on board the ship they have been forced to take after their plane crash-lands on an island in the Pacific, to a close-up freeze-frame of Beatty and Bening kissing superimposed over shots of the ship as it sails, accompanied by lush violins on the soundtrack. True to the film's trailer in spirit if not in actual dialogue, Bening's Terry McKay does not give in easily; when she finally does, it is not because she just wants to have sex with Mike, and he with her, but because they have fallen hopelessly in love.

The most notable event in this discourse surrounding the private life of Beatty in his films, however, is the reaction of the audience. In 1975, Beatty's orchestration of sexuality, which reworked the categories of what it was to be male and female by directly involving the construction of Beatty's own sexuality on and off the screen, was a hit.[9] The audience wanted to know. In 1994, however, the cinematic discourse about Beatty's "secret" life was rejected, despite the publicity and plot that promised some sort of revelation. According to the final analysis in the *New York Times*, two of the problems were directly related to the nature of Beatty's star discourse: "No one wants to see a married couple on screen" because "the sexual sparks don't fly," and "younger audiences were not especially interested in Mr. Beatty as a romantic lead."[10] The tease that attracted viewers to *Shampoo* failed.

While the film's critical and financial failure is one indication of the limits of Beatty's star image as a sex symbol, Beatty's curtailed presence in popular culture between 1994 and 1998 intimates that Beatty is at best a sex symbol with limited appeal, or perhaps is under no woman's desiring gaze at all (except, probably, his wife's), especially if that younger audience has no interest in Beatty that way. Peter Bart, in a 1996 article for the men's magazine *GQ*, sums up Beatty's problem on the cusp of age sixty: "He is suddenly a husband and father, not a lover-at-large.... Most daunting, as the utter failure of *Love Affair* (which Beatty produced as well as starred in opposite Bening) vividly demonstrated, he is no longer able to get away with playing the romantic lead" (78). This is not to say that there is a direct correspondence between the film's failure and Beatty's absence; he has taken long periods off between roles in the past. What is notable regarding these alterations in persona cited by Bart, however, is that when a potentially quite demystifying story about Beatty's body and sexual ability was published in 1995, there was very little public reaction vis-à-vis Beatty. In the book *You'll Never Make Love in This Town Again*, authored by several Hollywood prostitutes and women about town, one of the women deemed Beatty "nothing to write home about" either physically or sexually. Though the book appeared on the best-seller list, the revelation that Beatty was ostensibly not the Great Lover he is purported to be on screen and in gossip got almost no mention in the press. While *Esquire*'s "Don Juan in Turnaround" article (1996) includes Beatty's angry response to the book's "exploitation," "lies," and the alleged damage to his reputation, it is in the context of an argument with the book's publisher at a party (Hedley, 130). More important, the entire incident is relegated to the final pages of a ten-page article, superseded by the story of Don Simpson's life and death, and O. J. Simpson's take on the Hollywood "culture of whores" and sleaze.[11] The revelation simply does not matter as a revelation, nor is it worth first position in a story about 1990s sexual Hollywood. Since Beatty does not function as a visible star presence signifying sex *or* romance for an audience, who wants to know the "truth" of the person that much? In 1997, a *Marie Claire* piece on Beatty and Jack Nicholson posed the question, "Sexy at 60?" then suggested that since Beatty and Nicholson are turning 60, "for women the image of the Great Seducer needs adjustment"; even more so since Beatty is "in safe harbor, with a third baby on the way" (Howell, 34, 37). There is no tease left in Beatty's private life.

The failure to incorporate a discourse on sexuality that abides by its own rules to question the categories of "masculine" and "feminine," subject and object, through positing a desirable male and a desiring female into a discourse that involves the "law of marriage" raises larger questions about the cultural apparatus surrounding the star discourse that go beyond the methodological intent of this essay. The seeming contradiction of Beatty stems from an organization of desire that does not abide by "normative" rules, yet it expresses a decidedly "normal" heterosexual desire, to the point of marriage and several children. The vicissitudes of Beatty's star discourse and its polymorphous construction of sexuality indicate a fluidity and a susceptibility to outside discourses that defy a set reading. When Beatty constructs a manhood that corresponds more to the "norm," the reception is very different from when he breaks the rules, putting into question what the "rules" are at any given time. In order to avoid a tendency toward all-encompassing assumptions about sexuality and power, the qualities attached to male and female need to be mapped out as they are constructed in the star discourse itself, whether it is in a particular event or a series over time, before they can be determined, rather than the reverse of stating what the categories are and then deciding if the star "fits." Indeed, as the construction of Beatty as fantasy sexual object is fading another consistent aspect of his star text was positioned to take its place with the release of *Bulworth* in 1998: politics—a traditional bastion of male power regardless of liberal or conservative stance.

notes

I would like to thank Peter Lehman, Robert Sklar, and Alexandra Keller for their helpful suggestions in revising this essay.

1. See especially Mulvey 1988, 62–63, and Neale 1993, 17–18, for the early paradigms of Hollywood's representation of gender dictating that the male body "hides" from the gaze in order to preserve the norm of active male looking subject and passive female spectacularized object.
2. Rudolph Valentino is a clear antecedent in this regard. As both Miriam Hansen and Gaylyn Studlar assert, Valentino's image as a highly desirable man for women's eyes ultimately resisted recuperation into the "norm" of masculinity, rupturing the binary discourse of active/passive attached to gender in the realm of sexual desire. See Hansen 1986, 23; Studlar 1989, 31.
3. See Foucault 1990, especially 105–7.
4. This brings up the active/male passive/female binarism of Mulvey and Neale. Still, despite criticism that the sex assumed is male, Foucault's formulation suggests that this binarism is nor the overriding rule of Power and the Father. For that criticism see, for example, de Lauretis 1987, 14–15; Fuss 1991, 107.
5. The need to recuperate the epistemological rupture of an "objectified" or "feminized" male body through the intervention of various discursive

practices such as those suggested by Neale, Cohan, Studlar on Valentino, and Bingham on Jimmy Stewart points to the capacity for this type of star to cause this instability. See Studlar 1989, 26; Bingham 1994a, 24.

6. The other reviews include Kael 1975, 89; Michener 1975, 51; Sarris 1975b, 61.

7. Not that Beatty's physical sign of phallic masculinity has never been the object of public discourse. In an *Esquire* article titled "Beds" (Mansfield 1990) that consisted of a collection of quotes regarding Beatty's career in bed, Bianca Jagger and Mamie van Doren say, "It was very big," but Carole Mallory reports, "He's average in size but more friendly than most. It's not the size of Texas. More like the tip of Montauk" (156). Madonna nicely conflates size and performance when she tells the *Advocate* in 1991, "I haven't measured it, but it's a perfectly wonderful size" (Shewey 1991, 51). The woman in *You'll Never Make Love in This Town Again,* however, says nothing on the subject.

8. All of this could constitute its own more extensive study. It is the persistent intersection of film and life texts to construct notions of sexuality that are of interest here, but these extratextual influences needed to be acknowledged, especially given the different reactions of audiences to the discourse.

9. With a gross of more than $20 million in the first three months of release, "Distrib says the film 'is already one of the company's biggest grossing films in its 50-year history.'" From "*Shampoo* a Columbia Clean-Up," 1975, 6.

10. Weinraub 1994, C19. A detail that has too many implications to analyze beyond what is here. It is not possible to determine exactly why from the *Times,* but the few articles on Beatty between 1994 and 1998 do suggest that age can be just as epistemologically disruptive for the male sex symbol as the female, even if it is ostensibly used more as a yardstick in certain pieces for how long Beatty has been around.

11. Simpson qtd. in Hedley 1996, 129. No comment.

works cited

Adler, Dick. 1975. "Warren Beatty: The Star of *Shampoo* Lets Down His Hair." *Viva,* July 40ff.

Bart, Peter. 1996. "Warren Can Wait." *GQ,* April, 76–80.

Beatty, Warren, and Annette Bening. 1994. Interview with Oprah Winfrey. *The Oprah Winfrey Show.* ABC. WABC, New York. Oct. 21.

Bingham, Dennis. 1994a. *Acting Male.* New Brunswick: Rutgers University Press.

———. 1994b. "Warren Beatty and the Elusive Male Body in Hollywood Cinema." *Michigan Quarterly Review* 33 (winter): 149–76.

Chafe, William H. 1977. *Women and Equality: Changing Patterns in American Culture.* New York: Oxford University Press.

Cocks, Jay. 1975. "Blow Dry." *Time,* Feb. 24, 4–5.

Cohan, Steven. 1993. "Masquerading as the American Male in the 50s: *Picnic,* William Holden and the Spectacle of Masculinity in Hollywood Film." In *Male Trouble,* ed. Constance Penley and Sharon Willis, 202–32. Minneapolis: University of Minnesota Press.

Collins, Nancy. 1975. "Bad Boy Goes Good." *Women's Wear Daily,* Feb. 11, 16.

deCordova, Richard. 1990. *Picture Personalities: The Emergence of the Star System in America*. Chicago: University of Illinois Press.

de Lauretis, Teresa. 1987. *Alice Doesn't: Feminism, Semiotics, Cinema*. Bloomington: Indiana University Press.

Dunne, Dominick. 1994. "Love Story." *Vanity Fair*, Sept., 140ff.

Dyer, Richard. 1979. *Stars*. London: BFI Publishing.

Foucault, Michel. 1990. *The History of Sexuality, Vol. 1: An Introduction*. Trans. Robert Hurley. New York: Vintage Books.

Fuss, Diana. 1991. *Essentially Speaking*. New York: Routledge.

Gallagher, Tag. 1975. "Warren Beatty: The Stud as a Thoughtful Man." *Village Voice*, Feb. 24, 112, 60–62, 87.

Hansen, Miriam. 1986. "Pleasure, Ambivalence, Identification: Valentino and Female Spectatorship." *Cinema Journal* 25, 4 (summer): 6–32.

Hedley, Tom. 1996. "Don Juan in Turnaround." *Esquire*, September, 122–32.

Howell, Georgina. 1997. "Sexy at 60?: Warren & Jack." *Marie Claire*, Feb., 34–37.

Kael, Pauline. 1975. "Beverly Hills as a Big Bed." *New Yorker*, Feb. 17, 86–93.

Lehman, Peter. 1993. *Running Scared: Masculinity and the Representation of the Male Body*. Philadelphia: Temple University Press.

Mansfield, Stephanie. 1990. "Beds." *Esquire*, May: 151–57.

Michener, Charles. 1975. "Don Juan in Beverly Hills." *Newsweek*, Feb. 10, 51.

Muir, Florabel. 1961. "The New Great Lover." *The Sunday News*, Oct. 15, 100.

Mulvey, Laura. 1975. "Visual Pleasure and Narrative Cinema." *Screen* 16, 3 (autumn 1975). Reprinted in *Feminism and Film Theory*, ed. Constance Penley, 57–68. New York: Routledge, 1988.

Neale, Steve. 1983. "Masculinity as Spectacle." *Screen* 24, 6. Reprinted in *Screening the Male*, eds. Steven Cohan and Ina Rae Hark, 9–20. New York: Routledge.

Pacheco, Patrick. 1994. "Love Connection." *New York Newsday*, Oct. 16, 18ff.

Parker, John. 1993. *Warren Beatty: The Last Great Lover of Hollywood*. New York: Carroll & Graf Publishers.

Robin et al. 1995. *You'll Never Make Love in This Town Again*. Los Angeles: Dove Books.

Sarris, Andrew. 1975a. "The Blissful Servitude of Self-Indulgence." *Village Voice*, March 13, 71.

———. 1975b. "Studs Have Feelings Too." *Village Voice*, Feb. 24, 61.

Schell, Jonathan. 1975. *The Time of Illusion*. New York: Vintage Books.

"*Shampoo* a Columbia Clean-Up." 1975. *Variety* May 28, 6.

Shewey, Don. 1991. "The Saint, the Slut, the Sensation . . . Madonna." *Advocate*, May 7, 42–51.

Studlar, Gaylyn. 1989. "Discourses of Gender and Ethnicity: The Construction and De(con)struction of Rudolph Valentino as Other." *Film Criticism* 8, 2 (winter): 18–35.

Thompson, Thomas. 1968. "Under the Gaze of the Charmer." *Life*, April 26, 86–94.

Weinraub, Bernard. 1994. "This Year, Oscar Bets Won't Be Sure Ones." *New York Times*, November 29, C15ff.

Winner, Karin. 1974. "On Movies and Politics." *Women's Wear Daily*, May 24, 12.

Winsten, Archer. 1975. "Rages and Outrages." *New York Post*, March 3, 22.

james

bond's

penis

toby miller

Jane, 17, was quite indignant when I asked her if she found the films sexist. She replied sharply: "I think a lot of women would love Bond to have his wicked way with them, don't you?" It was a rhetorical question, so I didn't answer.

—Maria Manning (1990, 13)

The most successful saga in postwar popular culture got off to a start after breakfast on a tropical morning in Jamaica on January 16, 1952. Ian Fleming . . . knocked out about two thousand words on his Imperial portable . . . two months later, he was done, with Commander James Bond recovering from a near lethal attack on his balls and Vesper Lynd dead by her own hand. A major addition to the world's cultural and political furniture was under way.

—Alexander Cockburn (1987, 27)

You've caught me with more than my hands up.

—James Bond, *Diamonds Are Forever* (Guy Hamilton, 1971)

It's almost as if Bond was written for the purpose of being read for his ideological incorrectness by angsty academics who felt decidedly uncomfortable that they actually enjoyed these unsound films. Where could you find a better example of xenophobic, chauvinistic behaviour? Whether as a fantasy of post-colonial or masculine power, James Bond films are rampantly reactionary. So how do you explain their popularity?

—Suzanne Moores (1989, 44)

ADMIRAL ROEBUCK: With all due respect, M, sometimes I don't think you have the balls for this job.

M: Perhaps. The advantage is that I don't have to think with them all the time.

—*Tomorrow Never Dies* (Roger Spottiswoode, 1997)

The James Bond books and films are routinely held up as a significant contributor to, and symptom of, imperialism, sexism, Orientalism, class hierarchy, and jingoism—even as the first form of mass pornography (Baron 1994, 69–70; Bold 1993; Drummond 1986, 66–67; Moniot 1976, 29; Denning 1992, 225). And so they are. But frequently in a chaotic manner that is more complex and contradictory than teleological accounts of a phallic, hegemonic hero will allow. In this chapter, I follow up some previous work on men and culture, using methods that are comparatively rare in screen studies but are available in both popular culture (Cohen 1999; Paley 1999) and social theory (see Miller 1995; 1998, 101–40; and 1993, 49–94; for anthropology, see Beidelman 1997; for film, see Lehman and Hunt 1999 and Lehman 1998). These methods are not beholden to the unsaid, the repressed, or the hermeneutic turn. Instead, they are mundane, positive knowledges that work with conventional public truths as commonsense ways of making meaning. I will contend that (a) far from being the *alpha* of the latter-day Hollywood *macho* man, as per Sylvester Stallone, Bruce Willis, Arnold Schwarzenegger, and Wesley Snipes, Bond was in the *avant garde* of weak, commodified male beauty; (b) we can see this in the history of his penis; and (c) psychoanalysis doesn't help us to do so.

Bond's penis is a threat to him—a means of being known and of losing authority, a site of the potentially abject that must instead be objectified as an index of self-control and autotelic satisfaction. In the character's first film incarnation, Sean Connery's Bond was very much a spectator to his own, publicly shared penis, its stark movements between patriarchal power and limp failure anticipating the long, slow move that has gradually made the male body the object of routine speculation for commercial and governmental purposes, in a very conscious, highly unimaginary series of material encounters. Governmentality, the refinement of human bodies as part of rationalization and utilitarianism, connects to capital accumulation in a network of power dispersed across the conditioned and consuming body. The male body references these complexities of contemporary capitalism, played out over the public bodies of headlined workers. Bond's gender politics are far from a functionalist world of total domination by straight, orthodox masculinity. Excoriating evaluations of women's bodies have long been a pivotal node of consumer capitalism. Now, slowly in many cases but rapidly in others, the process of bodily commodification through niche targeting has identified men's bodies as objects of desire, and gay men and straight women as consumers, while there are even signs of lesbian desire as a target. Masculinity is no longer the exclusive province of men, either as spectators, consumers, or agents of power. And Bond was an unlikely harbinger of this trend.

Why not use the nineteenth-century metanarrative that claims to deal with repression and displacement? After all, the hermeneutics of spotting hidden genitals may be the most enduring Freudian legacy. People "effortlessly and unembarrassedly identify the phallus in dream objects, domestic objects, and civil objects" (Scarry 1985, 282), its real nature mystified by a metaphor that has distanced it from sex. Psychoanalysis holds that the phallus represents power. The phallus itself lacks a universal material sign. The closest signifier is the penis, given male social dominance (and Freudianism's dependency on sex as the epicenter of life and analysis). The penis fails to live up to this responsibility, however—it is not as powerful as the phallus. At the same time, its unsuitability as a signifier, and the taboo on its public emergence, is said to metaphorize phallic power. Suppression of penile representations is generally attributed in psychoanalytic cultural theory to castration anxiety and the formation of the superego. When the penis appears, foregrounding its sex, it becomes paradoxically difficult to know in this discourse, because it fails to conceal its true nature. Hence the problem of the filmic penis. What is to be done when the penis is encountered as an overt textual sign: not secreted behind phallic signifiers or sedimented psychic narratives, but straightforwardly present on-screen?

Psychoanalysis is a factor in what follows to the extent and on the occasions when Freudianism and its kind are invoked intratextually as systems of thought, but not as an extratextual truth to be used as a metacode. The position enunciated in *The Well-Tempered Self* and repeated here is that the human sciences (linguistics, psychoanalysis, and so on) divide the person into discrete entities that are set up as in need of amendment, reconciliation, and renewal because they are ethically incomplete. This search is asymptotic—it never reveals or creates that person's supposed expressive totality—but also productive, in that its legacy is a set of cultural norms that construct inadequacy. Such endeavors should be displaced by an historicized use of social theory to assist in the generation of new selves derived from the *detritus* of our present past. The penis is always already located in a symbolic order: distinctions between the imaginary and the symbolic, or the phallic and the penile, are distinctions of discourse. They reside in sometimes parallel, sometimes overlapping formations, with different material effects depending on their mobilization at specific moments and places.

In this chapter, I present myself as a vulgar sexual materialist concerned to comprehend man-as-commodity. Because Bond is such a complex series of social texts, his film *persona* needs to be understood across sites, starting with the originary novels. Their trace was significant to film reviewers of the day and also provides an abstraction from contemporary viewing positions in order to get at "the affective structure" of Bond (Bergonzi 1958, 221). This structure spoke to eight-year-old Jay McInerney when *Doctor No* (Terence Young, 1962) was released. Bond had come "to save America, and not incidentally to liberate me from my crew cut and help me to meet girls." McInerney's parents forbade him to see the film because it was said to be "racy" and because the father's domestic mastery was attested by the son's hairstyle (McInerney et al. 1996, 13). Now that's a male affective structure.

the novel bond

Many British critics of the mid-1960s interpreted Bond as a symptom of imperial decline, evidenced by his lack of moral fiber and an open sexuality that assumed the legitimacy of strong women desiring heterosexual sex outside marriage (Denning 1992, 223; Cannadine 1979, 49–50). This aspect made Bernard Bergonzi (1958) deride Bond as not "an ideal example for the young," because women are "only too eager to make love to *him*" (222, 225). The Salvation Army's *War Cry* journal objected to the same tendency (Woolf 1990, 86). Bond represented the casual pleasures that derived from a perverse intermingling of American consumer culture with European social welfare—what the *New Statesman*, in a celebrated essay on Bond (Johnson 1958), referred to as "our curious post-war society." Connery stood for the right and the space—for men *and* women, albeit in unequally gendered ways—to be sexual without being "committed," and he also symbolized polymorphous sexuality (Bold 1993, 320). In *Doctor No*, Fleming describes Honeychile Rider's buttocks as "almost as firm and rounded as a boy's." This drew a rebuke from Noël Coward: "Really, old chap, what could you have been thinking of?" (quoted in Richler 1971, 343). Any scan of the popular sociology and literary criticism of the time indicates how threatening this was to the right, which drew analogies between the decline of empire and the rise of personal libertarianism (Cannandine 1979, 46, 49–50; Booker 1969, 42–43; Houston 1964–65).

For all the supposed association with fast living, high-octane sex, and a dazzling life, Bond basically runs away from fucking in the novels, leaving the desiring women who surround him in a state of great anxiety. Attempts to match Bond with other literary-historical figures, notably via claims that the novels are based on either *Beowulf* or *Sir Gawain and the Green Knight*, explain this rejection of women as Fleming's "medieval blueprint" of chaste valor (Webb 1968; H. R. Harris 1990, 30–31). But it's more than that:

> God, it was turning towards his groin! Bond set his teeth. Supposing it liked the warmth there! Supposing it tried to crawl into the crevices! Could he stand it? Supposing it chose that place to bite? Bond could feel it questing amongst the first hairs. (Fleming, *Doctor No*, 65)

Of course, "it" is a centipede heading for "that place." Everyone recalls the spider doing the same in the film—after which, Connery runs to the bathroom and is violently ill. But the steadfast way with which Bond eschews sex in the original stories might as well have made it a human being that "liked the warmth there," for all the horror of intimacy.

Bond's terror about "that place" is also evident in *Casino Royale*. Le Chiffre tortures him with "a three-foot-long carpet-beater in twisted cane." The details are fetishistically enumerated in three pages of purple Fleming prose that describe the evil mastermind making his way across what he calls Bond's "sensitive part," while the latter awaits "a wonderful period of warmth and languor leading into a sort of sexual twilight where pain turned to pleasure and where hatred and fear of the torturers turned to a masochistic infatuation" (119–22).

In *Doctor No*, Bond is confronted with his desire for Honeychile Rider, her "left breast . . . hard with passion. Her stomach pressed against his." In response he "must stay cold as ice . . . Later! Later! Don't be weak" (142). Bond risks being taken down by desire, the threat of woman exhausting man's capacity to control his environs. This refusal draws a mocking retort when Honey addresses him in the third person:

> His arms and his chest look strong enough. I haven't seen the rest yet. Perhaps it's weak. Yes, that must be it. That's why he doesn't dare take his clothes off in front of me. (144)

Bond's struggle with the attraction he feels for women stands in contrast to Scaramanga, the villain of *The Man with the Golden Gun*, an assassin who "has sexual intercourse shortly before a killing in the belief that it improves his 'eye,'" according to a briefing provided by the British Secret Service (30).

the screen bond

Ayn Rand, who adored the 007 books for what she saw as their unabashed romanticism and heroic transcendence, was appalled by the films because they were laced with "the sort of humor intended to undercut Bond's stature, to make him ridiculous" (1971, 138). These qualities of self-parody are key aspects to the unstable masculinity on display. The technology of the penis is mockingly troped again and again in details and stories from the series. The film of *Doctor No* featured condoms as special-effects devices. Loaded with explosives, they blow up the sand in puffs when Bond and Honeychile are shot at (Barnes and Hearn 1998, 13). The producers, keen from the first to defray costs through product placement and merchandising, refused permission, however, for a line of 007 condoms, despite pressure from the Salvation Army to refer in the film to the use of prophylactics (Pfeiffer and Lisa 1995, 218–19).

Elsewhere in the movies, however, the penis comes out of this protective sheath, just as the literary Bond's ambivalence about commodities bursts onto the screen as joy through consumption. Connery's Bondian sex is fairly progressive for its day, with the sadomasochistic aspects, predictably, too much for U.S. critics: *Newsweek* condemned Connery in *Doctor No* as of interest solely to "cultivated sadomasochists" (quoted in Anez 1992, 314). Identical critiques came from the Communist Party youth paper *Junge Welt* in the German Democratic Republic, and from the Vatican City's *L'Osservatore Romano* (Sann 1967, 34). Britain's *Daily Worker* found an "appeal to the filmgoer's basest instincts" and "perversion," while on the other side of politics, the *Spectator* deemed the film "pernicious." *Films and Filming* called the "sex and sadism" a "brutally potent intoxicant" and identified Bond on-screen as a "monstrously overblown sex fantasy of nightmarish proportions." He was "morally . . . indefensible" and liable to produce "kinky families" (quoted in Barnes and Hearn 1998, 16–17, 26–27). But for Susan Douglas growing up, the film of *Doctor No*, for example, was a sign that "sex for single women [could be] glamorous and satisfying" (1994, 72).

The producers cast Connery knowing full well that he was not the ruling-class figure of the novels, in the hope that he would appeal to women sexually and encourage cross-class identification by men (Broccoli with Zec 1998, 171). Co-producer Albert Broccoli called this "sadism for the family" (quoted in Barnes and Hearn 1998, 20). Connery as Bond was frequently criticized as a wuss during the '60s, in keeping with the notion that his s/m style embodied the weak-kneed and decadent cosseting that was losing an empire. *Time* labeled him a "used-up gigolo" after *Doctor No* (quoted in Barnes and Hearn 1998, 16) while many U.S. magazines objectified him mercilessly by listing his bodily measurements (Dore 1996, 11). (Connery's successor, George Lazenby, was criticized by the producers for being too *macho* by contrast with the first film incarnation: "one could wish he had less *cojones* and more charm" [quoted in Barnes and Hearn 1998, 93].)

In *Doctor No*, Bond hands his card to a woman he meets in a club and invites her to come up and see him some time. This is an invitation for the woman, Sylvia Trench, to exercise her desire—which she does, astonishing him by breaking into his apartment within the hour. He encounters her practicing golf in his rooms, attired in just a business shirt. *Thunderball* (Terence Young, 1965) finds Bond chided by Fiona Volpe:

> I forgot your ego, Mister Bond. James Bond, who only has to make love to a woman and she starts to hear heavenly choirs singing. She repents, then immediately returns to the side of right and virtue. But not this one. What a blow it must have been—you, having a failure.

The equal legitimacy of male and female extramarital desire lives contradictorily within Bond's violent patriarchal attitudes. So it should be no surprise to find that the first *Sunday Times* magazine color supplement (1962) features Mary Quant clothing, worn by Jean Shrimpton and photographed by David Bailey; a state-of-the-nation essay on Britain; and a James Bond short story. Or that the inaugural *Observer* equivalent includes fashions from France and stills from the forthcoming Bond movie (Booker 1969, 49, 238).

This is the all-powerful brute at work, with women cowering defensively?

Connery's prior careers as Scottish Mr. Universe, Carnaby Street model, and Royal Court Shakespearian background the intersection of body, style, action, and performance perfectly. In gesturing against McInerney's father's crewcut, Connery showed that the look of a man could transcend his class background and *politesse*. This was a postmodern figure of beautiful male commodification *avant la lettre*, exquisitely attractive to many women and men who either shared or read through his sexism and racism to enjoy goodness, excitement, and parody (Synnott 1990; Manning 1990, 13; Bold 1993).

From the first, Connery was the object of the gaze, posing in 1966 besuited for *GQ* and bare-cleavaged for *Life*, making it clear that sexiness did not have to be associated with a choice between ruggedness and style (McInerney 1996, 26, 32)—the harbinger of a new male body on display. The style has become increasingly familiar across the '80s and '90s. Consider male striptease shows performed for female audiences. This fairly recent phenomenon references not only changes in the direction of power and money, but also a public site where "[w]omen have come to see exposed male genitalia; they have come to treat male bodies as objects only" (Barham 1985, 62). Something similar is happening in feminist "slash lit" fanzines that recode male bonding from TV action series as explicitly sexual, depicting hyperstylized, hugely tumescent cocks at play in sadomasochistically inflected pleasure (Penley 1992 and 1997). Such texts trope Cyril Connolly's 1963 spoof "Bond Strikes Camp," which finds M coming out as gay and 007 a transvestite.

Thirty years on, Connery's remains *the* style, the way to be. The *London Review of Books* published poetry about his Bond three decades after the fact (Crawford 1995). And when CNN devoted ten minutes to the summer 1995 release of a new book on the culture of the martini, the story was divided in two. The principal diegesis was the launch in a Manhattan bar. Increasingly unappealing-looking yuppies were interviewed after their first, second, and third martinis. As hair went askew, ashtrays overflowed, words slurred, and mascara ran, the viewer was offered another diegesis: Connery's martini order from each of his Bond films, lovingly edited together by the network.

connery goes gold/twenty years after

The Bond films make much play of the penis, spectacularly in *Goldfinger* (Guy Hamilton, 1964) and *Never Say Never Again* (Irvin Kershner, 1983). They do so parodically. Janet Thumim (1992) reads *Goldfinger* as a paean to "personal liberation . . . privileging the young and the new" through the blurring of espionage with comedy, where the unpacking of secrets is less important than the work of spectacle: luxury Miami hotel life, a personal jet plane, gold bullion holdings, private laser weaponry, and regal sports. The real "secret" is the capacities of Bond's Aston Martin (73–76). She is so right. Bond offers transcendence from the bonds of origin via a form of life that uses commodities and sex to go beyond, to another place, and then moves on, without any drive toward accumulating power and authority. He is the drifter in a tux whose body bears the signs of social stratification, but who never stays in one place long enough to adopt the mantle of patriarchy through its trappings of soil, blood, and home. "Why do you always wear that thing?" inquires a woman of Connery's shoulder holster in the pre-credits diegesis of *Goldfinger.* His reply—"I have a slight inferiority complex"—short-circuits the critique. Narratively, this exchange bespeaks a gratuitous self-confidence: he lets go of the gun and is subsequently exposed to peril. For alongside all his dexterity, the Connery body is on display as ever, notably in a terry-cloth jumpsuit that he dons in a subsequent scene. This is "major beefcake." A sequence in bed with Jill Masterson is initially characterized by smart-ass conduct during a phone call where he tells a CIA agent that they cannot meet immediately because "something big's come up." But this is followed by defeat: he is knocked senseless and Eaton is drowned in gold paint. Back in Britain, Connery beats his adversary in a round of golf. But then Oddjob squashes a golf-ball in front of his nose in reprisal. Bond's reaction is registered via a medium close-up on a very anxious face. For Anthony Burgess (1987), it shows Bond disconcerted rather than imperturbable. This quality of being "ironic, but never facetious," where "[h]e knows the world, but he is not knowing," makes Connery not only a star but a strangely esteemed public figure (117).

Bond is more directly at risk in the laser-castration scene, sensationalized on the poster advertising the film. Strapped to a table, Bond is taunted by Auric Goldfinger as an industrial laser cuts through wood and metal between his spread legs. As 007's muscles visibly tense, the two men engage in some *badinage,* and a close-up on Bond's face evidences further concern. He looks between his legs and across the room in a series of reverse shots with Frobe. As Bond is spread-eagled before the beam, John Barry's three-minute musical sequence "begins by simply sustaining and repeating, with characteristic punctuation from the xylophone, an F-minor added-second chord." As the beam heads for 007's wedding tackle, violins offer "an eight-note motif, harmonized by the same chord." It repeats in crescendo a dozen times, then returns to the opening two notes of the previous motif, which also repeats twelve times. Throughout, harmonies are sustained, with volume providing the chief dynamic (Brown 1994, 46–47; also see Smith 1998, 115–30). Throwing out a last suggestion that he knows something about "Operation Grand-Slam," Connery persuades his adversaries to turn off the band of light as it is about to reach his crotch. The segment illustrates Michel Chion's concept of "added value," the mix of information and expessivity with which sound enriches pictures. It is fully achieved at moments of "synchresis," when there seems to be "an immediate and necessary relationship" between what is seen and heard, an organic one-on-one correspondence of visual and aural signs that produces empirical faith in the listener-watcher (1994, 5).

Stunned by a tranquilizing dart, Bond awakens (as do we through subjective camera) to the face of Pussy Galore, as if to complete the point. His weakness is certainly signaled by the fortunes of his penis— a sign of lacking control. Caught up earlier by strong feelings over Jill Masterson's killing, he had failed to manicure his conduct as per the technologies of the self that should mark him out as an effective agent. He has risked reassignment away from the mission, faced a gendered death, and then confronted the eponymous Other. We receive some telling lessons in the management of nuclearity toward the climax of the text. The sure and certain hand of a nameless, speechless bureaucrat brushes confidently past 007's clammy paws to disarm the

251

bomb that threatens both them and Fort Knox. Smooth and direct, entirely free of the panic revealed on Connery's face via a series of cuts from ticking timer to sweating spy, this sober and anonymous administrative intellectual simply cuts off the device. For New York critics at the time of the release, this 007 was just too much of a failure for the film to appeal (Anez 1992, 317).

Never Say Never Again marks Connery's return to the role, some two decades after *Goldfinger*. It contrasts Bond with his colleague Nigel Small-Fawcett (Rowan Atkinson), an ineffectual bureaucrat abroad who represents the unearned decadence of the English ruling class. His name alone establishes this ineffectualness through a penile slight. Yet, throughout, Bond's own penis is a vehicle for investigation and doubt. Dispatched to a health farm for a thorough purgation and makeover, as per the shared storyline of *Thunderball*, 007 is required to provide a urine sample. He makes a joke of this to the nurse, but the text then cuts to a worm's-eye view from the stiletto heels of the villainous Fatima Blush (Barbara Carrera). And Bond's line "I was up all night," a knowing remark to his doctor made to be heard by the woman he has just slept with, is countered with the prescription of an herbal enema. Each triumphal moment is followed by a letdown. Even defeat of a muscle-bound enemy is only achieved by blinding the assailant with what turns out to be Bond's urine sample from the first morning. Breathlessly talking to Small-Fawcett over the phone while having sex, he quips: "Just be brief; I don't have too much time." As a woman moves astride Bond, Small-Fawcett offers: "Just want you to know that I'm on top of things." In their final confrontation, Blush orders 007 to "spread your legs" and sign a testament to her superior sexual skill before being shot ("Guess where you get the first one"). But he overcomes.

This mythic imbrication of sex, secrets, and the slide from an Empire to the Commonwealth of Nations, drawn across the body of Bond and his others, is quite overtly a "postimperial fantasy life" (Cockburn 1987, 30). Being dispatched to a health farm in search of renewal is an intervention, not a symptom (Harper 1969, 83–84). It's the fantasy life that saw huge public support in Britain for the folly of the Suez Canal in 1956, a folly that ended when Eisenhower told Prime Minister Anthony Eden to stop, and for the Falklands/Malvinas War of 1982, a farce that continued because Reagan told Thatcher to keep going. Bizarre sexual activities by politicians at home helped to bring down both British administrations, even as this desperate staging of global authority played out antediluvian hegemony.

The point is that viewers can *see* all this: there are no suppressed psyches here, clinging on to a lost world. Rather, Bond is the first screen action hero to embody and address the new, fragile pleasure of the commodity, where both his own form and the object he encounters are "mundane objects of desire" (Cockburn 1987, 31). What Michel Foucault called in the mid-1970s "the grey morning of tolerance" that seemed to be dawning for a diversity of sexual practice could never be wholly welcomed or welcoming. It was necessarily marked by anxieties over sudden change and the inevitability of cheapened commodification through a "movement of growth-consumption-tolerance" (1982, 73–74).

encoded psychoanalysis and the bodily commodity

Psychoanalysis has certainly been the preferred system of inscribing ethical incompleteness onto James Bond, Ian Fleming, and their male readers. Mythological and psychological criticisms of the series have been prominent for almost four decades now, stretching from Lacanian interrogations of woman and her lack to an object-relations account that says the gold in *Goldfinger* is feces, Goldfinger himself the father's cock, and spying a regressive primal-scene pastime that makes men gay. Such approaches have made their way so successfully into the language of Bond that *Goldeneye* (Martin Campbell, 1995) finds Pierce Brosnan alluding to the issue. Conversely, alternatives to Jungian and Freudian methods have generally involved either genre thematisation or ideology critique. Here the penis disappears beneath a welter of spy-story precedents, class politics, or international relations (Holbrook 1972; Cawelti and Rosenberg 1987, 126–55; Bennett and Woollacott 1987). Or does it? The gun as phallus is *encoded* in the textuality of Bond. It does not await the amateur-hour psychoanalytic textual analyst to uncover this fact. Rather, the symbolism is played with deliberately. In Fleming's *The Man with the Golden Gun*, a report is read that says "the pistol . . . has significance for the owner as a symbol of virility—an extension of the male organ—and that excessive interest in guns . . . is a form of fetishism" (35). Critics of the time recognized this. Sydney Harris (1965) regarded *Goldfinger* as giving permission "to eat our Freudian cake and keep our All-American frosting at the same time" and the *London Magazine* pointed to the "consciously Freudian structure of the fictions," evident in the father-son conflicts that Bond has with M and the master villains (Ormerod and Ward 1965, 42–43). *Newsweek's Goldfinger* review was titled "Oedipus Wrecks," referring to Bond's relations with his boss M and the title character. And Vincent Canby (1965) looked forward to a moment when writers would use these symbols as an alibi to uncover "some anxious, fundamental truth about our time." Where to now for the psy-complex hermeneut ablaze within us?

Instead, let us consider Joseph Maguire's four-part social typology of the body as a site of discipline, mirroring, domination, and communication. The *disciplined* penis is trained to be obedient, to transcend but also operate alongside biology—to be under control in a satisfactorily self-policed body, as per today's penile prostheses and Bond's time spent at the health farm recovering from his various excesses in *Never Say Never Again* and *Thunderball*. The *mirroring* penis is a desirable icon, used in the Bond saga to represent and produce excitement, anxiety, and failure, as per the bedroom triumph and decline of *Goldfinger*. The *dominating* penis is a physical sign and technique for exerting force over others, especially women—Bond's instant attraction to those he meets on the street or anywhere else, in all the films. And the *communicative* penis stands for a combination of the aesthetic and the sublime, as in the complex relations of size, race, sexual activity, and the Bondian organ's wry history—Bond sickened by desire and terror in the *Doctor No* spider sequence.

Commercial and historical shifts in the protocols of producing and viewing James Bond's penis seem to heed, however unconsciously, Félix Guattari's (1981) call to bring down the binary that divides people by sex. Guattari seeks to "destroy notions which are far too inclusive, like woman, homosexual." He argues that when these are "reduced to black-white, male-female categories, it's because there's an ulterior motive, a binary-reductionist operation to subjugate them" (86—87). This is not to suggest the prospect of transcendence through the discovery of an authentic self: that search is an unending one given the power of ethical incompleteness over the human sciences. Rather, it is to call for an engagement with the sometimes murky, sometimes clear, often unworthy, and frequently insignificant historicism of man and his penis, their thick and thin past—in a practical encounter with occasions of masculinity. The nature of these occasions will be decided by differential forms and uptakes of a text, based on the social formation and the reading protocol disposed at the time: 007 is decoded by different audiences as sadistic snobbery, modern transcendence, libertine promise, amateurish dash, organizational obedience, new technological heroism, and outmoded imperial folly (Denning 1992, 213)—and all through the lens of commodified male beauty. James Bond's penis comes in many sizes.

works cited

Anez, Nicholas. 1992. "James Bond." *Films in Review* 43, 9—10: 310—19.

Barham, Susan Baggett. 1985. "The Phallus and the Man: An Analysis of Male Striptease." In *Australian Ways: Anthropological Studies of an Industrialised Society*, ed., Lenore Manderson, 51—65. Sydney: Allen & Unwin.

Barnes, Alan, and Marcus Hearn. 1998. *Kiss Kiss Bang! Bang! The Unofficial James Bond Film Companion*. Woodstock: Overlook Press.

Baron, Cynthia. 1994. "*Doctor No*: Bonding Britishness to Racial Sovereignty." *Spectator* 14, 2: 68—81.

Beidelman, T. O. 1997. *The Cool Knife: Imagery of Gender, Sexuality, and Moral Education in Kaguru Initiation Ritual*. Washington, D.C.: Smithsonian Institution Press.

Bennett, Tony, and Janet Woollacott. 1987. *Bond and Beyond: The Political Career of a Popular Hero.* Basingstoke: Macmillan.

Bergonzi, Bernard. 1958. "The Case of Mr Fleming." *Twentieth Century*, March, 220–28.

Bold, Christine. 1993. "'Under the Very Skirts of Britannia': Re-Reading Women in the James Bond Novels." *Queen's Quarterly* 100, 2: 310–27.

Booker, Christopher. 1969. *The Neophiliacs: A Study of the Revolution in English Life in the Fifties and Sixties.* London: Collins.

Broccoli, Albert, with Donald Zec. 1998. *When the Snow Melts: The Autobiography of Cubby Broccoli.* London: Boxtree.

Brown, Royal S. 1994. *Overtones and Undertones: Reading Film Music.* Berkeley: University of California Press.

Burgess, Anthony. 1987. "Oh, James, Don't Stop." *Life* 10, 4: 114–20.

Canby, Vincent. 1965. "United Artists' Fort Knox." *Variety* 31, March, 3.

Cannadine, David. 1979. "James Bond and the Decline of England." *Encounter* 53, 3: 46–55.

Cawelti, John G. and Bruce A. Rosenberg. 1987. *The Spy Story.* Chicago: University of Chicago Press.

Chion, Michel. 1994. *Audio-Vision: Sound on Screen.* Trans. and ed. Claudia Gorbman. New York: Columbia University Press.

Cockburn, Alexander. 1987. "James Bond at 25." *American Film* 12, 9: 26–31, 59.

Cohen, Joseph. 1999. *The Penis Book.* Cologne: Könemann.

Connolly, Cyril. 1963. *Previous Convictions.* New York: Harper & Row.

Crawford, Robert. 1995. "Male Infertility." *London Review of Books* 17, 16: 22.

Denning, Michael. 1992. "Licensed to Look: James Bond and the Heroism of Consumption." *Contemporary Marxist Literary Criticism*, ed. Francis Mulhern, 211–29. London: Longman.

Dore, Katherine. 1996. "Public School Playboy: The Image of James Bond in America in the Sixties." Unpublished ms.

Douglas, Susan J. 1994. *Where the Girls Are: Growing Up Female with the Mass Media.* New York: Times Books.

Drummond, Lee. 1986. "The Story of Bond." *Symbolizing America*, ed. Hervé Varenne, 66–89. Lincoln: University of Nebraska Press, 1986.

Fleming, Ian. 1966. *Casino Royale.* London: Pan.

———. 1990. *Doctor No.* New York: Berkeley.

———. n.d. *The Man With the Golden Gun.* New York: Signet.

Foucault, Michel. 1982. "Grey Mornings of Tolerance." Trans. Danielle Kormos. *Stanford Italian Review* 2, 2: 72–74.

"*Goldfinger*: The New Brutalism." 1964. *Sight and Sound* 33, 3: 127–28.

Guattari, Félix. 1981. "Becoming-Woman." *Semiotext(e)* 4, 1: 86–88.

Harper, Ralph. 1969. *The World of the Thriller.* Cleveland: The Press of Case Western Reserve University.

Harris, H. R. 1990. "New Light on James Bond." *Contemporary Review* 256, 1488: 30–34.

Harris, Sydney. 1965. "Embarrassed, but He Did Like the Movie." *Citizen-News*, March 29.

Holbrook, David. 1972. *The Masks of Hate: The Problem of False Solutions in the Culture of an Acquisitive Society.* Oxford: Pergamon Press.

Houston, Penelope. "007." *Sight and Sound* 34, no. 1 (1964–65): 14–16.

Johnson, Paul. 1958. "Sex, Snobbery, and Sadism." *New Statesman* April 5: 430–32.

255

Lehman, Peter. 1998. "In an Imperfect World, Men with Small Penises are Unforgiven." *Men and Masculinities* 1, 2: 123–37.

Lehman, Peter, and Susan Hunt. 1999. "From Casual to Melodramatic: Changing Representations of the Penis in the 70s and 90s." *Framework* 40 (April): 69–84.

Maguire, Joseph. 1993. "Bodies, Sportscultures and Societies: A Critical Review of Some Theories in the Sociology of the Body." *International Review for the Sociology of Sport* 28, no. 1: 33–52.

Manning, Maria. 1990. "Futile Attraction." *New Statesman and Society* 3, no. 122: 12–13.

McInerney, Jay. 1996. "How Bond Saved America—And Me." *Dressed to Kill: James Bond the Suited Hero*. Jay McInerney, Nick Forllas, Neil Norman, and Nick Sullivan, 13–37. Paris: Flammarian

Miller, Toby. 1995. "A Short History of the Penis." *Social Text*, no. 43 (Fall): 1–26.

———. 1998. *Technologies of Truth: Cultural Citizenship and the Popular Media*. Minneapolis: University of Minnesota Press.

———. 1993. *The Well-Tempered Self: Citizenship, Culture, and the Postmodern Subject*. London: The Johns Hopkins University Press.

Moniot, Drew. 1976. "James Bond and America in the Sixties: An Investigation of the Formula Film in Popular Culture." *Journal of the University Film Association* 28, no. 3: 25–33.

Moores, Suzanne. 1989. "Britain's Macho Man." *New Statesman and Society* 2, no. 55: 44, 46.

"Oedipus Wrecks." 1964. *Newsweek*, Dec. 21, n.p.

Ormerod, David, and David Ward. 1965. "The Bond Game." *London Magazine* 5, 2: 41–55.

Paley, Maggie. 1999. *The Book of the Penis*. New York: Grove Press.

Penley, Constance. 1992. "Feminism, Psychoanalysis, and the Study of Popular Culture." *Cultural Studies*, ed. Lawrence Grossberg, Cary Nelson, and Paula A. Treichler, 479–94. New York: Routledge.

———. 1997. *NASA/TREK: Popular Science and Sex in America*. London: Verso.

Pfeiffer, Lee, and Philip Lisa. 1995. *The Incredible World of 007: An Authorized Celebration of James Bond*, updated ed. New York: Citadel Press.

Rand, Ayn. 1971. *The Romantic Manifesto: A Philosophy of Literature*, rev. ed. New York: Signet.

Richler, Mordecai. 1971. "James Bond Unmasked." *Mass Culture Revisited*, ed. Bernard Rosenberg and David Manning White, 341–55. New York: Van Nostrand Reinhold.

Sann, Paul. 1967. *Fads, Follies and Delusions of the American People*. New York: Crown.

Scarry, Elaine. 1985. *The Body in Pain: The Making and Unmaking of the World*. New York: Oxford University Press.

Smith, Jeff. 1998. *The Sounds of Commerce: Marketing Popular Film Music*. New York: Columbia University Press.

Synnott, Anthony. 1990. "The Beauty Mystique: Ethics and Aesthetics in the Bond Genre." *International Journal of Politics, Culture, and Society* 3, 3: 407–26.

Thumim, Janet. 1992. *Celluloid Sisters: Women and Popular Cinema*. New York: St. Martin's Press.

Webb, Bernice Larson. 1968. "James Bond as Literary Descendant of Beowulf." *South Atlantic Quarterly* 67, 1: 1–12.

Woolf, Michael. 1990. "Ian Fleming's Enigmas and Variations." *Spy Thrillers: From Buchan to le Carré*, ed. Clive Bloom, 86–99. New York: St. Martin's Press.

oliver stone's

nixon and

the unmanning

of the

self-made man

dennis bingham

"I let down my friends," former president Richard Nixon told David
Frost in a paid television interview two and a half years after his resignation. "I let down the country. I let down our system of government.... I let the American people down, and I have to carry that
burden with me for the rest of my life." In this carefully phrased
attempt at an apology, Nixon in 1977 only just approaches the emotional point where Oliver Stone begins his drama of the disgraced president's journey into self-understanding. While *Nixon* (1995) begins with
President Nixon eight months before his resignation listening to his
tapes and trying to comprehend how he lost his hold on the country,
David Frost's Nixon is out, but not down. "Let down" is a curious, non-
committal phrase meaning not much more than that Nixon disappointed his supporters, something all presidents could be said to do to
some extent. Like most of Nixon's utterances on Watergate, this one
sounds confessional, without confessing anything. The Nixon of the
Frost interviews is a New Old Nixon, embattled, struggling as always to

salvage his manhood. Because it must be protected and fiercely fought for, this masculinity is apparently either highly coveted or so fragile that it's constantly in danger of being shown up as an unapproachable illusion. It goes without saying that the actual Nixon held to the first view. He told Frost, "I brought myself down. I gave them the sword. And they stuck it in. And they twisted it with relish. And, I guess, if I'd been in their position, I'd have done the same thing."

Elsewhere in the same interview, he blamed his downfall on his *softness*: if only he hadn't sought to protect Haldeman, Ehrlichman, Mitchell, and others (i.e., the "real" culprits), he would have let *them* have them sooner and there would have been no cover-up. Very late in his life he told Monica Crowley, a sympathetic young biographer, that he was brought down because *they* changed the rules. Wiretapping and political skullduggery that were permissible when Democratic presidents engaged in them suddenly became criminalized when Nixon practiced them (Crowley 1996, 287). To the end of his life, Nixon, who continually worked football metaphors into his public remarks, needed to believe that Watergate was a rigged Super Bowl in which the opposing team stole the ball, kept his side illegally bottled up, got all the calls to go in their favor, and won the game by a point. "Nixon never did admit final defeat," according to one biography, "because he never believed that he was finally defeated, only temporarily set back" (Volkan, Itzkowitz, and Dod 1997, 105).

Stone's Nixon, on the other hand, is already defeated, undone, and unmanned; his White House is a hall of horrors. He's down, but not out (of office) as the film begins. When he is first shown, it is from the point of view of his chief of staff, Alexander Haig, a former general who manages to be at once obsequious and swaggering. It is this ambivalent figure—half-symbolic father, half-servant—whom Nixon sees as a "whole man" compared to himself. Nixon in the opening scenes cannot master the smallest physical competencies; he fumbles with the childproof cap on a bottle of pills and needs help disentangling a reel-to-reel tape. Haig stands over him holding incriminating tapes, the "sword" for which his enemies are clamoring. Nixon jokes that if Haig had wanted to be considerate to his employer, he might have brought him a pistol and then left him alone with it.

258

Behind nearly all of these Nixon's "crises" and "battles" is some weakness, or a potential or past defeat. His break-ins and wiretaps are motivated by fears that the opposition may have on him something worse than what he has on them. He sees himself as unwavering and strong in his prosecution of a war that was lost before he took office. What Nixon finds in listening to his tapes is that his tough masculine poses have all been unsuccessful covers for lost causes, fear of weakness, and plain mendacity (as in, "stonewalling," a macho euphemism for lying).

Stone's *Nixon* asks to be seen as a dissection, an examination of the continuity and coherence of Nixon's self-identity. The film does not demonize or vilify him but tries to understand the systems, ambitions, and ideologies that drove Richard Nixon. Oliver Stone himself is too masculinist to undertake a study of Nixon that would show him as a product of patriarchy and a servant of its interests. What he does make, however, is a biopic that connects the inner man to his external reactions and decisions. The film involves Nixon trying to understand what he has done to bring him to the point of resignation. The real process of understanding, of course, is undergone by the spectator, who must sort out the life of a leader who looms as too important an archetype of American manhood to be easily dismissed. Most importantly, the film takes Nixon to a deeper point of consciousness than he ever allowed himself to go. This Nixon is divested of his power, his prestige—all of which is to say, his manhood—and he spends the film trying to understand where it went.

In depicting a retrospective Nixon who has already lost when the film begins, Stone concentrates less on the physical Nixon. Of his three immediate predecessors, Eisenhower was a warm and confident father figure, Kennedy was suave and virile, and LBJ was roistering and overbearing. Nixon, however, didn't register under any signifier of masculine leadership. He appeared studious, introverted, and puritanical; he was lithe and thin, with long arms and legs. Stiff and awkward, he was a man who never seemed comfortable in his own body. His physical delicacy made his postures of tough masculinity transparently unconvincing.

Anthony Hopkins, who plays Stone's version of the thirty-seventh president, is very different from Nixon physically; he is stout and bull-necked with heavy features and a jutting jaw. Stone and Hopkins forget, probably deliberately, that after the debates with Kennedy in 1960, Nixon knew the damage a wan appearance can do to a candidate in the television age, and cultivated an impressively dignified look. In the 1968 campaign and as president, Nixon wore well-tailored, deep-blue suits, blindingly white shirts, and neat-patterned ties that made him appear more than sufficiently presidential on the then-new medium of color TV. Hopkins, by contrast, wears ill-fitting dark brown and black suits that make Nixon look as unworthy of his place in the world as the script shows him to feel.[1] It's not clear how this man ever won a single vote. But there are many "Nixons," and Nixon the successful politician is not this film's concern. In discussing his casting of Hopkins, Stone points out that the actor is not English but Welsh, and brings to the role a lonely isolation that fits his conception of Nixon as a castrated figure. The Stone-Hopkins Nixon is a graceless, sulking man who has already lost, not one who struggles against failure.

Like the historical Nixon, Stone's Nixon is defined by anger and pugnaciousness. Indeed Nixon's self-image as "a fighter"was the face he most often tried to show his "enemies." The difference again is of kind. The cinematic Nixon expresses anger out of impotence and helplessness, whereas the actual Nixon indulged his vengeful, vindictive rages. But these were based more in impotence than he knew. When Nixon refused to go into the hospital in the fall of 1974 after a renewed flareup of the phlebitis that plagued him the year of his resignation, he told an aide in his San Clemente exile, "You've got to be tough. You can't break, my boy, even when there is nothing left. You don't admit, even to yourself, that it is gone" (Volkan et al. 1997, 105). Stone has Nixon say these lines to Haig and Ron Ziegler in the White House just before the firing of special prosecutor Archibald Cox in October 1973, demonstrating the misplaced and self-destructive masculinism of Nixon's "fighting spirit." "A man doesn't cry," he adds, "I don't cry. You don't cry. You fight."

This obstinacy, which the culture is conditioned to admire in most men, was raised to such a pitch in Nixon that it looked like the hysterical overreaction of a man in denial. "Looking and listening to him," wrote Stanley Kauffmann (1996), "I used to wonder if everyone else thought he was as mentally ill as I thought him" (26). It's little wonder that I trace my realization of masculinity as a massive fabrication to Nixon's years as president. Time and again, his determination to "be a man" backfired on him, most spectacularly in his refusal to wear makeup during his first televised debate with Kennedy in 1960, one of a series of miscalculations by the Nixon campaign that may have cost him what turned out to be the closest presidential election in U.S. history. Nixon had just been hospitalized with a knee infection and looked ill and tired next to the tanned and ruddy Jack Kennedy; he declined makeup because, explained campaign manager Herb Klein, "to Nixon this made it look like he lacked macho, and Nixon was a very macho man." "It was a manhood thing," concluded Christopher Matthews, writing of this incident in his book *Kennedy and Nixon* (1996, 149). The script includes this dialogue in the control booth during the debate between Haldeman and longtime consultant Murray Chotiner, the last two lines of which were edited out of the film:

> CHOTINER: You could've at least gotten him a suit that fit, for Christ's sake, and slapped some makeup on him. He looks like a frigging corpse!
>
> HALDEMAN: He wouldn't do the makeup. Said it was for queers.
>
> CHOTINER: Kennedy doesn't look like a queer, does he? (*then*) He looks like a god. (Rivele, Wilkinson, and Stone 1995, 118)

Furthermore, while Nixon's attempts at a hard masculinity were comic when they involved his overstated predilection for football, they were dangerous at those times when he seemed to be exercising his war powers as commander in chief in order to prove his manhood. This more than any of the other "Nixons" is the one that has gone down in demonology. Michael Kimmel (1996) ties anger, frustration, and war to a quest for manhood in describing Nixon as "chronically afraid of appearing soft on communism—or on anything else." To Kimmel "Nixon's compulsive manhood formed an explosive amalgam with his political paranoia"; he "resolved to 'overcome the weak-kneed, jelly-backed attitude' of Congress and press ahead with escalating the war in Vietnam" (270).[2] Nixon's peculiar depression following his overwhelming 1972 reelection victory is interpreted by his psychoanalytic biographers as follows:

> Nixon's way of lifting himself out of a depression was to turn aggression outward. As President, the turning of aggression outward meant making a foreign policy/military decision. Nixon ordered a heightened bombing of North Vietnam in December, called "The Christmas Bombing," the intensity of which surprised even the military experts. Success, combined with the threat of humiliation, had made the President anxious, so he emerged fighting and killing. (Volkan et al. 1997, 131)

One of the greatest, and most needless, limitations of film biography has been its tendency to play out the story of a public "great man" in determined isolation from his historical, political, cultural, and gender-based circumstances. The film dramatizes what Volkan and his associates write about Watergate: "It demonstrates how the internal world of a political figure can intrude into his conscious world, intermingling with external factors . . . to affect a historical process" (4). Stone's complex editing style and a spiraling narrative structure that never places a spectator either entirely inside or outside Nixon's point of view, create an intricate stacking-doll experience. Nixon may have dominated the period from the late 1940s to the early 1970s, but he never made it look easy. In fact, Nixon's success often looked excruciating and compulsive. Even President Lyndon Johnson, a fellow overachiever out to prove his manhood, dubbed him "a chronic campaigner" (Wicker 1995, 457). Why would an era that appeared to mark the peak of white male dominance in modern America feature a man so obviously pained and torturously self-constructed as Richard Nixon as its most familiar political icon?

Nixon represents the epitome of the self-made man, the logical product of American democracy, a figure who, according to Michael

Kimmel, "derives identity entirely from [his] activities in the public sphere, measured by accumulated wealth and status, by geographic and social mobility" (1996, 17). The self-made man makes his own way in life on a path defined by continual self-betterment and self-control. His "success must be earned. Manhood must be proved—and proved constantly" (23). Nixon embodies the self-made man's determination never to fall below his own studied image of what he must become. We see this in young Nixon's self-abasement in the interests of "toughness," for instance, his persistence in staying on his college football team when the only position for him was that of "tackling dummy" against whom the "real" football players practiced. He attended hometown Whittier College because the family could not afford to send him to Yale or Harvard, where he had been invited to apply for scholarships.

Garry Wills, in *Nixon Agonistes: The Crisis of the Self-Made Man*, published in the second year of Nixon's presidency, tied Nixon's visible resentments and noisy strivings to the ubiquitous self-made man archetype. Such men are

> the Joneses we try to keep up with, whom we envy but imitate. We are told that it is easy to join their ranks— but that means it is easy, also, for them to slip down to our level, a fact that gives them their oppressively *scrambling* air. They are all runners who can never win the race, long distance runners, well-fed worriers; and they went to Miami [the site of the 1968 GOP Convention] to choose their very archetype, the longest-distance runner of them all. (1970, 584)

Nixon's emotional and psychological baggage became his political calling card. He presented himself as a man who had a love-hate relationship with his humble background and with the obstacles, real and perceived, that he had overcome. Many voters identified with these struggles. Theodore H. White (1975) wrote that even after his defeats for president in 1960 and California governor in 1962, Nixon "retained an invisible nationwide base. There were millions who admired him for his tenacity, pluck, and conservative politics, as well as for the stigmata of poverty and bitterness they shared with him" (76). This polarizing personality was not the president whom the already divided social climate called for, but perhaps no one of his generation who could have been elected in that passionate time would have been.

national insecurity and the family romance

Nixon completes a ten-year cycle that Oliver Stone had been working on since his first two films as director, *Salvador* and *Platoon* (both 1986).

This cycle also includes the Vietnam films *Born on the Fourth of July* (1989) and *Heaven and Earth* (1993), as well as *The Doors* (1991) and *JFK* (1991). Together these films weave a mammoth, complex, multiperspectived story of American anticommunism; the Vietnam War; the American government's response to Marxist regimes in our hemisphere, especially Cuba; the military-industrial complex and national security state; the assassinations of the Kennedy brothers and Martin Luther King Jr.; and the youth culture that coalesced around Vietnam protest. Stone's cycle dramatizes the consequences of the entire United States postwar Cold War philosophy, its attendant economic boom, and its burgeoning popular culture. This gigantic historical saga, culminating in the Nixon story and its all-too-human anticlimax of Watergate, gives meaning to a statement by George McGovern: "Vietnam will loom as the major tragedy, and Watergate—and the paranoia behind it—was one of the spin-offs from that. I have always thought the two were part and parcel of the same scenario" (Strober and Strober 1994, 525).

While Watergate is most often seen as a conspiracy spun from the paranoia of Richard Nixon, McGovern suggests that America's entire postwar policy was based on suspicion, secrecy, and distrust: There's always a story we don't know, a conspiracy we can't see. Communism, by this logic, must be behind domestic disputes, such as the civil rights movement and protests against the Vietnam War. Behind the international communist conspiracy, furthermore, must be a web of American treason. And the inverse of this was thought to be true: Only America can save the world from the spread of communism. Furthermore, it is hard not to see the American experience in Vietnam as a widespread effort to salvage America's manhood, as it were. To do this theme full justice would probably require the Stanley Kubrick of *Dr. Strangelove* (1964) and *Full Metal Jacket* (1987), two films that depict U.S. Cold War policies in satirical images in which male sexuality is displaced onto the desire to wage war and in which military preparedness calls for the obliteration of anything that smacks of "femininity."[3] Stone's depiction of an emasculated Nixon is consistent with Susan Jeffords's thesis that the loss in Vietnam left the country "demasculinized." However, *Nixon* depicts the condition of demasculinization and "explains" it as a motivation for the Watergate scandal. In ending Nixon's story with his resignation, and declining to depict his "comebacks" in the last twenty years of his life, Stone makes no effort to recover Nixon's lost masculinity, but leaves him and the audience to ponder the mad scramble for a sense of masculinity as a cause of his downfall.

Nixon was a part of systems that determined his responses as powerfully as his personality did. Stone connects his antihero to a confederation referred to in *Nixon* as *the beast*. In a January 1997 appearance before the American Historical Association, on a panel that included

McGovern and Arthur Schlesinger Jr., Stone described "the beast" as "a system ... of money, a system of the way things work. The system requires money, requires media, requires power and the perception of power." The military-industrial complex, the permanent government, the national security state: all are synonyms for "the beast."

Stone's two Vietnam biopics, *Born on the Fourth of July* (1989), about the American veteran Ron Kovic, and *Heaven and Earth* (1993), about a South Vietnamese woman, Li Haislip, take the form of maturation stories in which a young person, through harrowing experience, learns the truth about the Vietnam War and develops a mature attitude toward the experience. Non-biographical Stone films, such as *Platoon* and *Wall Street*, take similar tacks. Clearly, a *bildungsfilm* with a naive young protagonist would not work for *Nixon*. However, the idea of a young man led out into the world by the drive to go out and achieve *something* is swirled up somewhere within the spiral narrative structure that Stone uses.

Stone is drawn to oedipal narrative structures. In *Platoon* and *Wall Street* the young male protagonists, played in both films by Charlie Sheen, are confronted by a choice of fathers: a flashy, self-absorbed primal father who represents discredited ideals—murderous, warlike xenophobia in *Platoon*, unabashed greed in *Wall Street*—and quiet, sensible symbolic fathers. Stone even goes so far in *Wall Street* as to cast Sheen's own father, Martin, as the blue-collar good dad. While *Wall Street* was received in 1987 as part of a backlash against the get-rich-by-all-means ethic that dominated America during the Reagan administration, the film can also be seen as a working out of the director's relationship with his father, who was a Wall Street stockbroker. Louis Stone was no Gordon Gekko, the omnivorous tycoon of Stone's film; indeed, Stone's parents' divorce when he was sixteen revealed the upper-middle-class family to be awash in debt and launched Stone on a young adulthood of rootless wandering. According to Frank Beaver,

> Stone's masculine sensibilities resulted from deep-seated psychological ties to his father.... Lou Stone had chastised his son for dropping out of college, going to Vietnam as a soldier, and returning a drug-ridden, uneducated "bum." The elder Stone (who died in 1985, before *Salvador* or *Platoon*) reportedly never recognized his son's experience as a Vietnam soldier as valid. This refusal remained a painful gesture because, according to those closest to him, Oliver Stone had gone to Vietnam partly to prove himself to his father, a World War II veteran. (1994, 14)

Most of Stone's films can be seen, then, as resulting from what his wife, Elizabeth, called his "father complex," as his male protagonists feel "nagged on by a distant father" (14). Even when films depict weak fathers, such as *Born on the Fourth of July*, in which the protagonist's ineffectual father has for his son little advice as he unpacks cartons of toilet paper at the supermarket he manages, they portray the son as molded instead by formidable "national fathers" such as the Marine Corps, or, in *JFK*, the dead personage of President Kennedy, a national symbolic father of whose leadership the country has been robbed by the brutal primal fathers who may have had him assassinated. Thus even the conspiracy theorizing with which Stone's name became synonymous in 1990s popular culture is wrapped up with his "father complex."

Nixon, like *Wall Street* eight years earlier, is dedicated to Louis Stone. In his remarks in a supplement to the laser disc release of *Nixon* Stone said that his memories of his dad gave him

> a way of getting into the shoes of Richard Nixon, because I felt they were very similar. They both had suffered as young men coming out of college in the Depression and had felt in a sense screwed by the Roosevelt Administration.... My father was never wrong; he was never wrong about Vietnam; he was never wrong about the Cold War, about the Russians, and eventually he turned around on almost every issue. He was different from Nixon ... in that he was able to call himself wrong. I never saw Richard Nixon do that and that was what was almost the Greek [tragic] figure of Richard Nixon. He was so stubborn and strong and he never doubted himself, or pretended not to anyway.... So I could not have [made the film] without having been Lou Stone's son.

Nixon thus is portrayed as a failed national father who cannot "call himself wrong"—he even lies to his daughter Julie when she asks him about the Watergate cover-up, then tries to compensate with the language of the David Frost interviews: "I just hope I haven't let you down, kid." For the Stone who assesses these two father figures, Lou Stone and Nixon, the president is damned by his inability to admit his mistakes, to stop his lying to himself, his family, and the country. For Stone, Nixon's rigid, unwavering masculinism makes him a "Greek figure." His inability to bend from a firmly held determination to "act like a man" makes him ultimately a tragic figure. As a son himself, however, Nixon is depicted as scornful of a failed father. Unlike Stone's other characters, Nixon is unable to relegate his own angry, ineffectual father to the back of his mind; Frank Nixon is shown to be more of an influence on him than Richard would ever admit. Moreover, in speeches and in his writings it was Nixon's mother whom he revered as

265

a source of strength. This Nixon carries around with him wildly confused lessons from his parents.

Hannah Nixon (Mary Steenburgen) is shown as a sternly religious symbol of repression and self-denial. Drowning in Watergate, Nixon comes to grips with his profanity of mind when he madly rushes to cross out the "expletives" peppering the transcripts of the White House tapes, shouting that the world cannot hear that Mrs. Nixon's son has a filthy mouth. The film points out the lingering influence of Nixon's bitter father, a midwesterner for whom the promise of a golden life in California never panned out, and the initial source of Nixon's hatred of those he imagined "had things handed to them." While the mother represents rigid ideals that Nixon would betray, the father is the font of a liquid fear of failure and a loathing of those who succeed that spills onto everything it comes near. In Nixon, the film shows, the diatribes of the father hide out from the disapproving judgments of the mother. Both father and mother, at bottom, are patriarchal. The father illustrates the dark underside of the American Dream of the self-made man; the mother stands in for stiffly judgmental church fathers.

On election night 1960, Dick tells Pat that his defeat makes him think of his "old man . . . He was a failure too. Do you know how much money he had in the bank when he died? Nothing." Frank Nixon (Tom Bower) has an angry tirade in front of his sons about work and struggle as the only reasons for living. "Maybe a trip to the woodshed will straighten you out," he tells seventeen-year-old Harold, stressing that no one gets "something for nothing." The lesson is shown to have been learned—and misapplied—when President Nixon, in infamous remarks days before the Kent State shootings, is seen calling student protesters "bums . . . They call themselves 'flower children.' I call them spoiled rotten. And I tell you what would cure them—a good old-fashioned trip to my Ohio father's woodshed." Later in the film, however, Stone segues out of a childhood flashback with a Nixon stump speech, heard only in voice-over: "My old man struggled his whole life. You could call him a little man, a poor man, but they never beat him. I always tried to remember that when things didn't go my way."

This is a peculiar lesson. By biographical accounts, Frank Nixon was "an angry and essentially mean-spirited individual [whose] life, in fact, consisted of hardships, bad luck, and losses, leading him to know great frustration, discouragement, and humiliation" (Volkan et al. 1997, 25). Exactly how Frank Nixon went "unbeaten," who "they" are who never beat him, or why the son should remember this when things didn't go his way is not clear and Stone lets the line hang there for us to consider. (Nixon shouldn't let "them beat him" either.)

Apparently one of those Nixon wouldn't let beat him was his own wife, the former Thelma Patricia Ryan, whom Nixon pursued doggedly and largely unsuccessfully for two years. After she gave in and married him, in 1940, he repaid her elusiveness with coldness and distance. He could sometimes be seen in highly public situations, even when he accepted the vice presidential nomination in 1952, moving away from his wife on podiums when she tried to kiss or embrace him (Volkan et al. 1997, 49). "Nixon's fear of strong women and his desire to keep them in their place is suggested by his intense dislike of pant-wearing, opinionated women." For Nixon, "uncontrolled and uncontained, women are a potential source of shame and humiliation for men. Their job is to reflect their husband's glory, not to take away from it" (50). However, Stone and Joan Allen, who plays Pat, move "plastic Pat" out of the background and give her a voice and an attitude, making her Nixon's last reality checkpoint, the person who knows best how cut off from human contact and how obsessed with winning and maintaining control he has become. For Stone, who himself is known for treating women as little more than mannequins in his films, the portrayal of Pat Nixon as a woman who knows her husband better than anyone including himself, constitutes a breakthrough. It becomes clear that the rigid Hannah Nixon and a culture in which women are put on pedestals and kept out of the way have left Nixon unprepared for real women. There were few times that Nixon publicly referred to his mother without calling her "a saint." Allen's deep-voiced Pat, who has run out of the patience that political wives are supposed to possess in abundance, makes a compelling foil.

interior/exterior: *nixon* and "vertical editing"

As a man, Richard Nixon invites psychological probing because of the glimpses he shared of his pain and hostility. Stone's Nixon, as played by Hopkins, is brooding, introverted, and etched in sorrow. He is confused in the midst of a downfall that is both of his own making and wrought by forces that go far beyond one man, even the president. Ironically, the presidency took Nixon out of his element, so accustomed was he to running for things, scrambling toward a future position, rather than managing one in the present. The achievements for which Nixon's administration is remembered positively, particularly the strategy to thaw the Cold War by making overtures to both of the opposing communist superpowers, China and the Soviet Union, did involve the active pursuit of clear, linear goals. However, the dissent and unrest of the time, the no-win Vietnam War, along with his status as a minority president, continually placed him in passive, reactive, and directionless positions. Nixon's response was to fight, to hit back. With events like the Ellsberg psychiatrist break-in, the results were self-inflicted hits that Nixon experienced as blows from his enemies.

The film begins—outside Nixon, but really inside his soul—with the break-in at the Watergate; it then elides eighteen months to December 1973. It's a rainy night; the White House looks like The Old Dark House of horror films. A John Williams orchestral coda clashes away. Alexander Haig (Powers Boothe), who had replaced H. R. Haldeman as chief of staff, makes his way through darkened hallways. This credit sequence is punctuated by a drumbeat of authoritative news reports on the soundtrack and newspaper headlines, most of them from the *New York Times*. The scandal, as announced by the news media Nixon so despised, appears to grow closer to Nixon's door, as Haig does. The stentorian voiceovers signify *them*, Nixon's media enemies, coming to get him, proclaiming his criminality as gospel truth.

Haig, and the camera, find Nixon, a small, crumpled figure in retreat, huddled in a dark corner of the Lincoln Sitting Room. Haig comes bearing tapes. Nixon, in the film's version, then sits alone listening to the tape of the conversation of June 23, 1972, in which he directed Haldeman to order the FBI and the CIA not to investigate Watergate. This tape became the "smoking gun." It forced Nixon's resignation more than seven months later when the Supreme Court ruled that Nixon had no right to withhold it and it became public, withering even his Republican support in Congress.

The film's spiral structure begins here. Feeling buffeted from outside, Nixon looks inside, as Stone begins a revelatory dramatic process that is alternately external and internal. The camera appears to track through the mechanism of the tape recorder itself into Nixon's office in the Executive Office Building on that sunny June day. In this way, this biopic of Nixon is removed from the Great Man archetype, by which a man's great talent and vision drive him on to great accomplishments. Nixon's vision is obscured. He doesn't know what has brought him to this precipice, and he doesn't know what is causing him to topple. The "encounters" with the tapes are played as a continuing session with an analyst. Little wonder that Pat Nixon, who is portrayed as the conscience Nixon is determined to ignore, says of the tapes, "They're not yours. They *are* you." The film becomes, through this framing device, a conflict between Nixon and himself.

This is where Stone's evolving editing style becomes indispensible. "I don't know what to call this editing," Stone says,

> Some have called it vertical editing, insofar as we stop, and we go into a moment; we expand a moment by going into internal and external editing.... [A character] will say something on an external idea, but we will cut to a completely contrary look or feel, be it black and white or color. It comments on what's being said ...

268

So I call it exterior/interior. Sometimes we will go to
five or six images that will completely contradict or
perhaps supplement the external action. (*Nixon* laser
disc, side 5, chapter 33)

This technique might be seen as a new form of Eisensteinian juxtaposition, an expansion of cinematic "reality" that goes beyond the link-
ing of cause-and-effect events, as photographed by an "objective"
camera. In *Nixon* this jagged, free-form style lends itself to a whirlpool
of torturing memories. It serves well to illustrate a man, Martha
Mitchell (Madeleine Kahn) says to Nixon, whose smile and face "are
never in the same place at the same time." As Stanley Kauffmann
wrote, "*Nixon* assumes that a film biography cannot rightly be linear
because everyone carries his [sic] entire life with him all the time. The
backpack, ever present and always growing, is invisible in life but need
not be so in film" (1996, 26). Biography balances the public realm,
which is already familiar in the case of someone like Nixon, with the
private. The long-standing appeal of biography lies in its promise to
juxtapose the public and private selves, completing a full and satisfying
impression of the subject's personality and motivations. This promise
has sometimes led the biopic to extremes—either to sanitize a subject's personal life, as biopics of the studio era were often accused of
doing—or to "expose" a sensational and sordid personal life.

Even if a biopic hews to one of these extremes, however, it will probably do so through the essentially objective and linear structure of
mainstream cinema. *Nixon*'s editing elongates time, showing the feelings, thoughts, and associations behind Nixon's statements. It also
breaks into the carefully controlled facade that was both Nixon's *modus
operandi* and his biggest problem as a public figure, as well as what makes
him continually fascinating to us now—the surface that invites us to
peer beneath it while it forbids entrance. For example, in the sequence
depicting Nixon's acceptance of the Republican nomination in 1968,
Nixon's forceful delivery of his speech and the ecstatic response of the
convention, both filmed in color, are intercut, in lap dissolve, with a
shot showing Nixon, in black and white, looking uncertain, not knowing if he should smile, as if the "two-time loser," as my dad referred to
Nixon throughout 1968, wondered if this moment of triumph would
evaporate as others had.

It's worthwhile to study the entire sequence that includes this
moment because it shows Stone's associative, thematic method and
how it welds the personal and the historical. As the sequence opens, a
subtitle tells us we are in "1972: the President's Private Office," even
though the previous sequence showed the run-up to the nomination
in 1968. In '72 Nixon, wearing a red smoking jacket and sipping a

scotch, tells Haldeman about Track Two, which was a conspiracy to assassinate Fidel Castro conceived in the last months of the Eisenhower administration in 1960. It involved Nixon, then vice president, the Mafia, Cuban counterrevolutionaries, and, most significantly for Nixon in '72, CIA men, including Howard Hunt and Frank Sturgis, who were among those just arrested as Watergate burglars.

John Kennedy's ignorance of Track Two in his early days as president is, in Stone's version, one of the reasons for the botched Bay of Pigs invasion in May 1961. "I didn't want him to get the credit," Stone has Nixon saying, but only after Nixon says that the CIA didn't tell JFK either, "they just kept it going," stressing the theme of the "beast," the "permanent government" that operates independently of presidents. Nixon recounts how Kennedy called him to his office, "said I stabbed him in the back, called me a two-bit grocery clerk from Whittier."[4] A black-and-white cutaway to the same moment has Nixon stopped, pondering, as if JFK's remark continued to sting. A color reaction shot of Haldeman shows him obviously moved. All the while, there are cutaways to mob members (played by actors), stock shots of actual Cuban guerrillas, Castro, and atrocities, as well as a cut to Hopkins and Allen as Dick and Pat Nixon in the back seat of the car during the 1958 Caracas riots. All of these, plus what the script calls "a Rum and Coca-Cola song" on the soundtrack, take us well out of the 1972 diegesis and into the conspiratorial world Nixon describes (Rivele et al. 1995, 180). Moreover, early in the sequence, the Nixon of late 1973 is shown in the Lincoln Sitting Room hideaway listening to this conversation on tape.

Thus, when Nixon, in his talk with Haldeman, turns to the window, and away from his interlocutor, Stone is ready with the thematic thread that unites the entire sequence. "When I saw Bobby lying there on the floor"—shots and sounds of Robert Kennedy's assassination— "his arms stretched out, his eyes staring, I knew then I'd be president." Nixon stands at the window, fingers the lace curtains. "His death paved the way, didn't it? Vietnam, the Kennedys, cleared a path through the wilderness just for me." In black and white, Nixon is shown saying, "Over the bodies. Four bodies." A cut to a longer shot has Nixon on the left and Haldeman out of focus on the right. Fade to color and rack focus on Haldeman, who says, "You mean two." Rack focus back to Nixon as Haldeman continues: "two bodies."

"Four," answers Nixon in '73, also at the window, drinking. He moves to a painting of Lincoln. "How many did you have? Hundreds of thousands? Where would we be without death, Abe?" he asks. "Who's helping us? Is it God, or is it death?" Cut to a black-and-white shot of TB microbes under a microscope; then dissolve to an aerial view of a desert landscape. The eye requires a few seconds to perceive the difference. A subtitle reads: "1933. Arizona." This is the TB sanitorium where Harold Nixon spent his last days. (Earlier, the film cut from the death of JFK to the death in 1925 of Nixon's brother Arthur.) This scene, which plays in black and white, has Harold, in death throes, telling Dick that their parents will now have the money to send him to law school. Harold, scanning the desert, longs for death as Dick replies, "You're not gonna quit on me, are you," echoing Nixonian rhetoric; even in his resignation speech, Nixon insisted that he had never been "a quitter." The sound mix includes a distant train whistle, an image Nixon used in his speeches to evoke the American Dream that beckons the humblest, youngsters in remote places (like Whittier, California) to follow their ambitions.

Stone then cuts from trains to a toy plane that one of Nixon's two surviving younger brothers plays with following Harold's funeral. Richard will soon be leaving for Duke Law School. Hannah tells her son Richard, "God has chosen thee to survive," sounding a familiar theme of biopics, the idea that the Great Man "does not choose his way," as we have earlier heard Dick tell Pat to justify why he "had to" run in '68. The notion that the Great Man himself is a mere servant to his role in history and his significance as an icon—like Jesus the man in comparison to God the Son—becomes in Stone's rendering a delusion. It accounts for why as president, Nixon begins to refer to himself in third person. He tells John Mitchell, "I'd like to offer my condolences" [to the families of the students killed at Kent State]. "But Nixon can't." It is as if the man Richard Nixon has to wall himself off from feelings that the tough, masculine "Nixon" can't be shown betraying. And once "Nixon" the icon cuts himself off from feeling, Nixon the man does too.

Hannah admonishes Richard that he must seek "strength in this life, happiness in the next." The mother's words are often echoed ironically in Pat's. Pat speaks the word "happy" in two key scenes, first when Nixon tells Pat of his decision to run in '68 because he knows he can win. "Do you really want this, Dick? . . . And then you'll be happy?" Later, when as president amid the turmoil of Vietnam Nixon is too consumed with his enemies to want to make love to Pat, she says flatly, "It took a long time for me to fall in love with you, Dick. But I did. And if it doesn't make you happy . . ." From his mother's admonition, Nixon is next shown against a dark background, with random flashing lights and distorted sound. This is revealed to be the triumphant moment of his appearance before the '68 GOP Convention as its presidential nominee. As the hall turns up the lights, the candidate turns on his smile. However, what Nixon describes in his acceptance speech—illustrated by Stone in a cascading montage of stock shots in which the tumult of

271

the late 1960s builds to a frightening crescendo—is a country where hard work and sacrifice have not brought "happiness"; they have not been rewarded by any sense of contentment or stability.

Thus, Stone's style of montage conveys the Nixonian conviction that in the absence of happiness, one must be strong. Stone's montage then establishes this conviction as the foundation of Nixon's rhetoric, his sense of manhood, and his policies as president. Nixon sees the absence of happiness everywhere. The cut to an uncertain Nixon during one of the great moments of his life is steeped in the theme of Nixon as a beneficiary of death, and in the concept of a man who can't allow himself to enjoy his success, to feel secure in it, or to feel that he deserves it.

The logic of the cut that follows this is clear. Stone elides such details as Hubert Humphrey's near-upset in the 1968 election,[5] and waits to show Nixon in the White House until he had been president for fifteen months, in April and May 1970, the time of Cambodia and Kent State. More bodies. The president is shown overruling his secretary of state in pursuing a policy of terror in Vietnam designed to make his enemies, as Kissinger (Paul Sorvino) puts it, "fear the madman Richard Nixon." Thus when Stone says that Nixon "lied all his life," but "would never have identified it as such," he is referring, for instance, to Nixon's notion that a leader can achieve peace by becoming more war-like (*Nixon* laser disc). Anthony Hopkins said, "Stalin told Churchill, 'If you're ruling a country like the Soviet Union, you can't waste time on Christian ethics. You have to be brutal.' And I think Nixon must have taken a lot from Stalin; in order to achieve things, you have to be tough. And he was a tough man" (Pickle 1995, I–4). For many, Nixon's downfall was that once he attained his tough posture, he could not drop it when he needed to, even after it became self-parody. John Ehrlichman says in the film, "Dick Nixon say 'I'm sorry'? That'll be the day. His whole suit of armor would fall off."

More dangerously, the Hopkins quote reflects the film's depiction of a man whose thinking could slip too easily from that of a president in a democracy to that of a leader with a far less discriminating sense of power. When the president feels plagued by news leaks from within his administration, he declares (while standing under a painting of George Washington), "A leak happens, the whole damn place should be fired. Really. You do it like the Germans in World War II. If they went through these towns and a sniper hit them, they'd line the whole God-damned town up and say, 'Now until you talk, you're all getting shot.'" When Ehrlichman, whom the film poses as a kind of good angel, whispering intermittently in the president's ear, says, "We're not Germans," Nixon mutters, "Yeah," as he often does when dismissing inconvenient information.

Stone stages the meeting between Nixon and Mao Tse-Tung as a cauldron in which the Chinese communist leader and the leader of the free world melt together into one great, shapeless hunger for power. Stone suggests that while Nixon demonized Stalin, Khrushchev, Ho Chi Minh, Mao, Castro, and the rest, he also internalized them and emulated them. While this may make *Nixon* sound like a remake of *The Searchers*, it provides the film's ultimate juxtaposition, not the "bad Nixon" of break-ins and cover-ups with the "good Nixon" who made peace with China and the Soviets (Scheer 1995, xi), but Nixon the insecure, self-made man with Nixon the unconstitutional megalomaniac.

identifying with the other

In this way, the film's introspective aspect, letting Nixon search for and discover the truth about himself, leaving him to stew in his own juice, as it were, creates a vast tableau. It shows him as a product of failed American assumptions about political success and the wielding of power. I think Stone has been overly apologetic for making Nixon a "sympathetic" figure, which he isn't here, exactly. "We went so far," Stone says, "as to give this sad figure a consciousness of what he had missed. I don't think we were right in doing that, but we did it for movie reasons. We empathized with him and made him better than he was, which film tends to do because we [want] an audience to care about the protagonist" (Oliver Stone Session, Amer. Hist. Assoc., 1997). On the contrary, it's a brave thing Stone has done, identifying with the Other, adopting the point of view of someone who signifies for so many in the generations born since World War II everything sick and dangerous about the systems that drive us as Americans and that drive American men.

The film makes this point early. The Watergate burglars watch a Labor Department motivational film in which a counselor bucks up a salesman who has become unsure of himself. After saying, "I don't mean to pry, but is everything all right at home?" the man adds, "Remember what you're really selling—yourself." "You mean," says the salesman, echoing Arthur Miller's *Death of a Salesman*, "it doesn't matter what I say, but how I say it?" The counselor tells him, "always look 'em in the eye. Nothing sells," he says, smiling at the camera, "like sincerity."

This hackneyed training film with its parade of all-American clichés sets out a thematic agenda for the film. The Watergate scandal itself symbolizes a desperation beneath the American drive for success through persuasion and salesmanship, the "oppressively scrambling" air of the self-made man. "Everything" will be shown not to be "all right at home," whether the "home" is that of Hannah and Frank in

273

the 1920s, the repressed household of Dick and Pat, protests and division "on the domestic front" in America, or the psyche of Richard Nixon that is "home" to all of these traumas. As president, Nixon made policy out of the idea that it didn't matter what he said, because Nixon was saying it. He can desegregate schools and bargain with communists because of his image as a conservative and an anti-communist. "Don't worry about what we say; it's what we do," John Mitchell liked to tell reporters (Strober and Strober 1994, 108). Conservative Howard Phillips groused, "the conservatives got the rhetoric and the liberals got the government" (108). The flip side was that in practicing "politics as the art of compromise," as he says in the film, he gets little credit. "People have forgotten," the Nixon of late '73 tells Haig in their first scene. "Such violence. The tear gas, the riots, burning the draft cards, the Black Panthers.... We fixed it, Al, and they hate me for it. Because it's Nixon. They've always hated Nixon."

As the Watergate burglars wait and the Labor Department film unspools, the title "Nixon" appears over the projector beam, as if to cue the audience that what it's about to see is a series of projections both from and onto its tortured protagonist and that much of what he projects will disconcert even him. The man who boasts of "fixing" the violence will wince when his taped conversation reminds him of violence he perpetrated, such as the Ellsberg break-in ("I approved that?"), and violence from which he benefited, such as the shootings of George Wallace and the Kennedys. The man who takes offense when Nelson Rockefeller, his chief Republican nemesis, needles him at a 1963 party about the title of his book, *Six Crises* ("Sounds like you've got a crisis syndrome. Aren't you exaggerating a bit, Dick? Call it three and a half, maybe four ...") is capable of telling John Dean during Watergate, "Everything is a crisis to the upper intellectual types, the softheads. The average people don't think it's much of a crisis." Such contradictions dramatize Stone's belief that Nixon was "unconscious" of much about what he did. The projector is a metaphor for the public man as a projection, with the actual man an assemblage of a million fragments, most of them, in the media age, electronic, multiplied by six thousand hours of White House tapes. This charge to find the man behind the image is one of Stone's many indirect references to *Citizen Kane*. Moreover, the projector also symbolizes the beam whose object is never just interior or exterior. For Stone, the personal story is also the larger political and historical story. And for Nixon, the political is always the personal.

On the trip back from China, Nixon tells Pat, "Think of the life Mao's led. In '52, I called him a monster. Now he could be our most important ally. Only Nixon could have done that." The dialogue winds up being not about Mao at all, but about Nixon. In a rage following a stormy news conference Nixon thunders, "I did everything *The New York Times* editorial page said I should do. . . . So why are these assholes turning on me? Because they don't like the way I look. They don't like where I went to school," and ultimately these slights turn into a slam on America itself: "They don't—they don't trust America!" Even the film's Ehrlichman picks up this thread: "You think this is about politics," he asks Haldeman. "This is about Richard Nixon. You got people dying because he didn't make the varsity football team. You got the Constitution hanging by a thread because he went to Whittier and not to Yale." This is perhaps the most troubling revelation the film makes: that systems of government on which millions of lives depend turn finally on individual subjectivities—on men, mostly, who take vast systems personally and who are really not capable of understanding the large implications of what they do.

conclusion: atomic man, atomized

> Some mornings I linger
> in Pat's closet, among all the incompatible species
> of fox and alligator, ostrich and lamb.
> And I'm reminded of my Russian stacking dolls:
> how the smallest is absolutely empty
> but for silence, longing, a residue of perfume.
> —from "Nixon on the Pleasures of Undressing a
>   Woman," by Karen Kovacik

Nixon fascinates because he is a figure of such rigid masculinity, and yet he appears so insecure. He is a person who lied, and everyone seemed to know it but he. He appeared to be trapped by the limitations of his era, his masculinism, his ethnicity, and family background. He had aspirations as a national leader that went beyond his capacity to imagine many kinds of Americans other than himself. (Oddly, as a foreign policy enthusiast, he seemed to have less trouble with people of other nationalities.) He tried for unifying, Lincolnesque rhetoric, choosing the slogan, "Bring Us Together," as his administration's motto. Even if he believed in the idea, it was not in his nature to be capable of anything of the sort. Similarly, when he ventured out to the Lincoln Memorial in the middle of the night of May 9, 1970, to meet with protesting students, he was utterly unable to connect. To imagine Nixon, as the poet does, in his wife's closet, fingering her clothes, almost as if *he* might wear them, or to picture Nixon grooving on marijuana-laced cookies, as he does in *Dick*, or to submit him, as Stone does, to a combination of psychoanalysis and the kind of political re-education that the protagonists of *Platoon* and *Born on the Fourth of July* undergo, is to subvert his memory. However, it's also to stretch ourselves, to imagine possibilities beyond our own ideologically conditioned identities. This may well be why Nixon, the most willfully unmade, and remade, of self-made men, seems such an essential icon of American masculinity and why he is likely to remain so. Oliver Stone has shown that the way to approach this male product of Atomic Age fear is to atomize him. And why not? We're all living with the fallout.

notes

1. As I was finishing this essay in the summer of 1999, an endearingly odd little comedy titled *Dick* was released. It purports to tell the story of two teenage girls in 1972 who accidentally witness the Watergate break-in, befriend President Nixon, and end up accounting for nearly every unanswered question about Watergate, from the eighteen-and-a-half-minute gap to the identity of Deep Throat. Most reviewers noted that Dan Hedaya, who plays Nixon, is better suited to the role than Anthony Hopkins. And surely they're right. Hedaya has the right build and dark coloration. Writer-director Andrew Fleming and his team remembered the blue suits and stately appearance of President Nixon. Thus, ironically this piece of comic fluff conveys the contemporary public view of Nixon as president more acutely than Stone's historical biography does. Since the comedy stems partly from the girls' impression of Nixon, which turns from adulation and a teenage crush to indignation when he turns out to be "a bad man," *Dick* is concerned with Nixon's decorous public persona as opposed to the black-hearted schemer who emerges in private. Interestingly, although reviewers mentioned that Hedaya plays Alicia Silverstone's doting father in *Clueless*, they did not remember that he is also among the huge cast of *Nixon*. (Saul Rubinek, who played 1960 campaign manager Herb Klein in *Nixon*, gets a big promotion also; he's Kissinger.) As presidential buddy Bebe Rebozo (renamed "Trini Cordoza"), Hedaya has few lines but is in the background in many scenes. He emerges from the time he spent watching Hopkins play the role with a very different—and in some ways truer—Nixon, as if combining the haunted inner Nixon of Hopkins, the contemporary "Tricky Dick" caricatures, and the man Hopkins and Stone felt compelled to talk about in interviews who was "adored" by his daughters. Hedaya's Nixon is the one who did a guest cameo on *Laugh-In*. It all goes to show that there are many Nixons, and many ways of imagining him.

2. Nixon did not exactly escalate. He had been elected to find an end to the unwinnable morass that the war had become following the devastating surprise offensive launched by the North Vietnamese during the Tet holiday in January 1968, the turning point after which American efforts switched from winning the war to finding a face-saving exit. President Nixon took the most moderate, or equivocal course available: gradual withdrawal of troops and phasing out of the draft, accompanied by

negotiation, and punctuated by strategic, often savage strikes against key North Vietnamese positions, such as those in Cambodia. The actual terms of the treaty signed in January 1973 were not substantively different from those offered by North Vietnam in 1969. The difference was that because of "Vietnamization," Nixon was able to say that America had not abandoned an ally or walked away from a fight. Nixon managed to fight—and get more Americans and Vietnamese killed—and walk away at the same time.

3. See Paula Willoquet-Maricondi, "Full-Metal Jacketing, or Masculinity in the Making," *Cinema Journal* 33.2 (Winter 1994), 5–21.

4. This account of Nixon's post–Bay of Pigs meeting with Kennedy is fictional. Such a White House meeting did take place, but by Nixon's own account in his memoirs, Kennedy was very cordial. See Matthews 198–99; and Nixon 1978, 233. Also, an annotation in the published screenplay by Stephen J. Rivele, Christopher Wilkinson, and Oliver Stone concedes that JFK was told during the 1960 campaign about the plot against Castro. See Rivele, et al. 1995, 181.

5. Nixon won by approximately five hundred thousand votes out of some seventy-three million cast. However, this constituted a landslide compared to the one hundred thousand votes that separated Nixon and Kennedy in 1960.

works cited

Beaver, Frank. 1994. *Oliver Stone: Wakeup Cinema*. New York: Twayne Publishers.

Crowley, Monica. 1996. *Nixon in Winter*. New York: Random House.

Jeffords, Susan. 1989. *The Remasculinization of America*. Bloomington: Indiana University Press.

Kauffmann, Stanley. 1996. Review of *Nixon. The New Republic*. Jan. 22: 26.

Kimmel, Michael. 1996. *Manhood in America: A Cultural History* New York: Free Press.

Kovacik, Karen. 1998. *Nixon and I*. Kent, Ohio: Kent State University Press.

Matthews, Christopher. 1996. *Kennedy and Nixon: The Rivalry That Shaped Postwar America*. New York: Simon and Schuster.

Nixon, Richard. 1978. *RN: The Memoirs of Richard Nixon, Vol. I*. New York: Grosset and Dunlap.

Nixon laser disc. 1996. Burbank, Calif.: Hollywood Pictures Home Video. Supplemental material, introduced by Oliver Stone, side 5, chapter.

The Nixon Interviews with David Frost, Vol. 1: Watergate. 1992. VHS. Universal City, Calif.: MCA-Universal Home Video.

Oliver Stone Session. 1997. American Historical Association, New York, Jan. 4. Cablecast on C-Span, Feb. 17.

Pickle, Betsy. 1995. "Forget Looks: Hopkins Portrays Inner Nixon." Scripps-Howard News Service. In the *Indianapolis Star*, Dec. 31, Sect. I–4.

Rivele, Stephen J., Christopher Wilkinson, and Oliver Stone. 1995. "*Nixon*: The Original Annotated Screenplay." In *"Nixon": An Oliver Stone Film*, ed. Eric Hamburg, 81–318. New York: Hyperion.

Scheer, Robert. "Foreword." *Nixon: An Oliver Stone Film*, ed. Eric Hamburg, ix–xii. New York: Hyperion

Strober, Gerald S., and Deborah Hart Strober. 1994. *Nixon: An Oral History of His Presidency*. New York: HarperCollins.

Volkan, Vamik D., Norman Itzkowitz, and Andrew W. Dod. 1997. *Richard Nixon: A Psychobiography*. New York: Columbia University Press.

White, Theodore H. 1975. *Breach of Faith: the Fall of Richard Nixon*. New York: Atheneum.

Wicker, Tom. 1995. *One of Us: Richard Nixon and the American Dream, Revised Edition*. New York: Random House.

Wills, Garry. 1970. *Nixon Agonistes: The Crisis of the Self-Made Man*. Boston: Houghton Mifflin.

suck,

spit,

chew,

swallow

a performative

exploration

of men's bodies

tim miller

For almost twenty years I have been leading performance workshops for men all over the world. These workshops have been a place for men to physically explore in full-color real time their most intimate narratives, memories, dreams, and possibilities. While I have often done this work with mixed groups of straight, bisexual, and gay men, the majority of my efforts have been within the diverse gay men's communities in the United States, Australia, and the United Kingdom. A constant focus, the base note as it were, of all this work has been a commitment to discovering a more authentic and individualized way of being present within our deeply problematized men's bodies. I have taught such workshops in contexts ranging from the Men and Masculinities conference sponsored by the National Organization of Men Against Sexism (NOMAS) in Johnstown, Pennsylvania, to community-based gay men's groups in cities from Sydney, Australia, to Glasgow, Scotland. These workshops have developed strong communities of men, encouraged new artists, and functioned as the springboard for several gay men's performance collectives that have kept working together for years.

I was invited to the United Kingdom in 1999 to work with a group of gay men toward the creation of an original ensemble performance. Mark Ball, the director of Birmingham, England's Queerfest, an internationally significant festival of lesbian and gay culture, wanted me to work intensively with a group of men toward the creation of a performance. We hoped that this process would culminate in an ensemble-generated performance work culturally specific to Birmingham that would also enliven and encourage local artists. I arrived in London full of ideas for an exploration into gay men's embodiment, the place where our dreams and disappointments, desires and dreads really seem to constellate.

Allright, I admit it: had hoped my work there would offer the participants the opportunity to discover a new corporeal "discourse" of what it is to be men. Unfortunately for my highfalutin plans, the truth is that our bodies are much more layered and complex and messy than a nice tidy word like "discourse" could ever suggest. The flesh that men occupy stinks, fucks, shits, is written on, is blown apart, is fetishized, triumphs, fails, and eventually dies. It is so complex and multileveled that the more I approach this exploration the more humbled and silenced I feel in trying to talk about it.

On the plane ride from Chicago to London I devoured the research of Prof. Harrison Pope, a Harvard psychiatrist who has monitored the inexorable growth of G.I. Joe's biceps throughout the last thirty-five years. As a child, I was much more interested (and then powerfully disappointed) by the bulge in G.I. Joe's pants than I ever was in his upper arms. Imagine my profound deflation, if not gender confusion, when I slipped his Army fatigue pants down and saw no pillar of iron at his crotch but instead a gentle sloping mound of plastic, but that's another story. Since G.I. Joe was missing this standard male equipment, his biceps will have to serve as a measurement of society's representations of the male body.

Harrison Pope reports that in 1964 Joe begins with a svelte, normally proportioned man's body with a biceps circumference (when scaled to a life-size male) that measured 12.2 inches around. He has that long, shapeless look typical of late '50s TV sitcom fathers like Mr. Cleaver, the father of Beaver. That was a simpler time when the only iron that an adult male was supposed to pump was a 9-iron out on the golf course. Ten years later G.I. Joe's bulges start to show. They come in at 15.2 inches, and Joe looks like one of the tightly muscled kung fu fighters that I aspired to be in 1974. The next twenty years, Joe gained only a little more than an inch. However, between 1994 and 1998, G.I. Joe Extreme hysterically added ten inches to his biceps, attaining the cartoonish proportions of a 26.8-inch upper arm. These dolls—excuse me, I mean action figures—"display the physiques of advanced body builders and some display levels of muscularity far exceeding the outer limits of actual human attainment," as Pope's study dryly noted. Just as young girls and women have had to toil for decades under unrealistic and idealized physical images, now young boys also get to grow up feeling woefully inadequate when comparing their delicate carrot-stick arms to G.I. Joe's hefty honey-baked-ham biceps. There is a certain gleeful revenge fantasy that I am prone to indulge here as a properly trained feminist-identified queer boy. Part of me wants to gloat that at last men's bodies are as colonized and marketed as are women's, but I also know the enormous damage this is doing to men in general and to gay men in particular.

The giddy proliferation of homoerotic, idealized male images in advertising, TV, and film is triumphant in the complete objectification of all men's bodies, straight or gay, as something to be bought, taken home, eaten, and fucked. I acknowledge that straight men and boys are also subject to the slings and arrows of not meeting the grade of the perfected male body. However, they ultimately have the option of retiring to the nuclear bomb-proof cement bunker of straight male privilege if they are confronted with too much belly or not enough biceps. Gay men, on the other hand, whose bodies are endlessly contested and feminized by culture (and each other!) are in a real pickle. Gay men are forced to dodge a ricocheting male gaze that has created a marketplace where only the most perfect bodies get rewarded. If only these idealized male images stopped with G.I. Joe. In addition to this general trend of using hyperidealized male bodies to sell everything from personal computers to dish soap, gay men must also move in a sea of utopian physical representations advertising bars, treatment programs, and AIDS medications. Michelangelo Signorile is on target in his critique of this trend in his often annoying but always provocative book, *Life Outside,*

> Every major American city has one—or sometimes three or four—'bar rags' filled with images of 'perfect' gay men, the ideals that set the standard. Most of these images are being used to sell us something: gym memberships to the trendy gyms of choice; all night parties at nightclubs filled with near-naked, young-and-buff men; phone sex; and even actual sex in the guise of 'escorts.' These same images are played back to us again and again in gay porn, on safer sex posters, and in dozens of gay newspapers and several glossy national magazines that often sport pumped up cover-boys and fetching ads selling products and events, from underwear to hot parties. (1997, 25–26)

These images relentlessly discipline the narrowly defined ideal gay men's body: buffed and bronzed, stripped of humanizing body hair, extra flesh, and wrinkles. There are no boundaries too crass in this endless use of ideal male representations as the prime currency in the exchange of goods and services. One particularly disturbing advertisement for a suicide prevention program boasts a handsome young man being zipped into a body bag, his eyes softly and seductively closed as if he were Sleeping Beauty waiting for a wake-up call from some handy Prince. Even the corpses have to be beautiful in postmodern disembodied America!

suck, spit, chew, swallow

Dragging myself off the plane at London Heathrow Airport, my own personal gay body could barely stand upright after a few hours of tossing and turning in coach. I snared my luggage and found the car service that would take me to Birmingham. The project I was going to create in England with a group of gay men was festively called *Suck, Spit, Chew, Swallow*. A few hours later, I walked into the studio at the DanceXchange in Birmingham for the first meeting. The studios are perched over the Hippodrome Theater, whose marquee boasts larger-than-life billboards of almost-naked men for the coming attractions soon to play the Hippodrome: the gyrating men of Hen Party, a male strip show, joust with the Matthew Bourne Swan Lake and its sinewy men who look like butch satyrlike swans. I'm surrounded by the homoeroticized capitalist male body even at my workplace! There's no escaping! Leaving the mix of beefcake and fowl-muffin festooning the marquee, I trudge up the steep steps to the DanceXchange. I am always struck with a panic attack at the start of these projects. Who am I to gather men to dig deep into their hearts and memories and bodies? It helps that I know the men coming to these workshops are also frying in a griddle of panic and doubt. This evens the odds.

I watch the men one by one trudge up the landing as if they approach the gallows, their panic painfully obvious on their bodies. Later one of the men in the group, Carl Meigh, will say that as he walked up the steps, the four men waiting there seemed to be monsters, horrible beasts ready to devour him. It took all his self-control—not to mention my bounding down three steps to capture him in an overeager American handshake—to keep him from bolting.

Carl's intuitive image of other men as dangerous monsters is pretty much on the mark. Men are socialized to see one another as potential adversaries, strange creatures, bogeymen almost, to vanquish or die trying. For gay men this encounter with other men is a double danger zone since every other man is also a potential site of complex erotics.

Cast of *Suck, Spit, Chew, Swallow*. (Left to right) Ken Shields-Allen, Kuli Sohpal, Robert Shaw, Carl Meigh, and Tim Miller. (Photo: Joseph Potts)

Each man encountered is either an object that you desire who may well rebuff you, thus wreaking havoc on your self-esteem, or he is a predator who may want you even though you would rather eat fire than kiss him. These are the stakes that gay men dare to weather when they walk up those stairs. It's not surprising that such a gathering would be fraught with body terror and issues for days!

I have found that these workshops I lead for men almost inevitably revolve around the men in the group's experiences of their bodies sharing space with one another. There is something about gathering with gay men for this purpose that brings up both the terrors of PE and the pleasures of physical play as boys, the lost hell and the lost Eden. Regardless of what exercises I choose to lead, this raw physical proximity will almost always lead the men to an exploration of what it is like to be in their bodies and how they imagine the world judges/grades/ disciplines their bodies.

This particular gathering is small but interesting. These are the men in Birmingham, England, who are ready to work together every day for two weeks to create a project that already boasts a provocative title. What enormous courage and commitment it takes to jump in feet first!

Kuli Sohpal is a South Asian man, twenty years old, who is studying science at Warwick University. It will become clear over the first meetings that he is not "out" as a gay man and this in fact is the first time he has spent time in a self-identified group of gay men. His friends' nick-

283

name for him is "The Atom Bomb." His barely suppressed rage will be both a terror and an inspiration for this group.

Ken Shields-Allen, a man of color, is the oldest in the group at the age of fifty and arrives with an enormous flourish of confidence. He has lived his life as a performer, toured the world in productions of *Hair* and dozens of other shows. His bravado covers a very wounded and tender heart. His honesty and risk-taking will pull the work deeper.

There's Carl, the man with the vision of the monsters at the head of the stairs. He's a teacher of five-year-olds at a local primary school. Twenty-three years old and just out of college, he presents himself very slickly and middle class but is lucky to have a lot boiling inside. The look of panic is always darting around the corners of his eyes.

Robert Shaw has a lean and hungry look and is also my musical collaborator. He had quite some success with his New Wave band "Swann's Way" in the mid '80s and is now entering his 40s with his eyes open to the surprises of what new form his creativity may take. His quiet, grounded quality is a tonic dose of a man who is capable of watching and listening. He truly has an ear for what is going on in the community of men, and he will bring that to his music and sound-scapes for the piece.

My other collaborator is Joseph Potts, a talented young filmmaker and video artist who will work with us to create a rich décor of video images that will be projected at the DanceXchange during our performance. He and I have already plotted images of men's bodies detailed and examined under the relentless eye and bright light of a live feed

Kuli Sohpal performing his list Things I Hate written on his skin in *Suck, Spit, Chew, Swallow*. (Photo: Joseph Potts)

video camera for the performance. Joseph is the only non-gay man involved with the project at this point, though everyone assumes he is queer since he doesn't indulge the usual straight-man maneuver of broadcasting his heterosexuality. This gives Joseph the unusual experience of getting to "pass" as a gay man for the first few days of our work. His extraordinary intuition and sensitivity is a great wild card in the process.

Then, there's me. I'm in my fortieth year and feeling the miles. The odometer has been turned back more than once, believe me! As someone who has spent his life drawing from and marking on my body as a place for inspiration and narrative, I come to this work with a pocketful of agendas but also a healthy respect for the chaos that is likely to ensue. Like most men with more than a spoonful of the Peter Pan/*Puer Eternis*, whatever you want to call it, I have a ticking time bomb within me of having to confront getting older.

remapping men's bodies

I usually begin my work with groups of men by asking them to do some imagination work and to really visualize a new way of "mapping" their bodies. I invite them to put away for a time the received hegemonic maps of the male body: big dick, big muscles, hard flesh, hard heart, and so on. Instead I want them to see what metaphors their intuitive mind conjures of their embodied selves. Then they get the crayons and pens, and I ask them to draw these new and improved maps of the body.

Here in Birmingham I begin our work with this basic exercise. Suddenly the visual imagination goes wild and through the group's work we see dense and complex representations of how men actually experience being inside their bodies. The drawings explode into images of men with locks over their hearts, with wings sprouting from their backs, with hooks holding their flesh in equilibrium, with feet balancing precariously on a house of cards.

In each of the drawings, the penis, the most overdetermined body part known to humankind, surprises us with new potential. In the various maps, the phallus is covered with clouds, or propped up on a house of cards or is sending out roots to be more grounded to the earth. The exquisite caught-in-the-flashbulb vulnerability in these community-generated images of the penis touched me and reminded me how fragile and susceptible men's bodies really are (how subject to our most personal imagery and private experience of sexual being). It struck me that all the fuss about men's rigid strength (phallus as weapon, etc.), crashes against the sweet reality of the melancholic, almost Chekhovian, recumbent cock. The penis can be so accessible in its quiet moments, its

285

occasional tumescent shenanigans far in the distance. The softness of a man's dick can be tender and available, full of possibilities too. The flesh reminds me of Clark Kent the moment before he dashed into a phone booth to do his makeover. One must gently stroke and coax his penis to see if this is indeed a job for superman.

I find it very poignant how urgent it is for men, gay men in particular, to get the chance to "re-map" their bodies. My agenda is clear in the exercises I do in the workshops. To some extent this structure I have proposed to the performers clearly disciplines them to explore this more vulnerable and metaphoric potential body, but I actually find that it comes up and men want to do this regardless of what kind of exercise focus I suggest. The menu of potential representations offered to (imposed on) men is so oppressive and destructive of human life that I find in my workshops that the guys really grab the opportunity to reimagine their embodiment.

I am also reassured that plain folks want to do this and not just performance artists and those inclined to theorize! It's amazing how much the sharing of these very personal representations help men relate better to one another. Once we knew that Kuli saw himself as an atom bomb, or Carl saw his feet chained to the earth, it made it a much more honest place for the men to connect from. Claiming the power, the specificity and the vulnerability of your most private metaphorized physical self-image really unleashes a lot of psychic and creative juice.

body stories

The next day as I waited for the group to arrive for our second meeting I kept my fingers crossed that I hadn't scared anyone off. One by one they arrived at the DanceXchange, more grounded and confident than the night before. I could see how the participants had begun to claim this space and this process we were occupying.

I asked the men in Birmingham to look at these newly imagined maps of their bodies and to locate a story that lives somewhere on that map. I gathered the men in a circle holding hands (I am a Californian, never forget!) and told them to close their eyes and imagine they were traveling over the maps of their bodies. I asked them to really see the contours and canyons of the worlds they had imagined on their maps. I asked them to follow their nose, as it were, to the stories that each part of their bodies holds. What is the story of the elbow? What happened to make that scar? The story of the teeth? The eyes? The story of your genitals?

What part of our body has a story that really *needs* to be told? Is there a place on our bodies that carries a story so important that if it doesn't get told a person might burst? I invite the group to allow themselves to see their most idiosyncratic metaphors of their body as fully as possible. Our daily language is full of these expressions.

He has feet of clay.
I was caught red-handed.
He broke my heart.
My head is in the clouds.

I believe that hearts actually do break. I believe our heads actually can be in the clouds. I believe our feet can actually turn to clay. I believe that each of those things has probably happened to the men that I work with. As they open themselves to their stories, I asked them to really let those image associations leap forward uncensored by the practical mind. I want them to discover what kind of transformations the telling of this story might offer them. I want them to really find out what the legacy is of this place on their body that has a story that needs to be told. This could be either a positive or a negative legacy. In my experience with this exercise I have seen how these metaphors of our body are often the keys to knowing ourselves in a deep way. I asked the group to dig deep and find that embodied metaphor and that story of transformation that comes from this place. Then I gave the men the challenge of finding a physical action that expresses this story and then one at a time to go into the circle, perform that physical gesture as they tell the group these stories.

Carl Meigh performing the "body story" section in *Suck, Spit, Chew, Swallow.* (Photo: Joseph Potts)

Within the group in Birmingham the stories that came forward were revelatory. Where they had been a group of men socialized to fear and mistrust each other twenty-four hours before, suddenly there was a huge offering of these intensely intimate spaces within ourselves:

Carl told the story of his eyes, which loomed very large on his body map. When he was a small boy, Carl's father had become ill and died. No one would really tell him what had happened; the usual confusing platitudes were shoveled forth. He was not allowed to go to the funeral. This young boy kept looking around the house hoping that he might find his father hidden somewhere in the house. Carl told a story about his eyes that have looked for his father ever since.

The map that Robert had created showed a man's figure with hooks that were attached to his belly and lower back. It was unclear whether these hooks were holding him up or tearing him apart. Robert told the story of his guts and how troubled they have been in his life. When he was coming out as an adolescent, his intestines were troubling him so much that he couldn't control his bowels. He told in his performance how he felt that the shit inside him he felt as a queer boy was literally exploding out of him during his sixteenth year.

The next man began with his hands dancing in front of him. Ken told how his parents never touched him as a child. In fact, they barely noticed him at all and shipped him off to boarding school as soon as possible. He was saved by a special aunt who came from Jamaica and scooped him up and held him, gave him the touch he needed and let him know that he had healing power in his hands.

Kuli, the youngest of the group, did a piece about the time bombs inside him. All the feelings of being in the closet filling him with rage at the bullshit that just made him want to explode. As he told this story of all the things that he was sick of being fucked over by, he was slowly reaching his arm back as if to strike something. With a powerful integrated act, he made an explosive gesture as though slamming a door on all these voices that try to stifle the explosion he needed to make.

I told a story about getting hit in the hand by a bottle thrown at me in Montana two years ago when I was performing at Montana Pride in Bozeman. This was during a time when my boyfriend, Alistair, who is from Australia, had been refused a student visa by the U.S. government. I was feeling the absence of his hand in mine as well as the rage I have for the homophobic laws of my own country. I remember all the times my hand has been slapped: reaching for the cookie jar, touching myself as a child, and now struck by a bottle for wanting to hold the hand of another man.

One by one we participants in Birmingham told, chanted, sang these stories of the body. The room filled with the images of eyes looking for fathers, of children denied touch and affection, of bombs inside, of the shit in our guts, and the ways we get caught red-handed by an oppressive culture. These narratives that spring from our embodiment can lead a person to a deeper, more honest place within himself. Amid the distractions of making a living and keeping up appearances, men are unfortunately encouraged to be stoically alienated from the unpredictable heat of the narratives inside their bodies. As the group spelunked inside looking for the narratives of the body, it was a crucial beginning to a more intimate way of knowing our selves. Our vulnerabilities came forward and encouraged a tender empathy for our own embodied selves and the others gathered in the room. There is something about having these stories be told, "performed" as it were, and thus witnessed, that add to their resonance. Since performing is always an embodied act, it is particularly suited that this body narrative be physically performed as a direct line to owning the terrain of your own body and then have it be witnessed by the larger body of this community of gay men.

The vulnerability of our bodies (self-judgment, shaming, childhood wounding), which everybody is subject to, for gay men can be especially acute because of the fact that the physical body is such a persistent locus of where gay men's identity is constructed. These stories that come from the body are especially rich with metaphor and urgency. The group begins to really see each other, not as our tidy 8-by-10s with résumés on the back, but as fully alive and complicated body-selves that have *such* stories to tell. We start to see the way to escape from this culture of sameness that wants all of our bodies to be tamed of their uniqueness, fixed in the rigid caste system of the beauty myth, and disciplined to productivity and consumption. Such bodies won't rock the boat or upset the horses. The moment we begin to let these stories come forward, we start to unleash the anarchic energy that is held captive in the meat and blood of a more integrated physical self.

These stories, which carry both our pleasures and our pain, locate how our bodies occupy space and move in society. This is a crucial step to seeing how our narratives are shaped by how the world sees us as collections of data concerning race, age, size, and sexuality. The performing of these narratives creates and shares new potential models of resistance as we walk around in each others' shoes, see a dead father through a young boy's eyes, and carry each other's memory of unloving parents.

This creative reimagining and reimaging that came out of these two workshops in Birmingham was characteristic of many of the groups of men that I work with. I have seen the same issues come up again and again: the feelings of not quite making the grade, of not being properly parented, of some kind of residual trauma that ends up haunting men as adults. The themes are similar regardless of whether the men are

289

straight or gay. During some work I was doing with a group of straight and gay men at a conference sponsored by the National Organization of Men Against Sexism (NOMAS) I made these notes in my teaching journal:

Wow. This work the men have been doing this week has been really intense. Doing lots of body memory stuff. Male body image. This group is very ready to acknowledge their vulnerability as gay and non-gay men. Last night I had them create a solo performance about a site on their bodies that was a place of struggle, conflict, and hurt. Really amazing stuff came forward. One man did a piece about always feeling dirty, something he can't quite scrub away. A piece about parents forever sitting on your shoulders whispering nonstop criticism. Struggle with not living up to the prevailing ideal male body aesthetic (universal complaint!). Last night, they worked with each other to create group performances about what the teaching is from that place of hurt, struggle, etc. Where do they want to step forward from there? What transformation can come from that place on the body?

I had them imagine a drawing or sign that might represent that learning, healing, and to imagine where they would draw that on their body. They drew these symbols, these tattoos, with brightly colored magic markers on each other's bodies. Then they worked together to create group performances about where they want to go with the "teaching" from these embodied sites of struggle. Amazing collaborative pieces came forward. One man did an amazing piece where his partners had outlined every spot of his intense psoriasis all over his body with red magic marker. He exposed the thing he was most freaked out about in a room full of other men. He spoke how he wanted to stop seeing his skin as "wrong," wanted to include it as part of his sense of self. Another man, freaked out about getting older, created a performance with two other men where he talked with himself at the age of 7, and also at the age of 77. There was a gay man who had been covering his baldness with a toupee for twenty years and would never let men touch his head. He created a piece where his group touched his head while he told this story. Then he invited the whole workshop (30 fellows) to come into the middle and touch him there in this minefield spot. He breathed this in the moment poem/ chant about his heart and head as we did this.

It has been really great work. A little scary too to see how intense these clouds of self-loathing, judgment which hang over men's heads. Such a relief to air it out with each other. The group seems very drawn to allowing themselves to share their fragile embodiment with each other, the relief of letting down that defense that men usually pile up around one another.

I have often seen this exercise be a path for extraordinary revelation of humanness. The performances that came from this exercise in Birmingham were so full of the challenge of being men of flesh and blood. Often with these pieces, the last spoken words were the most important ones. The words that opened up the vulnerability and the potential space for empowerment and change, as did the last sentence of Carl's performance where he allowed himself to mourn for his eyes forever looking for his dead father. The naming of this personal mythos just might allow a man to see what further work needs to do humanly and creatively.

a night in a soho gay bar in london

The group has been brought together by the disarming intimacy of our several nights' work. Playfulness and hugs with one another now marked their arrival in the space. You could see the transformation in their bodies as the men bounded up the stairs or walked into the rehearsal room and began to warm up. Each person, I included, seemed to enter the workspace each night with a greater sense of empowerment and belonging. With the deepened sense of our own vulnerability of our individual bodies, I now wanted to place these gay men's bodies in the complex vortex of how our bodies are seen and disciplined by social forces outside of the protected specificity of our personal narratives. With my highly developed sadistic impulses as a teacher, I knew it was now time to invite the project participants to make a little visit into hell.

In the weeks before my arrival to England, I had been painfully aware that a right-wing nut had been setting bombs all over London during the spring of 1999. There had been horrific explosions in Brixton, a predominantly black neighborhood in South London as well as in the lively district of Indian and Pakistani shops in Brick Lane in the East End. Most deadly of all had been a bomb that exploded in a gay bar in Soho in London called the Admiral Duncan. A number of people had been killed and dozens terribly injured. This event had profoundly shocked

291

the gay community in the United Kingdom and fractured a feeling of safety and belonging that many gay people had experienced heretofore.

As we began our work this night I gathered the men in Birmingham very close into a circle with our heads touching. I asked them to list all the things they want from other men, the things they want from themselves as well.

> I want to be seen.
> I want to trust him.
> I want his touch on my body.
> I want his respect.
> I want him to open his heart to me.

This list of wants echoed in the new studio where we were working (we had been forced to evacuate DanceXchange by a flood and were now in a new rehearsal space at the Birmingham Ballet!). Then, from that place of desire and personal agency, I asked the men to imagine they had taken all those wants and had gone out on the town and had been there at the Admiral Duncan bar in Soho the night the bomb went off. I asked each man to detail the imaginary story of what his experience was that night. What they were wearing? Who they were going to meet there? How did they feel as they sipped their pint of lager? Then I wanted them to describe what it was like as the bomb went off. One by one we told these ground zero imagined stories to each other while Robert's minidisc recorded each of our voices on the descent into this imagined experience.

The most terrifying thing about this exercise was how *easy* it was for these men to imagine that they had been there. It took no effort at all to place themselves in a site where their body would be subject to the most extreme violation. The stark revelation here was that we gay men so often have the feeling of being physically endangered in the world that it takes no remarkable imagination at all for us to place ourselves in such a horrific moment.

Ken improvised a story of such disarming specificity that it was almost impossible not to believe that he had not actually been at the Admiral Duncan that terrible night. He very vividly described the observations, feelings, and desires that moved through him until the countdown to the explosion. His imagination got right to how he felt he was looking, what cologne was he wearing, who he wanted to chat up.

I clearly saw that the performance we would make over the next few days needed to be about these bodies full of desire and their encounter with disaster, the aspiration to love and companionship surrounded by the bombs without and within. I would gather together our newly mapped bodies, the recordings of our memories and imaginings, each man's story that he discovered on that map of his body, our lists of desires and an encounter with an explosion. The piece would mark the men's stories of their bodies, their search for love, the challenge of so many bombs, like the one in the bar in Soho, that the world tosses in our way as gay men. In the next days we would work very quickly to make space for each man's narrative and creativity, to conjure a full-evening performance called *Suck, Spit, Chew, Swallow.*

the performance

As we prepared for the one performance in Birmingham the intensity of our process hung around us like a dense fog. There had been huge performance anxiety, interpersonal dramas, and the insane creative challenge of creating a full-evening performance work in two weeks. The chaos that ensued when two of the members of the project slept together had been our own little bomb that ate up much of two rehearsals. The torrential rain had kicked us from space to space in Birmingham until I finally indulged one of my occasional righteous diva fits. Joseph couldn't find the proper video projector for the visual material (including close-ups of those body maps projected twenty feet tall on the scrim at the Dance Exchange) that he had conceived for Suck-Spit! The garden-variety slings and arrows that performance art is heir to!

In the hour before the performance I was afraid that Kuli, who was very nervous about his first time performing, would run for the hills. I thought seriously about hiding his backpack. I worried that the two lovebirds would start snarling at each other again. I feared that this time I was pushing my luck to think that I could gather five men at random, ask them to bare their most intimate selves, and that we would be able to make it into a performance for public consumption in only two weeks! Once the piece began, that forest fire in my head quieted down.

The piece began with five men "sleeping" in the space as the audience entered the theater at the DanceXchange. Outlined in a defined square of light, each man lay there under a blanket surrounded by a haunting ambient audio score. Over a rich musical environment, a collage of snippets cascade from each man's stories from intimate moments they had had with other men. Robert, who created all the music for the work, made an aural space that was simultaneously comforting and scary, cozy and funeral. Were these men in their beds or in their graves? Tucked in cozily or buried deep? The live-action video feed focused on parts of the men's bodies visible from under the blanket, a foot, a hand curled over the forehead, the gentle rise and fall of breath. The space was very alive with image, sound, and the embodied presence of these five men as the audience quietly entered a space that was already performative.

The audio score built to a chaos of the men's voices overlapping their desires and memories:

"I want to be held."
"I want his touch."
"I want his dick."
"I want him to look into my eyes."

Finally there is a little movement from the performers. Very slowly, the curtain going up as it were, from under the blankets, the performers, using a carefully concealed banana, slowly display a tent rising up over their blanket-covered pelvises. The men regard their mysterious erections, which seemingly had risen out of the cacophony of desire over the audio track. Then they reach down and pull the bananas out from under their blankets and proceed to energetically suck, spit, chew and swallow them. (Thus our title!) Giving the audience a moment to relax, the humor in the image introduced a sense of absurdity about the hyperdramatization that surrounds the revelation of men's bodies, "the melodramatic penis," as Peter Lehman aptly refers to it. The question that had hung in the air was "Are they naked under those blankets? When do we see some dick?" By frustrating that natural question with an almost summer camp stunt of childlike sleight of hand, the space was cleared for us to go about our business unencumbered by the penis-searching gaze of the audience.

The men shake out their blankets, fold them in a ritualistic manner, place them underneath a seat of the front row of spectators, then gather in a circle and perform a slow unison t'ai chi of gestures drawn from each man's story of an intimacy he has discovered with another man. A breath is held full in the body and then exhales into a mad game of cock-tag. This was drawn from a narrative that Robert had told of how his friends would gather in a vacant lot by the grim council houses and play their version of tag which was an excuse to grab one another's cocks. The crazy exuberance of this disappears as quickly as it arrived, and we launch into the individual narratives of each of the men. Carl is lying on his back, head tortured against the floor so he could see the audience.

"I wanted SEX!" he begins as he launches into a narrative of meeting a man over the chat telephone lines and meeting him at the Birmingham train station. Carl's piece was full of the local specifics of how men might connect in the Midlands of England. His narrative charts the dangerous DMZ where a sex hunt slowly begins to be about a search for greater intimacy. In the performance in Birmingham the audience recognizes a narrative of their own in Carl's words, a series of familiar spaces in their city that they also negotiate with their own bodies.

Kuli tentatively steps into center and asks to be heard. "I need to tell you something." His journey through this two-week process was his first time ever acculturated into a group of gay men. It would be a week of firsts for him: first gay tribe, first visit to a gay club, first gay sex. Kuli's body became the space for the Ur-queer narrative, the big daddy of coming out and into life! Kuli had literally been mutating in front of our eyes for two weeks, his body language and comfort level visibly altering by the second. His story in the performance was a reminder of this most fundamental step of claiming self. The story built to a wild Trip Hop club dance as he described his feelings of occupying queer space for the first night in his life.

The whole group dances wildly with Kuli on stage and then opens out into a circle as I take the space and told the story of my hand that I had begun from the mapping exercise. Each man slaps my hand as I tell the times I had been discouraged from reaching. This leads to the central story of the bottle hitting me in the hand, flung by the queer-basher in Montana as I longed for the touch of my boyfriend Alistair, in Australia, kept out of the United States by my own nation's homophobic immigration laws.

The group embraces and then from each of the hugs one man begins to fall as we hear Ken's harrowing imagination of the night of the bombing at the Admiral Duncan. The image of a fallen man from each couple echoes in the space as Robert begins his haunting song about the Admiral Duncan blast and indeed all bombs that go off around us.

Didn't I ever tell you, I'm not just zeros and ones
Didn't I ever tell you

Didn't I ever tell you, I just wanted some respect
Yea that's right, didn't I ever tell you

And it felt like a lifetime had passed us by,
Before our lovers could walk by our side

But we were new born in the City lights,
We were new born in those City lights

Then we walked in the darkness with a generation that got no bloom
A whole fucking generation got no bloom

And didn't I ever tell you
About the brothers and sisters that were blasted
Into fragments across the surface of a Soho bar,
Like pearls from a broken string

You said, my dear boy they're only Queers, why oh why all those tears,
Why oh why all those tears.

The fallen men are pulled in slow motion across the stage as Robert finishes his lament. We gather around Robert and place our hands, faces, on his body as the song echoes in the space. The performers face the audience. We check our bodies, as if for injury, pressing and touching to make sure we are still there. One by one we speak out the affirmative statement, "I'm gay." Slowly this segues to a more problematized question, *"I'm gay?"* as each performer shifted from checking that we were still breathing to madly checking to see if our hairlines were holding, crows feet spreading or love handles showing. This panic about our male bodies builds to a peak, and then Ken parades out and shouts, "I'm not gay!"

He slowly disrobes, regarding each revealed body part, as he performs a text explaining that his fifty-year-old body not only is no longer read as gay, but indeed compromises his claim on that identity:

> I'm not gay.
> I'm fifty years old.
> I'm not gay.
> The hair is gone. The face, oh God. I used to be a model. Was it really that long ago?
> I'm not gay.
> The body, my body.
> Chest? Tits. Gone.
> Stomach? 28 no more. Inches, years, what the hell gone is gone.
> Talking of gone ... HELLO DICK! ARE YOU AWAKE!
> I'm not gay.
> I want to be held, desired, loved.
> I am not gay.
> I want to feel skin upon skin. I want to lick his sweat, his cock, his balls.
> I want to smell him.
> I want to wake to his breath on my neck.
> I want to feel him deep inside me.
> I am not gay.
> I am. I am. *I AM A HOMOSEXUAL!*

Ken's piece ends with that declaration, which claims a more complex, less colonized way of being exactly the queer man that he is. He then wanders, a naked man among the clothed public, fresh from having revealed his vulnerabilities from asshole to belly, through the rows of the audience meeting and greeting. There is a great sense of liberation in Ken's gesture, of claiming a new way of seeing the embodied self. It made the audience deliciously nervous and giddy at the same time with the new set of possibilities that Ken offered.

The rest of the performers wander the stage, regard each other and

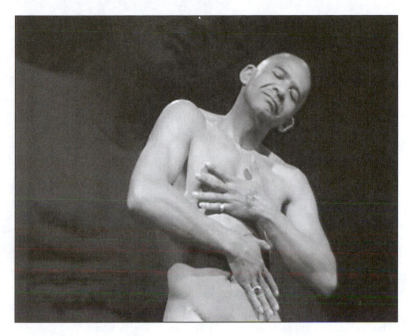

Ken Shields-Allen doing the "I Am Not Gay" body conversation in
Suck, Spit, Chew, Swallow. (Photo: Joseph Potts)

then face the audience. Each man offers a physical action, derived from
their maps of their bodies that taps into their deepest agency and aspiration for themselves, and offers the act with one sentence as *Suck, Spit,
Chew, Swallow* finishes:

> "I want to keep offering my heart to another man in my red, red
> hands."
> "I want him to respect me."
> "I want to feel safe to walk hand in hand."
> "I want my lover and I to grow old together!"

conclusion

As I climbed back on the plane to fly back to the States the day after the
performance, I felt almost more jet-lagged than the morning I had
arrived. The performers and I had undertaken such a deep inquiry of
how we see our bodies, found some narratives that live there, and built
a small community with one another to share these tales of men's
cocks and hearts. Not only that, we had also managed to create a
complex, performative representation of these body stories that we
could share with a larger community of people there in Birmingham,
England.

The performers at the conclusion of *Suck, Spit, Chew, Swallow.*
(Photo: Joseph Potts)

I knew we had done something very difficult and very much worth
doing. We had discovered that a man that becomes conscious of the
narratives within his body is more ready to look eye to eye with that
fucked-up legacy of embodied experience. Through our struggle and
drama with each other we had seen how the scarred and broken places
on the body could also let a little light in. We jumped into the abyss of
acknowledging the warfare that surrounds men's bodies, these bodies
trained to fear vulnerability and each other. I think this inquiry just
might prepare us for this raw activity of being a more conscious, less
colonized male of the species.

As I travel around the world performing and leading community-
based performance workshops, I see the need becoming ever greater
for theatrical, and experiential paratheatrical, spaces where people can
explore the complex human life going on within their bodies. A rigor-
ous and embodied participatory theater is one of the few ways these
bodies can gather with one another in our increasingly disembodied
culture. In the work I do with groups of artists and non-artists, I have
learned that finding a way to be more present in our bodies and open
to the narratives that we carry in our flesh and blood is the quickest
route to discovering the revelatory material about what it just might
mean to be human.

works cited

"As G.I. Joe Bulks Up, Concern for the 98-Pound Weakling." 1999. *New York Times*, May 30.

Lehman, Peter. 2000. "Crying Over the Melodramatic Penis: Melodrama and Male Nudity in Films of the 90s." In *Masculinity in Bodies, Movies, and Culture*, ed. Peter Lehman. New York: Routledge.

Signorile, Michelangelo. 1997. *Life Outside: The Signorile Report on Gay Men: Sex, Drugs, Muscles, and the Passages of Life*. New York: HarperCollins.

suck, spit, chew, swallow

299

contributors

AMY ARONSON holds a Ph.D. in American Literature and Culture from Columbia University and is U.S. editor of the journal *Media History*. She has taught humanities and media studies at New York University, Hofstra, Fordham, and Rutgers University. Her articles have appeared in *Ms.*, *Working Woman*, and *The American Prospect*.

AARON BAKER is an assistant professor and coordinator of film and media studies in the Interdisciplinary Humanities Program at Arizona State University. With Juliann Vitullo he has written on the Italian/American cinema for *Voices in Italian Americana*. He has also written about the representation of social and cultural identities in sports films *for Journal of Sport History*; for a collection of essays he co-edited with Todd Boyd entitled *Out of Bounds: Sports, Media, and the Politics of Identity* (Indiana, 1997); and for the forthcoming volumes *Classic Whiteness: Race and the Hollywood Style* (Minnesota) and *Basketball Jones: America Above the Rim* (NYU).

MAHER BEN MOUSSA has taught American and British literature in the English Department of the University of Tunis. He is currently completing his doctoral dissertation on "The Private Self and the Public Self in the Plays of Tennessee Williams" at Michigan State University. His interests include gender studies and queer theory.

DENNIS BINGHAM is an associate professor of English at Indiana University-Purdue University Indianapolis. The author of *Acting Male: Masculinities in the Films of James Stewart, Jack Nicholson, and Clint Eastwood* as well as many articles on film and gender, he is at work on a book on the post-studio era biopic.

LUCIA BOZZOLA recently completed her Ph.D. in cinema studies at New York University. Her dissertation is on Hollywood male sex symbols after 1960.

ROBERT EBERWEIN is a professor of English at Oakland University, where he teaches courses in film theory and history. He is writing a book on the combat film. His most recent book is *Sex Ed: Film, Video, and the Framework of Desire* (1999).

KRIN GABBARD teaches film, literature, and cultural studies at the State University of New York at Stony Brook. He is the author *of Jammin' at the Margins: Jazz and the American Cinema* (1996) and *Psychiatry and the Cinema* (1999). He is currently completing a book on masculinity and music in recent cinema.

MICHAEL KIMMEL is professor of sociology at the State University of New York at Stony Brook. His books include *Changing Men* (1987); *Men Confront Pornography* (1990); *Men's Lives* (5th edition, 2000); *Against the Tide: Profeminist Men in the United States 1776–1990* (1992); *The Politics of Manhood* (1996); *Manhood: A Cultural History* (1996); and *The Gendered Society* (2000). He edits *Men and Masculinities*, an interdisciplinary scholarly journal, a book series on men and masculinity at the University of California Press, and the Sage Series on men and masculinities. He is the spokesperson for the National Organization for Men against Sexism (NOMAS) and lectures extensively on campuses in the United States and abroad.

ROBERT LANG taught American Cinema at the University of Tunis in 1993–1994. He is currently translating Hédi Khélil's *Sens/Jouissance: Tourisme, erotisme, argent dans deux fictions coloniales d'Andre Gide*. His book *Masculine Interests* is forthcoming from Columbia University Press.

PETER LEHMAN is a professor in the Interdisciplinary Humanities Program and the Hispanic Research Center at Arizona State University. His books include *Running Scared: Masculinity and the Representation of the Male Body*; *Authorship and Narrative in the Cinema* (with William Luhr); *Blake Edwards*; *Returning to the Scene: Blake Edwards, Vol. 2*; and the textbook, *Thinking about Movies: Watching, Questioning, and Enjoying*. He is also editor of *Defining Cinema* and *Close Viewings: An Anthology of New Film Criticism*. He has served as President of the Society for Cinema Studies, editor of *Wide Angle*, and Director of the Ohio University Film Conference.

TIM MILLER is a solo performer and teacher. Miller's performance works Buddy Systems (1985), Sex/Love/Stories (1991), My Queer Body (1992), Naked Breath (1994), Fruit Cocktail (1996), Shirt & Skin (1997), and Glory Box (1999) have been presented all over North America, Australia, and Europe in such venues as Yale Repertory Theatre, the Institute of Contemporary Art (London), the Walker Art Center (Minneapolis), and the Brooklyn Academy of Music. He is the author of the book *Shirts & Skin* and his solo theater works have been published in the play collections *O Solo Homo* and *Sharing the Delirium*. Since 1990 Miller has taught performance in the theater and dance departments at UCLA and Cal State LA. He is a cofounder of Performance Space 122 on Manhattan's Lower East Side and Highways Performance Space in Santa Monica, California.

TOBY MILLER is professor of cultural studies and cultural policy at New York University. He edits the journals *Television & New Media* and *Social Text*. His books include The *Well-Tempered Self: Citizenship, Culture, and the Postmodern Subject*; *Contemporary Australian Television* (with S. Cunnigham); *The Avengers*; *Technologies of Truth: Cultural Citizenship and the Popular Media*; *Popular Culture & Everyday Life* (with A. McHoul); *SportCult* (with R. Martin); *A Companion to Film Theory* (with R. Stam); and *Film and Theory* (with R. Stam). He edits book series for the University of Minnesota Press, Routledge, and Peter Lang.

LEE PARPART is a doctoral candidate at York University in Toronto. Her critical work on Canadian cinema, culture and fine art has appeared in *The Globe and Mail*, *The Whig-Standard*, *POV* magazine, *Take One*, *Canadian Art*, *C* magazine and *The Journal of Canadian Film Studies*.

SALLY ROBINSON is associate professor of English at Texas A&M University. She is the author most recently of *Marked Men: White Masculinity in Crisis* (Columbia University Press, 2000).

CHRIS STRAAYER is an associate professor in the Department of Cinema Studies at New York University and author of *Deviant Eyes, Deviant Bodies: Sexual Re-Orientations in Film and Video* (Columbia University Press).

JULIANN VITULLO is an associate professor of Italian at Arizona State University. Her research focuses on questions of gender and ethnicity in Italian and Italian/American cultures. With Aaron Baker she has written on Italian/American cinema for *Voices in Italian Americana*. She has also written essays on Italian literature and a book titled *The Chivalric Epic in Medieval Italy*.

SUSAN WHITE is associate professor of English at the University of Arizona and film editor for *Arizona Quarterly*. She is the author of *The Cinema of Max Ophuls: Magisterial Vision and the Figure of Woman* (Columbia University Press, 1995), and of various essays on gender and cinema.

JOE WLODARZ is a Ph.D. candidate in film studies at the University of Rochester and is currently working on a study of masculinity and sexuality in U.S. cinema of the late '60s and '70s. His work has appeared in *camera obscura* and is often focused on queer cinema and spectatorship. In addition, he is assistant programmer of the Dryden Theatre film series at George Eastman House and chair of programming for ImageOut, the Rochester Lesbian and Gay Film and Video Festival.

AMY LOUISE WOOD holds an M.A. in southern studies from the University of Mississippi and is currently a doctoral candidate in the Graduate Institute of the Liberal Arts at Emory University. Her dissertation looks at racial violence as mass spectacle in relationship to public religious and visual practices in the American South at the turn of the nineteenth century.

JUSTIN WYATT is the author of *High Concept: Movies and Marketing in Hollywood* (University of Texas Press) and *Poison* (Flicks Books). He is the series editor for Commerce and Mass Culture at the University of Minnesota Press and a contributing editor for *Detour* magazine. His work has also been published in *Film Quarterly*, *Sight & Sound*, *Cinema Journal*, *The Velvet Light Trap*, and *Cineaste*.

index

Action Cop, 179
actors, 26, 31, 52
Adjuster, The, 169, 191n. 21
Adouani, Mustafa, 82
adultery, 35, 37
Affair to Remember, An, 236
Africa, 173, 1743
African Americans, 8, 13, 18, 98, 199, 203, 215, 217, 219–20; empowerment of, 19; lynching of, 193–211
African Caribbeans, 215
African Queen, 44
AIDS, 55, 63n. 1, 73, 238, 281
Al-Hassan Ibn Dhakwam, 88
Ali, Muhammad, 217
Allen, Joan, 267, 270
Allen, Woody, 26
Allport, G. W., 151
Ally McBeal, 37
Alton, Tom, 96
American Graffiti, 56
American History X, 68, 77, 188n. 2
Americans, 194, 205, 273, 275
Analyze This, 223, 224–25
Anderson, Paul Thomas, 37, 186–87
Anderson, Robert, 31
Andy Griffith Show, The, 21
Angels and Insects, 28, 33, 35–36, 39, 172, 188n. 2
Aniston, Jennifer, 48
Apollo 13, 21
Arnez, Desi, 155
Aronson, Amy, 3, 301
Astor, Mary, 10
Atkinson, Rowan, 252
audiences, 186–87, 229, 236–37, 239, 294, 297; female, 249; gay, 2, 52; straight, 2, 52
Australia, 279, 295
autonomy, 10, 83, 218

Babuscio, Jack, 60
Baby Boom, 47
Bacall, Lauren, 44
Backdraft, 21
Bacon, Kevin, 56, 70
Baker, Aaron, 5, 301
Baker, Bruce, 208
Baker, Ray Stannard, 197
Balfour, Ian, 189n. 8
Ball, Mark, 280
Barkin, Ellen, 56
Barretta, Bruno, 28
Barry, John, 251
Bart, Peter, 239
Barthes, Roland, 163n. 5, 207
Basic Instinct, 10, 37
Basinger, Kim, 96
Bataan, 155
bathhouses, 102–103
Bay of Pigs, 270, 277n. 4
Beatty, Ned, 133
Beatty, Warren, 5–6, 227–42; as a sex symbol, 233–36; as Don Juan, 236–40
Beaver, Frank, 264
Bederman, Gail, 137–38
Beefcake, 169
Being at Home with Claude, 172
Ben Moussa, Maher, 4, 301
Bendix, William, 156, 157
Bening, Annette, 6, 236–377, 238, 239
Bergman, Ingrid, 44
Bergonzi, Bernard, 246
Berry, Dave, 26
Bersani, Leo, 67, 72–73, 76, 145n. 9
Bérubé, Allan, 102–103, 159
Big Sleep, The, 44, 100, 107
Bingham, Dennis, 6, 228, 229, 301
Birdcage, The, 48
Birth of a Nation, 19

Black Rain, 52
black(s), 19, 214–15, 217; community, 208; lynching of, 193–211; masculinity (*see* masculinity, black)
blackness, 218
Bledsoe, Jerry, 144n. 1
Bly, Robert, 135
Bob & Margaret, 169, 189n. 5
Bob's Birthday, 169, 189n. 5
Bobbitt case, the, 26, 28, 40n.2
Bobbitt, John Wayne, 28
body: black man's, 196, 207; female, 2, 39; lynched, 195; male (*see* male body); maps of the, 293, 297; narratives, 289, 298; star's, 228; the, 9, 93
Body Heat, 10
Bogart, Humphrey, 9–10
Bond, James, 6; in novels, 246–47; on the screen, 248–50
Bonnie and Clyde, 10
Boogie Nights, 28, 33, 37, 39, 187
Boone, Joel T., 151
Boorman, John, 133–34, 139–40, 141, 143, 144n. 2, 145n. 7
Boothe, Powers, 268
Border Incident, 96
Born on the Fourth of July, 263, 264, 265, 276
Bouhdiba, Abdelwahab, 82, 83, 85, 88
Bourdieu, Pierre, 129n. 2, 201
Bouzid, Nouri, 4, 81–94; "On Inspiration," 83, 91
Bower, Tom, 266
boys, 54, 71, 74, 84–85, 88–89
Boys in the Band, The, 52, 53
Boys in the Sand, 52
Boys of St. Vincent, The, 72, 191n. 21
Bozzola, Lucia, 5, 301
Brass, Lorne, 181
Braveheart, 22n. 2
Britain, 174, 176, 177, 252, 279, 280, 282–83, 291, 292, 297
Broccoli, Albert, 248
Brontë, Charlotte, 44
Bronx Tale, A, 5, 213, 219–20, 223
Brosnan, Pierce, 26, 253
Brundage, Fitzhugh, 209n. 3

Brynner, Yul, 16
Buddies, 63n. 1
Bulworth, 5, 240
Burgess, Anthony, 251

camp, 60–61
Can't Buy Me Love, 45
Canada, 5, 172, 173, 174, 175–77, 179, 183, 186, 189n. 8
Canadians, 176, 178
Canby, Vincent, 253
capitalism, 198, 245
Carrera, Barbara, 252
Carrey, Jim, 45
Carried Away, 28, 33, 35–37, 39
Casablanca, 18, 20, 44
Casillo, Robert, 225n. 1
Casino Royale, 247
castration, 16, 39, 77, 79n. 9, 83–84, 88, 162n. 1, 174, 182, 204, 245
Castro, Fidel, 270, 273
Cato, Will, 197
characters: black, 15, 18–20; female, 3, 186; gay male, 3–4, 47–48, 53, 62, 67; heterosexual male, 32, 62; Italian-American, 215; lesbian, 48; male, 53, 170, 177, 214–15, 225, 264–65
Chase, Richard Volney, 50n. 4
Chicago Hope, 37
children, 82, 84, 89
China, 267, 273, 274
Chion, Michel, 251
Choirboys, The, 53
Chotiner, Murray, 260
Christie, Julie, 233
cinema (*see also* films): action, 17, 52; American, 5, 15, 169, 173, 174, 186; Arab, 89; British, 169; Canadian, 5, 167–92; Egyptian, 91; English-language, 175; European art, 28, 168, 169, 172–73; Hollywood, 40n.3, 168, 186; Italian-American, 219, 225n. 1; mainstream, 27, 168; narrative, 167, 168; Quebec, 181; queer, 167, 175–76, 178 (*see also* New Queer Cinema); Third World, 172; Tunisian, 81–94
circumcision, 84–85
Citizen Kane, 274

class, 4, 8, 14—15, 18, 115—32, 171,
    198—99, 244; difference, 117; iden-
    tity, 118
Clayburgh, Jill, 44
Clockers, 16, 21
Clover, Carol, 74—75
Clueless, 276n. 1
Cobb, 28, 33—36, 39, 40n.3, 188n. 2
Cobb, Ty, 34
Cock, Jay, 230
Cockburn, Alexander, 243
Cohan, Steven, 163n. 4, 228
Cold War, the, 12, 263, 265
Collins, Joan, 227
colonialism, 174, 188
Comstock, Gary David, 124—25
Connery, Sean, 244, 246, 247, 248—52
Connolly, Cyril, 250
Cook, Pam, 224—25
Coppola, Francis Ford, 214, 216
Corber, Robert J., 127
Coward, Noel, 246
Cox, Archibald, 260
Cox, Ronny, 139
Cronenberg, David, 33, 175, 178
Crowley, Monica, 258
Cruise, Tom, 9, 22n. 2, 45
Cruising, 47, 57—58
Crying Game, The, 3, 25, 28—30, 32—33,
    35—36, 39, 40n.2
Cuba, 263
cultural norms, 167, 170, 245
culture: African-American, 219;
    American, 10, 16, 104, 127, 186,
    191n. 21; Arab, 87; Canadian, 176;
    dominant, 18, 79n. 10; gay, 62—63,
    280; Islamic, 93; Italian-American,
    222; popular, 59, 239, 244, 263
Cusack, Joan, 48

D'Emilio, John, 61, 159
Daly, Timothy, 56
DanceXchange, 282, 284, 286, 292—93
Danson, Ted, 45
Darwinism, 138
Dave, 20
Davis, Geena, 20
Day of the Beast, The, 172, 173, 188n. 2
de la Iglesia, Alex, 172, 173
Dean, John, 274

Death of a Salesman, 273
Deathtrap, 58
Debord, Guy, 205
deCordova, Richard, 229
Deer Hunter, The, 149
DeFore, Don, 152
DeGeneres, Ellen, 49
Deliverance, 4, 68, 133—47
Delon, Alain, 118, *120*
Demme, Jonathan, 168
DeNiro, Robert, 69, 219—20, 223
Denny, Reginald, 157
desire, 52, 122, 185, 249; female, 99,
    236; heterosexual, 240; homo-
    erotic, 224—25; homosocial,
    95—96; representation of, 228; sex-
    ual, 119, 161, 224—25, 228
Destination Tokyo, 155
Di Leonardo, Micaela, 214, 219
Dick, 275, 276n. 1
Dick, Bernard, 163n. 1
Dickey, James, 7, 137—39, 141, 142,
    143, 145nn. 6
Die Hard films, 20—21
Die Hard with a Vengeance, 15
Dietrichson, Phyllis, 106
Diner, 4, 55—58, 62, 63n. 2
Dirty, 169
Disclosure, 44
Do the Right Thing, 19, 215—16, 224
Doctor No, 246—47, 249, 254
Doherty, Thomas, 164n. 8
Don Juan, 231, 236—40
Doors, The, 263
Dorian Grey, 184—85
Double Indemnity, 106
Douglas, Michael, 19
Douglas, Susan, 248
Dr. Strangelove, 263
Dream of a Common Language, 32, 38
Driver, Minnie, 38
Dunn, Irene, 44
Dyer, Richard, 27, 60, 63, 218

E.T., 45
Easthope, Anthony, 149, 150, 162,
    162n. 1
Eastman, George, 196
Eastwood, Clint, 9, 26
Eberwein, Robert, 4—5, 301

Eclipse, 172
Edelman, Lee, 77, 79n. 10
Edward II, 64n. 4
Egoyan, Atom, 175, 178, 191n. 21
Ehrlichman, John, 258, 272, 275
Eisenhower, President Dwight D., 259, 270
Eisenstein, Sergei, 184
Election, The, 187, 188n. 23
Ellen, 49
Elsaesser, Thomas, 30
emasculation, 68, 174; of black men, 196
embodiment, 286, 289
emotions, 135—36, 140
Eng, Lance, 184
eroticism, 80n. 12, 89—90, 104, 109; and violence, 104, 107
ethnicity, 3, 5, 11, 213—15, 219—20, 222—23, 275; and masculinity, 213; Italian-American, 213; urban, 222; white, 214, 219—20, 222
Everett, Rupert, 47
Eye for an Eye, An, 73
Eyes Wide Shut, 186

Falling Down, 19, 79n. 11
family, 8—11, 14, 17, 21, 22n. 5, 46—47, 54, 83, 91, 214—16, 225; gay, 54—55; values, 49, 222
Fanon, Frantz, 89, 173—74
Far and Away, 21
Farber, Stephen, 135
Farr, Kathryn Ann, 54
Farrell, Warren, 135
Fassbinder, Rainer Werner, 172
father complex, 264—65
fathers, 45—46, 49, 69, 72, 83, 288—89, 291
Favreau, Jon, 59, *60*
Faye, Alice, 158
feminine, the, 88, 155—56, 160, 222
femininity, 44, 49, 50n. 5, 107, 156, 159, 229—30; forms of, 107
feminism, 44, 78, 136—37
Fiedler, Leslie, 5, 23n. 10, 50nn. 4
Field of Dreams, 46
Fields, Barbara, 199
Fight Club, 187, 188n. 2, 191n. 20
film history, 19, 37, 178

film noir, 10, 96, 100, 106, 112n. 8, 118
film theory, 1—3, 8
films (*see also* cinema): 90s, 25—41; action, 26, 52, 141; American, 186; Angry White Male, 19; Arab, 81—94; Canadian, 170, 172, 190n. 10; contemporary, 43—50; experimental, 169; female rape revenge, 72, 74—75, 78, 79n. 9, 80n. 12; gay, 52, 64n. 4; Hollywood, 15, 18, 37, 141, 150, 164n. 8, 172—73; horror, 49n. 3; independent, 174; Italian-American, 215, 219, 223—24; James Bond, 243—56; lesbian, 64n. 4; male buddy, 52—53, 56, 150; male group, 52, 54, 56; male rape revenge, 12, 71, 73—78, 79n. 7, 80nn. 11; narrative, 169, 172; police/detective, 52; porn, 28 (*see also* pornography); sports, 52; straight, 52; training and documentary, 150—51, 156—57, 160; war, 5, 52, 149—66; Western, 17, 52, 107, 109, 113n. 13
Fine, David, 169
First Blood, 79n. 11
First Wives Club, The, 44
Fleming, Andrew, 276n. 1
Fleming, Ian, 243, 247, 253
Fonda, Henry, 157
Ford, John, 157
Ford, Wallace, 100
Forrest Gump, 19—20
Fortune and Men's Eyes, 172
Foster, Preston, 157
Fothergill, Robert, 177, 178
Foucault, Michel, 229, 231, 253
Four Weddings and a Funeral, 47
France, 174, 176, 249
Freeman, Morgan, 78n. 3
French, Marilyn: *The Woman's Room,* 134
Freud, Sigmund, 9, 104, 117, 128, 163n. 1, 231, 245, 253
Frost, David, 257, 265
Fuchs, Cynthia, 52, 180
Full Blast, 169, 170—72
Full Metal Jacket, 263
Full Monty, The, 33, 62
Fussell, Paul, 22n. 7

index

G.I. Joe, 280−81

G−Men, 96

Gabbard, Krin, 3, 302

Gable, Clark, 9, 37, 44

Gaffney, Oscar, 110

Gagnon, Madeleine, 176

Gallagher, Ted, 230

Gambril, Mike, 238

Gandolfini, James, 16, 223−24

Garnett, Tay, 155

gay: artifice, 115−32; audiences (*see* audiences, gay); characters (*see* characters, gay); community, 3, 63, 63n. 1, 103, 221, 292; cultural assimilation, 63; culture, 62−63; identity, 51−65, 91; male friendship, 4, 52−55, 63; representation, 52, 68; stereotypes (*see* stereotypes, gay)

gay men, 2, 47−49, 50n. 4, 54, 59, 61, 63n. 1, 67−68, 73, 75, 78, 80n. 12, 103, 111, 124−28, 184, 221, 245, 279, 281−86, 289−90, 293, 295; −straight woman pairing, 47−48; as nurturing role models in films, 47−48; bodies of, 281−86; masculinity of, 48; stereotypes, 73

gayness, 57−58, 60, 62

gaze, the, 14, 18−19, 229−30, 233−36, 239, 240n. 1, 249, 294; male, 70, 92−93, 110, 281

gender, 11, 38, 102, 176, 202, 219, 221, 228−29, 240n. 1, 280; and star discourse, 227−42; difference, 46, 54; dynamics, 17, 21; identity, 160, 176−77, 184, 187; roles, 5, 232

genitals, 39, 250

Get Shorty, 16

Gibson, Mel, 3, 7−8, 12−15, 21, 22n. 2

Gill, Aaron, 22n. 5

Gillis, Jamie, 26

Glenday, Michael, 137

Glimmer, Man, The, 20

Glover, Danny, 20

Go, 64n. 5

Godfather, The, 5, 11, 213, 214, 216, 219, 225n. 1; *Part II,* 213, 221, 225n. 1; *Part III,* 216

Goin' Down the Road, 177−78

Gold, Jonathan, 10

Goldbacher, Sandra, 28, 38

Goldberg, Herb, 134−36

Goldeneye, 253

Goldfinger, 250, 252, 253−54

Good Morning Vietnam, 64n. 2

Good Ole Boy Groups, 54, 56

Gooding, Cuba Jr., 45

Gould, Jason, 78n. 2, 79n. 4

Governess, The, 28, 33, 38, 39, 40n.5

Grable, Betty, 158

Grant, Cary, 155

Grant, Hugh, 47

Grant, Lee, 233

Gray, John, 46

Greenaway, Peter, 172

Greyson, John, 175, 183−85

Griffith, James, 137

Griffith, Melanie, 44

Groch, John, 19

Guadalcanal Diary, 156−57, 158

Guattari, Félix, 254

Gung Ho!, 21, 158

Guttenberg, Steve, 56

Hackman, Gene, 48

Haig, Alexander, 258, 260, 268, 274

Hair, 31, 284

Haislip, Li, 264

Haldeman, H. R., 258, 260, 268, 270, 275

Hale, Charlie, 199, *200,* 206

Hale, Grace, 209n. 3

Hall, Jacquelyn, 207

Hansen, Miriam, 98, 240n. 2

Hansen, Miriam, and Gaylyn Studlar, 240n. 2

Happy Days, 21

Harold and Maude, 170

Harris, Daniel, 63

Harris, Sydney, 253

Harrison, Russell, 123

Haskell, Molly: *From Reverence to Rape,* 84, 86

Hawn, Goldie, 233

Hayes, Sean, 48

He Walked by Night, 96

Heath, Stephen, 39

Heaven and Earth, 263, 264

Heaven Can Wait, 237

Hedaya, Dan, 13, 276n. 1

Hen Party, 282
Hepburn, Katherine, 44
heroes, 18; action, 18; American,
    9–10; official, 17; outlaw, 9, 17–18,
    20; Western, 107; white, 11, 19
heroism, 21
heteromasculinity, 115
heterosexuality, 27, 29, 62, 68, 75, 89,
    97, 111, 117, 121, 124–29, 135–36,
    154, 157, 159, 229, 234–35, 240, 285
Highsmith, Patricia, 4, 123–24,
    128–29
Highway of Heartache, 169
Higson, Andrew, 188
Hitchcock, Alfred, 34
Hoffman, Dustin, 45–46
Holden, William, 228
Holiday, Billie, 193
Hollywood, 8, 172, 174, 239
Holmes, John, 26
Holmlund, Chis, 52
Holocaust, the, 45
Holt, Sam, 197, 198
homme fatal, 118, 128
homoerotic, the, 52–53, 100, 111
homoeroticism, 69, 75–76, 97, 100,
    102, 109, 150, 162, 163n. 1, 224
homophobia, 2, 4, 47, 53, 62–63, 83,
    128, 221, 288, 295; homoerotic, 180;
    in Hollywood, 67–80
homosexual: behavior, 127; panic,
    117, 124–25, 131n. 11
homosexuality, 3–5, 27, 49, 50n. 5,
    51–65, 68, 70–74, 76, 78, 81, 89, 91,
    93, 100, 104, 115–17, 120, 122,
    124–29, 131n. 12, 145n. 8, 149–52,
    161–62, 163n. 3, 254; Islamic, 93;
    repressed, 116–18
homosexuals. *See* gay men
homosocial: anxiety, 185; bonding, 4,
    51–65, 104, 171–72; desire,
    116–17, 119, 121, 128; relation-
    ships, 214; the, 62, 95
homosociality, 51–52, 55, 71, 100,
    102, 111n. 1, 117, 122
Hoolboom, Mike, 169
Hopkins, Anthony, 259, 267, 270, 272,
    276n. 1
Hopper, Dennis, 36
Horner, James, 13

Houde, Germain, 181
Household Saints, 5, 213, 219, 221,
    222–23
Howard, Ron, 7, 21
Howells, Carol Ann, 174, 188
Huckleberry Finn, 20
Hudson, Rock, 44, 228
Hughes, Langston, 184
Hume, Cyril, and Richard Maibaum,
    22n. 6
Humphrey, Hubert, 232, 272
Hunt, Howard, 270
Hutcheon, Linda, 174
Hutton, Robert, 155
Hwang, David Henry, 26, 30, 33
hypermasculinity, 21, 104, 191n. 20,
    221–22; of white men, 196

I Love a Man in Uniform, 169, 183,
    185–86
I Spit on Your Grave, 75
identity, 5, 51–65, 115–16, 184–85,
    188, 215, 217, 289; ethnic, 219–21,
    223
Ignon, Alexander, 10
immigrants, 19, 138, 183; Italian,
    215–16
Immortal Sargeant, 157, 159, 161
In and Out, 48, 67
incest, 35, 37, 86, 173
India, 173, 174
innocence, 44–46, 48–49, 68–69, 73,
    78n. 1, 79n. 8; sexual, 160
Irey, 97
Islam, 81, 85, 93
It Happened One Night, 37
Italian American(s), 5, 214–16,
    219–20, 222–24; community, 218,
    220; identity, 213–15, 221
Italian-Americanness, 213–14, 224
Italians, 215

Jackson, Samuel L., 15, 20
Jaeckel, Richard, 158
Jane Eyre, 44
Jarman, Derek, 172
Jeffords, Susan, 52, 263
Jerry Maguire, 45
Jews, 84
JFK, 263, 265

Jim Crow laws, 195
Johnson, President Lyndon B., 259, 261
Johnson, Van, 152
Jones, Jacquie, 193–94
Jordan, Michael, 16
Jordan, Neil, 25–26, 29–30, 33, 40n.1

Kacmarczyk, Sgt. Alexandar, 153
Kahlo, Frida, 184
Kahn, Madeleine, 269
Kalthoum, Oum, 84
Kauffman, Stanley, 260, 269
Kaye, Tony, 77
Keaton, Diane, 47
Kennedy, Arthur, 107
Kennedy, President John F., 259, 260, 263, 265, 270–71, 274, 277n. 4
Kennedy, Robert, 270, 274
Kent State, 271, 272
Kid, The, 45
Killers, The, 10
Kimmel, Michael, 3, 6, 261–62, 302
Kinaae, Karethe, 169
King, Jr., Martin Luther, 263
Kinky Business 2, 168
Kiss Me Guido, 213, 219, 220–21, 223
Kiss of Death, 21
Kissed, 169
Kissinger, Henry, 272
Klein, Herb, 276n. 1
Kline, Kevin, 48
Koltnov, Barry, 37
Koppes, Clayton, and Gregory D. Black, 163n. 1
Kovacik, Karen, 275
Kovic, Ron, 264
Kramer vs. Kramer, 44, 45–46
Krutnik, Frank, 9–10, 96–97
Ksouri, Khaled, 81
Kubrick, Stanley, 186, 263

La Bruce, Bruce, 175
LaBute, Neil, 77
Ladd, Alan, 22n. 2
Laforet, Marie, 118
Lancaster, Burt, 10
Lane, Nathan, 48
Lang, Robert, 4, 302
Last Action Hero, 18

Last of the Mohicans, The, 20
Latinos, 98
Lauzon, Jean-Claude, 179
Lazenby, George, 249
Lebel, Roger, 179, *179, 180*
Lee, Spike, 19, 215, 224
Lehman, Peter, 80n. 12, 144n. 3, 230–31, 235, 294, 302; *Running Scared,* 26, 167, 168, 170, 172, 187, 189n. 3
LePage, Robert, 175
lesbians, 2, 48, 61, 245, 280
Lester, Richard, 53
Lethal Weapon, 20–21, 52
Levene, Sam, 158
Levinson, Barry, 4, 55–57, 63n. 2, 68
Levy, Shawn, 59
Liar Liar, 45
Liman, Doug, 55, 60, 64n. 5
Lindo, Delroy, 15–16, 20
Lipnicki, Jonathan, 45
Live Bait, 169, 170, *170*
Lockhart, June, 98
Loeser, Lt. Col. Lewis H., 163n. 3
Long Kiss Goodnight, The, 20
Loring, Francis, 184
Lorre, Peter, 26
Lott, Eric, 22n. 9, 100
love, 44, 111
Love Affair, 5, 228, 230, *236, 237,* 238–39
Lovett, Lyle, 25
Lovgren, David, *171*
Lucht, Richard, 40n.2
Luhr, William, 22n. 2
lynchers, 201–202, 204; masculinity of, 202
lynching, 193–211, *194, 200*; as ritual, 195–99, 201; as spectacle, 195, 206; photographs, 5, 193–211, *194*; victims, 196, 209n. 4

M. Butterfly, 26, 30, 32, 33, 37, 39, 40n.2
Maalal, Imad, 81
Mac, 213, 219, 221, 223
MacDonald, Heather, 32
MacDonald, Jeanette, 44
MacDowell, Andy, 47
Maddin, Guy, 175
Made in America, 45

Madonna, 47
Magnificent Obsession, 44
Maguire, Joseph, 253
Maheu, Gilles, 180, *181, 182*
Making Love, 58
male: -male interactions, 54, 99–100,
    103, 112n. 9; bonding, 4, 51–65,
    111, 112n. 10, 116–17, 130n. 7, 149,
    157, 162n. 1, 250; bravado, 21;
    desire, 9; dominance, 261; femi-
    ninity, 149, 155–56; friendship,
    52–55, 63, 84, 87, 125, 158; hysteria,
    141, 144; liberation, 133–47;
    masochism, 76, 141, 145n. 9; pair-
    ing, 55; power (*see* power, male);
    privilege, 38, 134, 136, 150, 233, 234,
    236, 281; psyche, 143, 145n. 6; rage,
    134, 140; rape (*see* rape, male);
    repression, 140, 142–43; ritual of
    joking, 54; sexual representation,
    170, 172–73, 176, 178, 180, 187–88,
    191n. 21; sexuality (*see* sexuality,
    male); socialization, 54, 63; specta-
    tors (*see* spectators, male); subjec-
    tivity, 67, 76–78
male body, the, 2, 4, 5, 25–41, 78,
    79n. 9, 80n. 12, 93, 99–100, 111,
    133–36, 138, 140–44, 145n. 6, 160,
    167–92, 228, 233–36, 240nn. 1, 244,
    249–50, 281, 285–86, 290; African-
    American, 195, 196, 207; and mas-
    culinity, 2, 40n.3; and
    performance, 279–99; colonial,
    178–79, 187; ideal, 281–86; nude, 5,
    25–41, 161–62, 164n. 11, 167–92;
    representation of, 174, 178, 183,
    188, 191n. 21; sexualized, 230; spec-
    tacle of, 167–92
male groups, 54, 55–57, 74; hetero-
    sexual, 55
maleness, 137
Malkmus, Lizbeth, and Roy Armes:
    Arab and African Film Making, 88–89
Maltese Falcon, The, 100, 107
mama boys, 151, 163n. 2
Man from Laramie, The, 107
Man of Ashes, 4
Man Who Shot Liberty Valance, The, 20
Man with the Golden Gun, The, 247, 253

Man without a Face, The, 22n. 2
manhood, 6, 8–9, 73, 77, 78n. 4, 84,
    137, 142, 150, 202, 228, 235, 240,
    258–59, 262, 272
manliness, 10, 1373
Mann, Anthony, 4, 95–114
Manning, Maria, 243
Mao Tse-Tung, 273, 274–75
Mapplethorpe, Robert, 40n.2
Margaret's Museum, 169, 170–72, 175
marriage, 82, 84–85, 91, 94, 240
Martinez, Cuca, 106
masculine: anxieties, 7–8, 81–94,
    215; autonomy, 9–11; exhibition-
    ism, 98; identity, 54, 216; privilege,
    54, 233; redemption in films,
    43–50; ritual, 202; role models, 16;
    southern white, 193–211
masculinity, 2, 4, 6, 10, 21, 22n. 2, 49,
    50n. 5, 68–72, 74–76, 78, 82,
    84–85, 93–94, 100, 115, 126,
    137–40, 144, 151, 156, 159–60, 161,
    168, 173–74, 177, 186–87, 196,
    203–204, 221, 228–29, 245, 248,
    254, 258–61, 263, 275; American,
    134; and ethnicity, 213; and space,
    95–114; and the male body (*see*
    male body, the); black, 3, 8, 50n. 5,
    195; black forms of, 22n. 9; Cana-
    dian, 177–78; colonial, 167–92;
    construction of, 134, 136, 141, 143,
    223; discourses on, 4; dominant, 5,
    8, 137, 176; ethnicized, 98; gay, 48;
    hegemonic, 177; heterosexual,
    50n. 5, 67, 77; Hollywood, 49; Ital-
    ian-American, 216, 224–25;
    masochistic, 76; myth of, 139–40;
    normative, 76; phallic, 26, 141;
    primitive, 137; redeemed, 10; rep-
    resentations of, 5, 224; repressed,
    133–47; sensitive, 69; sexuality
    and, 149–66; texts of, 149–50; tra-
    ditional, 10, 75; white, 3, 7–23,
    50n. 5, 71, 76, 80n. 11, 133–34,
    137–38, 141, 195, 207, 223, 225;
    working-class, 171
Masterson, Jill, 250–51
Matthew Bourne Swan Lake, 282
Matthew, Christopher, 260

Maunsell, Micki, 170
McCamus, Tom, 185−86
McCormick, Eric, 48
McGovern, George, 232, 263−64
McGraw, Charles, 107
McInerney, Jay, 246
McNally, Terence, 53
Meade, Mary, 106
Mean Streets, 213, 214−15, 225n. 1
Meigh, Carl, 282, *283,* 286, *287,* 288, 291, 294, 296
Mellen, Joan, 145n. 8
melodrama, 25−41
men, 1−2, 5, 16, 27, 31, 49, 83, 98, 111, 135, 151, 245, 279; American, 273; and power, 5−6; Arab, 82; black, 5, 11, 15−17, 20, 22n. 9, 71, 138, 193−211; ethnic, 219−21; friend-ship among, 3, 52−62; gay (*see* gay men); heterosexual, 29, 49, 54−55, 61, 68, 116, 126, 279, 281, 285, 290; Italian-American, 213−26; Mus-lim, 93; of color, 20; self-made, 257−78; southern white, 193−211; white, 3, 5, 7−23, 98, 134, 138, 156, 196, 201−202, 204, 207, 219−20, 261; working-class, 5, 22n. 9, 138, 171, 213−14
men's movement, the, 135
Menninger, William C., 159
Mensel, Robert, 209n. 8
metatext, 228−29
Mexicans, 215
MGM, 96
Miller, Arthur, 273
Miller, D. A., 68, 76
Miller, Tim, 2−3, 5, *283,* 302
Miller, Toby, 6, 303
Mishima, Yukio, 184
Mitchell, John, 258, 271, 274
Mitchell, Martha, 269
Mitchell, Thomas, 157
Mitchum, Robert, 10, 19
Moby Dick, 20
Modine, Matthew, 45
Mohr, Jay, 64n. 5
Montgomery, Robert, 158
Moore, Dudley, 26
Moores, Suzanne, 244
mother, the, 9−10, 46, 49, 88

Mrs. Doubtfire, 26, 46
Ms. 45, 75
Mulvey, Laura, 231, 240n. 4
Murdock, Tim, 152
Murray, Stephen O., and Will Roscoe: *Islamic Homosexualities,* 91, 93
Muslims, 85
Mustard Bath, 169
My Best Friend's Wedding, 3, 47, 67
My Own Private Idaho, 64n. 4

Nadeau, Chantal, 180
Naked City, The, 96
NAMBLA (North American Man-Boy Love Association), 73
narcissism, 116−17, 120; homo-, 120−22
Nardi, Peter, 54−55, 61
narratives: American, 9−10, 20−21; heterosexual, 86; revenge, 73
NEA Four, 2−3
Neal, Claude, 199
Neale, Steve, 99, 228, 233, 240n. 4
Never Say Never Again, 250−52, 254
New Queer Cinema, 3, 52, 62, 64n. 4 (*see also* cinema, queer)
Newland, Marv, 169
Newman, Paul, 22n. 2
Next Best Thing, The, 47
Night of the Hunter, 19
Nixon, 6, 257−78
Nixon, Frank, 265, 273
Nixon, Hannah, 266, 267, 271, 273
Nixon, Harold, 271
Nixon, Pat, 266−67, 270, 271, 274
Nixon, President Richard, 2, 232, 233, 257−61, 263, 265−75, 276nn. 1
No Skin off My Ass, 169
Nolan, Lloyd, 155, 156
Nolte, Brawley, 7
Nolte, Nick, 78n. 2
NOMAS (National Organization of Men Against Sexism), 279, 290
nonwhites, 217−19, 224
Novak, Kim, 237
nudity: frontal, 31, 34, 40n.2, 167, 186, 188n. 2, 235; male, 25−41, 161−62, 164n. 11, 167−92, 234
Nunn, Bill, 19

O'Hara, Maureen, 157
O'Keefe, Dennis, 96, 97
O'Shaunessey, Brigid, 106
Object of My Affection, The, 48, 67
Objective Burma, 159
Oedipal crises, 2, 3, 9–10, 83, 88, 90, 163nn. 1, 224–25, 253
Off Key, 169
Oh! Calcutta, 31
Oklahoma!, 179
oppression, 20, 134, 137, 194; institutionalized, 195, 198
Orbison, Roy, 25–26, 40n.1
Orientalism, 100, 112n. 8
Orsi, Robert, 215, 218, 219
Other, the, 11, 15, 50n. 4, 77, 181, 273–75; English Canadian, 179; gaze of, 14; paranoia about, 19; racial, 102; straight-as-, 53
Out of the Past, 10
Overman, Jack, 107

Pacino, Al, 22n. 2, 57–58, 220
Paisz, John, 175
Pakistan, 91
Pal, George, 12
Palace of Pleasure, 189n. 4
Panic in the Streets, 96
Paris Is Burning, 64n. 4
Paris, France, 169
Parpart, Lee, 5, 303
Parting Glances, 63n. 1
Partners, 58
patriarchy, 10, 40n.3, 45, 49n. 3, 69, 73–76, 78, 91, 93, 97, 137, 150, 168, 225, 250, 259
Patric, Jason, 68
pedophilia, 72–73
penis, the, 3, 27–28, 38–39, 40n. 3, 168–72, 180, 183–87, 189n. 6, 204–205, 245, 248, 250–51, 253, 254, 285; disciplined, 253–54; erect, 26, 27, 37; flaccid, 26, 37, 39, 186–87; images of, 5, 30–31, 33–34, 36–37, 38, 40n.3; James Bond's, 243–56; jokes about size of, 26, 27, 33; melodramatic, 3, 25–41, 168, 170, 172; phallic, 28, 33; representations of, 26–31, 33, 39, 245; size of, 26–27, 39; spectacle of, 35, 173

performance: and men's bodies, 279–99; artists, 2
Persons, Ells, 209n. 10
Pfeil, Fred, 21
phallic: authority, 10, 176, 183–86; masculinity, 26, 179, 186, 235, 241n. 7; power, 15, 33, 37, 76, 170, 173, 178, 187, 245; spectacle, 3, 26, 39
phallocentrism, 73
phallus, the, 16, 27, 40n. 3, 183, 189n. 6, 245, 285; symbolic, 27, 253, 285
Phifer, Mekhi, 16
Phillips, Howard, 274
photography, 5, 39, 196, 201–202, 205, 207; lynching, 193–211, *194*; snapshots, 202
Pink Komkommer, 169, 189n. 5
Pitt, Brad, 191n. 20
Platoon, 262, 264, 276
Podeswa, Jeremy, 175
Poison, 64n. 4
Polan, Dana: *Power and Paranoia,* 95
Polanco, Iraida, 11
Pool, Léa, 175
Pope, Harrison, 280–81
Porky's, 26
pornography, 27, 168, 208, 244; folk, 207–208; gay, 63, 169, 281; hard core, 26, 33, 39
Post-Mortem, 169
poststructuralism, 115–32
Potts, Joseph, 284–85, 293
power, 3–4, 18, 44, 228–29, 232, 250; and men, 5–6, 183; and sex, 232, 240; male, 4, 6, 134, 136, 138, 140, 207, 225, 233, 236, 240, 244; phallic (*see* phallic, power); sexual, 204; social, 134; white, 195
Praunheim, Rosa von, 172
Preston, Richard, 157
Price, Richard, 10, 21
Prince of Tides, The, 2, 4, 68, 75, 78nn. 1, 79n. 7
psychoanalysis, 162n. 1, 244–45, 253–54, 276
Puerto Ricans, 215, 221
Pulp Fiction, 68, 71, 79n. 8
Purple Noon, 115–32, *120*
Purvis, Kenneth, 136
Puzo, Mario, 214

Quaid, Randy, 45
queer cinema. *See* New Queer Cinema
Queerfest, 280
queerness, 51–65, 77, 104, 221
Quindlen, Anna, 43
Quinn, Anthony, 158

race, 3, 5, 8, 15, 17–18, 20, 102, 195–96, 219, 254
racial: distinction, 215; dynamics, 17, 21; ideology, 195–96; inbetweenness, 216–18, 220–21; superiority, 197; terrorism, 208
racism, 3, 17, 194, 206, 249
Raging Bull, 213, 214, 218, 224–25, 225n. 1
Rain Man, 64n. 2
Ramsey, Christine, 177
Rand, Ayn, 248
Ransom, 3, 5, 7–23
rape, 4, 79n. 8; homosexual, 4; male, 68, 72, 77–78, 79n. 9, 82, 83–85, 89–90, 99, 107, 133, 140–41, 143, 145n. 8, 180–81
Rat Pack Confidential, 59
Rat Pack, The, 59
Rat Pack, the, 58–59
Ray, Johnnie, 25
Ray, Robert B., 9, 17
Read, Allen, 173–74
Reconstruction period, 195, 198, 203
Reed, Donna, 158
Reid, Paul, 197
Reign of Terror, 100
Reinhold, Judge, 45
Reinke, Steve, 169
Reiser, Paul, 45
remasculization, 137, 141
Renfro, Brad, 70
Reynolds, Burt, 139, 140
Rhames, Ving, 79n. 8
Rich, B. Ruby, 64n. 4
Rickenbacker, Captain Eddie, 152–53, 154
Ridicule, 172, 188n. 2
Rih Essed/Man of Ashes, 81–94
Rioux, Marcel, 183
Ritz, The, 53

Robbins, Tim, 78n. 1
Roberts, Julia, 47
Robinson, Edward G., 26
Robinson, Sally, 4, 303
Rockefeller, Nelson, 274
Rocky, 5, 213, 214, 217, 219, 225n. 1
Rocky II, 213, 217–18, 225n. 1
Roeder, George, 161
Ronet, Maurice, 118
Rookie, The, 52
Ross, Irwin, 151
Roundy, George, 227
Rourke, Mickey, 56
Rozema, Patricia, 175
Running Scared, 2, 28
Russo, Rene, 7
Russo, Vito, 53
Rutledge, Vivian, 107
Ryan, Thelma Patricia, 266–67
Ryder, Alfred, 97

Salvador, 262
San Francisco, 44
Sandell, Jillian, 162
Sarris, Andrew, 227, 231
Saturday Night Fever, 221
Savalas, Telly, 16
Savran, David, 76, 79n. 11
Scarface, 98
Schehr, Lawrence R., 169
Schindler's List, 45
Schindler, Oscar, 45
Schlesinger, Jr., Arthur, 263
Scholte, Tom, 170, *171*
Schwarzenegger, Arnold, 26, 244
Sea of Love, 21
Searchers, The, 273
Secter, David, 189n. 4
Sedgwick, Eve Kosofsky, 62, 95, 116–17, 128, 129n. 4
Segal, Alex, 22n. 6
Segal, Lynne, 163n. 1
Selleck, Tom, 48
Seven, 188n. 2
sex, 6, 17, 67, 93, 195, 231–32, 245, 247, 248, 252, 254; anal, 4, 67, 68, 74, 79n. 9, 80n. 12 (*see also* sodomy); gay, 67–68, 78, 102, 184, 295; symbols, 227–42
sexism, 63, 244, 249

sexual: ideology, 195—96; power, 204, 208, 235; practices, 185, 253; roles, 4, 228

sexuality, 2, 6, 16, 49, 57, 81, 83, 89, 91, 116—17, 134—37, 150, 154, 156, 157, 161—62, 202—203, 217, 219, 221, 228—30, 231, 238, 240, 246, 289; black men's, 5, 196; female, 2, 136; gay, 90; in films, 1, 149—66; male, 4, 6, 79n. 9, 135, 144n. 3, 150, 151, 154, 161—62, 168

Shakur, Tupac, 16

Shallow Grave, 188n. 2

Shampoo, 5, 227, 230, 231—32, 234—35, 236, 237, 238—39

Shane, 17

Shaw, Robert, *283*, 284, 288, 292, 294, 296

Shawshank Redemption, The, 3, 8, 68, 75, 78nn. 1, 79nn. 7

She's Gotta Have It, 44

Sheen, Charlie, 264

Shields-Allen, Ken, *283*, 284, 288, 292, *297*

Shipp, Thomas, *194*

Shire, Talia, 214

Shock of Recognition, The, 31

Shohat, Ella, 18

Signorile, Michelangelo, 281

Silence of the Lambs, 47, 168

Silverman, Kaja, 76, 145n. 9

Simpson, Don, 239

Simpson, Mark, 149—50, 162, 162n. 1

Simpson, O. J., 239

Sinise, Gary, 11

Sirk, Douglas, 228

Six Crises, 274

Slap Shot, 53

slavery, 203

Sledge, Percy, 25

Sleepaway Camp, 40n.2

Sleepers, 4, 64n. 2, 68—77, 79n. 7, 80n. 12

Slotkin, Richard, 50n. 4

Smith, Abram, *194*

Smith, Paul, 141

Snipes Wesley, 244

Snowden, Alice, 169

Sobchack, Vivian, 49n. 3

social: formations, 61; identities, 213, 223; norms, 52; relations, 136

society: Arab-Muslim, 83—84, 91; dominant, 55, 63, 68; patriarchal, 72, 168; straight, 54, 60—61, 63; Western, 169

sodomy, 77, 89 (*see also* sex, anal)

Sohpal, Kuli, 283, *283, 284*, 286, 288, 295

Sontag, Susan, 59

Sopranos, The, 223—25

Sorvino, Paul, 272

South, the, 193—211

Soviet Union, 267

spectators: female, 25, 229, 235; gay, 102; male, 77—78, 80n. 12, 229, 235

Spielberg, Steven, 45

Stage Fright, 34

Stallone, Sylvester, 26, 217, 244

Star Wars, 18

stars: construct of, 229; discourse, 239—40; male, 16, 227—42; porn, 26; sexuality of, 229

Steenburgen, Mary, 266

Steichen, Edward, 153—54

stereotypes: gay, 48, 54, 126; racial, 214

Stern, Daniel, 56

Stewart, Jimmy, 107

Stone, Louis, 264

Stone, Oliver, 6, 257—78

Stone, Sharon, 37

Story of a Transport, The, 156—57

Stouffer, S. A., 151

Straayer, Chris, 4, 303

Streep, Meryl, 46

Streisand, Barbra, 78n. 4

Studlar, Gaylyn, 145n. 9, 240n. 2

Sturgis, Frank, 270

suburban spaces, 222—25

Suck, Spit, Chew, Swallow, 279—99, *283, 284, 287*, 293, *297, 297, 298*

Sudden Impact, 75

Summer of Sam, 224, 225

Summer Place, A, 56

Sweeney, Bruce, 169

Swingers, 3, 51—65, *60*

T-Men, 4, 95—114, *105, 108, 109, 110*

taboos, 28, 39, 81

Talented Mr. Ripley, The, 4, 115—32

Tarantino, Quentin, 112n. 10

Tasker, Yvonne, 52

Taylor, Lili, 11

Taylor, Robert, 44

Tea and Sympathy, 86

Thaxter, Phyllis, 152

The Blue Ghost, 153

Thelma and Louise, 44

They Were Expendable, 158, 164n. 7

Thirty Seconds over Tokyo, 152, 154

This Is the Army, 156

Thompson, Kristen, 34

Three Men and a Baby, 45

Thumin, Janet, 250

Thunderball, 249, 252, 254

Thunderbolt and Lightfoot, 53

Till, Emmett, 209n. 10

Time Machine, The, 12, 14

Time to Kill, A, 73

Tin Men, 63n. 2

Tin Pan Alley, 158

To Have and Have Not, 44

Tobias, George, 159

Tolnay, Stewart E., and E. M. Beck, 208n. 2

Tom Paine, 31

Towne, Robert, 231, 235

Trachtenberg, Alan, 209n. 8

Tracy, Spencer, 44

transvestism, 35, 37, 156

Travers, Peter, 77

Tricarico, Donald, 214

Trier, Lars von, 172

Trudeau, Pierre, 176

Tunisia, 84

Turkey, 91

Turkish Delight, 168

Two Years before the Mast, 20

Tyre, Nedra, 203

Un Zoo, la nuit, 172, *179,* 180, *181, 182, 183*

Unforgiven, 20

United Artists, 58

United States, 76, 174, 176, 177, 186, 215, 263, 274, 279; Army, 151–52, 156

Unmarried Woman, An, 44

Urinal, 183–85

Valentino, Rudolph, 240n. 2

Van Horn, Patrick, *60*

Vaughn, Vince, *60*

venereal disease, 150–51, 156–57, 160

Vergès, Françoise, 89

Verhoeven, Paul, 168

Vice Versa, 45

Victor/Victoria, 58

Vietnam War, 19, 76, 217, 261, 263–65, 267, 270–72, 276n. 2

vigilantism, 73

violence, 8, 20, 30, 36, 77, 99, 103, 105, 107, 116, 119, 136–37, 139, 143–44, 145nn. 7, 186, 198, 201, 204, 206, 216, 221, 224; and sex, 73, 137; anti-gay, 181; fratricidal, 214–15; racial, 193–211, 220; rituals of, 197, 201; vigilante, 195

Vitullo, Juliann, 5, 303

Voight, Jon, 139

Waiting to Exhale, 44

Wake Island, 157

Walker, Robert, 152, 155

Wall Street, 264–65

Wallace, George, 274

Warner, Michael, 117

Watergate, 257–58, 261, 263, 265–66, 268, 270, 274, 276n. 1

Waugh, Tom, 175, 178, 185

Way Down East, 30

Wayne, John, 9, 26, 158, 164n.7

Weaver, Signourey, 44

Weigman, Robyn, 21

Weintraub, Bernard, 21

Well-Tempered Self, The, 245

Wellington, Peter, 175, 183, 186

Wellman, William, 163n. 1

Wells, H. G., 12, 15

Welsh, Kenneth, 171

West Indies, the, 173, 174

Weston, Kath, 54

Whalberg, Mark, 37, 187

Wheeler, Anne, 175

white(s), 15, 20, 22n. 9, 208; commu-nity, 206–208, 221; male stars, 16; masculinity (*see* masculinity, white); men (*see* men, white); Southerners, 5, 193–211; supremacy, 196, 199, 204, 208; vic-timization, 76, 79n. 11

White, Susan, 4, 303

White, Theodore H., 262
whiteness, 214, 216, 219–20, 222–23
Wiest, Diane, 48
Wilde, Oscar, 184
Will and Grace, 48
Willeman, Paul, 95, 100
Williams, Linda Ruth, 39, 133–34
Williams, Pat Ward, 209n. 10
Williams, Robin, 46, 48
Willis, Bruce, 9, 15, 18–19, 45, 244
Willis, Sharon, 18, 21, 50n. 5, 112n. 10
Wills, Garry, 262
Wincester 73, 107
Winfrey, Oprah, 237
Wing and a Prayer, 158
Winter Kept Us Warm, 189n. 4
Wittson, C. L., 151
Wlodarz, Joe, 4, 303
Wolf, Scott, 64n. 5
women, 1–2, 6, 19, 25–27, 31, 49, 81,
    97, 136, 245, 254; black, 196; het-
    erosexual, 48–49; Italian-Ameri-
    can, 214, 216; white, 195, 202, 204,
    207
women's: bodies, 245; liberation, 4;
    love, 44; movement, 38, 232

Woo, John, 162
Wood, Amy, 5, 304
Wood, Robin, 224–25
Woolf, Virginia, 44
working class, the, 11–14, 19, 22n. 9,
    198, 219, 221, 223
Working Girl, 44
World War I, 153
World War II, 272, 273; films (*see*
    films, war)
Wright, Robin, 19
Wyatt, Justin, 3–4, 304
Wyle, Florence, 184
Wylie, Philip: *Generation of Vipers,* 151,
    163n. 2
Wyman, Jane, 44
Wynette, Tammy, 25

*You Know I Can't Hear You when the Water
    Is Running,* 31
Your Friends and Neighbors, 68, 77

Zellweger, Renee, 45
Zero Patience, 190n. 11
Ziegler, Ron, 260
Žižek, Slavoj, 100–101

index